Deployment Psychology

Deployment Psychology

Evidence-Based Strategies to Promote Mental Health in the Military

Edited by

Amy B. Adler, Paul D. Bliese, and Carl Andrew Castro

American Psychological Association • Washington, DC

Published by
American Psychological Association
750 First Street, NE
Washington, DC 20002
www.apa.org

To order
APA Order Department
P.O. Box 92984
Washington, DC 20090-2984
Tel: (800) 374-2721; Direct: (202) 336-5510
Fax: (202) 336-5502; TDD/TTY: (202) 336-6123
Online: www.apa.org/pubs/books/
E-mail: order@apa.org

In the U.K., Europe, Africa, and the Middle East, copies may be ordered from
American Psychological Association
3 Henrietta Street
Covent Garden, London
WC2E 8LU England

Typeset in Goudy by Circle Graphics, Inc., Columbia, MD

Printer: Maple-Vail Book Manufacturing Group, York, PA
Cover Designer: Mercury Publishing Services, Rockville, MD

The opinions and statements published are the responsibility of the authors, and such opinions and statements do not necessarily represent the policies of the American Psychological Association.

Library of Congress Cataloging-in-Publication Data

Deployment psychology : evidence-based strategies to promote mental health in the military / edited by Amy B. Adler, Paul D. Bliese, and Carl Andrew Castro. — 1st ed.
    p. cm.
Includes bibliographical references and index.
ISBN-13: 978-1-4338-0881-4
ISBN-10: 1-4338-0881-1
ISBN-13: 978-1-4338-0882-1 (e-book)
ISBN-10: 1-4338-0882-X (e-book)
1. Psychology, Military. 2. Soldiers—Mental health services—United States. 3. Soldiers—Mental health—United States. 4. Veterans—Mental health services—United States.
5. Veterans—Mental health—United States. 6. Post-traumatic stress disorder. 7. War—Psychological aspects. 8. Combat—Psychological aspects. I. Adler, Amy B., 1963- II. Bliese, Paul D. III. Castro, Carl Andrew.

U22.3.D47 2011
355.3'45—dc22

2010012107

British Library Cataloguing-in-Publication Data

A CIP record is available from the British Library.

Printed in the United States of America
First Edition

To Dylan, Jason, and others who follow Bella's dream
—*Amy B. Adler*

To Marta, Emma, and Ellie
—*Paul D. Bliese*

To Louise
—*Carl Andrew Castro*

CONTENTS

CONTRIBUTORS

Amy B. Adler, PhD, Clinical Research Psychologist and Chief of Science, U.S. Army Medical Research Unit–Europe, Walter Reed Army Institute of Research, Heidelberg, Germany

George N. Appenzeller, MD, Lieutenant Colonel, U.S. Army, and Deputy · Commander for Clinical Services, Winn Army Community Hospital, Fort Stewart, GA

Paul D. Bliese, PhD, Colonel, U.S. Army, and, Director, Center for Military Psychiatry and Neuroscience, Walter Reed Army Institute of Research, Silver Spring, MD

Jill E. Breitbach, PsyD, Major, U.S. Army, Clinical Neuropsychologist, Evans Army Community Hospital, Fort Carson, CO

Thomas W. Britt, PhD, Professor, Department of Psychology, Clemson University, Clemson, SC

Carl Andrew Castro, PhD, Colonel, U.S. Army, and Director, Military Operational Medicine Research Program, Medical Research and Materiel Command, Fort Detrick, MD

Jennifer L. Francis, PhD, Psychologist, Department of Medicine, Uniformed Services University of the Health Sciences, Bethesda, MD

Neil Greenberg, BM, BSc, MMedSc, ILTM, MRCPsych, Surgeon Commander, Royal Navy, and Defence Professor of Mental Health, Academic Centre for Defence Mental Health, King's College, London, England

Charles W. Hoge, MD, MPH, Colonel (retired), U.S. Army, and Senior Scientist, Center for Military Psychiatry and Neuroscience, Walter Reed Army Institute of Research, Silver Spring, MD

Norman Jones, BSc (Hons), MSc, RGN, RMN, CBT, Major, British Army Medical Services, and Nurse Lecturer, Academic Centre for Defence Mental Health, King's College, London, England

Terence M. Keane, PhD, Associate Chief of Staff for Research and Development, VA Boston Healthcare System, and Director, Behavioral Science Division, National Center for Posttraumatic Stress Disorder, Boston, MA

Jennifer T. Lange, MD, Lieutenant Colonel, U.S. Army, and Medical Director, Behavioral Health Clinic, Walter Reed Army Medical Center, Washington, DC

Julie C. Merrill, PhD, Research Associate, Military Psychiatry Branch, Center for Military Psychiatry and Neuroscience, Walter Reed Army Institute of Research, Silver Spring, MD

Angela Mobbs, PsyD, Captain, U.S. Army, and Group Psychologist, 7th Special Forces Group, Fort Bragg, NC

Barbara L. Niles, PhD, Researcher, Behavioral Science Division, National Center for Posttraumatic Stress Disorder, VA Boston Healthcare System, and Assistant Professor of Psychiatry, Boston University School of Medicine, Boston, MA

John D. Otis, PhD, Director of Pain Management Psychology Services, VA Boston Healthcare System, and Assistant Professor of Psychology and Psychiatry, Boston University, Boston, MA

Stephen J. Quinn, PhD, Researcher, Behavioral Science Division, National Center for Posttraumatic Stress Disorder, VA Boston Healthcare System, Boston, MA

Lyndon A. Riviere, PhD, Research Sociologist, Military Psychiatry Branch, Center for Military Psychiatry and Neuroscience, Walter Reed Army Institute of Research, Silver Spring, MD

Michael J. Roy, MD, MPH, Colonel, U.S. Army, and Department of Medicine, Uniformed Services University of the Health Sciences, Bethesda, MD

Christopher H. Warner, PhD, Major, U.S. Army, and Chief, Department of Behavioral Medicine, Winn Army Community Hospital, Fort Stewart, GA, and Assistant Professor of Clinical Psychiatry and Mental Medicine, Medical College of Wisconsin, Milwaukee

Kathleen M. Wright, PhD, Supervisory Research Psychologist, U.S. Army Medical Research Unit–Europe, Walter Reed Army Institute of Research, Heidelberg, Germany

Mark Zamorski, MD, MHSA, Head, Deployment Health Section, Canadian Forces Health Services Group Headquarters, Ottawa, Ontario, Canada

ACKNOWLEDGMENTS

There are many people we would like to thank for their contributions to this volume. In particular, we thank our colleagues at the Walter Reed Army Institute of Research and, especially, Charles Hoge and Dennis McGurk for their support in putting together this volume and Robert Klocko for his technical support. Note that the views expressed in these chapters are those of the authors and do not represent the official policy or position of the U.S. Army medical command or the U.S. Department of Defense. We also recognize the contributions of hundreds of military clinicians and researchers working to address the issues of combat-related mental health. Above all, we recognize the sacrifices that service members and their families make every day.

Deployment Psychology

AN INTRODUCTION TO DEPLOYMENT PSYCHOLOGY

AMY B. ADLER, PAUL D. BLIESE, AND CARL ANDREW CASTRO

Combat changes the lives of those involved. When soldiers reflect on surviving combat, they do not necessarily focus on the glamour of war; neither do they focus on how combat has broken them. Instead, soldiers reflect on how they have changed. We have asked them to write about how they think combat has changed them, and we have collected thousands of accounts from soldiers returning from war. Many of these accounts were written by soldiers who anticipated returning to combat within the year.[1]

When soldiers take the opportunity to reflect on the experience, they write about how they have changed and how, at the same time, they are trying to move on. In an example of reflecting on personal change, one soldier wrote, "As far as emotions are concerned, I have grown weary." Another wrote,

---

The views expressed in this chapter are those of the authors and do not reflect the official position of the Walter Reed Army Institute of Research, the U.S. Army, or Department of Defense. This chapter was authored or coauthored by an employee of the United States government as part of official duty and is considered to be in the public domain. Any views expressed herein do not necessarily represent the views of the United States government, and the author's participation in the work is not meant to serve as an official endorsement.
[1]Quotes are taken from soldier essays completed under Walter Reed Army Institute of Research [WRAIR] Protocol 1171, "Transition Strategies and soldier Behavioral Health Following Combat Deployment," by Amy B. Adler and Paul D. Bliese, principal investigators, WRAIR.

"I can tell my thought process . . . changed." Another soldier described trying to benefit from his experiences: "I would like to make my experience help make me better. My attempts at this so far are not successful. I have become bitter and rude." The accounts also illustrated how soldiers changed in relation to those around them: "You have to realize you don't talk to civilians the same way you do your battle buddies because they [civilians] don't understand."

A military service occupation requires a commitment to a demanding profession. Soldiers must grapple with emotional tasks that are exempt from most occupations. One soldier, reflecting on the possibility of dying in combat, wrote, "I didn't fear dying, I fear not being a part of my daughters' life." Another occupational reality is that after returning from deployment, soldiers must prepare to return again to combat. One soldier reflected, "I will drive on, go on another deployment, accept my responsibilities, will not cave." Another soldier explained that deployment can also have underlying benefits by honing one's life to a single-minded focus:

> When I was down range, life was good for me, as well as hard. But it was full, with little time . . . to feel sorry for myself. I like the serenity I felt where I was preparing my equipment and myself for patrol.

Combat also means coming to terms with loss and grief over the death of buddies and leaders, encompassed in a fundamental sentiment expressed by one soldier: "We lost so many great people." The significance of this loss is a reflection of deep connections that can be forged during deployment. One soldier wrote, "I love the brotherhood and camaraderie we have as soldiers," and another wrote about how he had matured: "From being in combat you realize how much more important your friends, family, and battle buddies are . . . you realize how much more life should be treasured."

Clinicians, military professionals, and anyone working or living closely with service members returning from combat will likely recognize these perspectives. These perspectives reflect the professionalism, the toll, and the dedication of today's volunteers, and this multidimensional reality underlies the chapters in this volume.

THIS VOLUME

Goal

The goal of this volume is to guide the field of military psychology in the development of evidence-based support for service members. Many psychological studies have described the mental health toll of combat as a warning about its cost in terms of human suffering. It is amazing that fewer studies have focused on evidence-based attempts to prevent mental health problems and enhance service member well-being and resilience. This volume is designed to fill this gap. The authors in this volume represent perspectives from clinical and research psychologists, physicians, and sociologists, and although the focus is largely the United States and primarily the army, international perspectives from the United Kingdom and Canada are included as well. The authors are a unique group of specialists who, as clinicians and researchers, are addressing the challenge of sustaining service member mental health. These authors share the goal of developing and implementing evidence-based interventions.

Using the perspective of an occupational health model, the chapters in this volume emphasize the way in which the military organization can moderate the impact of combat on service member mental health through individual screening, training, peer support, leadership, and organizational policies. The chapters range from clinically based reflections on how to manage service member mental health during deployment to proposals for reconceptualizing service delivery, the role of peers, and what it means to transition home. This volume emphasizes what is known—and not known—about evidence-based approaches for early interventions and mental health resilience training conducted with service members. Throughout, the authors, all specialists in the field of military mental health, consider both the positive and negative impact that combat can have on service members and their families. The chapters also establish an agenda for research designed to support and promote the well-being of service members and their families.

Structure

This volume is divided into two main sections. The goal of Part I, Supporting Resilience in a Deployment Context, is to highlight the most recent clinical and research approaches within the military to support deployed soldiers and units. Part II, Transitioning Home From Deployment, has as its goal reviewing the broad way in which the experience of deployment affects service members after the deployment.

There are five chapters in Part I. Chapter 1 outlines the key public health strategies that have served as the crux of the military's response to mental health problems arising from deployment. Chapter 2 proposes the way in which mental health support should be broadened and reconceptualized for a deployed environment. Chapter 3 demonstrates and discusses the value of focusing the approach used in the United Kingdom on peer support and leaders. Building on the importance of peer support and leadership, Chapter 4 focuses on the role of the occupational context and social group in supporting military mental health. Chapter 5, the final chapter in this section, discusses the question of how deployments affect military families.

Part II of this volume addresses the transition home. Chapter 6 establishes a model for conceptualizing the psychological transition home. Chapter 7 reviews the goals and research behind the large-scale psychological assessment of service members returning from deployment. Chapter 8 tackles the topic of behavioral health considerations for service members physically wounded in combat. Chapter 9 proposes a new conceptualization of posttraumatic stress disorder (PTSD) symptoms from an occupational perspective. Chapter 10, the final chapter in this section on transitioning home, addresses the question of mental health in veterans and the way in which the veterans' administration has responded to the need for validated mental health treatment.

Key Themes

Each chapter examines combat-related mental health problems, defines the scope of the problem, and reviews interventions designed to address these problems. Throughout, key themes emerge: (a) the need for evidence-based interventions, (b) the need for definitional clarity in understanding post-deployment health, and (c) positive aspects of deployment.

First, despite the existence of some promising evidence-based interventions, the chapters highlight critical gaps in our knowledge. Few studies demonstrate the efficacy of interventions with military units, at-risk service members, and their families, and this reality requires mental health professionals to rely on their personal judgment. For example, in Chapter 2, Warner and colleagues tackle the issue of how to provide mental health interventions in a combat environment when standard clinical practice borders on irrelevance in the face of conducting therapy in remote forward operating bases. In contrast, as Keane and coauthors note in Chapter 10, even under traditional treatment circumstances, providers may choose not to use evidence-based treatment, highlighting the point that even though there may be acceptable treatments for PTSD, there are still important challenges to be faced when integrating consistent state-of-the-art treatment practices into the Veterans Affairs system. Furthermore, as Roy and Francis discuss in Chapter 8, postdeployment treatment does not begin with the Veterans Affairs system. For many of the physically wounded, mental health treatment begins in military hospitals, and there are no randomized controlled trials that guide this kind of support. There are also no evidence-based psychological treatments for managing amputations or mild traumatic brain injury in service members.

Second, some clinical definitions need to be clarified. For example, the importance of a clear definition of mild traumatic brain injury is raised in Chapters 1, 8, and 10. The need for definitional clarity is also indicated by

Castro and Adler in Chapter 9, which proposes a reconceptualization of PTSD. By more accurately describing the experience of service members who are most at risk, the field of combat-related mental health can establish meaningful diagnostic criteria that may prompt the development of innovative interventions.

Third, most of the chapters point out that although combat affects everyone, not all combat-related outcomes are negative. The transition home can be positive and an opportunity for personal growth (see Chapter 6), the family can grow and develop new skills (see Chapter 5), and peers and leaders are afforded the opportunity to provide meaningful support to unit members (see Chapter 3). By emphasizing these positive considerations, the goal is moved beyond a traditional discussion of combat stress and instead focus on the way in which combat deployment can have both a positive and negative impact on individuals, families, and units.

Just like their counterparts in World War II, the authors of the chapters in this volume are part of their nation's consultation services responsible for developing programs to identify service members in need, to maintain the mental health of service members, and to treat those with significant mental health problems. And like their counterparts of more than 50 years ago, the authors of these chapters note that the military cannot rely on selection alone to remove the risk of mental health problems following combat. The focus instead is on designing large-scale programs that increase the resiliency of personnel serving in the military. Nevertheless, the challenge of balancing the need to deliver mental health programs quickly with the need to establish their efficacy has remained. Despite this level of urgency, several recent mental health initiatives have been based on research evidence. Whether it is developing validated mental health assessments (as described in Chapter 4), establishing the rates of mental health problems (as described in Chapter 1), or creating valid mental health training, military mental health has set a new standard for evidence-based initiatives. Although the standard has been set, there is still much to be done to ensure optimal mental health support for service members and their families.

FOCUSING ON U.S. ARMY RESEARCH

This volume was drafted in the spirit of Stouffer's hallmark four-volume series, *The American Soldier* (e.g., Stouffer et al., 1949; Stouffer, Suchman, DeVinney, Star, & Williams, 1949), which reported on data collected by army researchers on the attitudes and experiences of U.S. soldiers during World War II. Although we did not try to approach the depth of detail and scope of Stouffer's work in our modest volume, we have tried to reflect the spirit of Stouffer's accomplishment by recording the work done for soldiers by military researchers. We have thus brought army researchers and clinicians together to benchmark the psychological effects of war on service members and to establish an agenda from researchers and clinicians working directly with the military.

Walter Reed Army Institute of Research

Given the focus on army research in this volume, it follows that many of the chapters highlight studies conducted by WRAIR. WRAIR is an army research asset that, particularly in the early days of the wars in Iraq and Afghanistan, was a core source for epidemiological studies, assessment research, and mental health resilience training research conducted with soldiers.

In considering these accomplishments, it is important to acknowledge that much of this work was made possible by the military's willingness to maintain a long-term focus on the importance of mental health research. Prior to the wars in Afghanistan and Iraq, much of the research infrastructure was well-established and focused on studying a variety of topics that included examinations of the mental health of peacekeeping personnel (Bartone, Adler, & Vaitkus, 1998; Bliese, Halverson, & Schriesheim, 2002; Britt & Adler, 2003), the impact of high operations tempo (Castro & Adler, 2005; Dolan, Adler, Thomas, & Castro, 2005; Huffman, Adler, Dolan, & Castro, 2005; Thomas, Adler, & Castro, 2005), the leadership and training effects on well-being (e.g., Chen & Bliese, 2002; Jex & Bliese, 1999), and the mental health effects on service retention (Hoge et al., 2002). In addition, the research programs had been addressing analytic and theoretical issues that exist in hierarchically nested military data, specifically, issues revolving around having nonindependent data sets in which individual service member responses were influenced by the groups to which they belong (Bliese, 2000; Bliese & Jex, 2002; Bliese & Hanges, 2004; Bliese, 2006).

The fact that active research programs were in place with an in-house tradition of research and scientific publications allowed the U.S. Army to mobilize efforts in support of soldiers serving in the wars in Iraq and Afghanistan almost immediately. Just as important, the research staff understood the practical logistics of conducting research in applied military settings: from navigating the approval process to deploying to Iraq and Afghanistan; from providing feedback to military leaders to measuring psychological and organizational variables in a deployment context. It is certainly our opinion that the military's long-term investment in maintaining this core competency paid off. Although the findings from WRAIR research can be found in peer-reviewed medical and psychological journals, army technical reports, and military briefings, this volume provides a broader platform for army research and WRAIR research in particular. Furthermore, the American Psychological Association encouraged the development of this volume as a showcase for work conducted by researchers directly connected to the military.

Army Resilience Training: Battlemind

One of WRAIR's major accomplishments was the development of a resilience training system called *Battlemind Training*. Training content was developed on the basis of WRAIR research, and studies found an association between predeployment Battlemind Training and soldier mental health during deployment (Mental Health Advisory Team V, 2008). Moreover, postdeployment modules were found to be effective in three group randomized trials (Adler, Bliese, McGurk, Hoge, & Castro, 2009; Adler, Castro, Bliese, McGurk, & Milliken, 2007; Thomas et al., 2007). Initially, Battlemind Training was the only army-wide resilience training initiative, and at the direction of the secretary of the army, Battlemind Training was integrated into the institutional army through the Deployment Cycle Support Program and the army's formal officer and noncommissioned officer career training courses (Department of the Army, 2007).

It is important to note that prior to Battlemind Training, none of the services in the U.S. military had developed an empirically based mental health training program for preparing service members for the psychological demands of combat. The task confronting the mental health community was by no means an easy one. Imagine a brigade combat team comprising more than 3,500 soldiers getting ready to deploy to combat for over a year. What should these soldiers be told in 1 hour about the psychological demands of combat to prepare and sustain them for that year? That was one of the challenges we faced.

Of course, before the development of Battlemind, some service members did receive mental health training prior to deploying, but this training was generic and nonspecific to the actual demands of the combat environment and was not conducted in a systematic manner or validated (e.g., McKibben, Britt, Hoge, & Castro, 2009). Typically, the mental health training consisted of home-grown PowerPoint presentations containing theoretical information on stress that had unknown value to service members getting ready to go into combat. These programs may have been of no value, or they may have been of high value, but there was no research basis on which to make this determination. Thus, Battlemind was the first systematic attempt to create a research-based mental health training initiative, and a few years later, the army broadened its approach and launched a more comprehensive resilience training program.

In 2009, the Battlemind Training System was selected as one of three programs to be absorbed by the army's Comprehensive Soldier Fitness initiative.

Comprehensive Soldier Fitness is based on the principles of positive psychology (Seligman & Csikszentmihalyi, 2000; see also Cornum, Matthews, & Seligman, 2009; Lester, McBride, Bliese, & Adler, 2009; Novotney, 2009; Peterson, Park, & Castro, 2009; Reivich & Seligman, 2009). Besides offering an online self-assessment of resilience and online training modules designed for self-development, the program also includes in-depth resilience training. This training integrates (a) fundamental resilience skills based on training developed by researchers at the University of Pennsylvania (Gillham et al., 2007), (b) performance psychology techniques developed by the Army Center for Enhanced Performance, and (c) resilience skills oriented toward the military and deployment context based on training developed by WRAIR (i.e., adapted from Battlemind Training).

To facilitate integration of Battlemind Training into this large-scale effort, the name *Battlemind* was replaced with the term *resilience training*. This development reflects the priority given to resilience training by the military. Although research is currently underway to assess the efficacy of this wide-ranging effort, as of the writing of this volume much of the previous army research has been centered on the efficacy of Battlemind Training. Before the Battlemind Training studies, there was little evidence in the scientific literature to suggest that 1-hour public health programs could have a significant impact on the resilience of service members (Sharpley, Fear, Greenberg, Jones, & Wessely, 2007). Thus, Battlemind Training is repeatedly cited by many of the chapter authors as an example of an army program developed specifically for soldiers and validated as an early intervention. Recurring reference to Battlemind Training in this volume reflects the fact that there were no other validated programs in the army and that study results suggested benefits from public health-style interventions that support soldier resilience.

CONCLUSION

This volume is intended to convey the breadth and depth of behavioral science research conducted to support service members who have deployed to Iraq and Afghanistan. Research gaps remain, and it may take years before conclusive evidence of efficacy for some programs is established. Taken as a whole, however, we believe mental health research has played a critical role in providing care to service members and their families by producing (a) societal-level awareness of the mental health consequences of combat, (b) army-specific preventive mental health programs, (c) advances in how behavioral health care is practiced in combat environments, and (d) theoretically and empirically driven insights into the nature of mental health problems associated with combat.

Each of these objectives is designed to help service members, their families, and military units meet significant challenges inherent in military life. There is potential for soldiers to falter psychologically in response to a deployment. As one soldier reflected in his written account, "Soldiers are tough and strong, but it's my belief that we can only take so much before we break down and lose all control." And there is also potential to demonstrate resilience, commitment to battle buddies, and personal growth in the face of these demands. As one soldier wrote after returning from 15 months in combat,

> I like living and if I die in combat . . . so be it, but [I] know that my best chance for staying alive is keeping my buddy alive, so I'll do my best but my best is all I can give.

And despite frustration with organizational bureaucracy, one soldier summarized the deployment experience by writing the following:

> I feel now that it has made me a better and stronger person. I know now that I can deal with some pretty fucked up shit and get through it. The relationships with my friends and family have gotten stronger from these experiences.

REFERENCES

Adler, A. B., Bliese, P. B., McGurk, D., Hoge, C. W., & Castro, C. A. (2009). Battlemind Debriefing and Battlemind Training as early interventions with soldiers returning from Iraq: Randomization by platoon. *Journal of Consulting and Clinical Psychology, 77,* 928–940. doi:10.1037/a0016877

Adler, A. B., Castro, C. A., Bliese, P. D., McGurk, D., & Milliken, C. (2007, August). The efficacy of Battlemind Training at 3–6 months postdeployment. In C. A. Castro (Chair), *The Battlemind Training System: Supporting soldiers throughout the deployment cycle.* Symposium conducted at the meeting of the American Psychological Association, San Francisco, CA.

Bartone, P. T., Adler, A. B., & Vaitkus, M. A. (1998). Dimensions of psychological stress in peacekeeping operations. *Military Medicine, 163,* 587–593.

Bliese, P. D. (2000). Within-group agreement, nonindependence, and reliability: Implications for data aggregation and analysis. In K. J. Klein & S. W. Kozlowski (Eds.), *Multilevel theory, research, and methods in organizations* (pp. 349–381). San Francisco, CA: Jossey-Bass.

Bliese, P. D. (2006). Social climates: Drivers of soldier well-being and resilience. In A. B. Adler, C. A. Castro, & T. W. Britt (Eds.), *Military life: The psychology of serving in peace and combat: Vol. 2. Operational Stress* (pp. 213–234). Westport, CT: Praeger.

Bliese, P. D., Halverson, R. R., & Schriesheim, C. A. (2002). Benchmarking multilevel methods on leadership: The articles, the models, the data set. *The Leadership Quarterly, 13*, 3–14. doi:10.1016/S1048-9843(01)00101-1

Bliese, P. D., & Hanges, P. (2004). Being both too liberal and too conservative: The perils of treating grouped data as though they were independent. *Organizational Research Methods, 7*, 400–417. doi:10.1177/1094428104268542

Bliese, P. D., & Jex, S. M. (2002). Incorporating a multilevel perspective into occupational stress research: Theoretical, methodological, and practical implications. *Journal of Occupational Health Psychology, 7*, 265–276. doi:10.1037/1076-8998.7.3.265

Britt, T. W., & Adler, A. B. (2003). *The psychology of the peacekeeper: Lessons from the field.* Westport, CT: Praeger.

Castro, C. A., & Adler, A. B. (2005). Operations tempo (OPTEMPO). *Military Psychology, 17*, 131–136. doi:10.1207/s15327876mp1703_1

Chen, G., & Bliese, P. D. (2002). The role of different levels of leadership in predicting self and collective efficacy: Evidence for discontinuity. *Journal of Applied Psychology, 87*, 549–556. doi:10.1037/0021-9010.87.3.549

Cornum, R., Matthews, M. D., & Seligman, M. E. P. (2009). *Comprehensive soldier fitness: Building resilience in a challenging institutional context.* Manuscript submitted for publication.

Department of the Army. (2007, March). *Deployment Cycle Support (DCS) directive.* Retrieved from http://www.apd.army.mil/pdffiles/ad2007_02.pdf

Dolan, C. A., Adler, A. B., Thomas, J. L., & Castro, C. A. (2005). Operations tempo and soldier health: The moderating effect of wellness behaviors. *Military Psychology, 17*, 157–174. doi:10.1207/s15327876mp1703_3

Gillham, J. E., Reivich, K. J., Freres, D. R., Chaplin, T. M., Shatté, A. J., Samuels, B., . . . Seligman, M. E. P. (2007). School-based prevention of depressive symptoms: A randomized controlled study of the effectiveness and specificity of the Penn Resiliency Program. *Journal of Consulting and Clinical Psychology, 75*, 9–19. doi:10.1037/0022-006X.75.1.9

Hoge, C. W., Castro, C. A., Messer, S. C., McGurk, D., Cotting, D. I., & Koffman, R. L. (2004). Combat duty in Iraq and Afghanistan, mental health problems, and barriers to care. *The New England Journal of Medicine, 351*, 13–22. doi:10.1056/NEJMoa040603

Hoge, C. W., Lesikar, S. E., Guevera, R., Lange, J., Brundage, J. F., Engel, C. C., . . . Orman, D. T. (2002). Mental disorders among U.S. military personnel in the 1990s: Association with high levels of health care utilization and early military attrition. *The American Journal of Psychiatry, 159*, 1576–1583. doi:10.1176/appi.ajp.159.9.1576

Huffman, A. H., Adler, A. B., Dolan, C. A., & Castro, C. A. (2005). The impact of operations tempo on turnover intentions of army personnel. *Military Psychology, 17*, 175–202. doi:10.1207/s15327876mp1703_4

Jex, S. M., & Bliese, P. D. (1999). Efficacy beliefs as a moderator of the impact of work-related stressors: A multi-level study. *Journal of Applied Psychology, 84,* 349–361. doi:10.1037/0021-9010.84.3.349

Lester, P. B., McBride, S. A., Bliese, P. B., & Adler, A. B. (2009). *Bringing science to bear: An empirical assessment of the Comprehensive Soldier Fitness Program.* Manuscript submitted for publication.

McKibben, E. S., Britt, T. W., Hoge, C. W., & Castro, C. A. (2009). Receipt and rated adequacy of stress management training is related to PTSD and other outcomes among Operational Iraqi Freedom Veterans. *Military Psychology, 21,* S68–S81. doi:10.1080/08995600903249172

Mental Health Advisory Team V. (2008). *Mental Health Advisory Team (MHAT) V Operation Iraqi Freedom 06-08: Iraq, Operation Enduring Freedom 8: Afghanistan.* Retrieved from http://www.armymedicine.army.mil/reports/mhat/mhat_v/mhat-v.cfm

Novotney, A. (2009, December). Strong in mind and body. *Monitor on Psychology, 40,* 40–43.

Peterson, C., Park, N., & Castro, C. A. (2009). *Assessment for the U.S. Army Comprehensive Soldier Fitness Program: The global assessment tool.* Manuscript submitted for publication.

Reivich, K., & Seligman, M. E. P. (2009). *Master resilience training in the United States Army.* Manuscript submitted for publication.

Seligman, M. E. P., & Csikszentmihalyi, M. (2000). Positive psychology: An introduction. *American Psychologist, 55,* 5–14. doi:10.1037/0003-066X.55.1.5

Sharpley, J. G., Fear, N. T., Greenberg, N., Jones, M., & Wessely, S. (2007). Predeployment stress briefing: Does it have an effect? *Occupational Medicine, 58,* 30–34. doi:10.1093/occmed/kqm118

Stouffer, S. A., Lumsdaine, A. A., Williams, R. B., Smith, M. B., Janis, I. L., Star, S. A., & Cottrell, L. S. (1949). *The American soldier: Vol. 2. Combat and its aftermath.* Princeton, NJ: Princeton University Press.

Stouffer, S. A., Suchman, E. A., DeVinney, L. C., Star, S. A., & Williams, R. A. (1949). *The American soldier: Vol. 1. Adjustment during army life.* Princeton, NJ: Princeton University Press.

Thomas, J. L., Adler, A. B., & Castro, C. A. (2005). Measuring operations tempo and relating it to military performance. *Military Psychology, 17,* 137–156. doi:10.1207/s15327876mp1703_2

Thomas, J. L., Castro, C. A., Adler, A. B., Bliese, P. D., McGurk, D., Cox, A., & Hoge, C. W. (2007, August). The efficacy of Battlemind at immediate post deployment reintegration. In C. A. Castro (Chair), *The Battlemind Training System: Supporting soldiers throughout the deployment cycle.* Symposium conducted at the meeting of the American Psychological Association, San Francisco, CA

I

SUPPORTING RESILIENCE
IN A DEPLOYMENT CONTEXT

1

PUBLIC HEALTH STRATEGIES AND TREATMENT OF SERVICE MEMBERS AND VETERANS WITH COMBAT-RELATED MENTAL HEALTH PROBLEMS

CHARLES W. HOGE

We are always dealing with dirty data. The trick is to do it with a clean mind.
—Mike Gregg, Epidemiologist,
Centers for Disease Control and Prevention

Research to assess the mental health impact of wartime military service has often been conducted years or decades after the return home (Jordan et al., 1991; Kang, Natelson, Mahan, Lee, & Murphy, 2003; Prigerson, Maciejewski, & Rosenheck, 2002), with the notable exception of the wars in Iraq (Operation Iraqi Freedom; OIF) and Afghanistan (Operation Enduring Freedom; OEF) in which the Department of Defense (DoD) and Veterans Affairs (VA) leadership promoted research early in the war to inform health policy (Hoge et al., 2004). This chapter details the unique interface between research, policy, and clinical services to address the mental health needs of service members and veterans deployed to combat zones, with particular emphasis on the importance of epidemiological research findings from the wars in Iraq and Afghanistan. These wars have led to important insights about the mental health impact of combat and the development of new education, prevention, and clinical care

The views expressed in this chapter are those of the author and do not reflect the official position of the Walter Reed Army Institute of Research, the U.S. Army, or Department of Defense. This chapter was authored by an employee of the United States government as part of official duty and is considered to be in the public domain. Any views expressed herein do not necessarily represent the views of the United States government, and the author's participation in the work is not meant to serve as an official endorsement.

strategies. They have also highlighted challenges in delivering evidence-based treatment for war-related mental health problems.

The largest sustained U.S. ground operations since the Vietnam War were initiated in October 2001 in Afghanistan and in March 2003 in Iraq. One of the first indications of potential deployment-related mental health problems that made national headlines was a cluster of suicides and homicides at Fort Bragg among soldiers involved in early operations in Afghanistan (U.S. Surgeon General, 2002). An epidemiological investigation suggested that the cluster was associated with high deployment-related work stress (i.e., "operational tempo") combined with marital difficulties. On the basis of this investigation, the DoD responded in 2003 by establishing the Deployment Cycle Support Program to address mental health problems and ensure that service members who return home from the combat environment due to serious family stressors are evaluated on return. A hallmark feature of this program was the implementation of the Post-Deployment Health Assessment (PDHA), a standardized population-wide screening for deployment-related health concerns, including posttraumatic stress disorder (PTSD), depression, and marital or relationship problems. The PDHA program was implemented in time to screen soldiers returning from their first rotation to Iraq but prior to any systematic validation of the mental health screening items. This reflects a relatively common occurrence: Public health policies in military and veteran populations, such as postdeployment screening, may be implemented due to a perceived need to address an urgent health concern before adequate scientific evidence is available. The perceived urgency of the health concern may preclude a full analysis of the potential risks and costs associated with such policies (Rona, Hyams, & Wessely, 2005). Research and program evaluation after implementation, therefore, become high priorities.

The foundation of population health strategies depends on well-conducted epidemiological studies. Epidemiological methods are used to define the extent of disease burden in a population and identify risk and protective factors that may be the focus of prevention and treatment interventions. These methods are also important in establishing case definitions and outcome measures that can be studied systematically and used to evaluate the effectiveness of health policies implemented on a population level. One of the unique features of the wars in Iraq and Afghanistan has been the extensive application of epidemiological methods to assess the mental health impact of deployment as the wars were progressing, as well as the willingness of the senior DoD leaders to implement new health policies on the basis of the findings from those studies.

Epidemiological methods used in the wars in Iraq and Afghanistan have included surveys, program evaluation of population-based screening, and health care utilization studies. Surveys of representative samples of military personnel have been used to assess the prevalence, risk factors, and predictors of mental disorders. These surveys have combined classic epidemiological analyses of patterns of disease expression in the population with traditional psychological assessment techniques from social, organizational, educational, and behavioral psychology perspectives. This integration has allowed analysis of moderating variables, such as cohesion and leadership, on the expression of traditional mental disorders, such as PTSD, and behavioral outcomes, such as aggression or misconduct, in military units. Population-based deployment mental health screening has been used as a key strategy to mitigate mental health problems, and epidemiological methods have been applied to understand the lessons learned, assess effectiveness, and contribute to improvements. Studies of rates of use of mental health services have provided key data on access to care and burden of treatment in the population and have led to changes in allocation of mental health resources to improve care.

LAND COMBAT STUDY

One of the most widely cited epidemiological studies of the mental health impact of OIF and OEF is the Walter Reed Army Institute of Research (WRAIR) Land Combat Study, established in early 2003 just before the start of the ground invasion of Iraq (Hoge et al., 2004). This study stemmed from a recommendation issued by a 2003 epidemiological consultation team that assessed the causes of a cluster of homicides and suicides involving service members returning to Fort Bragg from Afghanistan. This assessment quickly developed from a one-time survey into an ongoing effort measuring the mental health impact of the war in Iraq and Afghanistan.

The foundation for the Land Combat Study, however, was laid long before OIF and OEF with an army investment in deployment-related research, to include uniformed military research psychologists deploying with operational units on peacekeeping, humanitarian, and combat operations. During the Persian Gulf War (Operations Desert Shield and Desert Storm), military psychology research teams from WRAIR assessed the psychological well-being of unit members in theater and postdeployment (Gifford, Marlowe, Wright, Bartone, & Martin, 1992; Martin et al., 1992; Stretch, Bliese, et al., 1996; Stretch, Marlowe, et al., 1996). WRAIR Teams also conducted in-theater research with units deployed to Operation Just Cause in Panama in 1989 (Kirkland, Ender, Gifford, Wright, & Marlowe, 1996), Operation Restore Hope in Somalia in 1993 (Gifford, Jackson, & DeShazo, 1993), Operation Uphold Democracy in Haiti in 1994 (Halverson & Bliese, 1996), and throughout the Balkans in the 1990s, including Operation Provide Promise in Croatia (Bartone, Adler, & Vaitkus, 1998), Operation Joint Endeavor in Bosnia (Bartone, 1997), and Operation Joint Guardian in Kosovo (Castro, Bienvenu,

Huffman, & Adler, 2000). The experience in the Balkans provided the foundation for the development of the PDHA. When troop mobilizations began for both OEF and OIF, researchers at WRAIR were in a unique position to develop and execute a comprehensive research plan. Military research psychologists formed a multidisciplinary collaboration with clinicians and epidemiologists to examine the mental health impact of the current combat operations.

The Land Combat Study involved anonymous cross-sectional surveys of service members in combat infantry brigades before, during, and after deployment to Iraq or Afghanistan. The surveys included validated measures of depression, PTSD, and other mental health problems. In addition, they incorporated measures of combat experiences, unit cohesion, leadership, and family functioning derived from assessments conducted by research psychologists during prior deployments. A novel feature of the Land Combat Study was the inclusion of measures of mental health care use, stigma, and barriers to care.

In July 2004, findings from some of the first units returning from Iraq and Afghanistan deployment were published in the *New England Journal of Medicine* (Hoge et al., 2004). The results were widely disseminated in the news media and led to congressional hearings and increased funding for the VA and DoD to improve mental health services for returning service members and veterans. The wide-spread attention on the findings reflected the degree to which the mental health care of troops had become a national priority. The study indicated that 12% to 20% of soldiers and marines from combat units met the definition of PTSD 3 to 4 months after returning from Iraq, compared with 5% to 9% prior to deployment, with the lower prevalence estimates based on a stringent cutoff criteria (PTSD Checklist score of 50 or higher) and the higher prevalence based on the presence of symptom criteria consistent with the definition in the *Diagnostic and Statistical Manual of Mental Disorders* (4th ed., American Psychiatric Association, 1994). Overall, 16% to 29% of service members met criteria for PTSD, depression, or generalized anxiety 3 to 4 months postdeployment.

Although the news headlines associated with this article highlighted the finding that one in six service members had PTSD or other mental health problems, the news articles also included remarkably detailed discussions about the findings related to stigma and barriers to care. Less than half of service members with serious mental health problems reported receiving professional help, generating a spirited discussion in the medical community and the media about the pervasive nature of stigma both in the military as well as in society at large. This discussion contributed to the development of population-wide postdeployment training to reduce stigma and encourage service members to seek care. The attention on stigma also led to new efforts to expand mental health services in primary care.

Since the initial publication of these cross-sectional data, a number of other studies using different methods have found similar prevalence estimates. These studies were based on postdeployment population screening results, random telephone surveys of military populations, health care utilization records from DoD and VA, and longitudinal studies of military populations with combat exposure (Hoge, Auchterlonie, & Milliken, 2006; Milliken, Auchterlonie, & Hoge, 2007; Seal, Bertenthal, Miner, Sen, & Marmar, 2007; Smith et al., 2008; Tanielian & Jaycox, 2008). Rates of mental health problems in U.K. service members have been reported to be lower (Hotopf et al., 2006), but this was likely due to the lower frequency and intensity of combat experiences in Southern Iraq, where the U.K. units were based (Hoge & Castro, 2006). Studies have consistently shown that the frequency and intensity of combat experiences were the most important correlates of PTSD and other mental health problems. The aggregate data point to a substantial burden of combat-related mental health problems.

Adding to the overall mental health burden of combat duty is the profound association demonstrated in many studies of PTSD with generalized health problems (Boscarino, 2004). PTSD is associated with neuroendocrine, autonomic nervous system, and cell-mediated immune dysregulation (Boscarino, 2004). One study, based on Land Combat Study data, confirmed that soldiers who screened positive for PTSD were much more likely than other soldiers from the same units to report missed workdays, medical appointments, and high ratings of somatic symptoms (Hoge, Terhakopian, Castro, Messer, & Engel, 2007). These findings were independent of being wounded in combat and contributed to new programs within DoD to enhance collaborative care efforts within primary care settings (Engel, 2007).

MENTAL HEALTH ADVISORY TEAMS

Another unique epidemiological effort in OIF and OEF was the implementation, sponsored by the army surgeon general, of annual assessments of the mental health and well-being of deployed troops. Using the same methods as in the Land Combat Study, researchers from WRAIR deployed to Iraq and Afghanistan and conducted anonymous assessments throughout the operational theaters, focusing on infantry units (i.e., brigade combat teams; Mental Health Advisory Team [MHAT] 2003; MHAT II, 2005; MHAT III, 2006; MHAT IV, 2006; MHAT V, 2008). The MHATs also assessed the distribution and availability of in-theater behavioral health resources.

The MHATs showed that 15% to 20% of deployed soldiers in brigade combat teams met criteria for PTSD (termed *acute stress* in the operational environment) or depression, and 20% of married soldiers reported marital problems during deployment. Marines from regimental combat teams experienced similar prevalence rates of mental health concerns as army soldiers after controlling for deployment length (MHAT IV, 2006). They also showed that multiple deployments, longer deployments, greater time performing missions outside the wire (i.e., away from the base camp), and combat intensity and frequency all contributed to higher rates of PTSD, depression, and marital problems.

One of the unique assessments conducted by the MHAT survey teams, at the request of senior military leaders, concerned battlefield ethics, including self-reports of mistreating noncombatants or damaging Iraqi property unnecessarily (MHAT IV, 2006; MHAT V, 2008). The study of battlefield ethics exemplified the need to adapt classic epidemiological approaches to the reality of field research. Battlefield ethics had not been previously assessed; there were no standardized approaches, and questions had to be generated that addressed these concerns. Results showed that soldiers with mental health problems were much more likely to report committing ethical violations than soldiers without mental health problems, a demonstration of the relationship between mental health problems and mission-related behaviors. The MHAT studies also demonstrated the strong protective effect of leadership. Strong leadership was associated with improved morale and cohesion, lower rates of mental health problems, and a lower likelihood of ethical misconduct during deployment.

As a direct result of the MHATs, the army revised the Combat and Operational Stress Control (COSC) doctrine (Headquarters, Department of the Army, 2006), mandated COSC training for all mental heath professionals deploying to Iraq or Afghanistan, and used MHAT data to determine the optimal allocation of mental health professionals in the deployed environment. The MHATs determined that the optimal ratio of mental health personnel to service members in-theater was 1:1,000, with about half of the personnel being credentialed independent practitioners and the other half enlisted mental health technicians. Most important, the findings led to increased colocation of mental health personnel with operational units, as well as improved outreach by mental health professionals to units in remote locations with limited access to care. The MHAT findings, together with those from the Land Combat Study, contributed to the development and fielding of a comprehensive army mental health training program called *Battlemind*, also developed by WRAIR researchers (Adler, Bliese, McGurk, Hoge, & Castro, 2009). Battlemind was designed as a risk communication and training strategy that frames mental health issues within the context of the skills and strengths that soldiers exhibit in combat that help them to survive. The training normalizes the transition process and identifies ways that soldiers can check themselves and each other for signs that they may benefit from professional assistance. A primary goal is to reduce the stigma of mental health care. Battlemind was mandated army-wide as part of the Deployment Cycle Support Program in 2007 and was scheduled to occur at the same time as the PDHA and PDHRA screening programs.

POSTDEPLOYMENT MENTAL HEALTH SCREENING PROGRAM EVALUATION

Postdeployment psychological screening for mental health problems was first required by DoD in 1996 with the deployment of U.S. forces to Bosnia. Although the requirement was not renewed during the subsequent deployment to Kosovo, it continued at the request of operational commanders, and the experience in Bosnia and Kosovo provided the foundation for the development of the PDHA program (Wright, Huffman, Adler, & Castro, 2002; Wright, Thomas, et al., 2005).

The PDHA was implemented in April 2003, 1 month after the Iraq ground war began. This program generated controversy because of the lack of evidence to support DoD-wide mental health screening (Rona et al., 2005; Wright, Bliese et al., 2005), and WRAIR researchers extended previous screening research from Bosnia and Kosovo to assess the utility of the program.

Three research initiatives provided key data to inform the PDHA program. The first initiative compared screening responses of soldiers immediately after return from deployment with responses to a second screen 3 to 4 months later. The study found that rates of reporting mental health problems increased 2 to 5 times during this period, indicating that the timing of the PDHA screening process immediately after return from deployment was not optimal (Bliese, Wright, Adler, Thomas, & Hoge, 2007). The data were presented to DoD leadership in 2005 prior to publication and led to an immediate mandate by the DoD to expand the PDHA program and add a second screening, the Post-Deployment Health Reassessment (PDHRA), 3 to 6 months after return from deployment (Assistant Secretary of Defense, Health Affairs, 2005; U.S. Department of Defense, n.d.).

A second research initiative provided validation of the mental health questions included on the PDHA and PDHRA by comparing survey results with results from structured clinical interviews conducted by providers unaware of the service member's original survey results (Bliese, Wright, Adler, Hoge, & Prayner, 2005; Bliese et al., 2008). The study demonstrated that the sensitivity and specificity of the PDHA questions were comparable with accepted standardized mental health screening instruments and led to more specific recommendations regarding the scoring of the instruments, including an interview guide for clinicians.

The third study involved a program evaluation of a cohort of nearly 90,000 soldiers who had completed both the PDHA and the PDHRA (Milliken et al., 2007). Screening results from the PDHA were linked to referral information, mental health care use, and data from the subsequent PDHRA screening (averaging 6 months after the PDHA). One of the most important findings from this longitudinal assessment was that soldiers in reserve component (RC) units showed markedly higher rates of all health concerns (both physical and mental) at the time of the PDHRA compared with their active component (AC) counterparts. RC and AC soldiers reported similar rates of combat experiences and health concerns (both physical and mental) immediately on return from deployment as measured by the PDHA, suggesting that RC and AC soldiers had comparable levels of mental fitness and resiliency. However, marked differences emerged several months later at the time of the PDHRA screening. The most likely explanation for this finding pertained to the expiration of full civilian (TRICARE) insurance benefits 6 months after return from deployment for RC soldiers, although other considerations, such as differences in unit cohesion and support after reintegration may have also played a role. Shortly after this finding was published, the VA expanded the duration of health benefits for all OIF and OEF veterans in VA facilities.

The longitudinal study of soldiers who completed both the PDHA and PDHRA provided the first opportunity to evaluate the effectiveness of the PDHA program. Contrary to expectations, this evaluation showed no direct relationship between screening results, referrals, and improvement in PTSD symptoms (Milliken et al., 2007). Among AC soldiers referred for PTSD symptoms on the PDHA, those who failed to follow up with their mental health appointment actually had higher rates of improvement 6 months later on the PDHRA than soldiers who kept their appointments. This counterintuitive finding was most likely due to the fact that this was an observational program evaluation, not a randomized controlled trial, in which soldiers who had more severe illnesses self-selected themselves to keep their appointments after referral. However, the study also highlighted challenges in population screening, the evaluation of screening efficacy, and the treatment of PTSD.

PUBLIC HEALTH AND CLINICAL CHALLENGES

Several factors may contribute to the difficulty of demonstrating the efficacy of postdeployment screening in reducing the mental health impact of combat. These factors include the low predictive value of the screening instruments in population samples, the high rate of comorbid medical and mental health problems associated with PTSD, and the low to moderate effectiveness of treatment modalities for PTSD (Terhakopian, Sinaii, Engel, Schnurr, & Hoge, 2008).

Even the best diagnostic tools for PTSD and other mental disorders have limited sensitivity and specificity and demonstrate low positive predictive value (less than 50%) when they are applied on a population level (Terhakopian et al., 2008). The fact that over half of service members who screen positive for PTSD will not have the condition is a product of the low-moderate prevalence of the condition in the population at large as well as the inherent test properties (sensitivity and specificity) of the screening instrument. It is important to note that there are differences between epidemiological approaches and psychometric approaches in characterizing the utility of standardized mental health measures. Psychometricians tend to focus on various types of reliability and validity, whereas epidemiologists take a decidedly pragmatic approach to determine whether a test will have clinical utility when applied to a population of interest. Standardized measures with high reliability, validity, and efficiency between sensitivity and specificity are frequently found to have low clinical utility when applied on a population level.

PTSD comorbidity also likely limits the overall effectiveness of current treatment approaches. PTSD is strongly associated with alcohol misuse and depression and coexists with other combat-related social and behavioral issues that may impair functioning (e.g. anger, aggression, relationship problems; Hoge et al., 2004; Milliken et al., 2007). In addition to the association of PTSD with physical symptoms, work absenteeism, and increased medical appointments, PTSD has been implicated as the underlying etiology of persistent symptoms among service members who report concussions (i.e., mild traumatic brain injuries) during deployment. Two studies have shown that postconcussive symptoms were much more strongly associated with PTSD than with the concussions themselves (Hoge et al., 2008; Schneiderman, Braver, & Kang, 2008).

Other public health challenges relate to identifying effective treatments for combat-related mental health problems. In 2007, the Institute of Medicine (IOM) published a comprehensive assessment of the evidence supporting various treatment modalities for PTSD. This report, which used a high standard to assess the evidence, concluded that exposure therapy was the only treatment category in which there was a sufficient quality and confidence of evidence for effectiveness. Most exposure modalities include a combination of in vivo and imaginal exposure, with the term *imaginal* referring to the process of the client recounting his or her story multiple times until the reactivity and symptoms subside. Imaginal exposure may involve keeping ones eyes closed, speaking in present tense, and completing homework assignments that include listening to recordings of the in-person sessions to additionally desensitize the client to their own stories (Foa, Hembree, & Rothbaum, 2007). The IOM committee considered the evidence for all other commonly used psychotherapy or psychopharmacological treatments inadequate, including selective serotonin reuptake inhibitors (SSRIs), cognitive restructuring, eye movement desensitization and reprocessing, coping skills therapy, group therapy, and other modalities. One committee member dissented on the conclusion that the evidence was insufficient for SSRIs, the most commonly prescribed pharmacotherapy for PTSD. However, his suggested changes to the evidence statement, which were included as an appendix to the report, added little to the overall conclusion that the evidence is insufficient to conclude that SSRIs are effective. He requested that the IOM conclusion be changed to, "The evidence is suggestive but not sufficient to conclude efficacy of SSRIs in general populations with PTSD. The available evidence is further suggestive that SSRIs are not effective in populations consisting of predominantly male veterans with chronic PTSD" (IOM, 2007, Appendix H, p. H-1).

It is important to note that the IOM's assessment of evidence was not intended as a guideline for clinicians. Clinical practice guidelines (CPGs) combine the best available evidence with expert consensus so that clinicians have something to guide their clinical decision making. Clinical decisions often have to be made with suboptimal levels of evidence. Nevertheless, the IOM report highlights some fundamental issues with the state of treatment for combat-related PTSD. Notably, the overall effect sizes are modest at best for all treatment modalities, including exposure therapy. A rough expectation is that as many as half of treated patients will continue to meet criteria for PTSD or have ongoing significant symptoms, even if they are able to remain in treatment for the full duration.

Most clinical trials have relied on waiting-list designs in which a treatment modality of interest is compared with essentially no treatment at all (IOM, 2008). There have been few studies involving head-to-head comparisons to determine which components of treatment are most effective. A conflicting observation, for example, is that cognitive processing therapy (CPT), a manualized form of cognitive restructuring, was the only cognitive therapy modality considered to have sufficient evidence for effectiveness by the IOM committee because the treatment incorporated a written exposure component (IOM, 2008). However, in a dismantling study by the creators of CPT, the written exposure component added no additional benefit compared with cognitive restructuring alone (Resick et al., 2008).

The field remains in need of high-quality clinical trials that address key combat-related mental health problems. For example, although virtual reality has been widely promoted in the news media as a novel form of exposure treatment for PTSD, there is a lack of head-to-head comparisons with evidence-based imaginal exposure techniques. This lack of evidence precludes concluding that this technology adds value to exposure treatment. Most important, there have been few studies in military populations, particularly those of service members recently returned from the combat environment; thus, studies to date are not necessarily generalizable to this population.

TREATMENT CONSIDERATIONS

Despite the absence of strong evidence for effectiveness of standard treatment modalities recommended in clinical practice guidelines for PTSD, clinicians must decide how to treat individual service members and veterans experiencing combat-related mental health concerns. The current evidence indicates that exposure therapy (i.e., in vivo and imaginal) is an essential ingredient of PTSD treatment (Hoge, 2010). However, given the high comorbidity of PTSD with other mental health problems after deployment, particularly depression and substance use disorders, clinicians need to use a range of evidence-based treatments beyond those designed for PTSD. These treatments can include cognitive behavioral therapy for depression; medication treatment that addresses both PTSD and depressive symptoms, particularly SSRIs and serotonin–norepinephrine reuptake inhibitors; and stress inoculation training to reduce physiological reactivity. It is critical to address sleep disturbance through sleep hygiene education, psychotherapy such as imagery rehearsal, and pharmacological interventions. Comorbid physical health problems, which are strongly associated with both depression and PTSD, also need to be addressed to increase the likelihood of treatment success.

Rage, guilt, and grief will interfere with successful therapeutic outcomes if they are not included as a focus of therapy for combat veterans. The avoidance and emotional numbing symptoms of PTSD can be particularly debilitating for relationships and occupational functioning, and clinicians should be attentive to the possibility that guilt and grief may be underlying these reactions. To minimize the impact of mental health problems on family and social functioning, it is helpful to involve spouses and other family members, with the patient's permission, both to assist in educating them about the nature of combat-related reactions and to facilitate better understanding of the important areas to focus on in treatment. There also may be behavioral issues that present in a manner similar to Axis II personality disorders. However, Axis II labels should be applied cautiously because of their pejorative nature and the potential negative implications that they may have with regard to establishing and maintaining a strong therapeutic rapport.

A number of other barriers exist to providing effective evidence-based treatment for PTSD and other combat-related mental health problems. Less than half of service members and veterans with serious combat-related mental health problems seek care, and many who do start treatment fail to follow through on a sufficient number of sessions to achieve a successful outcome (Hoge et al., 2004; Tanielian & Jaycox, 2008). This lack of follow-through is in part related to the stigma of treatment as well as to difficulties with access to care, difficulties getting time off from work, and the considerable number of sessions required for current psychotherapy modalities to be effective. Heightened physiological reactivity and avoidance also present a symptom-based barrier to following through with treatment, and combat veterans may be reluctant to talk about their experiences to civilian mental health professionals.

When a service member or veteran does make it into treatment, it is essential that the therapeutic alliance is established quickly to facilitate continued engagement with care. To enhance the alliance, mental health professionals should acknowledge honestly any lack of understanding of military experiences. Even providers with a history of deployment are not likely to have experienced the same kind of combat or the same kind of deployment-related conditions as service members seeking care. Respecting the unique nature of the combat veterans experience is an important step for establishing authenticity in the therapeutic relationship. The treatment plan should be tailored to the individual patient on the basis of the range of symptoms and comorbid problems. Key to establishing the alliance early on is to normalize the symptoms through psychoeducation, such as by providing information on how the symptoms of PTSD have an adaptive physiological and neurobiological basis in a highly threatening environment such as a war zone. For example, hypervigilance, emotional numbing, and anger are essential survival reactions in combat but become symptoms if they persist and interfere with functioning after the return home. Psychoeducation that highlights these issues can help in the development of a strong therapeutic alliance and provides a way to explain how treatment, such as in vivo or imaginal exposure therapy, will help to reduce reactivity that may be impairing function.

Clinicians also should be aware that combat-related PTSD may have unique features compared with PTSD associated with other traumas. Service members and veterans who have deployed to a combat zone may have been exposed to multiple traumatic events, and the intensity of these events may be of a magnitude that is rarely seen in civilian settings. There is evidence that responses to trauma among service members may be distinct from responses in victims of other types of trauma because of the context of their occupational duties (Adler, Wright, Bliese, Eckford, & Hoge, 2008;

see also Chapter 9, this volume). Service members undergo rigorous training on how to respond in combat events, training that is similar to that of police officers or firefighters. Clinicians can use this knowledge to help veterans with PTSD understand how their symptoms exist on a spectrum that includes normal reactions to traumatic events occurring as part of their occupation.

Improving the treatment of combat-related mental health problems will require new clinical trials research that uses rigorous study methodology, similar to those outlined in the IOM report. Key priorities in clinical trials research include the following: (a) testing evidence-based interventions (both pharmacotherapy and psychotherapy) earlier in the course of PTSD, including immediately after trauma and in the early posttrauma period (e.g., during the first few months after coming home from combat); (b) developing and testing novel pharmacotherapeutic agents; (c) dismantling studies that identify which components of psychotherapy are most effective; (d) determining whether combinations of psychopharmacology and psychotherapy offer improvements; (e) developing group treatment modalities that are as effective as individual modalities; and (f) developing and testing novel approaches to treatment, such as complementary alternative medicine strategies (e.g., mindfulness training, acupuncture).

TOWARD A MODEL OF EPIDEMIOLOGY FOR PSYCHOLOGY AND PSYCHIATRY IN THE MILITARY

Public health epidemiology is critical for defining the extent of the problem in a population, creating priorities for research and intervention, and establishing targets to measure the impact of program and policy changes. In the case of applying epidemiological approaches to understanding the mental health impact of war, no wars prior to Iraq and Afghanistan produced the wealth of population and unit-based research and program evaluation data directly relevant to health care policies. Several principles have emerged from the wars in Iraq and Afghanistan that are important in ensuring relevant outcomes and recommendations. First, assessments should be conducted as close to the time of exposure as possible. In the case of the deployments to Iraq and Afghanistan, this approach has meant deploying research teams to combat to ensure adequate understanding of the nature of combat exposures and outcomes in the operational environment, and fortunately this capability has been institutionalized. Second, standardized assessment tools are cornerstones of epidemiological research. However, clinical utility is as important a consideration, if not a more important one, than validity and reliability; the predictive value of even the best tools is limited when they are applied on a population level. In some cases standardized measures may not exist to assess meaningful problems, as in the case of ethics on the battlefield and barriers to care. Third, the research needs to focus on questions with direct relevance to organizational policies and programs. For example, data from existing DoD databases have been used to measure the effectiveness of postdeployment health assessments, to generate improvements, and to identify challenges in establishing effective interventions. Specifically, the MHATs have assessed the distribution of deployed mental health assets in meeting behavioral health care needs in theater and have led to improved allocation of resources and training. Fourth, epidemiological research is a critical platform for establishing organizational priorities and new interventions. These principles provide a model for future research of important military public health outcomes.

REFERENCES

Adler, A. B., Bliese, P. B., McGurk, D., Hoge, C. W., Castro, C. A. (2009). Battlemind Debriefing and Battlemind Training as early interventions with soldiers returning from Iraq: Randomized by platoon. *Journal of Consulting and Clinical Psychology*, 77, 928–940. doi:10.1037/a0016877

Adler, A. B., Wright, K. M., Bliese, P. D., Eckford, R., & Hoge, C. W. (2008). A2 diagnostic criterion for combat-related posttraumatic stress disorder. *Journal of Traumatic Stress*, 21, 301–308. doi:10.1002/jts.20336

American Psychiatric Association. (1994). *Diagnostic and statistical manual of mental disorders* (4th ed.). Washington, DC: Author.

Assistant Secretary of Defense, Health Affairs. (2005, March). *Policy implementation guidance* (Health Affairs Policy 05-011). Retrieved from http://www.ha.osd.mil/policies/2005/05-011.pdf

Bartone, P. T. (1997). American IFOR experience: Stressors in the early deployment period. In J. L. Soeters & J. H. Rovers (Eds.), *NL Arms: The Bosnian experience* (pp. 133–139). Breda, the Netherlands: Royal Netherlands Military Academy.

Bartone, P. T., Adler, A. B., & Vaitkus, M. A. (1998). Dimensions of psychological stress in peacekeeping operations. *Military Medicine*, 163, 587–593.

Bliese, P. D., Wright, K. M., Adler, A. B., Cabrera, O., Castro, C. A., & Hoge, C. W. (2008). Validating the primary care posttraumatic stress disorder screen and the posttraumatic stress disorder checklist with soldiers returning from combat. *Journal of Consulting and Clinical Psychology*, 76, 272–281. doi:10.1037/0022-006X.76.2.272

Bliese, P. D., Wright, K. M., Adler, A. B., Hoge, C., & Prayner, R. (2005). *Postdeployment psychological screening: Interpreting and scoring DD form 2900* (U.S. Army Medical

Research Unit–Europe [USAMRU–E] Research Report 2005-03). Heidelberg, Germany: USAMRU–E.

Bliese, P. D., Wright, K. M., Adler, A. B., Thomas, J. L., & Hoge, C. W. (2007). Timing of postcombat mental health assessments. *Psychological Services, 4*, 141–148. doi:10.1037/1541-1559.4.3.141

Boscarino, J. A. (2004). Posttraumatic stress disorder and physical illness: Results from clinical and epidemiological studies. *Annals of the New York Academy of Sciences, 1032*, 141–153. doi:10.1196/annals.1314.011

Castro, C. A., Bienvenu, R., Huffman, A. H., & Adler, A. B. (2000). Soldiers' dimensions and operational readiness in U.S. army forces deployed to Kosovo. *International Review of the Armed Forces Medical Services, 73*, 191–199.

Engel, C. C. (2007, August). *Bringing best practices and research together in primary care to improve soldier-centered care*. Paper presented at the 10th Annual Force Health Protection Conference, Louisville, KY.

Foa, E., Hembree, E., & Rothbaum, B. (2007). *Prolonged exposure therapy for PTSD: Emotional processing of traumatic experiences: Therapist guide*. New York, NY: Oxford University Press.

Gifford, R. K., Jackson, J. N., & DeShazo, K. B. (1993, March). *Report of the human dimensions research team, Operation Restore Hope*. Retrieved from Defense Technical Information Center website: http://handle.dtic.mil/100.2/ADA274340

Gifford, R. K., Marlowe, D. H., Wright, K. M., Bartone, P. T., & Martin, J. A. (1992, December). Unit cohesion in Operation Desert Shield/Storm. *Journal of the U.S. Army Medical Department*, 11–13.

Halverson, R. R., & Bliese, P. D. (1996). Determinants of soldier support for operational uphold democracy. *Armed Forces and Society, 23*, 81–96. doi:10.1177/0095327X9602300104

Headquarters, Department of the Army. (2006, July). *Combat and operational stress control field manual 4-02.51 (8-51)*, Washington, DC: Author.

Hoge, C. W. (2010). *Once a warrior—Always a warrior: Navigating the transition from combat to home—Including combat stress, PTSD, and mTBI*. Guilford, CT: GPP Life.

Hoge, C. W., Auchterlonie, J. L., & Milliken, C. S. (2006). Mental health problems, use of mental health services, and attrition from military service after returning from deployment to Iraq or Afghanistan. *JAMA, 295*, 1023–1032. doi:10.1001/jama.295.9.1023

Hoge, C. W., & Castro, C. A. (2006). Posttraumatic stress disorder in U.K. and U.S. forces deployed to Iraq [Letter to the editor]. *The Lancet, 368*, 837. doi:10.1016/S0140-6736(06)69315-X

Hoge, C. W., Castro, C. A., Messer, S. C., McGurk, D., Cotting, D. I., & Koffman, R. L. (2004). Combat duty in Iraq and Afghanistan, mental health problems, and barriers to care. *The New England Journal of Medicine, 351*, 13–22. doi:10.1056/NEJMoa040603

Hoge, C. W., McGurk, D., Thomas, J., Cox, A., Engel, C. C., & Castro, C. A. (2008). Mild traumatic brain injury in U.S. soldiers returning from Iraq. *The New England Journal of Medicine, 358,* 453–463. doi:10.1056/NEJMoa072972

Hoge, C. W., Terhakopian, A., Castro, C. A., Messer, S. C., & Engel, C. C. (2007). Association of posttraumatic stress disorder with somatic symptoms, health visits, and absenteeism among Iraq war veterans. *The American Journal of Psychiatry, 164,* 150–153. doi:10.1176/appi.ajp.164.1.150

Hotopf, M., Hull, L., Fear, N. T., Browne, T., Horn, O., Iversen, A., . . . Wessely, S. (2006). The health of U.K. military personnel who deployed to the 2003 Iraq war: A cohort study. *The Lancet, 367,* 1731–1741. doi:10.1016/S0140-6736 (06)68662-5

Institute of Medicine. (2008). *Treatment of posttraumatic stress disorder: An assessment of the evidence.* Washington, DC: National Academies Press.

Jordan, B. K., Schlenger, W. E., Hough, R., Kulka, R. A., Weiss, D., & Fairbank, J. A. (1991). Lifetime and current prevalence of specific psychiatric disorders among Vietnam veterans and controls. *Archives of General Psychiatry, 48,* 207–215.

Kang, H. K., Natelson, B. H., Mahan, C. M., Lee, K., & Murphy, F. M. (2003). Posttraumatic stress disorder and chronic fatigue syndrome-like illness among Gulf war veterans: A population-based survey of 30,000 veterans. *American Journal of Epidemiology, 157,* 141–148. doi:10.1093/aje/kwf187

Kirkland, F. R., Ender, M. G., Gifford, R. K., Wright, K. M., & Marlowe, D. H. (1996). Human dimensions in force projection: Discipline under fire. *Military Review, 76,* 57–64.

Martin, J. A., Vaikus, M. A., Marlowe, D. H., Bartone, P. T., Gifford, R. K., & Wright, K. M. (1992, September/October). Psychological well-being among U.S. soldiers deployed from Germany to the Gulf war. *Journal of the U.S. Army Medical Department,* 29–34.

Mental Health Advisory Team. (2003). *Operation Iraqi Freedom (OIF) Mental Health Advisory Team (MHAT) Report.* Retrieved from http://www.armymedicine.army. mil/reports/mhat/mhat/mhat_report.pdf

Mental Health Advisory Team II. (2005). *Operation Iraqi Freedom (0IF-11) Mental Health Advisory Team (MHAT) Report.* Retrieved from http://www.armymedicine. army.mil/reports/mhat/mhat_ii/OIF-II_REPORT.pdf

Mental Health Advisory Team III. (2006). *Mental Health Advisory Team (MHAT) III Operation Iraqi Freedom 04-06.* Retrieved from http://www.armymedicine.army.mil/ reports/mhat/mhat_iii/MHATIII_Report_29May2006-Redacted.pdf

Mental Health Advisory Team IV. (2006). *Mental Health Advisory Team (MHAT) IV Operation Iraqi Freedom 05-07.* Retrieved from http://www.armymedicine.army.mil/ reports/mhat/mhat_iv/MHAT_IV_Report_17NOV06.pdf

Mental Health Advisory Team V. (2008). *Mental Health Advisory Team (MHAT) V Operation Iraqi Freedom 06-08: Iraq, Operation Enduring Freedom 8: Afghanistan.*

Retrieved from http://www.armymedicine.army.mil/reports/mhat/mhat_v/MHAT_V_OIFandOEF-Redacted.pdf

Milliken, C. S., Auchterlonie, J. L., & Hoge, C. W. (2007). Longitudinal assessment of mental health problems among active and reserve component soldiers returning from the Iraq war. *JAMA, 298,* 2141–2148. doi:10.1001/jama.298.18.2141

Prigerson, H. G., Maciejewski, P. K., & Rosenheck, R. A. (2002). Population attributable fractions of psychiatric disorders and behavioral outcomes associated with combat exposure among U.S. men. *American Journal of Public Health, 92,* 59–63. doi:10.2105/AJPH.92.1.59

Resick, P. A., Galovski, T. E., O'Brien Uhlmansiek, M., Scher, C. D., Clum, G. A., & Young-Xu, Y. (2008). A randomized clinical trial to dismantle components of cognitive processing therapy for posttraumatic stress disorder in female victims of interpersonal violence. *Journal of Consulting and Clinical Psychology, 76,* 243–258. doi:10.1037/0022-006X.76.2.243

Rona, R. J., Hyams, K. C., & Wessely, S. (2005). Screening for psychological illness in military personnel. *JAMA, 293,* 1257–1260. doi:10.1001/jama.293.10.1257

Schneiderman, A. I., Braver, E. R., & Kang, H. K. (2008). Understanding sequelae of injury mechanisms and mild traumatic brain injury incurred during the conflicts in Iraq and Afghanistan: Persistent postconcussive symptoms and posttraumatic stress disorder. *American Journal of Epidemiology, 167,* 1446–1452. doi:10.1093/aje/kwn068

Seal, K. H., Bertenthal, D., Miner, C. R., Sen, S., & Marmar, C. (2007). Bringing the war back home: Mental health disorders among 103,788 U.S. veterans returning from Iraq and Afghanistan seen at department of Veterans Affairs facilities. *Archives of Internal Medicine, 167,* 476–482. doi:10.1001/archinte.167.5.476

Smith, T. C., Ryan, M. A., Wingard, D. L., Slyman, D. J., Sallis, J. F., & Kritz-Silverstein, D. (2008). New onset and persistent symptoms of posttraumatic stress disorder self-reported after deployment and combat exposures: Prospective population-based U.S. military cohort study. *British Medical Journal, 336,* 366–371. doi:10.1136/bmj.39430.638241.AE

Stretch, R. H., Bliese, P. D., Marlowe, D. H., Wright, K. M., Knudson, K. H., & Hoover, C. H. (1996). Psychological health of Gulf war era military personnel. *Military Medicine, 161,* 257–261.

Stretch, R. H., Marlowe, D. H., Wright, K. M., Bliese, P. D., Knudson, K. H., & Hoover, C. H. (1996). Posttraumatic stress disorder symptoms among Gulf war veterans. *Military Medicine, 161,* 407–410.

Tanielian, T., & Jaycox, L. H. (Eds.). (2008). *Invisible wounds of war: Psychological and cognitive injuries, their consequences, and services to assist recovery.* Santa Monica, CA: RAND Corp.

Terhakopian, A., Sinaii, N., Engel, C. C., Schnurr, P. P., & Hoge, C. W. (2008). Estimating population prevalence of posttraumatic stress disorder: An example using the PTSD checklist. *Journal of Traumatic Stress, 21*, 290–300. doi:10.1002/jts.20341

U.S. Department of Defense. (n.d.). *Enhanced postdeployment health assessment process (DD Form 2796).* Retrieved from http://www.pdhealth.mil/dcs/dd_form_2796.asp

U.S. Surgeon General (Ed.). (2002, October). *Fort Bragg epidemiological consultation report.* Fort Bragg, NC: Author.

Wright, K. M., Bliese, P. D., Adler, A. B., Hoge, C. W., Castro, C. A., & Thomas, J. L. (2005). Screening for psychological illness in the military [Letter to the editor]. *JAMA, 294*, 42–43. doi:10.1001/jama.294.1.42-b

Wright, K. M., Huffman, A. H., Adler, A. B., & Castro, C. A. (2002). Psychological screening program overview. *Military Medicine, 167*, 853–861.

Wright, K. M., Thomas, J. L., Adler, A. B., Ness, J. W., Hoge, C. W., & Castro, C. A. (2005). Psychological screening procedures for deploying U.S. forces. *Military Medicine, 170*, 555–562.

2

THE CARE FRAMEWORK: THE BROADENING OF MENTAL HEALTH SERVICES IN A DEPLOYED ENVIRONMENT

CHRISTOPHER H. WARNER, GEORGE N. APPENZELLER,
JILL E. BREITBACH, ANGELA MOBBS, AND JENNIFER T. LANGE

The psychological effects of warfare have been well documented throughout history. Since World War I, the United States Army has been deploying mental health assets to the front lines for treatment of combat operational stress and to advise unit commanders on mental health issues and on the effect of war on soldiers. Currently, commanders of combat units are being encouraged to attend to the overall health of their soldiers, including their psychiatric well-being.

There are unique challenges in the care of soldiers in the deployed environment and for the mental health professionals who provide that care. This chapter outlines prevention and treatment strategies, command consultation, traumatic event management, and the care of psychological casualties on the modern battlefield. It includes a review of existing literature and incorporates the opinions and experiences of the five authors who, combined, have been deployed more than 85 months as mental health providers in a combat environment. We also present a framework of interdependent elements that support the overall mission of mental health care that we have termed the *CARE framework*.

COMBAT AND OPERATIONAL STRESS REACTIONS

During deployments, service members face a myriad of physical and psychological stressors in such difficult environments: sleep deprivation, fatigue, dealing with organizational dynamics, performing duties outside one's normal area of concentration, and being separated from friends, family, and support groups. Service members may respond to these stressors along a continuum of physical and psychological adaptation that ranges from adaptive to maladaptive (Figure 2.1). There are two classes of maladaptive responses to combat operational stress: misconduct behaviors and combat operational stress reactions. *Misconduct behaviors* can range from minor violations of unit

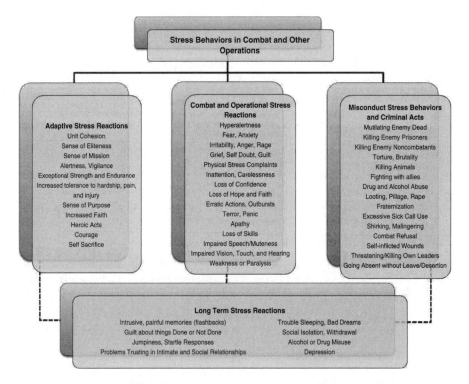

Figure 2.1. Stress behaviors in combat and other operations. Adapted from *Field Manual (FM) 4-02.51. Combat and Operational Stress Control,* by the Department of the Army, 2006, Washington, DC: Headquarters, Department of the Army. In the public domain.

orders to serious violations of the laws of land warfare. *Combat operational stress reactions* are defined as "expected, predictable, emotional, intellectual, physical, and/or behavioral reactions of soldiers who have been exposed to stressful events in combat or military operations other than war" and include physical, emotional, cognitive, and behavioral responses (Department of the Army, 2006). The goal of combat operational stress control measures is to help promote the development of adaptive stress reactions and identify and treat maladaptive responses early (Department of the Army, 2006).

Service members may experience *physical reactions* to the physical and/or psychological stressors of deployment. These physical reactions are the result of the body's physiological stress response to changes in one's internal and/or external environment. Common physical symptoms of combat operational stress include muscle aches, sleep disturbance, hyperarousal, altered sensory experiences, and headaches. Compared with psychological reactions, service members may be relatively apt to report physical symptoms to their medical provider. Thus, these signs often serve as the first opportunity for intervention, and general medical providers need to be trained to recognize these opportunities.

Emotional responses to deployment stressors may include fear, anxiety, irritability, anger, grief, apathy, depression, and guilt. However, individual differences in how service members respond emotionally can lead fellow unit members and leaders to be less tolerant of some reactions. This lack of understanding can reinforce problems because the affected service members may feel more isolated when their experience is not normalized by their peer group. Thus, these psychological reactions can be relatively difficult to identify because individuals may be reluctant to identify themselves for fear that fellow service members will perceive them as weak.

Cognitive responses to deployment stressors include the schematic organization of events by an individual and their subsequent belief systems about the military event, the environment (e.g., "The world is not safe"), others (e.g., "They don't care about my well being"), oneself (e.g., self-doubt and the "I shoulda, coulda . . . "), and/or altered spiritual beliefs (e.g., "Bad things are only supposed to happen to bad people"). Many times service members have limited insight about how these responses affect their well-being and how the responses alter their fundamental beliefs about the world around them.

Behavioral responses include the variety of actions, or lack thereof, that an individual has to an event. Common behavioral responses may include increased aggressive behaviors (e.g., fighting, yelling), impulsive behaviors (e.g., drinking alcohol, spending money), isolative behaviors, and/or compulsive behaviors (e.g., checking behaviors). These behaviors will often first capture the concern of an individual's peers or leaders. However, the behaviors may not be recognized as symptomatic of combat operational stress.

An individual's physical, emotional, cognitive, or behavioral responses to combat operational stress are influenced by many variables. Specifically, each service member brings a unique set of personality, physiological, and personal history factors to each potential stressor. All of these factors mediate and moderate the individual's stress response either by enhancing resiliency or decreasing the effectiveness of coping mechanisms.

Furthermore, an individual's perceived support network (i.e., unit) can also mediate his or her stress response. Much of what is currently understood about preventing combat operational stress casualties comes from the work of Menninger, who identified that a failure to meet basic needs such as food, water, and sleep, in addition to not providing respite from isolation and boredom, contributed significantly to the incidence of combat operational stress casualties in combat (Menninger, 1948). Also, unit cohesion and morale have been repeatedly found to be important in supporting individual coping behavior and unit performance both in wartime and in peacetime (Gal & Jones, 1995; Tischler, 1969). Although *morale* remains difficult to define operationally, it may be considered to represent the general sense of unit cohesion, confidence in ability, and overall well-being of a unit. Low morale, whether due to poor integration with the group or to inadequate leadership causing decreased order and decreased perceived security, has been associated with psychiatric referral, at least on initial deployment (Tischler, 1969). Development and reinforcement of high morale and strong unit cohesion is one of the greatest defenses against breakdown in combat (Glass, 1966).

In addition, it has been well documented throughout history that time spent exposed to combat correlates with higher rates of combat operational stress casualties (Appel, 1966; Gal & Jones, 1995; Group for the Advancement of Psychiatry, 1960; Glass, 1966; Mental Health Advisory Team [MHAT] III, 2006; MHAT IV, 2006; MHAT V, 2008; Tischler, 1969). The impact of time in a combat theater on visits to the mental health unit has been seen in operations in Iraq and Afghanistan, where multiple studies have noted an increase in combat operational stress reactions after 6 months of deployment (MHAT III, 2006; MHAT IV, 2006; Warner et al., 2007). It has been shown that soldiers deployed more than 6 months were 1.5 to 1.6 times more likely to screen positive for acute stress, depression, and/or anxiety than those deployed for less than 6 months (MHAT III, 2006). In addition, a higher number of combat experiences positively correlated with an increase in acute stress responses (MHAT IV, 2006). There are also data suggesting a link between the number of deployments and increased combat stress-related symptoms (MHAT V, 2008). This indicates that there is a link between cumulative time of exposure and severity of experiences and the likelihood of maladaptive stress reactions. Understanding these factors, as well as their historical context, provides a framework for application of current principles, recognition of high-risk groups, and targeted preventive interventions.

THE CARE FRAMEWORK

The CARE framework consists of four interdependent elements that form the basis of battlefield mental health care. These are consultation, availability, resiliency/prevention training, and early intervention. Although all of these elements are discussed in the following sections, the concept of CARE gives a base from which to plan and evaluate courses of action and programs. The concepts are also summarized in Table 2.1.

The first element is *consultation*. The military mental health provider is the subject matter expert and must act as a consultant to the leaders and medical providers on the battlefield. The command–consultant relationship is critical. Through this relationship, the provider not only promotes prevention and resiliency development programs but can also have a direct impact on combat power through communication about the unit's status, issues, and possible interventions. A good relationship with the commander is the primary means of decreasing the stigma associated with mental health care and increasing overall unit mental health. This consultant role also extends to the medical leadership, who may not have clinical experience or more than elementary training in mental health. Last, consultation to the other care providers on the battlefield in both individual cases and in procedures, policies, and training will greatly extend the potential effectiveness of the mental health system.

Availability does not refer just to an open clinic but also to the perceived presence of the military mental health provider throughout the battlefield. As is discussed in more detail later in this chapter, it is critical that the mental health providers be available to commands in the field, to service members when it is convenient given their mission requirements, and at locations away from the clinic and large base camps. This availability can be the most difficult element to achieve because the military mental health provider may be the only credentialed provider over a large geographic area. Creating this level of accessibility may require use of paraprofessionals and primary care providers for more basic clinical work while the mental health provider attends to those activities that require his or her expertise.

Resiliency and preventive training refers to providing coping skills training for managing reactions to the stressors associated with deployment. The effectiveness of resiliency and preventive training is directly affected by the military mental health provider's relationship and credibility with the unit leadership. This training should go beyond educational initiatives and

TABLE 2.1
Key Mental Health Provider Considerations During Deployment: Implementing the CARE Model

CARE topic	Actions to optimize provider efficacy
Consultation	Prioritize the development of good relationships with unit command.
	Preserve credibility through military appearance (e.g., uniform).
	Educate commanders about what mental health professionals can provide.
	Use numbers; quantify needs and accomplishments.
	Adapt interventions to unit needs, schedule, and situation.
	Participate in battlefield circulation.
	Make action-based recommendations for every problem identified.
	Conduct follow-up assessments and feedback.
Availability	Be ready to work 24/7; there are no real "days off."
	Be visible; get out of the office.
	Go to where the service members are, but avoid unnecessary risks.
	Assume everything is being observed or evaluated by a potential patient and/or leader.
Resilience training	Target stigma reduction in all education.
	Build service member confidence that most reactions are normal.
	Identify adaptive reactions to ongoing threats.
	Develop psychoeducation that matches the environment; use a discussion format.
Early intervention	Remember PIES, but be ready for other stress-related issues.
	Recognize the unusual nature of boundaries on deployment.
	Balance on-the-spot interventions with setting aside a place and time.
	Find colleagues and friends for support.
	Remember that restoration programs can have repercussions when service members return to their unit.
	Adapt clinical interventions for one session; do not assign homework.
	Remember that some service members just need help getting through a difficult period.
	Remember to work with your mental health technicians, chaplains, unit medical personnel, and unit leaders.
	Consider assessments of threats to self and other given availability of weapons and the need to respond to an attack.

Note. PIES = proximity, immediacy, expectancy, simplicity.

psychological screenings and should include unit-wide mental health assessments and data that can be used to make evidence-based recommendations to the commander, who in turn can implement preventive programs.

These assessments may also identify issues before they become significant unit problems, allowing for *early intervention*. The most notable aspect of this component of the CARE concept is the forward psychiatry principles that detail the approach to mental health interventions at the frontline. However, early interventions also include developing care plans prior to deployment, treating unit cohesion issues and proactive needs assessments, facilitating systems development, and conducting provision of full-spectrum care on the battlefield.

RESILIENCY AND PREVENTIVE MENTAL HEALTH

Military mental health providers were the first to focus on the total social environment of the individual in establishing programs for not only the treatment but also the prevention of mental illness (Bourne, 1970). This shift came in 1944, when the army began using psychiatrists in a preventive fashion, reshaping the role of combat mental health care from straight disposition of personnel into one in which consultants recommend how to use marginal personnel and implement mental hygiene training programs (Appel, 1966). Thus, the role of military mental health providers in providing primary, secondary, and tertiary prevention based on understanding biopsychosocial influences on behavior was established. The effectiveness of preventive psychiatry was later shown by the Group for the Advancement of Psychiatry (1960) when they reported that preventive military mental health care can reduce combat ineffectiveness through early recognition and prompt outpatient treatment of emotional difficulties during combat and noncombat situations.

Although this preventive approach is recognized as important, actual implementation can be problematic because of time constraints and misperceptions about what mental health professionals can provide. Time is a critical resource in the combat environment, and it can be difficult to obtain the required time for prevention efforts. Similarly, commanders must weigh competing priorities. Many commanders and service members may not have a solid understanding of the impact prevention can have on the unit. Furthermore, the commander's perception of the provider can help or hinder the provider's ability to implement effective programs. Credibility with commanders and the ability to provide coherent, evidence-based recommendations in terms commanders understand and that meet commander's priorities are essential. Last, there may not be acceptance of mental health's contributions from the nonmental health medical leadership and providers. Here the relationship between the military mental health provider and the senior medical officer is critical. These officers have many of the same concerns as commanders, including concerns about time and priorities, and may also have a lack of understanding about how mental health initiatives can enhance mission readiness.

Despite these obstacles, prevention work is not optional and cannot be left solely to the chaplains and other supporting services. Mental health providers must work with unit medical personnel and command regarding what they can do to prevent mental health casualties. This cooperative approach does not mean that mental health support requires continuous formal screening of all unit members but rather involves consistent awareness of the unit as a whole through interacting with leaders and unit members and through attending key unit events.

For example, in working with one unit, mental health personnel attended more than 40 memorial services over the course of a year in Iraq. The mental health personnel were typically the first to arrive and the last to leave these services. Mental health personnel not only participated in the services as affected soldiers but also used the opportunity to watch for signs that unit members might be in distress. They were direct with soldiers in expressing their concern for all unit members, asking questions about sleep, anger, and whether they had concerns about their fellow unit members. Initially, unit leaders did not pay particular attention to the providers; however, over time, leaders used these informal moments to identify who needed their additional support. Leadership outreach showed unit members that command cared, and, in our opinion, potential problems were addressed early.

PRIMARY PREVENTION

Primary prevention measures in combat operational stress control are designed to prevent the development of combat operational stress reactions in service members by minimizing the stressors and encouraging the development of adaptive stress responses and resiliency. This prevention is predominantly conducted through various aspects of health promotion. We discuss two types of primary prevention during combat operations: psychoeducation and battle-field circulation. Note that we recognize there is a distinction between psychoeducation and mental health training. *Training* implies the intent to impart specific skills and provide opportunities for practicing those skills, whereas *education* implies the general imparting of knowledge. For the purposes of this chapter, we have combined the two concepts.

Psychoeducation/Mental Health Training

Most military units regularly use 1- to 2-hour courses on a quarterly or yearly basis on topics such as prevention of sexual assault, suicide, and substance abuse. The U.S. Army medical department has also designed a resiliency-based psychoeducational series titled *Battlemind Training*, with specific modules administered before and after deployments. These modules, now adapted and incorporated as resilience training as part of the army's Comprehensive Soldier Fitness Program, build on a soldier's inner strength, help soldiers develop resiliency in stressful situations, and teach them how to use their strengths during times of transition.

During deployment, psychoeducation should be continued but needs to be modified in terms of content and delivery style. First, psychoeducation should focus on key deployment issues that service members encounter, including home front stressors, failing relationships, disciplinary problems, combat, casualty exposure, and ongoing peer or unit problems. Sessions should focus on early recognition of maladaptive stress responses, appropriate actions for peers and leaders, and how to access available resources. Currently, there is little objective data showing the effectiveness of these training sessions. However, initial research on the effectiveness of the resiliency-based Battlemind Training appears promising, and in our subjective experience, these deployment sessions help to decrease barriers to mental health care and increase soldiers' willingness to seek care (Adler, Bliese, McGurk, Hoge, & Castro, 2009; Castro & Thomas, 2007; MHAT IV, 2006; Warner, Appenzeller, Mullen, Warner, & Greiger, 2008).

As with other preventive and intervention efforts, significant barriers to providing education must be overcome to make Battlemind Training successful. The greatest obstacle is time constraints because of competing priorities. Secondary to this, education can be viewed as an unwelcome disruption (e.g., "Just one more thing taking me from the mission") or as useless (e.g., "We don't need that"). For these reasons, it is critical to quantify for the commander what is being done and to provide evidence-based recommendations. These recommendations need to be presented in a nonconfrontational manner, with an emphasis on how the recommendation will increase unit effectiveness or how it will directly affect mission capabilities. When making these recommendations, it must also be stressed that flexibility on the part of the mental health provider is paramount, and all education efforts should be coordinated with the unit's schedule. It is much easier to gain support from a commander when psychoeducation is brought to a unit at a time and place convenient to the unit.

In addition, the majority of education in theater is not traditional classroom education. It is often performed in austere circumstances, and the efforts should be tailored to them. Thus, handouts, formal presentations, and the classroom setting are unlikely to be successfully received. Small-group discussions are preferred, and whenever possible, mental health providers should have leaders and unit members help facilitate the training.

The most productive and accepted training shows immediate impact on specific issues, emphasizing "this is what you can do right now." Also, providers should brief commanders after the training. These briefs should focus on what was accomplished in the training, highlight unit mental health issues, and suggest recommendations. This information supports commanders in their decision-making process regarding further training, resource management, and support to programs. Problems identified by the mental health provider need to have a corresponding recommendation for action. Recommendations should be specific and action based. For example, instead of informing commanders that "service members are fatigued," mental health providers might suggest specific work and rest cycles and sleep hygiene interventions that can then be reassessed to determine whether they were effective.

One education initiative in Iraq that demonstrates these principles of psychoeducation addressed problematic ethical attitudes toward the treatment of noncombatants. After anonymous in-theater assessments documented significant levels of problematic ethical attitudes of soldiers in the combat zone (MHAT IV, 2006; MHAT V, 2008), we presented a plan for psychoeducation to their division commander in theater. On the basis of the recommendations, the division commander directed his combined staff to develop and implement training to address the issue. *Chain teaching* was chosen as the method of training. Chain teaching is the term used to describe a top-down approach to education in which each level of leadership is responsible for training service members under their direct command. This method was chosen to facilitate small group discussion and to allow training to be conducted at convenient times. Chain teaching also emphasizes how important a topic is to the leadership and allows leaders to more directly gauge unit member attitudes. The staff developed a training package using popular movie clips to illustrate points and as a guide to facilitate discussion. The commanding general emphasized the training publicly at weekly updates. After the training was complete, ethical attitudes were reassessed, and the results provided to commanders showed a significant reduction in unethical attitudes and an increased willingness to report ethical violations. These data provided support for continued educational efforts (Warner, Appenzeller, Mobbs, & Grieger, 2008).

One other consideration when conducting training in theater is to ensure that education is appropriate to the unit's stage in the deployment cycle. In an example of mismatch between educational content and deployment cycle phase, one deployed unit received psychoeducation about posttraumatic stress disorder that included a discussion of redeploying home and issues encountered during family reunions. Although this was appropriate for units nearing return to home, this unit had more than 8 months before returning home, and unit members voiced significant dissatisfaction with the training. This type of asynchronous training increases the possibility not only of being ineffective but also discrediting future training and the mental health providers.

In contrast, an example of psychoeducation appropriate to the deployment cycle was the creation of a "going home" video by a unit's deployed medical and mental health providers. Embedded in a music and video presentation were training materials on what to expect when reintegrating with family and noncombat life. The video was also designed to illustrate the great work unit members had performed during their deployment and to reinforce positive feelings about their sacrifice. The video was presented to soldiers while they were waiting to go through customs en route to coming home. This timing presented an opportunity to provide training without adding a burden to the unit. Anecdotally, the soldiers reported that they enjoyed the training, and many requested copies of the video to take home with them.

Battlefield Circulation

Battlefield circulation is a term used to describe a unit commander's time spent traveling around his or her unit gaining insight into the overall situation and the needs of subordinate commanders and service members. An effective way for mental health providers to gain not only insight into the conditions and issues at the subordinate unit levels but also credibility in the eyes of both commanders and service members is to accompany the commander on battlefield circulation when possible.

Credibility is acquired on multiple levels. The individual provider gains credibility with both the commander and service members by leaving the relative safety of the large base and going to small outposts to visit the service members. The service members recognize the military mental health provider's willingness to place service members' well-being over personal risk in making the site visits. Commanders recognize the military mental health providers "on the ground" opinion as more valid than one formed from a distance. In addition, the mere presence of the mental health provider travelling with the commander shows the importance that is placed on mental health care. This presence indirectly reduces the stigma of seeking care and promotes acceptance of the provider as "part of the team."

Primary prevention can be performed during battlefield circulation in two additional ways. Through direct interaction with the unit at the field site, the mental health provider is available to educate, counsel, and advise junior leaders and service members on applicable mental health topics and coping strategies. Sometimes referred to as a "ministry by presence" by military chaplains or "therapy by walking around" by military mental health professionals, getting out to the areas where the service member works allows the mental health provider direct observation of the current situation and the ability to break down negative attitudes toward military mental health personnel. During these visits, providers might meet individually or with a group of service members and junior leaders to get a "dipstick" on the current situation and to provide psychoeducation on relevant topics, such as sleep hygiene, dealing with loss, and anger management. This time can also be used to collect information and conduct needs assessments without placing additional burdens on a unit.

The second form of primary prevention specific to battlefield circulation is senior command advisement and mental health advocacy. While visiting any unit, particular attention should be paid to living conditions, morale concerns, work/rest cycles, service members who do not appear to be integrated into the group, overall unit cohesion, and the opinions of leaders and soldiers. Time should be spent listening to soldiers and junior leaders. This information, along with recommendations to ameliorate problems, should then be prepared for the senior commander in the form of an executive summary. This brief document should be nonjudgmental, factual, and focused on corrective measures; it should not simply be a list of complaints. Ideally, this assessment of environmental conditions should be done routinely.

For example, during a deployment to Iraq, a military mental health provider accompanied the senior mission commander on a battlefield circulation trip to a remote patrol base. During the time at the base, the provider noted there was a general lack of comfort items, the generator was not functional, there was limited communication capability with families, there were no bathing facilities, and laundry services were infrequent. Although the provider noted good group cohesion, the group's overall morale was low. The soldiers felt they had been "forgotten by command." Although there were not significant combat stress casualties, the military mental health provider felt that this environment was at great risk of developing decreased combat effectiveness, high levels of combat operational stress, and potential misconduct behaviors. On return from the visit, the provider prepared a report delineating the concerns. The senior commander was able to correct and improve the majority of issues, including refrigeration, resupply frequency, Internet service, air conditioning, and shower facilities. During a visit 2 months later, both soldiers and leaders noted improved morale, health, trust in leadership, and combat effectiveness.

The preceding example demonstrates the importance of broadening the traditional scope of military mental health providers. Military mental health providers can have more of a significant impact through their demonstrated availability, adapted use of psychoeducation, and consultation with leadership than if they maintain a strictly clinical or treatment role. However, the importance of balancing these activities with more traditional clinical practice and forward psychiatry must be emphasized. Concentrating on one tenet of the CARE framework to the exclusion of the others is detrimental to the overall well-being of the unit. One method of improving this balance is using helping resources and paraprofessionals to provide care within their scope, leaving the mental health provider to perform those activities only they can provide.

Battlefield circulation should also be used to collaborate and consult with medical providers, consulting on patients as well as educating medical personnel (i.e., both soldier–medics and providers) on important mental health problems.

SECONDARY PREVENTION

Secondary prevention involves the early identification of those service members who are at risk of developing mental health problems and applying interventions to prevent the worsening or the development of symptoms after exposure. These types of procedures are accomplished both through individual and unit level screening as well as through interventions such as traumatic event management.

Individual Screening

Military units conduct medical evaluations prior to their deployment to ensure that service members are capable of performing their duties during the deployment and that continued medical care can be provided for their respective condition. In 2006, the U.S. Department of Defense developed a minimum mental health standard for deployment. This policy outlines mental health criteria for deployability, identifying conditions that can be managed in theater and what level of treatment can be provided during a deployment (Assistant Secretary of Defense, 2006). Other than psychosis and bipolar disorder, this policy does not identify specific mental health conditions as preventing an individual from deploying. Instead, this decision is based on symptom severity and the level of care required. The key points and limitations of this policy are outlined in Table 2.2.

To determine whether service members meet the minimum mental health standards for deployment, deploying units are incorporating mental health screening into their predeployment medical screening process. That process allows the deploying unit's medical personnel to be aware of all service members who have active mental health diagnoses, are currently undergoing treatment, and who are taking psychotropic medications. This tracking allows the medical team to develop a continuation of treatment plan, assist in linking the service member to the necessary mental health resources during the deployment, and to put in place measures to ensure appropriate safety precautions are enacted. For example, service members who are identified as taking a benzodiazepine, a potentially sedating medication, may be deployed but restricted to duties within a headquarters facility where they can have a more consistent routine and not be expected to make rapid decisions about rules of engagement or about whether an individual is an enemy or noncombatant. In addition,

TABLE 2.2
Key Points in the November 2006 "Policy Guidance for
Deployment Limiting Psychiatric Conditions and Medications"

Limiting condition	Deployability criterion
Nondeployable diagnoses	Service members currently being treated for psychosis or bipolar disorder were not deployable.
Axis I diagnoses	Service members with significant ongoing mental health conditions (Axis I diagnosis) must be stable for at least 3 months prior to deployment.
Medication monitoring	Service members who are taking medications that require laboratory monitoring, such as lithium or valproic acid, are not deployable.
Antipsychotic medications	Service members who are taking antipsychotic medications to control psychotic, bipolar, or chronic insomnia conditions are not deployable.
Medication considerations	Continued use of psychotropic medications (e.g., short half-life benzodiazepines and stimulants) should be balanced between the need for successful functioning in the theater of operations and the ability to obtain the medication, the potential for withdrawal, and the potential for abuse.
Psychotropic medication	If service members are placed on a psychotropic medication within 3 months of deployment, then they must be improving, stable, and tolerating the medication without significant side effect to deploy.

Note. Adapted from *Policy Guidance for Deployment Limiting Psychiatric Conditions and Medications*, by the Assistant Secretary of Defense, 2006, Washington, DC: Department of Defense. In the public domain.

medical personnel can ensure that service members have continued access to appropriate mental health care and can monitor soldiers to ensure they have necessary mental health follow-ups. Establishing continuity of care between military mental health providers at home and during deployment can help prevent mental health conditions from deteriorating and can assist in ensuring service member and unit safety.

Failure to perform these actions can be detrimental to the unit and to service members and can consume inordinate amounts of time for deployed providers. Implementing the predeployment screening process appropriately is critical. One of the authors was deployed with a unit that had five soldiers who were recommended for separation from military service prior to deployment because of mental health problems. However, these soldiers were deployed, and the theater providers were not notified. Although the soldiers arrived in theater and appropriately sought treatment, there was no continuity of care, and theater providers had to recreate care plans. In addition, two of the soldiers were suicidal and had to be evacuated. Had the continuity of care been established, care plans could have been in place, and the two cases may not have escalated to the point of evacuation. In another example of mismanaged continuity of care, patients may arrive at clinics in theater requesting refills of antipsychotics or lithium, which were not available in or appropriate to the combat environment. These situations can be contrasted to those in units in a division, in which soldiers were screened more carefully and treatment plans were put into place prior to deployment. This division deployed with more than 20,000 soldiers, and more than 90 soldiers had care plans in place, and all of these soldiers successfully completed their 15-month deployment.

Unit Behavioral Health Needs Assessments

An additional method of prevention is the role of military mental health providers in consulting with the unit. In conducting a broad needs assessment, use of standardized tools is recommended. An example of this is the U.S. Army's Unit Behavioral Health Needs Assessment (UBHNA). This tool allows the consultant to survey a sample of unit members using standardized measures that assess morale, cohesion, stressors, and service member concerns, as well as current levels of need for mental health support and barriers to care. The mental health consultant can then provide the commander with clear, objective findings and customized recommendations specific to the unit. In addition, if repeated in the same unit over time, the survey can be used to track changes over time. Finally, the UBHNA has comparison data from units at different stages throughout Operation Iraqi Freedom that can help gauge a unit's relative status (MHAT III, 2006).

Traumatic Event Management

Exposure to combat-related potentially traumatic events such as a unit member being seriously injured or killed, being ambushed by the enemy, or having an improvised explosive device or booby trap explode nearby is one of the principle risk factors for behavioral health problems in a combat setting (Fontana & Rosencheck, 1998). *Traumatic event management* (TEM) involves intervening after a potentially traumatic event has occurred with the purpose of seeking to decrease the negative effect of the event on mental health and prevent long-term negative sequelae.

Initially, the TEM process is conducted at the request of a unit leader. The goal is to help the unit proactively manage the psychological effects of the traumatic experience. The military mental health provider begins by conducting a general needs assessment to determine whether service members need immediate mental health care for combat operational stress reactions. The general needs assessment also helps the military mental health provider to provide consultation and education to the unit leaders. The TEM process can reinforce perceptions that leaders are supportive of mental health care; it can also educate soldiers on how to access resources and can provide soldiers and leaders with recommendations on actions to take in response to potentially traumatic events, including the use of leader-led, after-action reviews encouraging soldiers to talk about the event.

In addition, in conjunction with the unit leader, the military mental health provider will determine whether and when a group psychological debriefing should be conducted. Psychological debriefings have historically differed depending on the model being used, but each involves some structured set of phases in which there is psychological recognition of the traumatic event and some degree of cognitive and/or emotional processing of reactions to the event. Unlike leader-led, after-action reviews, these sessions are led by trained mental health providers or chaplains.

There have been different models for debriefings. Most models evolved from Marshall's work in World War II, when he attempted to record accounts of unit operations for historical purposes (Koshes, Young, & Stokes, 1995). It is interesting that those initial sessions were not for the expressed purpose of providing psychological benefits to the involved parties. However, Marshall noted that during the process of debriefing, many misperceptions were corrected by other individuals involved in the traumatic event, and the debriefing appeared to render social support and decrease the development of combat stress reactions (Koshes et al., 1995).

Despite the tradition of debriefing in the military, there is considerable debate among both military and civilian mental health providers about the utility and efficacy of debriefings. Although psychological debriefings have been used throughout military conflicts, their effectiveness has not been well documented in research studies. There has been little data gathered on the risks and benefits of psychological debriefings performed on combat soldiers, but civilian studies of victims have demonstrated benefits as well as negative outcomes (Jacobs, Horne-Moyer, & Jones, 2004; MacDonald, 2003; Mitchell & Mitchell, 2006; Rose, Bisson, Churchill, & Wessely, 2002). Part of the problem in examining the utility of debriefings is the evolution of what TEM actually entails. In fact, "debriefings" are now thought to take many forms commonly used by all military personnel, including after action reviews, which are a standing operating procedure for all U.S. Army teams and small units following any training exercise (Koshes et al., 1995). Furthermore, there are multiple models for debriefings, including critical event debriefings, critical incident stress debriefings, psychiatric debriefings, historical debriefings, and intelligence debriefings. Thus, one of the inherent problems in determin-

TABLE 2.3
Phases of Debriefing Methods

Phase	After-action debriefing	Critical event debriefing	Critical incident stress debriefing	Battlemind Psychological Debriefing (in theater)
1	Purpose and ground rules	Introduction	Introduction	Introduction
2	Event reconstruction	Chronological reconstruction	Fact	Event
3	Group consensus of event	Cognitive–affective reactions	Thought	Reactions
4	Thoughts and feelings		Reaction	
5	Emotional validation	Symptoms	Symptom	Self and buddy aid
6	Prevention of scapegoating	Teaching	Teaching	
7	Symptoms	Wrap-up	Reentry	Battlemind (resiliency) focus
8	Lessons learned			

Note. Adapted from "Time-Driven Battlemind Psychological Debriefing: A Group-Level Early Intervention in Combat," by A. B. Adler, C. A. Castro, and D. McGurk, 2009, *Military Medicine, 174*, pp. 21–28. Copyright 2009 by IngentaConnect. Adapted with permission.

ing the effectiveness of TEM is the lack of consistent, standardized protocols across providers and across organizations. Table 2.3 compares and contrasts the different models.

Despite all of the inherent problems in definition, standardization, and demonstrable utility, psychological debriefings remain a common consultation task that is requested of military mental health providers as military leaders have become more aware of the potential long-term impact of traumatic events and have begun taking a proactive stance in helping their soldiers. Thus, it is imperative that all military mental health providers be aware of the current evidence-based practices and be proficient in all aspects of TEM, not just psychological debriefings. Currently, the Department of the Army's *Combat Operational Stress Control* field manual (4-02.51; 2006) provides a standardized outline and structure for TEM operations but leaves the decision of conducting a psychological debriefing and the method of debriefing open to the mental health provider.

This guidance on debriefing is still evolving. In 2007, the army introduced a new debriefing model termed *Battlemind Psychological Debriefing*, which is taught to all deploying mental health providers (Adler, Castro, & McGurk, 2009; MHAT IV, 2006). This debriefing model takes into account military rank and structure and incorporates resiliency-based education principles that help to build on the soldier's strengths during the process. It was specifically designed for use with soldiers in a combat environment and is focused toward equipping soldiers with the skills to help cope with the impact of the potentially traumatic event, enhancing cohesion within the group and preparing soldiers to return to the battlefield. Whereas all other models are designed to be implemented after a potentially traumatic event, Battlemind Psychological Debriefings have both a typical event-driven format and a time-driven format that occurs at regular intervals to review key potentially traumatic events that may have occurred over the course of several months. These sessions incorporate and build on the Battlemind (e.g., resilience) principles that all soldiers are taught prior to deployment and emphasize the importance of buddy care.

As with other debriefing methods, the effectiveness of this process has yet to be studied; however, a group randomized trial of Battlemind Psychological Debriefing conducted immediately after a 12-month combat deployment demonstrated this technique to be effective in reducing mental health symptoms over time compared with traditional postdeployment stress education (Adler, Bliese, et al., 2009). Furthermore, we have conducted more than 200 Battlemind Psychological Debriefings during deployment and note higher levels of participation during these sessions in contrast with other models. We have also noted increased levels of commander satisfaction with the debriefings, improved communication and cohesion amongst the soldiers involved in the event, and an enhanced understanding of the Battlemind principles. Positive provider perceptions were also systematically documented in the MHAT V report conducted in Iraq (MHAT V, 2008).

TERTIARY PREVENTION

If untreated, combat operational stress reactions can have a significant impact on a unit's ability to complete its mission. A review of the use of one division mental health provider team's activity during its deployment to Operation Iraqi Freedom in 2005 noted that in 1 year the five providers saw more than 5,000 of their 25,000 soldiers in a clinical setting at least once. Nearly one third (29.8%) of these first-time clinical contacts were for preexisting mental health disorders, with combat operational stress reactions accounting for the rest of the encounters (Warner et al., 2007). Home-front stressors, such as failing relationships and financial problems, were the largest factors associated with combat operational stress; combat experiences were the second most prominent cause.

In addition, the two most common preexisting mental health disorders encountered were generalized anxiety disorder (GAD) and major depressive disorder (MDD). GAD accounted for 42.4% of preexisting mental health encounters and 12.6% of all in-theater clinical encounters. MDD accounted for 33.4% of preexisting mental health encounters and 10.0% of all clinical encounters (Warner et al., 2007). Given these rates, it is clear that the principles of forward psychiatry must not only incorporate the treatment of traditional combat operational stress but must also include early intervention strategies for treating premorbid psychiatric conditions that are exacerbated by deployment.

FORWARD PSYCHIATRY

The current principles of combat operational stress control continue to use the principles originally developed by Thomas W. Salmon. The implementation of these principles, commonly termed *PIES* (proximity, immediacy, expectancy, simplicity), has evolved throughout the 20th century and has become known as *forward psychiatry* (Jones & Wessely, 2003).

Proximity refers to psychiatric casualties being treated as close to their units as possible to maintain unit cohesion and the individual's bond with his or her unit. One of the challenges for military mental health providers in combat is to balance provider availability and far-forward treatment while taking into account the safety issues associated with travelling to remote sites. That is, providers need to be available to remote units even though travelling across a wide area presents significant logistical and safety problems that can interfere with effectively adhering to the principle of proximity. In 2007, the U.S. Army increasingly embedded brigade behavioral health officers (i.e., social workers and psychologists) within combat units, which has not only facilitated adherence to the principle of proximity but also increases the chance that service members are treated by providers assigned to their unit, thus providing consistency and greater availability of provider staff.

The principle of proximity has been observed in other conflicts. During the Yom Kippur and Lebanon Wars, for example, Israeli researchers noted that evacuation of individuals with mild combat operational stress injuries worsened their prognosis and further complicated their recovery (Belenky, Tyner, & Sodetz, 1983). Specifically, evacuated individuals increasingly reported physical and psychological complaints as the time for rejoining their unit on the battlefield drew near. This finding highlights the significance of forward treatment. In contrast, service members with moderate to severe combat operational stress injuries who cannot be returned to their unit require early mental health intervention to help the service members cope with the difficult transition of returning home from combat without the assistance of their unit support group (Jones, 1995).

Facilitated by the concept of proximity, *immediacy* refers to psychiatric casualties being treated as soon as possible, allowing for early intervention. Distributing small teams of mental health providers throughout the battlefield ensures rapidly available and easily accessible care. In addition, if military mental health providers develop credible relationships with unit leaders through their battlefield circulation and psychoeducation initiatives, then leaders can have a better understanding of the mental health provider's mission and are more apt to get service members into care rapidly.

Expectancy refers to "prescribing health," and facilitating the service member's expectation of returning to duty. In essence, the mental health provider must make clear early that the treatment goal is for the service member to return to duty in the combat role. This principle is especially important given that once service members view themselves as "injured patients," they make cognitive shifts in role and expected outcome. Thus, it is important to refer to service members by their military title and refrain from using the term *casualty* or *patient*.

The significance of this particular principle was demonstrated in World War I. At that time, soldiers with combat operational stress symptoms were diagnosed as being ill with *shell shock*. This labeling appeared to provide an honorable escape from combat. As a result, shell shock resonated as a "contagious" disease requiring an increased number of soldiers to be evacuated from the battlefield (Jones, 1995). Other accounts have suggested that evacuation for mental illness may inadvertently increase identification with the patient role to justify leaving the unit. This identification then decreases the soldier's chance of recovery (Department of the Army, 1994). Thus, emphasizing and promoting a service member's value to the unit and mission, both in treating the service member and in consulting with the unit's leadership, fosters a sense of belonging and support that encourages return to full duty. In the majority of cases, the sense of accomplishment gained by completing the mission and the deployment will be psychologically beneficial and should result in improved postdeployment adjustment.

Simplicity refers to keeping treatment to the basics to emphasize the normality of the service member's experience rather than implying some significant level of mental illness (Jones, 1995). For instance, treatment might consist of the "five Rs": (a) rest from extreme stress, (b) rehydration and replenishment of nutrients, (c) restoration of confidence through work activities, (d) reassurance that the service member will be okay, and (e) return to duty. In 2008, the U.S. Army added a sixth "R," which stands for remind (Marr, 2008). In the combat zone, where all service members have the capability of deadly force at their fingertips, military mental health providers must be aware of the risk of potentially violent behaviors in combat operational stress casualties. It is imperative that the provider reminds service members that they are expected to follow the rules of engagement and "serve with honor." As part of this principle, military mental health providers should conduct a risk assessment for potential violent behaviors to determine whether additional safety measures should be taken, such as invoking weapons restrictions and unit watch (i.e., the individual is literally watched at all times by another unit member until the period of crisis has passed).

Despite the widespread acceptance of these principles, studies have not assessed the impact of forward psychiatry on long-term outcomes (Jones & Wessely, 2003). Critics have noted varying rates of combat stress relapse associated with forward psychiatry and that some symptomatic service members are eventually evacuated from the combat theater despite forward psychiatric treatment (Jones & Wessely, 2003). Further studies are needed to determine the overall short- and long-term effectiveness of forward psychiatry.

Although forward psychiatry principles are not the only element of early intervention, they do represent the cornerstone of battlefield mental health intervention. In rapid moving, high intensity combat this level of intervention may be the only one that can be provided. However, as a theater matures or additional mental health resources become available it is imperative that additional interventions be incorporated into the care that is provided.

PSYCHOTHERAPY IN THEATER

Balancing all aspects of the CARE framework can make providing therapy in theater challenging. Moreover, treatment approaches conducted in theater need to be adapted to respond to constraints inherent in a deployed environment. This section highlights some of the psychotherapy treatment interventions that may be most appropriately applied in a deployed environment and the specific limitations inherent in deployment psychotherapy.

Arguably, the most pressing constraint is time. Providers have to coordinate psychotherapy treatment with the mission requirements of the service member's unit and with their own availability, given that they will need to travel to remote sites to be available to units and to provide command consultation. On deployment, most military mental health providers will find themselves on call 24 hr a day, 7 days a week, with the time available in a stationary clinic limited by their travel schedule. Furthermore, the ongoing risk of potential enemy contact and traumatic events can result in both the provider and the service member being unable to meet as scheduled.

Thus, trying to schedule treatment times with military personnel is difficult; the ability to capitalize on brief treatment modalities is paramount. Accordingly, it is often helpful to adapt to a single-session model of treatment. That is, therapists should not assume they will have another opportunity for intervention. They need to prioritize potential issues and target interventions that can provide the most immediate and beneficial changes. For instance, we have found it helpful to attend to more basic survival needs such as sleep and ensuring service members engage in adequate self-care (e.g., nutrition) before attending to other issues, such as feelings of isolation and peer conflict.

We have experienced treatment success with such brief interventions as solution-focused therapy, cognitive–behavioral therapy, and aspects of cognitive processing therapy. It is important to note, however, that research on treatment effectiveness in a deployed environment is lacking and adaptations need to be made for traditional therapies. These adaptations, outlined as follows, were developed on the basis of our observations and collective experience. For example, particular therapies appear to help the mental well-being of service members immediately through techniques such as reframing, refocusing on long-term goals, and confronting maladaptive beliefs. Although the basic outlines of these therapies are not altered from traditional methods, the vehicle for therapeutic change in each modality is often shifted from external homework assignments to more immediate demonstrations and application. In general, the portions of these therapies that facilitate "in-session homework" completion are most helpful given that the scheduling of the next therapy session is unpredictable. Further, many deployment environments are not conducive to some "homework" interventions because basic supplies, privacy, time, and safety are often limited. However, for those therapists treating service members in a more stationary deployment role (i.e., both service member and therapist are not routinely leaving their location), traditional and nonbrief psychotherapies might be more applicable, depending on the demands placed on the behavioral health provider and the level of threat.

Common treatment topics during deployment include bereavement, relationships, and the management of many different reactions including anger and aggression, depression, anxiety and panic, and acute stress and post-traumatic stress symptoms. However, several distinguishing characteristics inherent in a deployed environment direct the way in which these topics are addressed.

First and foremost is the need to maintain combat readiness of the individual and the unit, which can conflict with individual needs. At times during the deployment, the individual identity of deployed service members shifts to a more universal or group identity. As a result, individuals may be reluctant to seek treatment for individual problems, such as anger issues, because they do not want their stress or seeking help to detract from their unit's mission capability. Individuals may also find it difficult to manage home front and/or relationship issues because they tend to compartmentalize deployed life separately from life at home. This compartmentalization has benefits in helping service members cope with immediate threats to survival, but, as a result, home front issues may be ignored. This may result in a loss of a potential source of support and might create a mounting stressor.

Further, service members have valid negative perceptions about their life in a combat situation, and this reality shifts the focus for behavioral health providers toward helping service members tolerate distress rather than point out cognitive distortions. For example, it is appropriate for an individual to have anxiety and hypervigilance about leaving a forward operating base and routinely patrolling a dangerous route. Thus, treatment may focus less on changing the beliefs that a situation is dangerous, because in reality it is dangerous, and focus more on how to channel energy from anxiety into improving combat effectiveness through healthy nutrition, physical activity, and sleep routines. Behavioral health providers must carefully consider what they are defining as "maladaptive" because healthy behaviors and beliefs held on deployment are often different than what would be considered healthy in a garrison environment.

Group sessions targeting relationship stress in terms of distance from family members and children may also be helpful. The focus of these groups is often establishing effective and assertive communication with family members at home and managing grief that can be associated with leaving loved ones behind. Mood management groups targeting anger, depression, and anxiety may also be useful. The focus of these groups is to understand the effects of the deployment cycle on an individual's mood and to find effective ways to manage the symptoms and resulting behaviors (e.g., assertiveness training for dealing with anger at higher ranking soldiers).

Groups integrating a health psychology focus may also be helpful. These groups focus on establishing sleep hygiene in a deployed environment, reducing the effects of preexisting conditions, maintaining adequate self-care, and establishing healthy routines. These health-related behaviors can prove quite challenging given the level of noise, work/rest cycles of units, and the inherent safety risk. Although perhaps not a priority in some settings, groups can help service members use the time on deployment to make healthy lifestyle changes, such as tobacco use cessation.

Bereavement groups may also be useful for service members who have lost a comrade and who may need assistance through their grieving process. It is important to note that many of the young service members who deploy have no previous experience with losing a loved one and often will not have a frame of reference on "how to grieve."

Each of the groups described here has been conducted by us in deployed settings. Ongoing groups have been both open and closed to new members, although they are typically open given how difficult it is to predict attendance. In addition, it is recommended that groups be independent of each other.

That is, groups should not rely on cumulative psychoeducation to adapt to the changing composition of group membership over time.

Given the large overlap of physiological and psychological symptoms experienced in response to deployment stress, therapy targeting an individual's physical response to stress can prove invaluable. This is especially salient given that a majority of service members are routinely exposed to high-risk situations and are often in a continued state of vigilance, creating significant wear and tear on the body and one's mental health. Thus, techniques such as relaxation training, deep breathing, progressive muscle relaxation, and guided imagery can be useful. By teaching these techniques, providers can help service members capitalize on opportunities in which they are under relatively less threat and can relax and physically unwind.

These techniques may be useful in helping service members whose level of vigilance or anxiety has become maladaptive and is interfering with their ability to do their job effectively. For instance, one service member who experienced a blast attack but did not sustain physical injuries developed significant anxiety. He began to experience panic symptoms whenever he had to leave the forward operating base for patrol. Through the use of deep breathing and imagery, he was able to harness his anxiety and continue to perform his patrolling mission effectively, maintaining his confidence, his identity as a service member, the confidence of other unit members, and his command.

Finally, some military mental health providers have been able to acquire biofeedback equipment to assist with the reduction of physiological symptoms. Using biofeedback equipment can be helpful because it allows service members to use computer output to visualize how their mind and body are connected and how controlling the mind can help reduce the physiological stress on the body. However, it is important to note that electronic equipment can often be unreliable during deployment given the environment's impact on electronic equipment (i.e., effects of sand and dust) and the constraints of using electronic equipment (i.e., using electronic converters and having unreliable power).

MEDICATION MANAGEMENT IN THEATER

Multiple factors affect the dispensing of medications in the deployed environment. Providers need to ensure that they are able to follow up with individuals who are started on medications and that resupply is available. The method for dispensing psychotropic medications in theater is determined by several factors including the service member's access to mental health services, service member reliability, and the proximity of pharmacy services. For example, on the basis of lessons from Iraq, medication management can include providing service members with a bottle of medication, providing a starting dose and a prescription to take to the local aid station or pharmacy, or just providing a prescription that the patient takes to a local aid station, pharmacy, or hospital. In general, to ensure adequate follow-up, service members should not be provided more than a 1-month supply of medication.

Clinicians must make decisions regarding the extent of services they can safely and effectively provide their units. Providers must recognize the limitations of their resources, capabilities, and situation and make the decision to treat in theater, return the service member to home station, or delay treatment until the service member returns home as scheduled. The decision to continue to treat or to evacuate service members depends on which medications are available, how significant the symptoms are, how the service member initially responds to treatment, how significantly the symptoms are interfering with the service member's assigned duties, and what duties and responsibilities the service member is expected to perform.

RESTORATION AND DISPOSITION FROM THEATER

A mental health provider in a combat theater has few options for disposition. The majority of service members will be treated locally and, if required to spend a night away from their unit, will do so at the local medical aid station. Service members who present a safety risk concern will be placed on a unit watch. Service members with more pronounced symptoms or whose symptoms do not begin resolving within 72 hr can be sent to a restoration center. The centers are located within the theater of operations but are farther away from the units and the front lines. Here, service members can receive intensive outpatient treatment for up to a week. The majority of the service members seen and treated at the restoration center are returned to duty, but service members whose symptoms persist can be evacuated from theater and returned to their home station for further care. It is important to note that there are few, if any, inpatient mental health capabilities available in a deployed environment.

One of the challenges observed in operations in Iraq and Afghanistan is the effect of evacuation on an individual's recovery. Specifically, when service members are evacuated out of theater, they have often reported feeling not only geographically isolated but also emotionally isolated from their unit. This isolation can lead to the development of perceived helplessness (e.g., "I can't get back to my unit . . . there's nothing I can do") and personal failure (e.g., "I've let my unit down"). Perceived isolation can be detrimental to morale and can negatively affect recovery even if early psychiatric treatment is offered. Thus, units should be encouraged to take an active role in facilitating recovery of evacuated service members through outreach and maintenance of unit cohesion, even after a unit member is evacuated from theater. Fortunately, advancements in technology can facilitate this cohesion through telephone calls, electronic mail, and in some instances, video teleconference.

SUMMARY

Military mental health care has evolved significantly since World War I, when Salmon implemented the first forward psychiatry principles. With the establishment of combat operational stress teams there has been an increasing focus on prevention and on the role of the mental health provider as a consultant to commanders. The CARE model discussed in this chapter provides the deployed military mental health provider with a framework for organizing their efforts. It is imperative that military mental health providers be comfortable with and aware of all the prevention and resiliency development tools they have at their disposal and that they actively engage with unit commanders as consultants in support of the deployed soldier. At the same time, it is important to realize that although units can become increasingly resilient, there will continue to be combat operational stress casualties. Therefore, early intervention and forward treatment mechanisms with a goal of return to duty will continue to be required.

RISKS AND ETHICAL CONCERNS TO THE MENTAL HEALTH PROVIDER

Serving in the role of a deployed mental health provider is different from a typical doctor–patient encounter. The unique situation of providing mental health treatment in a combat environment can present personal risk and, at times, ethical challenges and difficult situations.

Personal Safety

The mental health provider on the battlefield has a unique role that will require, at times, a level of personal risk beyond that experienced by most providers in a noncombat setting. It is not uncommon for providers to be asked to travel into areas that may be subject to enemy fire or to use air travel with its concomitant risks. Although willingness to put personal safety aside for the needs of the service members and unit will gain the provider credibility and trust, it must be tempered with good judgment. The urge to "sightsee" or place oneself at unnecessary risk should be resisted. This urge may stem from a combination of enthusiasm for the job, curiosity about being in a foreign country, a sense of adventure, a desire to be a hero or accumulate "war stories," or a protective denial of the real dangers inherent in combat and travel. In most instances, the mental health provider is the single source of credentialed mental health care for the unit. Because his or her injury or death would adversely affect the entire unit, the provider should ensure that he or she has all the appropriate safety equipment and knows how to use it. Providers need to be adequately trained and well-rehearsed in what to do in an emergency prior to any mission. There must be a balance between the responsibility to maintain the safety of a limited resource (i.e., the mental health provider) and the requirements of caring for a unit on the battlefield.

Patient Safety

Safety measures for at-risk patients in the deployed environment are different from those in the home environment. First, because they are in a combat zone and need to be prepared to respond to potential enemy attack, service members are armed with automatic weapons and ammunition at all times. Several studies have suggested that access to weapons places people, with or without mental health problems, at higher risk of committing suicide (Kellermann et al., 1992; Marzuk et al., 1992). Immediate access to weapons must be considered in every mental health contact, and military mental health providers need to determine whether service members should be disarmed during each encounter. The fact that both the patient and provider are armed during a session also heightens risk when dealing with intensely angry, homicidal, or suicidal service members.

Evacuating service members to a safer location where weapons are less likely to be required is a possible intervention for those who may be dangerous and/or have poor impulse control. Another intervention is to have their weapons confiscated or the firing mechanism removed. Taking away a weapon is complicated, however, by the stigmatization service members experience and the threat to their safety if they cannot defend themselves from attack. Safety must be the primary consideration, yet the psychological sequelae of being unarmed also become a therapeutic issue.

It should be clarified that mental health providers do not have direct authority over a service member's mission status but rather make recommendations to commanders. Providers do not remove, stockpile, or store suicidal patients' weapons. Instead, mental health providers must engage and ally with the unit to keep service members safe. In making their recommendations, however, providers can work with unit leaders to help them maintain an appropriate balance of limits and support. Providers must also deal with the fact that leaders may need clinical support.

For patients who require inpatient psychiatry, other solutions need to be found. Inpatient psychiatry does not exist in a combat theater, as it is known in the United States. Inpatient psychiatric beds, of which there are few, are beds in a medical ward with a sitter. Restoration programs provide a therapeutic milieu in a day-treatment, or partial hospitalization setting, with service members living at the facility but not typically in a fully supervised or locked setting. Service members with suicidal or homicidal thoughts that are not resolved by being temporarily removed from the immediate situation and setting require urgent evacuation. In summary, treatment options are limited in a combat theater and require creative solutions and flexible treatment planning.

Double-Agency

During deployment, military mental health providers are frequently called on to simultaneously address the needs of both the unit and the soldier–patient. This dual responsibility is termed *double-agency*. Sometimes, the only "patient" is the unit, and there is not an identified individual. In other cases, service members are identified as patients, and providers have a responsibility to treat them and, at the same time, to advise the commander on the military's most favorable course of action. The majority of times, these two priorities are synchronous: Frequently, what is good for the service member is also good for the military. However, a mutually beneficial course of action does not always exist. For example, when a soldier confides to a mental health provider that he "just can't take it anymore [and is] going AWOL [absent without leave]," the provider must weigh the relative risks and benefits to the patient and the military. Cases of service members reporting war crimes to mental health providers are another example. In these situations, there may not only be an emotional conflict for the service member but also a leadership problem within the unit.

When making recommendations about treatment, duty limitations, and separation or evacuation, the mental health provider must keep in mind the service member's ability to perform his or her assigned job in a combat environment. This assessment becomes more difficult in the case of service members who are struggling with the psychological effects of combat. The provider may find it difficult to determine the proper time to recommend that a unit commander remove a service member from continued combat exposure while also keeping in mind the unit's mission and current needs.

These situations must be carefully examined and, as with many ethical issues, there is no single right answer. Discussion with colleagues or senior mental health providers is recommended and can be helpful in processing the issues and arriving at a course of action.

Confidentiality

Service members, especially those in combat, have lower expectations of privacy. These expectations are realistic given that their commander has a right to know their diagnosis, prognosis, treatment plan, and recommended duty limitations. Beyond these concise issues, however, the mental health provider should not disclose other details. In contrast, the commander is under no such restriction and can provide a wealth of information to the mental health provider, including reports about the service member's ability to function at work, relationships with peers and supervisors, past occupational counseling, and sometimes the "other side" of the story. If approached as partners on a team, rather than as adversaries, the consulting relationship between mental health providers and commanders can be beneficial to each party, as well as to service members.

Though a commander has a right to know some treatment-related details, mental health providers certainly do not contact every patient's commander with that information. If a service member has mild symptoms that do not impair occupational functioning or require duty limitations, there is no need to contact the commander. However, if there is risk to the unit, mission, or service member, the provider has a responsibility to make certain that command is aware to ensure not only the ongoing safety and treatment of the patient but also the safety and mission effectiveness of the unit. This includes making commanders aware of a service member beginning a new medication that could affect duty performance.

Boundaries

When providers live and work in a small community with other service members whose mental health is also their responsibility, the issue of a dual relationship frequently arises. Providers can manage this issue by categorizing relationships into *nonpatient* or *potential patient*. Care needs to be taken in establishing social relationships with fairly stable, resilient service members who are not likely to become patients in the future. Perhaps the most challenging request a deployed provider may face occurs when a previous nonpatient, such as a tent mate, exercise partner, or friend, comes to need mental health care. If there are no other mental health providers to whom to refer, then the social relationship changes, which can be awkward and isolating for a provider and for the new patient as well.

Furthermore, with some regularity, senior officers and supervisors of the mental health provider request treatment. Depending on the situation, there may be no other provider to refer the individual to, and providing treatment is not only in the senior officer's best interest but also in the best interest of the entire unit. In cases of potential dual relationship, boundaries must be clearly discussed at the outset of treatment, separating the treatment from the professional relationship and establishing expectations on both sides.

Finally, many providers will be deployed to relatively remote areas with a patient population similar to a small community. Whenever possible, the military mental health provider should arrange a specific time and place for conducting therapy sessions, even if the sessions are not in an office setting or during traditional office hours, to help demarcate the session as a therapeutic encounter for the service member. This type of session is not in contrast to the availability principle but rather emphasizes the importance of differentiating therapeutic from social encounters. At the beginning of treatment, the provider should discuss with the service member how both parties will handle daily interactions such as seeing each other at the dining facility, the gym, or in the general living area. Key areas to be discussed include whether and how each party would like to be recognized and greeted in a nonclinical setting and appropriate times to approach with nonemergency questions or concerns. If not discussed, these boundaries can negatively affect the therapeutic alliance between the service member and the military mental health provider. In many cases, approaches for mental health support outside a clinical setting can be met by briefly listening and arranging an appropriate place and time for further treatment, if the issue cannot be resolved in this brief encounter.

Provider Resiliency

Medical providers are at the same risk of stress-related illness and fatigue as any other service member exposed to combat or deployment conditions. Care must be taken to maintain appropriate work/rest cycles, sleep habits, nutrition, regular exercise, attendance to spiritual needs, stress-relief activities, and contact with loved ones at home. Providers must pace themselves to ensure they are functional for the full length of the deployment, which can be as long as 15 months. The urge to work continuously must be avoided, and appropriate boundaries must be maintained. This balance can be difficult when the provider eats, sleeps, showers, and works in the same place as their potential or active patients.

In many cases, mental health providers are placed in their unit at the time of deployment, so not only do they not have the support networks they did at home but they also may not have had time to develop relationships within their new unit. Providers should establish mentor and peer relationships, both military and medical, in the unit to which they are assigned, in addition to networking with other units and higher level headquarters. As service members and as individuals great benefit is derived from the emotional support of peers in times of stress. Meeting regularly with friends for dinner, exercise, or fun can significantly improve a provider's quality of life during a deployment. Furthermore, continuing to maintain good contact with friends, family, and mentors who are not deployed can allow for ongoing support and objective opinions.

Detainee Care

Most deployed military mental health providers have limited contact with detainees. In general, the only interactions that occur are those that happen when a detainee is displaying odd behavior or there is concern about suicidal or homicidal thoughts. In these cases, the provider conducts a safety assessment and determines whether appropriate measures are being taken. This also ensures that necessary facilities and equipment are available at the location to safely care for the detainee. If they are not, the necessary safety requirements should be clearly stated so the detainee can be transferred to an appropriate facility. These evaluations can be difficult because there are likely to be language barriers requiring evaluations to be conducted through an interpreter. Furthermore, there are often cultural barriers and a lack of trust by both the provider and the detainee.

In some instances, deployed military mental health providers serve in hospitals, where their primary mission is to care for the medical needs of the detainee. Prior to this assignment, the provider is given specialized training on interacting and caring for detainees. An additional challenge in these settings is caring for the service members who serve as guards. Working as a guard can be stressful, and it is imperative that the mental health providers assigned to detention centers help the service members develop adaptive responses. This development is accomplished not only through ensuring that readily accessible care is provided but also through frequent circulation throughout the unit's area to help identify detention facility guards and other personnel who may be developing a combat operational stress reaction.

It is notable that many nonmedical personnel may not be aware of the scope, capabilities, and limitations of a deployed mental health provider. At times, the provider may be asked to participate in or review an interrogation to provide insight. The provider may also be asked to give information from a patient encounter with a detainee so that the information can be used during an interrogation. In these instances, the provider should reject this request and set clear boundaries. The provider needs to be sure that the mental health staff and the leadership understand that providers cannot be involved in these activities at any level and that both the American Psychological Association and the American Psychiatric Association have published position statements against these actions (American Psychiatric Association, 2006; Behnke, 2006).

FUTURE DIRECTIONS

Military mental health providers give commanders a unique and critical perspective on the health and care of their service members. This consultation not only provides direct care to patients in a high stress environment but can also play a pivotal role in the prevention of psychological casualties. However, the effectiveness of forward psychiatry principles and their impact on long term outcomes are not well established. Research is required to determine the overall effectiveness of forward psychiatry. Such research should examine the mental health status of service members throughout the military deployment cycle and revisit fundamental assumptions about the mental health of deploying service members, such as the impact of preexisting psychological conditions on psychiatric attrition in a combat zone. Research should also examine the effectiveness of resiliency training, such as the army's resiliency-based Battlemind Training program or the Master Resiliency Trainer program. Finally, development of a full spectrum framework, such as the CARE model of consultation, availability, resiliency training, and early intervention, should be pursued. Training programs, policies, and research should target different facets of the CARE model to optimize the efficacy of battlefield mental health providers.

REFERENCES

Adler, A. B., Bliese, P. D., McGurk, D., Hoge, C. W., & Castro, C. A. (2009). Battlemind Debriefing and Battlemind Training as early interventions with soldiers returning from Iraq: Randomization by platoon. *Journal of Consulting and Clinical Psychology, 77*, 928–940. doi:10.1037/a0016877

Adler, A. B., Castro, C. A., & McGurk, D. (2009). Time-driven Battlemind Psychological Debriefing: A group-level early intervention in combat. *Military Medicine, 174*, 21–28.

American Psychiatric Association. (2006). Position statement on detainee interrogation. *Psychiatric News, 41*, 10.

Appel, J. W. (1966). Preventive psychiatry in neuropsychiatry. In A. J. Glass & R. J. Bernucci (Eds.), *World War II* (pp. 373–416). Washington, DC: Office of the Surgeon General.

Assistant Secretary of Defense. (2006). *Policy guidance for deployment limiting psychiatric conditions and medications*. Washington, DC: Department of Defense.

Behnke, S. (2006). Ethics and interrogations: Comparing and contrasting the American psychological, American medical, and American psychiatric association positions. *Monitor on Psychology, 37*, 66.

Belenky, G. L., Tyner, C. F., & Sodetz, F. J. (1983). *Israeli battle shock casualties: 1973 and 1982* (WRAIR NP-83-4). Washington, DC: Walter Reed Army Institute of Research.

Bourne, P. G. (1970). Military psychiatry and the Vietnam experience. *The American Journal of Psychiatry, 127*, 481–488.

Castro, C. A., & Thomas, J. L. (Chairs). (2007, August). *The Battlemind Training System: Supporting soldiers throughout the deployment cycle*. Symposium conducted at the meeting of the American Psychological Association, San Francisco, CA.

Department of the Army. (1994). *Field manual 8-51. Combat stress control in a theater of operation, tactics, techniques, and procedures*. Washington, DC: Headquarters, Department of the Army.

Department of the Army. (2006). *Field Manual 4-02.51. Combat and operational stress control*. Washington, DC: Headquarters, Department of the Army.

Fontana, A., & Rosencheck, R. (1998). Psychological benefits and liabilities of traumatic exposure in a war zone. *Journal of Traumatic Stress, 11*, 485–503. doi:10.1023/A:1024452612412

Gal, R., & Jones, F. D. (1995). A psychological model of combat stress. In F. D. Jones, L. R. Sparacino, V. L. Wilcox, J. M. Rothberg, & J. W. Stokes (Eds.), *War psychiatry* (pp. 133–148). Washington, DC: Office of the Surgeon General—Borden Institute.

Glass, A. J. (1966). Lessons learned in preventive psychiatry. In A. J. Glass & R. J. Bernucci (Eds.), *Neuropsychiatry in World War II* (pp. 989–1027). Washington, DC: Office of the Surgeon General.

Group for the Advancement of Psychiatry. (1960). *Preventive psychiatry in the armed forces: With some implications for civilian use* (Report 47). New York, NY: Group for the Advancement of Psychiatry.

Jacobs, J., Horne-Moyer, H. L., & Jones, R. (2004). The effectiveness of critical incident stress debriefing with primary and secondary trauma victims. *International Journal of Emergency Mental Health, 6*, 5–14.

Jones, E., & Wessely, S. (2003). "Forward psychiatry" in the military: Its origins and effectiveness. *Journal of Traumatic Stress, 16*, 411–419. doi:10.1023/A:1024426321072

Jones, F. D. (1995). Psychiatric lessons of war. In F. D. Jones, L. R. Sparacino, V. L. Wilcox, J. M. Rothberg, & J. W. Stokes (Eds.), *War psychiatry* (pp. 1–33). Washington, DC: Office of the Surgeon General—Borden Institute.

Kellermann, A. L., Rivara, F. P., Somes, G., Reay, D. T., Franciso, J., Gillentine Banton, J., . . . Hackman, B. B. (1992). Suicide in the home in relation to gun ownership. *The New England Journal of Medicine, 327*, 467–472.

Koshes, R. J., Young, S. A., & Stokes, J. W. (1995). Debriefing following combat. In F. D. Jones, L. R. Sparacino, V. L. Wilcox, J. M. Rothberg, & J. W. Stokes (Eds.), *War psychiatry* (pp. 271–290). Washington, DC: Office of the Surgeon General—Borden Institute.

MacDonald, C. M. (2003). Evaluation of stress debriefing interventions with military populations. *Military Medicine, 168,* 961–968.

Marr, K. (in press). "Remind": Addressing the risk of illegal violence in military operations. *U.S. Army Medical Journal.*

Marzuk, P. M., Leon, A. C., Tardiff, K., Morgan, E. B., Stajic, M., & Mann, J. J. (1992). The effect of access to lethal methods of injury on suicide rates. *Archives of General Psychiatry, 49,* 451–458.

Menninger, W. C. (1948). *Psychiatry in a troubled world.* New York, NY: MacMillan.

Mental Health Advisory Team III. (2006). *Mental Health Advisory Team (MHAT) III Operation Iraqi Freedom 04-06.* Washington, DC: Office of the Surgeon General.

Mental Health Advisory Team IV. (2006). *Mental Health Advisory Team (MHAT) IV Operation Iraqi Freedom 05-07.* Washington, DC: Office of the Surgeon General.

Mental Health Advisory Team V. (2008). *Mental Health Advisory Team (MHAT) V Operation Iraqi Freedom 06-08: Iraq, Operation Enduring Freedom 8: Afghanistan.* Washington, DC: Office of the Surgeon General.

Mitchell, S. G., & Mitchell, J. T. (2006). Caplan, community, and critical incident stress management. *International Journal of Emergency Mental Health, 8,* 5–14.

Rose, S., Bisson, J., Churchill, R., & Wessely, S. (2002). Psychological debriefing for preventing posttraumatic stress disorder (PTSD). *Cochrane Database of Systematic Reviews, 2.* Retrieved from http://www2.cochrane.org/reviews/en/ab000560.html

Tischler, G. L. (1969). Patterns of psychiatric attrition and of behavior in a combat zone. In P. G. Bourne (Ed.), *Psychology and physiology of stress* (pp. 19–44). New York, NY: Academic Press.

Warner, C. H., Appenzeller, G. N., Mobbs, A., & Grieger, T. (2008, August). *Effectiveness of battlefield ethics chain teaching.* Paper presented at the U.S. Army Force Health Protection Conference, Albuquerque, NM.

Warner, C. H., Appenzeller, G. N., Mullen, K., Warner, C. M., & Greiger, T. (2008). Soldier attitudes towards mental health screening and seeking care upon return. *Military Medicine, 173,* 563–569.

Warner, C. H., Breitbach, J. E., Appenzeller, G. N., Yates, V. D., Greiger, T., & Webster, W. G. (2007). Division mental health: Its role in the new brigade combat team structure: Part I. Predeployment and deployment. *Military Medicine, 172,* 907–911.

3

OPTIMIZING MENTAL HEALTH SUPPORT IN THE MILITARY: THE ROLE OF PEERS AND LEADERS

NEIL GREENBERG AND NORMAN JONES

Hey, Hoot, why do you do it, man? Why? You some kind of war junkie?
I won't say a goddamn word. Why? They won't understand. They won't
understand why we do it. They won't understand it's about the men next
to you . . . and that's it. That's all it is.
—U.S. soldier, Mogadishu, Somalia, 1993

Military personnel are required to carry out dangerous tasks that often take them into highly hazardous locations. The duties they undertake will most likely place them at considerable risk of exposures to traumatic stimuli. When at home, personnel can access support from multiple sources, including family and friends; however, operational deployments make accessing such support difficult and in some cases impossible. Furthermore, even though there are likely to be caring professionals available, such as medical staff, chaplains (also known as "padres"), or mental health providers in theater, such resources are often limited and the tactical situation and geographical constraints may render them difficult to access. Therefore, there appears to be a mismatch between a probable increased need for support while deployed and an increased difficulty in accessing such support.

When personnel join the military, they do so having at least some understanding that their operational duties will put them at risk of physical

This chapter was authored or coauthored by an employee of the United States government as part of official duty and is considered to be in the public domain. Any views expressed herein do not necessarily represent the views of the United States government, and the author's participation in the work is not meant to serve as an official endorsement.

injury and that they may be asked to carry out physically arduous duties in regions of the world far from their home. In fact, the desire to challenge oneself and to embrace chaos as part of the work are probably among the reasons why many join. However, the same factors may also be the reasons why many military personnel retire from service earlier than they anticipated when joining. Unlike personnel employed in other high-risk occupations, once service personnel join up and have signed on the dotted line, they lose a substantial degree of autonomy and choice. Having done so, some will realize that the realities of war are different from their fantasies prior to, and during, the early stages of service. Thus, although all organizations that predictably place their employees in danger have a duty of care toward their employees, military commanders can rightly be said to owe a great deal more toward their subordinates than managers in other such organizations. Given that military personnel have a limited opportunity to refuse highly dangerous tasks, the service member's psychological health should be a key mission objective for leaders at all levels. This point is simply summed up in the moral principle of proportionality: The more you ask of those who work for you, the more you owe them.

This chapter sets out the relevant issues that influence how military leaders should discharge their duty of care toward subordinates. The chapter takes a primarily preventative approach to the management of psychological injury. A prime goal of an effective leader should be the ongoing assessment of psychological threat and, where possible, its mitigation. Furthermore, for those service members who need it, the responsible leader should ensure the provision of effective early interventions. We argue that this leadership is best achieved, at least in the operational setting, by fostering an environment in which peer support flourishes. The chapter covers both the science behind the provision of effective social support and describes some of the innovative ways in which this support can be optimized. In particular, we discuss a United Kingdom model of early intervention called *Trauma Risk Management* (TRiM), which was developed by the authors. We also discuss a series of American resilience interventions centered on a psychological and behavioral concept known as *Battlemind*. Although we support the notion that psychological health professionals have a role in treating personnel who are unwell and a role in providing support to commanders, within most military services, including the U.K. Armed Forces, policy and doctrine support the notion that the psychological welfare of troops is primarily a command and leadership responsibility. This chapter therefore argues that, wherever possible, responsibility lies with the chain of command to provide for service members' needs in the aftermath of traumatic events and for medical and mental health services to act in support of them. Thus, however well resourced, skilled, and expert a military health service might be, we suggest that unless unit commanders adopt the right approach to dealing with psychological distress in their units and, in particular, minimizing stigma, no amount of mental health support will be effective.

SOCIAL SUPPORT

Social support is a term that has been widely used by social and psychiatric researchers. It refers to a construct that has, at its core, elements that link one person to another. Social support research has been conducted in both civilian and military populations although in the military samples such research is usually termed *unit cohesion* (Bartone, Ursano, Wright, & Ingraham, 1989) or is incorporated into the wider construct of morale (Grinker & Spiegel, 1945); both constructs are closely related to social support (Siebold, 2007).

Social Support: General Concepts

Military organizations are discreet and in some ways unique social con-structs. Service personnel use an idiosyncratic language, usually distinct from the day-to-day language of civilians, and have evolved patterns of behavior that are often at odds with those found in the majority of general society. For instance, within most military forces, there is a need to maintain high levels of physical fitness, to be willing to obey orders whatever they may be, and to regularly endure adversity, including the threat to one's life; the same is not the case for the majority of the general population. Part of being socialized into the military culture involves learning to rely on team members and to look out for them in order to accomplish the mission.

The process of military socialization begins with basic military training that aims to indoctrinate recruits into the military culture and lifestyle that will continue throughout a soldier's career and often into life as a veteran (McGurk, Cotting, Britt, & Adler, 2006). Socialization is a key element of any socially supportive environment. The benefits of socialization were first noticed by social scientists, including Durkheim (1951), who found that suicide was more common in those who had fewer social ties. Although suicide is thankfully a rare event in most military forces, a substantial amount of research has confirmed the psychological benefits of social contact in both military and nonmilitary populations (Lerner, Kertes, & Zilber, 2005; Orsillo, Roemer, Litz, Ehlich, & Friedman, 1998; Thomas & Znaniecki, 1920). In fact, numerous research articles have established that lack of social support is a highly important, albeit hard to measure, risk factor for physical, as well as psychological, morbidity and mortality (Berkman & Syme, 1979; Helgeson, Cohen, & Fritz, 1998; House, Robbins, & Metzner, 1982; Reifman, 1995).

Thus, it follows that encouraging socialization in military forces should have significant benefits for psychological and physical health. However, doing so requires planning at two levels. First, the process of military indoctrination should formally incorporate socialization as a stated aim. Second, during training and operational deployments, commanders should ensure that opportunities for socialization are formally planned even when the tempo of operations is high.

Nevertheless, the effects of social support are not always beneficial to health; designers of military mental health support frameworks should remain cognizant of potential iatrogenic effects. Although many authors have reported the beneficial effects of socialization, as described earlier, others have suggested that an overly social environment is not associated with good functioning and enhanced well-being (Cohen & Wills, 1985; Schwarzer & Leppin, 1989). Furthermore, Beehr, Bennett, and Bowling (2007) investigated the elements of social support that might be detrimental to mental health in a nonmilitary environment and suggested three main explanations. First, social interactions with potentially supportive people may lead personnel to focus on just how stressful the workplace really is, which may have the effect of increasing anxiety rather than reducing it. Second, some help from other people can, perhaps unintentionally, undermine an individual's self-concept in that it may cause him or her to feel inadequate. In a military sense this could happen when a buddy takes over a command task because it is not working out well or a leader overrides an order given by a junior commander because "they know better and want the mission to succeed." Last, Beehr et al. suggested that help from others that is unsolicited or unwanted for any reason may also have an adverse impact on mental health.

One well-researched example of social and environmental interaction and its impact on individual psychology is reflected in the concept of *expressed emotion*. Although expressed emotion has been more traditionally studied in relation to its adverse effects on serious mental health problems such as schizophrenia (Flanagan, 1998; Leff, 1994), the research carried out may have relevance for military forces. One interpersonally toxic element of expressed emotion is overinvolvement, which may parallel the thoughts of Beehr et al. (2007) concerning the provision of well-intended help even when this is not wanted and when it is delivered in a way that focuses on the inadequacy of the individual to whom it is delivered. So although leaders and colleagues may intend their advice or help to be useful, it may be linked to poor psychological health outcomes in recipients (Leff, 1994). Although this over-involvement is regarded as particularly negative for individuals with tenuous mental health and weak emotional boundaries, the concept demonstrates the difficulty socially cohesive units might encounter in trying to provide appropriate levels of emotional support to a struggling team member. Thus, commanders cannot simply place a potentially emotionally distressed sailor, soldier, or airman with any team member and hope that the distressed person will benefit as a result. Careful thought needs to be given as to how social support is provided.

We argue that any peer-delivered program should be carefully planned and executed so as to have a beneficial effect on mental health and general functioning. This means that those who provide support as part of such a program must be able to fulfill the role; it is not something that can be done by just anyone. For instance the United Kingdom's TRiM program, described later in this chapter, relies on an assessment of a service member's state of mind carried out by a trained peer. Our experience is that some service personnel, in particular those who do not have a "personnel-focused" attitude, cannot carry out the TRiM role successfully. Carrying out an effective TRiM assessment requires an ability to listen calmly, to remain focused on what is being said, and to pick up on nonverbal cues. Furthermore, an effective TRiM interview should use the service member's language and avoid potentially negative effects such as retraumatization, which has been cited as one of the reasons for poor outcomes after psychological debriefing (Sijbrandij, Olff, Reitsma, Carlier, & Gersons, 2006). Thus, although the provision of social support by peers and commanders may often be useful, it is also a topic that must be considered and planned in detail to maximize the effectiveness of such support.

Structural and Functional Social Support

Social support has been conceptualized in two broad ways, structural and functional support, and these models have led to the development of two hypotheses about how social support may work. This next section describes the basic science behind the different models and indicates how this information applies to military forces.

Structural support refers to the availability of social ties and is often grouped into four categories: marriage-related, family-related, church-related, and that related to other group affiliations (McNally & Newman, 1999). In the military, the most important social ties are with other unit members, which can be categorized as *other affiliation*. However, many service members also view the military as their family; this may be especially true for younger personnel with adverse childhood experiences (Iversen et al., 2007). In keeping with McNally and Newman's (1999) work, religious personnel are also important providers of support for some, and even indirect communication with spouses during a deployment via telephone, mail, or e-mail can be important sources of support for many. The structural support model, with its emphasis on the availability of social ties, has also been validated in longitudinal studies (Berkman & Syme, 1979).

Thus, the structural way of thinking about support describes belonging to any group that brings with it a set of shared values or beliefs that can influence the cognitions, affect, behavior, and even the biological responses of those in the group. Belonging to a group, be it a family, a police force, a battalion, or the heavy-weapons section of a support company, involves interacting with other members of the group and, to some degree, developing, contributing to, and also conforming to the group norms. This process, if successful, brings with it a sense of belonging; a feeling of increased self-worth and conforming to group norms may have implications for health. Conversely, a failure to integrate with other group members may be detrimental in terms of psychological health for both the group and the individual (Loo, Lim, Koff, Morton, & Kiang, 2007).

The structural model has given rise to what is called the *main effect hypothesis*, which purports that there are beneficial effects of social support, whether or not someone is under the effect of stress (Cohen & Wills, 1985). As a result, the potential beneficial effects of social support on health are not just useful following adversity. Access to a network of social contacts may affect the way that people exercise, the sorts of foods they eat, and other health-related behaviors, such as smoking or the use of intoxicants. On operations, the group to which service members belong also may affect the way they carry out their duties.

Other studies have suggested that being part of a social network can reduce psychological despair (Thoits, 1985) and improve the motivation to care for oneself (van Dam et al., 2005). It is even possible to demonstrate the effects of one's social network on an individual's neuroendocrine and immune system (Cohen, Clark, & Sherrod, 1986; Uchino, Cacioppo, & Kiecolt-Glaser, 1996). According to the main effect hypothesis, belonging to a group such as the military, which has an ethos of easily accessible support and a proactive approach to dealing with stressors, may in itself reduce the likelihood that someone will experience mental health problems even in the face of adversity. As described later, both the TRiM model and the Battlemind system are proactive models that aim to ensure that service personnel know that their psychological needs matter both on operational deployments and also when at home in barracks.

The structural support model does not, however, take into account the receiver's subjective evaluation of the available support. In addition, an individual may have access to a potentially supportive network, such as the platoon, but may not benefit from belonging to the group because of dysfunctional relationships or difficult personal attributes and temperament (McNally & Newman, 1999).

Another, perhaps more intuitive, way of looking at social support is to take a functional rather than structural approach, that is, to ask what function support has rather than simply whether it is there. Within a military unit, for example, having a small number of good buddies might be sufficient to meet a service member's support needs even though that individual does not necessarily "gel" with all team members. At its core, the *functional support model* considers not just whether support is present but whether the support provides what an individual might need at a particular time. Such functions may include aiding emotionally focused coping, giving relevant information, or assisting with problem solving. This model therefore assumes that social support acts to fulfill a need, either overt or implicit, which if not met will lead to an exacerbation of distress and which, if met, will lead to amelioration. Given that the military abounds with rules and regulations, which if broken can often have serious consequences for both the individual and the organization, it is easy to see why functional support can act to reduce distress. Being able to gain information from a supportive colleague or commander could, for instance, inform the service person that he or she is entitled to additional allowances or leave, which may be beneficial.

Functional support is linked with what is known as the *stress-buffering hypothesis*. This hypothesis was first suggested in the mid-1970s by two social scientists, John Cassel and Sydney Cobb, who identified that people with strong social ties were protected against the adverse effects of being exposed to stressful events (Cassel, 1976; Cobb, 1976). They hypothesized that stressors that place individuals at risk of developing mental, and most probably physical, disorders are often characterized by confusing or absent feedback from a person's social environment. In contrast, the effect of these stressors is attenuated, or even negated, in individuals who understand what is expected of them and who have easy access to support and assistance with tasks. Furthermore, the stress-buffering hypothesis suggests that it is helpful if individuals receive appropriate feedback on their performance and appropriate rewards (Cassel, 1976). Thus, when a leader or colleague lets someone know that they have done a good (or bad) job and suggests ways in which they might carry out a task, it may have consequences in terms of both skills acquisition and mental health. Put simply, those who deliver a clear and understandable message are more likely to be perceived as supportive than those who do not.

The relevance of stress buffering is perhaps best exemplified by the need of combat troops to have their actions validated following contact with the enemy or after having been engaged in prolonged difficult, dangerous, or gruesome tasks. Such feedback, which may be available from their peers or their commander, may serve to aid the troops to find meaning in what has happened to them, which can, in turn, reduce their risk of experiencing a psychological injury (Galea & Resnick, 2005). Therefore, commanders should be aware that after-action reviews should act as a vehicle not just to review the mission's tactics, techniques, and procedures but also to validate actions, give praise, and normalize the reactions that occur in response to combat and difficult military duties.

Stress buffering has also been postulated to help with major life transitions (Cobb, 1976), which in a military sense include both deploying and recovering from operational duties. The Battlemind program, which aims to foster resilience, specifically addresses the difficulties in transitioning from the "war zone" to the "home zone," and thus is consistent with the stress-buffering hypothesis. Belonging, feeling valued, and being cared for by a social network means those within the network are to some extent "emotionally protected" and better able to cope and adapt to stressful situations. Fostering a sense of belonging is important in a military context not just for personnel engaged in hazardous duties but also because a military lifestyle entails a relatively nomadic existence with frequent postings worldwide. This lifestyle may affect not only the service members but also their family unit, be it their spouse and children or their wider immediate family such as parents, brothers, and sisters. It is crucial, therefore, to ensure personnel posted away from geographically accessible support can still access it by other means, and those who organize postings should keep this issue in mind.

Since Cassel's (1976) and Cobb's (1976) original findings, research has found that effective stress buffering is related more to perceived availability of social resources than actual availability and that to be effective the support needs to be suited (or "matched") to the needs elicited by the stressful event (Cohen & Wills, 1985; Cutrona & Russell, 1990). This matching reinforces the point that for the benefits of social support to be realized, commanders need to consider how best to provide social support rather than leave its provision to chance. For instance, senior personnel may be better able to assist with practical problem-solving difficulties, whereas same rank peers who are personnel focused may be more effective at providing a "listening ear."

At this point it is appropriate to mention the needs of leaders. There can be no doubt that the attitudes and mental health of those in command are of paramount importance to the health of their subordinates. Leaders' beliefs and actions are likely to influence the way other unit members deal with those who experience operational stress reactions and unit member willingness to admit to psychological distress. It is perhaps not surprising that perceived quality of leadership has been found to be an important factor for the mental health of those being led (Bliese & Britt, 2001; Bliese & Castro, 2000; Bliese & Halverson, 2002; Iversen et al., 2008; Jones & Wessely, 2005).

However, being in charge can also make it tough to access support oneself. For instance, a study by Cawkill (2004) on the attitudes of U.K. leaders about stress found that although most leaders reported that they would be sympathetic to those they commanded who experienced a stress-related problem, they would be unlikely to seek help themselves if they were experiencing stress. For leaders to be able to access functional support from those with whom they serve, it is likely that they will have to access different elements of support from different team members. It may be that a successful battalion commander would rely on their regimental sergeant major, medical officer, padre, and the second-in-command for different support functions, depending on the nature of the support that they needed. It may also be that the needs of leaders may be met by talking with others of a similar rank. However, this is likely to be difficult when on operations because battalion headquarters are not often located together, and in any case the rivalry between higher ranked leaders for the limited opportunities for promotion may limit the desire to open up to those with whom they are in competition. Although some nations, such as the United States, aim to provide a VIP service for leaders to support their mental health, the effectiveness of such programs has not been evaluated.

In summary, a considerable body of research suggests that social support is an important factor that can bolster resilience before traumatic events (main effect hypothesis) as well as mitigate the effects of critical incidents or operational deployments (stress-buffering hypothesis). Support does not need to be universal from all those within a unit; however, successful provision of support requires commanders to consider the ranks, personal qualities, and experiences of those who may provide support and ensure that it is matched to those who may need it. It is likely, for instance, that assistance with problem solving provided by a subordinate may be unsuccessful because such an individual may not have a firm grasp of issues associated with higher command or an appreciation of the difficulties of leadership. We consider that unless such issues are reviewed and addressed, the potential abundance of support within military units may not be optimally effective in offsetting the psychological impact of the hazardous duties that military personnel undertake. Although the military family may well be highly supportive, it is also possible that the military hierarchy can act as a barrier to effective stress buffering in some circumstances. As we argue later on in the chapter, the theory and research discussed earlier support the development of a peer support system that uses stress-buffering theory as its conceptual driver and that is provided by a pool of appropriately trained practitioners.

Combat Motivation, Unit Cohesion, and Morale

Prior to World War II (WWII), it was thought that men fought wars because of patriotism or pride or because of good leadership. Nationalistic motivations, as epitomized in the U.K. military by still-quoted militarisms such as "for Queen and country," "taking the bayonet to Her Majesty's enemies," and "defeating Her Majesty's enemies at sea," were thought to be of paramount importance in determining what drove sailors, soldiers, or airmen who were facing battle to "do their duty." Although these potential motivators might have been important for some personnel, it was not until after WWII that the roles of small group psychology and unit cohesion in influencing combat motivation were fully considered (Wessely, 2006). After WWII, a series of publications examined what motivated men to continue to fight when their own survival might have been better served by fleeing and saving themselves (Marshall, 1947; Shils & Janowitz, 1948; Stouffer, 1949). These publications, sponsored by the U.S. military, found that membership in a *primary group*, a term borrowed from psychoanalytic theory, was the strongest determinant of whether military personnel kept going when the going was tough (Smith, 2002). The primary group was made up of those individuals with whom service members mixed on a regular basis, that is, their regular and immediate unit. The operational relevance of primary group loyalty is well illustrated by a quote from S. L. A. Marshall (1947): "I hold it to be one of the simplest truths of war that the thing which enables an infantry soldier to keep going with his weapons is the near presence or presumed presence of a comrade" (p. 42).

The concepts of unit cohesion and morale are predicated on loyalty to the primary group and are fundamental to operational effectiveness and good mental health of unit members. Unit performance in both wartime and peacetime has been directly linked to both factors (Bartone et al., 1989; Manning & Ingraham, 1987; Shirom, 1976; Stouffer, 1949). Morale has been described as having faith in each other, in the leadership, and in the common purpose and as being able to get a balance of rest along with work (Grinker & Spiegel, 1945). Faith in each other is the strongest of these principles.

In terms of unit cohesion, psychological breakdown was considered to occur, or was deemed more likely to occur, when service members' links to their primary group were severed or disrupted. Currently, many military forces, including those of the United Kingdom and the United States, operate under doctrines that emphasize the importance of a robust primary group within command training (known in the U.K. Armed Forces as the "moral component of warfare"). Much in keeping with the main effect theory of social support, lack of a robust primary group can have negative effects for service members deployed on operations, especially those who do not benefit from the effects of group membership (e.g., individual reinforcements) or those belonging to specialist units (e.g., medics or forward artillery observers who deploy with other units in small numbers; Ismail et al., 2000; Jones, Roberts, & Greenberg, 2003).

Good morale has been demonstrated to enhance functioning both while deployed on and following recovery from operations. In a study of troops deployed on peacekeeping operations, morale was strongly related to the perception that they were engaged in meaningful work, and those with high levels of morale had confidence in unit functioning and leadership (Britt, Dickinson, Moore, Castro, & Adler, 2007). Higher levels of morale measured during the deployment were also related 6 months later to perceiving benefits from having been deployed. Furthermore, in a study of unit cohesion as a moderator of posttraumatic stress disorder (PTSD) symptoms, perceived high levels of unit cohesion reduced the impact of previous traumatic life experiences (a powerful risk factor for PTSD) on the development of PTSD symptoms in military personnel after return from operations (Brailey, Vasterling, Proctor, Constans, & Friedman, 2007).

Thus, purely from the viewpoint of military effectiveness, group loyalty, unit cohesion, and morale, terms used to describe related constructs, operate to ensure that military personnel continue to function. However, as Wessely (2006) pointed out in his essay on combat motivation and breakdown, social cohesion does not always serve the best interests of the military. At times, the needs of the troops can prevail over the needs of the military. Such may have been the case for U.S. troops toward the end of the conflict in Vietnam who were more focused on staying alive and not complying with orders that they saw as unreasonable rather than furthering the aims of the U.S. military in a war that most service personnel, and indeed many U.S. citizens, saw as futile.

Social Support and the Military

Although social support and unit cohesion may not typically be discussed together, we argue that measurements of unit cohesion are in reality measurements of both structural and functional social support. Stress buffering can occur through interactions with military colleagues who are close to hand whatever the nature of the operational duty. The informal sharing of experiences with friends who are able to understand could have important health benefits, and there are many plausible reasons why military colleagues may be better placed to offer support than nonmilitary colleagues or professional providers (e.g., medics, chaplains). This peer advantage is borne out by the research of Greenberg et al. (2003), who found that in a sample of U.K. military peacekeepers the majority spoke about their experiences to colleagues who had deployed with them as opposed to their chain of command, medical personnel, or social workers. The same study also found that those peacekeepers who had spoken about their experiences were less distressed than those who had not. The reliance on colleagues may be especially useful because the jargon inherent within close-knit military communities may not be understood by those seen as outsiders.

The main effect hypothesis would predict that belonging to a hardy and resilient organization has a positive impact on service member well-being. In the United Kingdom, military recruiters readily exploit this element of military life in the use of their recruiting slogans. The Royal Navy adver-tisements state "the team works," the Royal Marines Commandos state that "99.9% need not apply" (i.e., because they are not hardy enough), the British Army states that one should join the army to "be the best," whereas the Royal Air Force recruiters tell potential candidates that they will "rise above the rest." Therefore, even early on in their careers military personnel are given an image of teamwork and robustness to which they should aspire. This idealized team working and sense of hardiness may have direct health benefits.

There are other positive physical and psychological health benefits to military life as a result of belonging to the "military family." These benefits include an expectation of physical fitness and assertiveness, which are inherent in all military promotion courses. Conversely, there are numerous potentially negative consequences of belonging to the military family. These consequences include a propensity to value risk-taking behaviors, ready access to low-priced alcohol and cigarettes, the potential stigmatization of vulnerability, and a dis-dain for overt expressions of emotion (often referred to as the "stiff upper lip"; Bowyer, 2005).

For instance, within both the U.K. and U.S. armed forces, the risk of dying as a result of a road traffic accident in the year following return from an operational deployment is significantly raised (Fear et al., 2008). In the United Kingdom, troops who return home are now shown a relatively shocking film called the *Grim Reaper* (Services Sounds and Vision Corporation, 2007), which, although lasting only 6 min, attempts to vividly portray the real risk of dying as a result of a road traffic accident after deployment. The film tries to communicate a simple message to the homecoming troops: "You're tough, but you're not invincible." This is an example of the military trying to change the group norm about risk-taking through education. Whether this strategy will be successful is unclear.

Thus, although military science may jargonize the principles of social support and use such terms as *operational effectiveness* and *small group motivation*, we believe the concepts of social support theory are central to any Western military force. Military forces have always relied on socially supportive groups being able to undertake difficult duties in the face of adversity. Although skills and experience are important determinants of mission success and mental health, so is the provision of support, which is nicely encapsulated by the words of the French colonel Ardant du Picq, who, according to Labuc (1991), stated the following in 1880:

> Four brave men who do not know each other will not dare attack a lion. Four less brave men, but knowing each other well, sure of their reliability and consequently their mutual aid, will attack resolutely. This is the science of the organization of armies in a nutshell. (p. 486)

STIGMA

Our discussion thus far has concentrated on the various forms of support available to military personnel and how that support may be best used to facilitate positive psychological adjustment in response to military stressors. Our contention is that social support in its various forms can be a powerful informal and formal intervention in military stress and strain. However, just because support is available, it does not follow that military personnel will necessarily use it. Members of robust organizations, including the military, often do not seek help because of a variety of potential psychological and practical barriers. This next section describes some of the theory behind stigma and other barriers to care and examines how the theory of stigma applies to military life.

Conceptualization of Stigma

Stigma has been defined as "an attribute that is deeply discrediting" (Goffman, 1963, p. 3) and the stigmatized individual as "the bearer of a mark that defines him or her as deviant, flawed, limited, spoiled, or generally undesirable" (Jones et al., 1984, p. 6). Corrigan (2004) proposed that stigma can operate across three levels that interact and augment each other: (a) *public stigma*, the treatment the marked individual or group receives when the public endorse prejudices; (b) *self-stigma*, the internalizing of public stigma; and (c) *structural stigma*, economic and political forces operating on the culture. These three levels can be thought to operate on an individual so as to produce either *internal stigma* (e.g., the fear that if service members ask for help, their career will be over or they will not be trusted by their peers or leaders) or *external stigma*, which describes the beliefs held by others that dictate how people treat others who have mental health problems (e.g., believing that such people cannot be trusted or that the military should discharge personnel with mental health problems).

The consequences of stigma associated with mental illness have been well documented. For instance, it has been shown that having a psychiatric history can lead to negative evaluations and treatment by others (Britt, 2000; Mehta & Farina, 1997). Stigma may occur at all stages of mental illness, from help seeking to treatment and discharge (Byrne, 2001), and it has been suggested that the effects of stigma may be longer lasting, more life limiting, and more devastating than the primary mental illness itself (Schulze, Richter-Werling, Matschinger, & Angermeyer, 2003). However, it is important to remember that much of the work on stigma and mental health has been in relation to patients with more serious mental health problems (e.g., schizophrenia) rather than military personnel who may have difficulty coping with less serious mental health problems or even intense symptoms of distress (and concomitant irritability, poor sleep, and so on). However, military service, especially on operations, means that personnel need to be highly functional at all times and therefore even low-level mental disorder is likely to attract some degree of stigma within military settings.

Others have questioned the conceptual framework of stigma and its relationship with mental illness by arguing that stigma implies that the source of the problem is with the individual, and therefore it is the stigmatized individual's responsibility to sort out the problem (Sayce, 1998). In some circumstances, thankfully not a characteristic of modern military forces, external stigma has led to those with mental health problems being publically ridiculed or rejected. For instance, General Patton, who was a most successful World War II leader, was temporarily removed from command after slapping a soldier who was probably experiencing an operational stress injury while in a military hospital in Italy. Clearly, if senior leaders are highly dismissive of mental health issues, it is inevitable that those in less senior positions of command are likely to view these beliefs as acceptable. However, as stated earlier, more recent research suggests that extreme external stigma is no longer a prevalent problem within Western military forces, although the validity of such research may be hampered because of people's propensity to answer questions on such matters in a socially desirable manner (Cawkill, 2004).

Stigma and Seeking Care in the Armed Forces

Reluctance to seek help has been well documented in the general population, and evidence suggests that civilian men are less likely to seek help than women (i.e., the male:female ratio is 1:2; e.g., Meltzer et al., 2003; Wells, Robins, Bushnell, Jarosz, & Oakley-Browne, 1994). This may be due to the social norms of traditional masculinity (Möller-Leimkühler, 2002), and, given the high proportion of men within most armed forces, this is particularly relevant to the military. Military culture has been described as masculine-warrior culture dominated by stereotypical masculine norms (e.g., toughness, physical strength), psychological health, and resiliency (Dunivin, 1994). Indeed, in 1940, the Royal Air Force introduced the term "lack of moral fiber" (i.e., a loss of courage and resolution; wavering), an example of external stigma with the explicit intention to humiliate those who refused to fly without a valid medical reason, to encourage aircrew to keep flying, in spite of the high risk of being shot down, because their country needed them (Jones, 2006). Although, as discussed earlier, external stigma is less prevalent now, it still exists; for example, a staff sergeant in the U.S. forces was charged with cowardice after he attempted to seek help for a combat stress reaction (Robinson, 2004).

In 2002, ex-service personnel brought a class action suit against the U.K. Ministry of Defense (MoD) for the failure to detect PTSD problems at an early stage and provide effective treatment. During the hearing, an exhaustive examination of issues surrounding PTSD was conducted, with world experts discussing historical and current research data. From the outset, the claimants did not argue that they should never have been exposed to military trauma, because they accepted that being in the military brings with it the expectation of exposure to difficult situations. Instead, they argued that they were inadequately prepared and supported by the military and also, of relevance to this chapter, that they were unable to ask for help because of fear of being stigmatized. Although the case went on for over a year, the judgment was finally delivered in favor of the MoD on the basis that what was done at the time was legally sufficient (McGeorge, Hacker Hughes, & Wessely, 2006). However, the judge was clear that posttraumatic stress reactions were, and indeed remain, an organizational issue for the military and that there must be sufficient training for military commanders to ensure that they are able to exercise their duty of care with respect to traumatic exposures faced by their personnel. Although the judge ruled that the MoD had discharged its duty of care for the time period in question (1960 to the late 1990s), the judge instructed that the MoD keep pace with current evidence-based interventions and strategies. In his deliberations, the judge, Mr. Justice Owen, highlighted that considerable stigma is attached to revealing a psychiatric or psychological disorder, which is seen in military circles as a sign of weakness that might expose an individual to ridicule and that would have a negative influence on his or her military career (Jones & Wessely, 2005).

One of the other interesting findings from the case was that the judge made it clear that individuals did not have an absolute duty toward their comrades during war. Therefore, although the traditional buddy system is accepted practice in the U.K. Armed Forces, it is a voluntary, and not a statutory, duty. The findings of the case specifically stated that a soldier does not owe a fellow soldier a duty of care in law when either (one or other or both) is engaged with an enemy in the course of combat. Furthermore, the MoD is not under a duty to maintain a safe system of work for service personnel engaged with an enemy in the course of combat. Given the chaotic nature of military operations, this judgment came as somewhat of a relief for the MoD. Despite that relief, the judgment also served as an impetus to develop mechanisms that would support buddy-to-buddy care and decrease stigma. As described later, since the judgment, the U.K. Armed Forces have adopted a relatively novel formal mechanism of peer support as one of the important support provisions for service personnel in the wake of traumatic events.

Stigma Research

Research has shown that the decision to disclose mental health problems and engage in help seeking is affected by how individuals think they might be perceived and treated as a result of the disclosure (Cepeda-Benito & Short, 1998). Following this work, Britt (2000) explored the concept of stigma relating to psychological problems in U.S. military peacekeepers returning from Operation Joint Endeavor in Bosnia. Britt also assessed whether personnel would be more likely to follow through with a psychological referral or a medical referral and examined whether concerns about stigma varied depending on whether the individual was screened alone or in his or her unit.

The study examined a screening process whereby service members completed standardized medical and psychological questionnaires either alone or with their unit (depending on operational rotations). Stigma was then measured using a four-item scale that was found to have good reliability. The screening procedure dictated that individuals who scored above the cutoff points on the standardized health questionnaires would be referred to a medical or psychological professional and asked to wait in line in full view of others.

Although in general all participants indicated that being screened was a stigmatizing experience, Britt found that those who admitted to a psychological problem reported that doing so was much more stigmatizing than did those admitting to a medical problem. Furthermore, over half of those surveyed indicated that they believed their career would be adversely affected if they disclosed a psychological problem. There were significantly more concerns about stigma when individuals were screened with their unit, and individuals were less likely to follow through with a psychological referral than with a medical referral. Although this study raised a number of ethical concerns (e.g., group screening, confidentiality), the results clearly demonstrated the presence of pervasive concerns about help seeking for a psychological problem in the military. Cawkill (2004) found that seeking help for psychiatric problems is also perceived as detrimental to a military career in U.K. forces. Stigmatization appears to be an international problem; a study of Canadian forces also demonstrated that service personnel perceived a number of obstacles to engaging with services including a lack of trust in military health, administrative, and social services, and despite efforts to destigmatize mental health problems and treatments, unmet needs for mental health services remained a significant problem (Fikretoglu, Guay, & Pedlar, 2008).

Hoge et al. (2004) investigated help seeking and barriers to care among U.S. soldiers and marines after deployment to Iraq (Operation Iraqi Freedom) and Afghanistan (Operation Enduring Freedom). The researchers developed Britt's four-item stigma measure (Britt, 2000) into an 18-item scale that included practical concerns about help seeking, defined as barriers, and six items about stigma ("It would be too embarrassing," "It would harm my career," "Members of my unit might have less confidence in me," "My unit leadership might treat me differently," "My leadership would blame me for the problem," and "I would be seen as weak"). Personnel completed this questionnaire along with a range of medical and psychological screening measures. The study revealed that of those who scored above the cutoff on screening, only 38% to 45% indicated an interest in receiving help, and only 23% to 40% had sought mental health care. Concerns about stigmatization were almost twice as likely among personnel who scored above the cutoff: Those who were most in need of care were least likely to seek help for their problems. The three most common concerns were being perceived as weak, being treated differently by unit leadership, and believing that members of one's unit would have less confidence in one. In light of this finding, the authors proposed that the military needed to make the reduction of stigma and barriers to care through outreach programs, education, and changes in health care delivery a priority.

Attitudes of Military Personnel Toward Mental Health Problems in Others

Stigma can thus be a strong obstacle to seeking help. Stigma can be felt by the person him- or herself (e.g., "I am weak if I ask for help" or "My leadership would treat me differently," examples of internal or self-stigma) or about others (e.g., "People who suffer mental health problems are not to be trusted," an example of external stigma). Both attitudes potentially dissuade someone experiencing a mental health problem from coming forward and engaging in a potentially helpful therapeutic relationship. This is unfortunate for many reasons but especially because early treatment, if successful, can prevent a whole series of secondary problems such as poor performance at work, poor relationships (with family, colleagues, and bosses), and an increased potential to abuse substances and create disciplinary problems, all of which can damage careers or reputations. However, it is important to remember that stigma is not the only obstacle that may prevent those who need help from receiving it. Other barriers include military practices (e.g., having a regimented daily routine) and procedures (e.g., being away from a base camp for long periods of time). In addition, help-seeking is affected by the attitudes of those who have to agree to the help-seeking (e.g., one's chain of command) and those in the medical chain who eventually provide the help; they may themselves hold externally stigmatizing beliefs (Robinson, 2004). Clearly, the military system is awash in potential obstacles that can impede help-seeking and that reinforce the need for commanders to address the issue.

Thus far, we have focused on research assessing internal stigma and barriers to care. Contemporary research that examines the attitudes that military personnel actually hold about mental illness in others (i.e., external stigma) is quite limited. One study found that U.S. Air Force personnel held relatively liberal attitudes toward psychiatric patients (Rosen & Corcoran, 1978). However, research on attitudes toward combat stress in U.S. military ground forces found that only 35% believed that they or someone else in their platoon might experience combat stress and that 40% would not trust a returning casualty to be an effective colleague (Schneider & Luscomb, 1984). Another study examined Israeli Defense Force officers' attitudes to combat stress reactions using vignettes and attitude questionnaires (Inbar, Solomon, Aviram, Spiro, & Kotler, 1989). The results showed that an officer was expected to be more responsible than an ordinary soldier for his own recovery and that the higher the rank of the respondent, the less he viewed psychological help as effective and the more he advocated disciplinary methods. In contrast, Porter and Johnson (1994) surveyed U.S. Navy and U.S. Marine Corp commanders and executive officers ($N = 138$) about the competence (i.e., qualification to do the job) and reliability (i.e., trustworthiness) of a hypothetical service member who had received mental health care. Responses tended to be neutral (as measured by a 5-point Likert scale) with few negative evaluations. These results are consistent with a more recent assessment of 172 NATO operational leaders asked about their attitude toward unit members with mental health problems (Adler et al., 2006). With some exceptions, respondents reported that experiencing stress problems on operations was normal, and they considered seeking help to be a positive sign.

Although leaders may report tolerant attitudes, they are concerned about the response of other leaders. Cawkill (2004) conducted a triservice study in the U.K. Armed Forces (i.e., Royal Navy/Royal Marines, army, and Royal Air Force) using an anonymous questionnaire sent to those who were deemed to be leaders or commanders. Responses showed that although most considered it acceptable for their colleagues to experience stress, they did not trust that others would hold the same view. Therefore, most reported that they would not disclose any difficulties they might have themselves. Eighty-five percent thought that seeking in-service support for stress and stress-related problems would have some detrimental effect, including reducing their chances of being promoted and being given roles of responsibility, being perceived as weak, and not being trusted by their peers.

Such concerns about stigma are not limited to leaders. A review of attitudes about PTSD in the Canadian Armed Forces found that soldiers felt stigmatized and abandoned after seeking help and many had not sought help for fear of being ostracized and "shown the door" (Marin, 2002). The report concluded that members of the Canadian Armed Forces were generally poorly informed about mental health issues and did not understand the link between physical and mental health. It further noted an "appalling" lack of knowledge about mental health that permeated the ranks at all levels. The report suggested that mental health education should be a mandatory component of all leadership courses to counter ill-informed attitudes. Cawkill (2004) concurred:

> The macho military culture still prevails and stress and stress-related problems are still viewed negatively. The Armed Forces as a whole need to be seen as more accepting of stress and stress-related problems, so that when personnel are adversely affected by stress they are more likely to seek help and be open about their difficulties without fear of prejudice or perceived negative effects on their career. This cultural shift can be brought about by more and better stress education, preferably early on in a Service person's career so that positive attitudes can be formed and negative attitudes changed. (p. 95)

Thus, there appears to be a considerable body of evidence that many personnel within the armed forces believe that if they were in need of psychological help—and if they sought it—their career would be adversely affected. However, the reality is that their military colleagues and commanders do not, in the main, report that seeking help would be considered as a definitive sign of weakness and therefore a barrier to career progression. Thus, it appears that internal stigma appears to be a much bigger barrier to care than external stigma.

There is evidence that breaking down barriers to care, such as stigma, can be worthwhile and can assist military personnel to get back to full fitness quickly. In a study of 1,068 personnel referred for mental health assessment and treatment, Rowan and Campise (2006) demonstrated that cases of self-referral were more likely to have a transitory problem, were less likely to have their confidentiality broken, and had fewer career-affecting recommendations made about them than those that were ultimately told to report sick or were referred by their commander. Breaking down barriers to care and enabling early assessment therefore appears to be less stigmatizing than allowing a problem to get so complex that it comes to the attention of the chain of command and may ultimately result in a mental health referral anyway (Rowan & Campise, 2006).

Greene-Shortridge, Britt, and Castro (2007) proposed a model for managing stigmatizing beliefs held by military personnel about others. Their ideas centered on three strategies: providing a strong argument against holding stigmatizing views and suppressing such views wherever possible, establishing a strategy of education across the forces to counter stigma, and exposing personnel to those who had experienced mental health problems to directly confront personnel with those that they might stigmatize. It is interesting that it is only the last of these strategies that has any real evidence of being effective. However, many forces do not make widespread use of involving personnel who have been successfully treated for mental health problems in their anti-stigma programs. An exception to this is the Canadian forces, which run a peer support program called Operational Stress Injury Social Support, set up in 2001, that uses retired military personnel to mentor military personnel and veterans who have operational stress injuries (and their families). However, the efficacy of the program has not yet been evaluated.

ARGUMENT FOR PEER SUPPORT

The sections of this chapter on social support and stigma have aimed to highlight that although one's colleagues are a potentially useful resource, stigma and other military barriers to care, can prevent people from making good use of the support available. With physical injuries, even if someone is not keen to seek help, colleagues should be able to spot that their buddy is in need of help, especially for more serious physical problems. Even the hardiest of troops are unlikely to allow a colleague with a fractured leg to hobble about; for both operational and health reasons the afflicted individual would be most likely dragged to a medical center. However, personnel with psychological problems who suffer in silence may not be spotted as being unwell and any decrease in performance might be wrongly attributed to lack of motivation or disinterest, which would understandably lead to poor annual performance ratings.

Addressing mental health problems directly may also be an efficient way to improve job performance. Dunmore, Clark, and Ehlers (1999) reported a variety of cognitive problems in those who experience PTSD, including a sense of ongoing or heightened potential threat. There is little doubt that handling weapons or partaking in arduous training exercises, both of which are essential for a successful military career, would be difficult for those who perceive being at constant threat. Unless such an individual was able to overcome any barriers to help seeking, it is hard to see how he or she might be successful in continuing in service.

However, it seems both logical and practical that as well as trying to get those with mental health problems to overcome any stigma and other potential barriers to care, those close to them could be proactive in providing them with social support and appropriate advice. Certainly, within the U.K. Armed Forces the psychological welfare of troops is primarily a command and leadership responsibility. For those service members who are spotted as functioning less well than is normal, it would be expected that their colleagues and leaders would support them. The challenge, of course, is for those who are proximal to the affected individual to know that he or she needs their help; many who suffer do so in silence.

Social support is also critical in the immediate aftermath of a potentially traumatic event. A meta-analysis of the risk factors for PTSD by Brewin, Andrews, and Valentine (2000) found that factors relating to the postincident environment, namely, provision of social support and a reduction in other life stressors, were more important in predicting who developed PTSD than factors before or during the event. It therefore follows that if the postincident environment can be positively manipulated by colleagues and leaders who are sensitively aware that an individual needs help, then it may be possible both to minimize the nature or severity of trauma-related psychopathology and, where necessary, to encourage those who remain distressed to seek help.

ROLE OF THE MILITARY COMMANDER

Effective military command is a critical component in ensuring that military units function effectively. Leader attitudes and behaviors can be crucial factors in determining whether a unit will fight effectively in combat as well as whether unit personnel will seek help for mental health problems. Leaders are pivotal in the effective functioning of the military group and have been described as having two distinct roles: (a) organizing and completing group tasks and (b) facilitating social and emotional functioning within the group (Bales, 1950). It could be argued that an effective commander must be competent at carrying out both roles for the group to be successful. However, the psychological support of troops may be seen as a "soft" skill and is not always embraced by commanders despite the fact that provision of support can be viewed as a force multiplier. Therefore, the first requirement of a peer-delivered psychological support program is that it is credible to the commander. The commander needs to see the program's tangible benefits, operationally as well as psychologically.

Our experience of introducing just such a system, TRiM, into the Royal Marines Commandos serves as an example of how a structured peer support program can be implemented. The commandos approached one of the authors and requested that a training system be developed within a peer support framework. The request resulted from the recognition that a small number of marines were experiencing psychological difficulties both in response to operational deployments and in response to infrequent but devastating training accidents. At the time, the Royal Marines had no organized system outside the medical and welfare route to deal with this perceived need. As mentioned previously, U.K. research has found that military personnel do not prefer to talk with medical or welfare staff (Greenberg et al., 2003). Thus, the new program needed to create an alternative mechanism for support.

During initial training sessions for the new program, the trainers were also faced with a number of seasoned warrant officers who were deeply skeptical of psychology and external support generally. Three factors determined the positive outcome of these early interactions. The first was the presence of a highly experienced and respected commando officer who had previously voiced his support for the project. The second was the operational experience of the trainers, which gave credibility to the training system. The third factor was the conversion of the most senior warrant officer present from a skeptic to a supporter of the training philosophy. This senior warrant officer's assent effectively unlocked the group, and the atmosphere of the training changed palpably, with each course member participating more fully. Sufficient interest was generated from the initial course to allow the training to progress and evolve over time into what is now termed *Trauma Risk Management*. Without the direct support of commanders and, critically, the senior noncommissioned officers, it is likely that the project would have foundered.

It is notable that the system of TRiM is now run internally by Royal Marine warrant officers with support as required from military mental health professionals who provide audits and quality assurance for the training courses. Within the Royal Marines, the concepts of TRiM are taught during basic training to all marine recruits so that when it is suggested that they interact with TRiM practitioners during their service, it is not seen as stigmatizing but merely as part of military life. The TRiM principles are also taught to commanders, both junior and senior, by experienced, nonmedical TRiM practitioners. It is the ongoing support at all levels that has made peer psychological support an acceptable component of the commander's operational toolbox. It has also resulted in routine psychological risk assessment and support and has become part of a commander's routine ongoing assessment of psychological threat on operational deployments.

MILITARY STRESS MITIGATION AND SOCIAL SUPPORT MODELS

Before moving on to describe both TRiM and Battlemind in more detail, we suggest that social support provision within the military can be viewed as being part of a wider model of stress mitigation. We consider two such models here.

The first model we propose is a propositional model with an operational focus that synthesizes the various components described in this chapter so far (see Figure 3.1). It suggests that leadership style, stress control policy, leadership training, cohesion, and morale all influence whether someone is prepared for exposure to psychological threat both through modification of risk factors (e.g., ensuring personnel experience sufficiently arduous and realistic training opportunities that will bolster self-esteem, confidence, and skills prior to deployment) and through modification, or at least mitigation, of military risk factors, such as time away from loved ones (e.g., providing sufficient support for families at home, which will decrease service members' concerns about

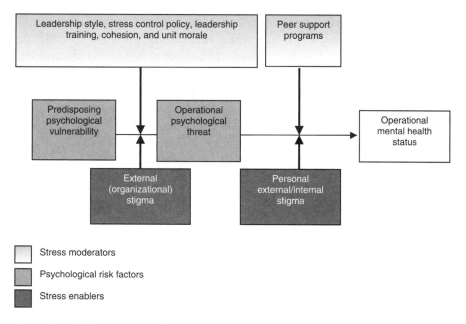

Figure 3.1. Military stress mitigation and social support model.

how their families are coping without them) or working in adverse climatic conditions (e.g., providing suitable training about dealing with extreme heat or cold, providing water coolers as far forward as possible). The same factors also influence a unit's acceptance of peer support and indeed the culture within the unit in relation to stigma and other barriers to care. This model suggests that although peer support can mitigate and influence the effects of exposure to traumatic stressors, it can only do so if the culture set by the unit leadership facilitates such support. Therefore, according to this model, successful peer support can overcome stigma and result in a positive outcome.

Another way of conceptualizing stress moderation that complements our proposed model is the *soldier adaptation model* (Bliese & Castro, 2000). The soldier adaptation model views stressors such as work overload or role ambiguity as leading to strains such as poor health, poor attitude, or poor performance. The link between stressors and strains is moderated by both individual factors, such as involvement with the mission and perceived self-efficacy, and unit factors, such as leadership and social support. This model therefore views the social environment of a military unit as moderating the effect of a whole variety of stressors whether related to an operational environment or not. Our opinion is that however it is viewed, social support appears to facilitate military personnel reasserting control over highly chaotic circumstances. For instance, military personnel deployed on peacekeeping operations are not infrequently constrained by restrictive rule of engagement from using controlled aggression when negotiating with hostile civilians. Although such situations might cause individuals to experience distress and frustration, being able to discuss the emotional (and quite possibly behavioral) consequences of being in such situations with their colleagues is likely to be beneficial in a way that talking to professionals or indeed nonmilitary family members could not.

TRAUMA RISK MANAGEMENT AS A MODEL OF PEER SUPPORT

Although TRiM began within the Royal Marines Commandos, elite amphibious troops, it is now being rolled out across the majority of the U.K. Armed Forces, apart from some Royal Air Force units. Many other nonmilitary organizations use it, including the police, the Foreign & Commonwealth Office, the British Broadcasting Corporation, and a number of emergency services. TRiM is compliant with the United Kingdom's National Institute for Health and Clinical Excellence standards (National Collaborating Center for Mental Health, 2005; Greenberg, Cawkill, & Sharpley, 2005; Jones et al., 2003).

The model bases itself on keeping personnel functioning after traumatic events by providing support, advice, and education to those who require it. In addition, TRiM practitioners identify those who are not coping after potentially traumatizing events and ensure they are referred to professional sources of help. TRiM practitioners are embedded within units, so even where there is limited, or no, access to medical or mental health assets, as is often the case in forward operating bases, even small units will have someone who can provide a psychological focus and ongoing mentoring on behalf of the commander. Such personnel can also act as the eyes and ears of the medical and mental health services to alert them to those who might benefit from their services.

TRiM practitioners are nonmedical personnel who have received between 2 and 5 days of training that enables them to identify psychological risk factors that might otherwise go unnoticed. The training covers the basics of trauma psychology and how to plan for managing traumatic events and combat incidents before they occur. Preplanning entails having trained TRiM practitioners within the unit and ensuring that unit personnel are aware of TRiM and its aims and therefore do not see its use as indicative of a special situation. The training also covers how to manage events immediately afterward and how to conduct a psychological risk assessment. Practitioners are encouraged to use already existing personnel management systems to assist in the recovery of normally distressed individuals and, where necessary, to ensure that those who require it are referred for appropriate treatment at an early stage.

A major component of the program is that TRiM enables practitioners to be reactive to the ebb and flow of activity in any operational theatre in a way that externally delivered systems cannot. Often, the level and nature of psychological threat are only apparent to those who understand the current operational environment and how this interacts with groups and individuals in the unit. The TRiM system emphasizes careful planning at the unit level, which can take place only when the subtle interactions of personal and group history, personality, group dynamics, and the current state of threat are known. This insider knowledge allows for a flexible response that might range from watchful waiting and purposeful inactivity to a full psychological risk assessment, psychoeducation, and ongoing peer support. The importance of ongoing and reactive threat assessment cannot be overstated, and we hope that by having this in place, chronic psychological illness can be prevented by timely psychological intervention.

The TRiM process is layered and has the following discreet stages:

1. initiating the management of risk by attempting to offset potential problems through general support at the site of the traumatic or combat event (e.g., ensuring that those personnel who do not need to be exposed to corpses are not);
2. organizing a formal planning session as soon as possible after the event(s) to identify those involved in the event, even those at the periphery, using a structured template;
3. identifying those who require no intervention and grouping the remainder (using objective criteria) into those who will participate in a peer-delivered semistructured interview to assess risk and those who will receive education in a larger group;
4. conducting a psychological risk assessment using a 10-item risk scale at an early stage and again a month later to identify how personnel are psychologically adjusting to the potentially traumatic event; referral is encouraged if early problems persist; and
5. providing continuous mentoring, general support, and advice about self-management and referral when and if required.

Within the U.K. military, TRiM is routinely used in the current theaters of operation, where the system aims to help overcome stigma while mobilizing social support. Units that have adopted the system report that it is a useful tool for helping to discharge a commander's duty of care toward his or her subordinates and that it may also help to change a unit's culture toward stress in general. By giving personnel the skills to recognize distress in others and the knowledge to help such people in practical and commonsense ways, TRiM may act as a catalyst to a unit's destigmatizing of operational stress reactions. TRiM has been subject to a group randomized trial and has not been found to cause harm, a prevailing concern in the United Kingdom because of the use of previous models of single-session psychological debriefing (van Emmerik, Kamphuis, Hulsbosch, & Emmelkamp, 2002). Also, TRiM has the advantage of being able to respond to changes in the form of support techniques over time; that is to say, to make use of the locally available best support mechanisms. Because it is a peer-delivered system, the practitioners can be updated in the same way as those trained in immediate medical responses are updated in resuscitation protocols.

BATTLEMIND

Battlemind is a holistic set of resilience building strategies devised by researchers in the U.S. Army. The aim of the various Battlemind interventions is to help military personnel adopt a resilience-based attitude toward the possible effects of operational stress. For instance, postdeployment Battlemind aims to help troops transition from the "war zone" to the "home zone." The word *Battlemind* is an acronym: For instance, the B refers to buddies, and in a postdeployment sense, it is important for soldiers to recognize that while they were in operational theatres they, quite correctly, relied heavily on their buddies for their physical and psychological safety. However, on returning home, it is essential that soldiers understand that although they might want to continue to spend time with their buddies because this kept them safe for the period of deployment, doing so prevents them from reestablishing their supportive home relationships with family and friends. The other letters of the Battlemind acronym all relate to important transitions that personnel have to undergo to have a successful homecoming experience.

Battlemind has been found to be of benefit to the psychological health of U.S. troops (Adler, Bliese, McGurk, Hoge, & Castro, 2009; Adler, Castro, Bliese, McGurk, & Milliken, 2007; Adler et al., 2006), and its approach builds on peer support because the Battlemind principles reinforce the need to pay attention to fellow unit members' states of mind and emphasizes the point that stigma prevents many who need it from seeking help. Furthermore, the Battlemind modules also emphasize the role of the leader in establishing the unit environment in terms of stress-related issues. Such is the utility of the Battlemind approach that Canadian forces also use the Battlemind intervention for troops who are returning from operations, and the U.K. Armed Forces are embarked on a trial to investigate whether the system will be of benefit to their personnel.

Taken together, TRiM and Battlemind represent the formalization of the importance of peer support and leadership in optimizing the mental health of service members. Both systems emphasize the role of the other team members in caring for one another and the importance of the leader in establishing a supportive unit climate. Through this formal recognition, and by training identified practitioners and incorporating these concepts into the military's socialization process, the strength of social support can be leveraged to support military mental health.

CONCLUSIONS

This chapter set out to demonstrate that peer-delivered support systems are good practice and are pragmatic, especially within military systems in which professional assistance may not always be easily accessible. For peer support to be effective, it requires that commanders are supportive of its concepts and sensitive to the needs of those they lead. Social support can prove beneficial not just in helping to deal with stressful circumstances after events but also before events occur. Military forces rely heavily on colleagues and leaders supporting each other operationally, and we believe that such support is of equal importance in terms of psychological well-being. There is clearly a need to continue to refine the understanding of what it is about social support that is beneficial in terms of mental health; the results of future studies might be able to influence basic training and leadership courses to attempt to capitalize on what is useful and minimize what is not. However, as is the case with most interventions, it would be important to show that any changes were beneficial and that the "law of unintended consequence" did not lead to an unpredicted reduction in performance or health. Furthermore, it may be that what is useful in a garrison setting may not be ideal on the battlefield. However, in general, this chapter aimed to show that although there will always be a place for the provision of formal services by medical, psychiatric, and chaplaincy personnel, we believe that the immediate management of distressed personnel is best achieved within that person's unit. This is likely to be less stigmatizing than simply referring any distressed individual for "outside" help, and it avoids unnecessary labeling of distressed personnel as being anything other than normal people going through unpleasant times.

REFERENCES

Adler, A. B., Bliese, P. D., McGurk, D., Hoge, C. W., & Castro, C. A. (2009). Battlemind Debriefing and Battlemind Training as early interventions with soldiers returning from Iraq: Randomization by platoon. *Journal of Consulting and Clinical Psychology, 77,* 928–940. doi:10.1037/a0016877

Adler, A. B., Castro, C. A., Bliese, P. D., McGurk, D., & Milliken, C. (2007, August). The efficacy of Battlemind Training at 3–6 months post deployment. In

C. A. Castro (Chair), *The Battlemind Training System: Supporting soldiers throughout the deployment cycle*. Symposium conducted at the meeting of the American Psychological Association, San Francisco, CA.

Adler, A. B., Castro, C. A., McGurk, D., Bliese, P. D., Wright, K. M., & Hoge, C. W. (2006, November). *Postdeployment interventions to reduce the mental health impact of combat deployment to Iraq: Public health policies, psychological debriefing and Battlemind Training.* Paper presented at the International Society for Traumatic Stress Studies, Hollywood, CA.

Bales, R. F. (1950). A set of categories for the analysis of small group interaction. *American Sociological Review, 15*, 257–263. doi:10.2307/2086790

Bartone, P. T., Ursano, R. J., Wright, K. M., & Ingraham, L. H. (1989). The impact of a military air disaster on the health of assistance workers: A prospective study. *Journal of Nervous and Mental Disease, 177*, 317–328. doi:10.1097/00005053-198906000-00001

Beehr, T. A., Bennett, M. M., & Bowling, N. A. (2007). Occupational stress and failures of social support: When helping hurts. In T. A. Beehr & M. M. Bennett (Chairs), *New developments in social support research.* Symposium conducted at the meeting of the Society for Industrial and Organizational Psychology, New York, NY.

Berkman, L. F., & Syme, S. L. (1979). Social networks, host resistance, and mortality: 9-year follow-up study of Alameda County residents. *American Journal of Epidemiology, 109*, 186–204.

Bliese, P. D., & Britt, T. W. (2001). Social support, group consensus and stressor–strain relationships: Social context matters. *Journal of Organizational Behavior, 22*, 425–436. doi:10.1002/job.95

Bliese, P. D., & Castro, A. C. (2000). Role clarity, work overload, and organizational support: Multilevel evidence of the importance of support. *Work and Stress, 14*, 65–73. doi:10.1080/026783700417230

Bliese, P. D., & Halverson, R. R. (2002). Using random group resampling in multilevel research: An example of the buffering effects of leadership climate. *The Leadership Quarterly, 13*, 53–68. doi:10.1016/S1048-9843(01)00104-7

Bowyer, A. (2005). Keep a stiff upper lip. *New Scientist, 188*, 26.

Brailey, K., Vasterling, J. J., Proctor, S. P., Constans, J. I., & Friedman, M. J. (2007). PTSD symptoms, life events, and unit cohesion in U.S. soldiers: Baseline findings from the neurocognition deployment health study. *Journal of Traumatic Stress, 20*, 495–503. doi:10.1002/jts.20234

Brewin, C. R., Andrews, B., & Valentine, J. (2000). Meta-analysis of risk factors for posttraumatic stress disorder in trauma exposed adults. *Journal of Consulting and Clinical Psychology, 68*, 748–766. doi:10.1037/0022-006X.68.5.748

Britt, T. W. (2000). The stigma of psychological problems in a work environment: Evidence from the screening of service members returning from Bosnia. *Journal of Applied Social Psychology, 30*, 1599–1618. doi:10.1111/j.1559-1816.2000.tb02457.x

Britt, T. W., Dickinson, J. M., Moore, D., Castro, C. A., & Adler, A. B. (2007). Correlates and consequences of morale versus depression under stressful conditions. *Journal of Occupational Health Psychology, 12,* 34–47. doi:10.1037/1076-8998.12.1.34

Byrne, P. (2001). Psychiatric stigma. *The British Journal of Psychiatry, 178,* 281–284. doi:10.1192/bjp.178.3.281

Cassel, J. (1976). The contribution of the social environment to host resistance. *American Journal of Epidemiology, 104,* 107–123.

Cawkill, P. (2004). A study into commanders' understanding of, and attitudes to, stress and stress related problems. *Journal of the Royal Army Medical Corps, 150,* 91–96.

Cepeda-Benito, A., & Short, P. (1998). Self-concealment, avoidance of psychological services, and perceived likelihood of seeking professional help. *Journal of Counseling Psychology, 45,* 58–64. doi:10.1037/0022-0167.45.1.58

Cobb, S. (1976). Social support as a moderator of life stress. *Psychosomatic Medicine, 38,* 300–314.

Cohen, S., Clark, M. S., & Sherrod, D. R. (1986). Social skills and the stress-protective role of social support. *Journal of Personality and Social Psychology, 50,* 963–973. doi:10.1037/0022-3514.50.5.963

Cohen, S., & Wills, T. A. (1985). Stress, social support, and the buffering hypothesis. *Psychological Bulletin, 98,* 310–357. doi:10.1037/0033-2909.98.2.310

Corrigan, P. (2004). How stigma interferes with mental health care. *American Psychologist, 59,* 614–625. doi:10.1037/0003-066X.59.7.614

Cutrona, C. E., & Russell, D. (1990). Type of social support and specific stress: Toward a theory of optimal matching. In I. G. Sarason, B. R. Sarason, & G. R. Pierce (Eds.), *Social support: An interactional view* (pp. 319–366). New York, NY: Wiley.

Dunivin, K. O. (1994). Military culture: Change and continuity. *Armed Forces and Society, 20,* 531–547. doi:10.1177/0095327X9402000403

Dunmore, E., Clark, D. M., & Ehlers, A. (1999). Cognitive factors involved in the onset and maintenance of posttraumatic stress disorder (PTSD) after physical or sexual assault. *Behaviour Research and Therapy, 37,* 809–829. doi:10.1016/S0005-7967(98)00181-8

Durkheim, E. (1951). *Suicide: A study in sociology* (J. A. Spaulding & G. Simpson, Trans.). Glencoe, IL: Free Press.

Fear, N. T., Iversen, A. C., Chatterjee, A., Jones, M., Greenberg, N., Hull, L., . . . Wessely, S. (2008). Risky driving among regular armed forces personnel from the United Kingdom. *American Journal of Preventive Medicine, 35,* 230–236. doi:10.1016/j.amepre.2008.05.027

Fikretoglu, D., Guay, S., & Pedlar, D. (2008). Twelve month use of mental health services in a nationally representative, active military sample. *Medical Care, 46,* 217–223. doi:10.1097/MLR.0b013e31815b979a

Flanagan, D. A. (1998). A retrospective analysis of expressed emotion (EE) and affective distress in a sample of relatives caring for traumatically brain-injured (TBI) family members. *The British Journal of Clinical Psychology, 37*, 431–439.

Galea, S., & Resnick, H. (2005). Posttraumatic stress disorder in the general population after mass terrorist incidents: Considerations about the nature of exposure. *CNS Spectrums, 10*, 107–115.

Goffman, E. (1963). *Stigma: Notes on the management of spoiled identity*. Englewood Cliffs, NJ: Prentice Hall.

Greenberg, N., Cawkill, P., & Sharpley, J. (2005). How to TRiM away at posttraumatic stress reactions: Traumatic risk management—now and in the future. *Journal of the Royal Naval Medical Service, 91*, 26–31.

Greenberg, N., Thomas, S., Iversen, A., Unwin, C., Hull, L., & Wessely, S. (2003). Do military peacekeepers want to talk about their experiences? Perceived psychological support of U.K. military peacekeepers on return from deployment. *Journal of Mental Health, 12*, 565–573. doi:10.1080/09638230310001627928

Greene-Shortridge, T., Britt, T. W., & Castro, C. A. (2007). The stigma of mental health problems in the military. *Military Medicine, 172*, 157–161.

Grinker, R. R., & Spiegel, J. P. (1945). *Men under stress*. London: J. & A. Churchill. doi:10.1037/10784-000

Helgeson, V., Cohen, S., & Fritz, H. L. (1998). Social ties and cancer. In J. C. Holland (Ed.), *Psycho-oncology* (pp. 99–109). New York, NY: Oxford University Press.

Hoge, C. W., Castro, C. A., Messer, S. C., McGurk, D., Cotting, D. I., & Koffman, R. L. (2004). Combat duty in Iraq and Afghanistan, mental health problems, and barriers to care. *The New England Journal of Medicine, 351*, 13–22. doi:10.1056/NEJMoa040603

House, J. S., Robbins, C., & Metzner, H. L. (1982). The association of social relationships and activities with mortality: Prospective evidence from the Tecumseh community health study. *American Journal of Epidemiology, 116*, 123–140.

Inbar, D., Solomon, Z., Aviram, U., Spiro, S., & Kotler, M. (1989). Officers' attitudes towards combat stress reaction: Responsibility, treatment, return to unit, and personal distance. *Military Medicine, 154*, 480–487.

Ismail, K., Blatchley, N., Hotopf, M., Hull, L., Palmer, I., Unwin, C., . . . Wessely, S. (2000). Occupational risk factors for ill health in Gulf veterans of the United Kingdom. *Journal of Epidemiology and Community Health, 54*, 834–838. doi:10.1136/jech.54.11.834

Iversen, A. C., Fear, N. T., Ehlers, A., Hacker Hughes, J. L. Hull, L., Earnshaw, M., . . . Hotopf, M. (2008). Risk factors for posttraumatic stress disorder among U.K. armed forces personnel. *Psychological Medicine, 38*, 511–522. doi:10.1017/S0033291708002778

Iversen, A. C., Fear, N., Simonoff, E., Hull, L., Horn, O., Greenberg, N., . . . Wessely, S. (2007). Preenlistment vulnerability factors and their influence on health outcomes in U.K. military personnel. *The British Journal of Psychiatry, 191*, 506–511. doi:10.1192/bjp.bp.107.039818

Jones, E. (2006). LMF: The use of psychiatric stigma in the Royal Air Force during the Second World War. *The Journal of Military History, 70,* 439–458. doi:10.1353/jmh.2006.0103

Jones, E. E., Farina, A., Hastorf, A. H., Markus, H., Miller, D. T., & Scott, R. A. (1984). *Social stigma: The psychology of marked relationships.* New York, NY: Freeman.

Jones, N., Roberts, P., & Greenberg, N. (2003). Peer-group risk assessment: A post-traumatic management strategy for hierarchical organizations. *Occupational Medicine, 53,* 469–475. doi:10.1093/occmed/kqg093

Jones, E., & Wessely, S. (2005). *From shellshock to PTSD: Military psychiatry from 1900 to the Gulf War.* Hove, England: Psychology Press.

Labuc, S. (1991). Cultural and societal factors in military organizations. In R. Gal & A. D. Mangelsdorff (Eds.), *Handbook of military psychology* (pp. 471–489). London, England: Wiley.

Leff, J. (1994). Working with the families of schizophrenic patients. *The British Journal of Psychiatry, 164,* 71–76.

Lerner, Y., Kertes, J., & Zilber, N. (2005). Immigrants from the former Soviet Union, 5 years postimmigration to Israel: Adaptation and risk factors for psychological distress. *Psychological Medicine, 35,* 1805–1814. doi:10.1017/S0033291705005726

Loo, C. M., Lim, B. R., Koff, G., Morton, R. K., & Kiang, P. N. C. (2007). Ethnic-related stressors in the war zone—Case studies of Asian American Vietnam veterans. *Military Medicine, 172,* 968–971.

Manning, F. J., & Ingraham, L. H. (1987). An investigation into the value of unit cohesion in peacetime. In G. Belenky (Ed.), *Contemporary studies in combat psychiatry* (pp. 47–67). Westport, CT: Greenwood Press.

Marin, A. (2002). Systemic treatment of CF members with PTSD. *National Defence and Canadian Forces Ombudsman.* Retrieved from http://www.ombudsman.forces.gc.ca/sr-er/ptsd-sspt-eng.asp

Marshall, S. L. A. (1947). *Men against fire: The problem of battle command in future war.* New York, NY: Morrow.

McGeorge, T., Hacker Hughes, J., & Wessely, S. (2006). The MOD PTSD decision: A psychiatric perspective. *Occupational Health Review, 122,* 21–28.

McGurk, D., Cotting, D. I., Britt, T. W., & Adler, A. B. (2006). Joining the ranks: The role of indoctrination in transforming civilians to service members. In A. B. Adler, C. A. Castro, & T. W. Britt (Eds.), *Military life: The psychology of serving in peace and combat: Vol. 2. Operational Stress* (p. 13–31). Westport, CT: Praeger.

McNally, S. T., & Newman, S. (1999). Objective and subjective conceptualizations of social support. *Journal of Psychosomatic Research, 46,* 309–314.

Mehta, S., & Farina, A. (1997). Is being "sick" really better? Effect of the disease view of mental disorder on stigma. *Journal of Social and Clinical Psychology, 16,* 405–419.

Meltzer, H., Bebbington, P., Brugha, T., Farrell, M., Jenkins, R., & Lewis, G. (2003). The reluctance to seek treatment for neurotic disorders. *International Review of Psychiatry, 15,* 123–128.

Möller-Leimkühler, A. M. (2002). Barriers to help-seeking by men: A review of socio-cultural and clinical literature with particular reference to depression. *Journal of Affective Disorders, 71*, 1–9. doi:10.1016/S0165-0327(01)00379-2

National Collaborating Center for Mental Health (2005). *Posttraumatic stress disorder: The management of PTSD in adults and children in primary and secondary care.* London, England: National Institute for Clinical Excellence.

Orsillo, S. M., Roemer, L., Litz, B. T., Ehlich, P., & Friedman, M. J. (1998). Psychiatric symptomatology associated with contemporary peacekeeping: An examination of postmission functioning among peacekeepers in Somalia. *Journal of Traumatic Stress, 11*, 611–625. doi:10.1023/A:1024481030025

Porter, T. L., & Johnson, W. B. (1994). Psychiatric stigma in the military. *Military Medicine, 159*, 602–605.

Reifman, A. (1995). Social relationships, recovery from illness, and survival: A literature review. *Annals of Behavioral Medicine, 17*, 124–131. doi:10.1007/BF02895061

Robinson, S. L. (2004). *Hidden toll of the war in Iraq: Mental health and the military.* Washington, DC: Center for American Progress.

Rosen, H., & Corcoran, J. F. T. (1978). Attitudes of USAF officers toward mental illness: Comparison with mental health professionals. *Military Medicine, 143*, 570–574.

Rowan, A. B., & Campise, R. (2006). A multisite study of Air Force outpatient behavioral health treatment-seeking patterns and career impact. *Military Medicine, 171*, 1123–1127.

Sayce, L. (1998). Stigma, discrimination and social exclusion: What's in a word? *Journal of Mental Health, 7*, 331–343. doi:10.1080/09638239817932

Schneider, R. J., & Luscomb, R. L. (1984). Battle stress reaction and the United States Army. *Military Medicine, 149*, 66–69.

Schulze, B., Richter-Werling, M., Matschinger, H., & Angermeyer, M. C. (2003). Crazy? So what! Effects of a school project on students' attitudes towards people with schizophrenia. *Acta Psychiatrica Scandinavica, 107*, 142–150. doi:10.1034/j.1600-0447.2003.02444.x

Schwarzer, R., & Leppin, A. (1989). Social support and health: A meta analysis. *Psychology & Health, 3*, 1–15. doi:10.1080/08870448908400361

Services Sounds and Vision Corporation (2007). *The grim reaper.* England: Ministry of Defence.

Shils, E., & Janowitz, M. (1948). Cohesion and disintegration in the Wehrmacht in World War II. *Public Opinion Quarterly, 12*, 280–315. doi:10.1086/265951

Shirom, A. (1976). On some correlates of combat performance. *Administrative Science Quarterly, 21*, 419–432. doi:10.2307/2391852

Siebold, G. L. (2007). The essence of military group cohesion. *Armed Forces and Society, 33*, 286–295. doi:10.1177/0095327X06294173

Sijbrandij, M., Olff, M., Reitsma, J. B., Carlier, I. V., & Gersons, B. P. (2006). Emotional or educational debriefing after psychological trauma. Randomised controlled trial. *The British Journal of Psychiatry, 189*, 150–155. doi:10.1192/ bjp.bp.105.021121

Smith, D. (2002). The Freudian trap in combat motivation theory. *The Journal of Strategic Studies, 25*, 191–212. doi:10.1080/01402390412331302815

Stouffer, S. A. (1949). *The American soldier: Combat and its aftermath.* Princeton, NJ: Princeton University Press.

Thoits, P. A. (1985). Self-labeling processes in mental illness: The role of emotional deviance. *American Journal of Sociology, 91*, 221–249. doi:10.1086/228276

Thomas, W. I., & Znaniecki, F. (1920). *The Polish peasant in Europe and America: Monograph of an Immigrant Group.* Chicago, IL: University of Chicago Press.

Uchino, B. N., Cacioppo, J. T., & Kiecolt-Glaser, J. K. (1996). The relationship between social support and physiological processes: A review with emphasis on underlying mechanisms and implications for health. *Psychological Bulletin, 119*, 488–531. doi:10.1037/0033-2909.119.3.488

van Dam, H. A., van der Horst, F. G., Knoops, L., Ryckman, R. M., Crebolder, H. F. J. M., & van den Borne, B. H. W. (2005). Social support in diabetes: A systematic review of controlled intervention studies. *Patient Education and Counseling, 59*, 1–12. doi:10.1016/j.pec.2004.11.001

van Emmerik, A. A., Kamphuis, J. H., Hulsbosch, A. M., & Emmelkamp, P. M. (2002). Single session debriefing after psychological trauma: A meta-analysis. *Lancet, 360*, 766–771. doi:10.1016/S0140-6736(02)09897-5

Wells, J. E., Robins, L. N., Bushnell, J. A., Jarosz, D., & Oakley-Browne, M. A. (1994). Perceived barriers to care in St. Louis (USA) and Christchurch (NZ): Reasons for not seeking professional help for psychological distress. *Social Psychiatry and Psychiatric Epidemiology, 29*, 155–164.

Wessely, S. (2006). Twentieth-century theories on combat motivation and breakdown. *Journal of Contemporary History, 41*, 268–286. doi:10.1177/0022009406062067

4

RESEARCH-BASED PREVENTIVE MENTAL HEALTH CARE STRATEGIES IN THE MILITARY

PAUL D. BLIESE, AMY B. ADLER, AND CARL ANDREW CASTRO

Toward the end of World War II, it was clear that a focused effort to reduce mental health problems by selecting only resilient individuals for service was not particularly effective (Berlien & Waggoner, 1966; Egan, Jackson, & Eanes, 1951; Glass, 1966). Maladjustment to military service continued, and stringent selection programs made it difficult to recruit sufficient numbers of personnel. As it became evident that the military was unlikely to create a resilient force through recruiting alone, mental health professionals began to focus attention on programs designed to prevent mental health problems among those already serving. These programs were designed to "maintain the mental health of trainees and [facilitate] the early recognition of emotional disability" (Glass, 1966, p. 750). It is important, however, as Glass (1966) noted, that "no convincing evidence was ever submitted to indicate that such

The views expressed in this chapter are those of the authors and do not reflect the official position of the Walter Reed Army Institute of Research, the U.S. Army, or Department of Defense. This chapter was authored or coauthored by an employee of the United States government as part of official duty and is considered to be in the public domain. Any views expressed herein do not necessarily represent the views of the United States government, and the author's participation in the work is not meant to serve as an official endorsement.

indoctrination or orientation lectures reduced the incident of maladjustment disorders in trainees" (p. 750).

Decades after World War II, preventive efforts in the U.S. military are again largely focused on programs to maintain the resilience of personnel, and questions about the efficacy of these programs are a central issue. The purpose of this chapter is to discuss the efficacy of large-scale preventive mental health programs in support of the war efforts in Iraq and Afghanistan. In considering program efficacy, we explore the link between different types of research (i.e., surveillance and randomized trials), with an eye on both statistical issues associated with program effectiveness and the pragmatic realities facing decision makers who implement policies that lead to large-scale preventive programs.

Our central argument is that research data have demonstrated that mental health variables from individuals in the same work group are more similar than would be expected by chance. These *group-level properties* associated with the mental health variables provide a basis to expect that even short universally applied interventions can be effective if such interventions leverage the existing small-group social structure. That is, intervention efficacy can be maximized if it builds on the small-unit social structure in a way that does things such as encouraging team members to look out for each other and support each other during stressful transitions. Research suggests, however, that the effectiveness of large-scale preventive interventions will almost certainly be small when evaluated against traditional statistical effect size criteria. Rather than dismiss the value of preventive measures because of small effects, we provide reasons why such programs should be emphasized and supported.

ROLE OF SURVEILLANCE DATA

Surveillance-related mental health research is designed to document rates of mental health problems and provides one of the key foundations underlying preventive mental health programs. Fundamentally, surveillance programs define the need that, in turn, provides the impetus for implementing preventive programs. Surveillance has been a cornerstone of mental health-related research in support of the wars on Iraq and Afghanistan. In 2004, for instance, Hoge and colleagues published an article in the *New England Journal of Medicine* detailing the psychological effects of combat in Iraq and Afghanistan. The high degree of press visibility was surprising; after all, it is certainly well known that combat exposure leads to increased risk of mental health problems such as posttraumatic stress disorder (PTSD) symptoms. What the Hoge et al. article did, however, was to quantify this risk in the context of Iraq and Afghanistan and show that between 15% and 17% of those exposed to combat in Iraq were at risk of PTSD, major depression, or generalized anxiety.

Statistically estimating the extent of the problem made it subsequently possible to estimate the need for services and the need for potential preventive programs designed to reduce the mental health impact on service members.

The Hoge et al. (2004) article is an early example of a much larger mental health surveillance research effort. The research protocol on which the 2004 article was based ultimately resulted in surveys from close to 70,000 soldiers returning from combat and produced a variety of surveillance-based publications (e.g., Cabrera, Hoge, Bliese, Castro, & Messer, 2007; Eaton et al., 2008; Hoge et al., 2008; Killgore et al., 2008; Thomas et al., 2010). The protocol also provided the research basis for a fundamental part of the army's ongoing surveillance effort: the Mental Health Advisory Teams or MHATs.

Throughout the Iraq and Afghanistan wars, MHATs have played a key role in the mental health surveillance of service members (see also Chapter 1, this volume). MHATs deploy to combat theaters to evaluate both (a) the mental health status of deployed service members and (b) the status of the mental health care delivery system. The first MHAT mission took place in the 1st year of the ground invasion of Iraq in 2003 and detailed both high rates of mental health problems and difficulties with providing behavioral health care in deployed situations (MHAT, 2003). Recommendations made by the initial MHAT team and subsequent teams (e.g., appointing a theater-wide behavioral health consultant to coordinate the distribution of behavioral health assets) have had a large impact on the delivery of behavioral health care in theater.

Subsequent MHATs continued to examine current conditions in both Iraq and Afghanistan. By the end of 2009, six MHATs had been sent to Iraq and three to Afghanistan. One noteworthy aspect of the MHATs is that all MHATs were requested by operational commanders. In other words, MHATs were initiated because senior operational leaders in Iraq and Afghanistan requested the teams. In this way, the MHATs were supported, but not driven, by the army's medical and research communities.

In each MHAT, core surveillance items remained constant (e.g., measures of PTSD symptoms and depression). Just as important, however, is that the survey instruments were easily modifiable to allow teams to assess emergent issues including deployment length (i.e., when the army began 15-month deployments), dwell time (i.e., when concerns were raised about the amount of time soldiers had between deployments), and the treatment of concussive events (i.e., when improvised explosive devices became major concerns). Over the course of the MHAT, analytic and sampling approaches were refined as conditions in theater made it possible to support designs with increased scientific rigor. For instance, MHAT VI (2009) began to conduct sampling using a random, cluster-based approach to help reduce any possibility that bias was being inadvertently introduced by the data collection procedures. This refinement was made possible by an infrastructure that was well established after 5 to 6 years of conflict and that facilitated delivering surveys to pre-selected platoons.

The recurrent nature of the MHAT deployments made it possible to compare mental health statistics by year and across theaters (Iraq and Afghanistan); the interpretation of the results had implications for broad policy decisions, such as deployment lengths and period of dwell time between deployments. In addition to tracking rates of mental health problems and providing data on emergent issues, each MHAT assessed the status of recommendations from previous years. Thus, the MHAT process represented a recurrent feedback system with high transparency, with reports made available to the media and public through an army medical link (http://www.armymedicine.army.mil/).

The influence of the MHAT reports was significant. The information in the reports was routinely provided in briefs to the highest levels of the medical and military leadership (including the secretary of the army, the chief of staff of the army, and the Joint Chiefs of Staff). Recommendations carried considerable weight and were tracked by the military, media and Congress. Indeed, as the MHAT process matured, it became important to be judicious in terms of the number and nature of recommendations because there was a tendency among the media and others to use the number of implemented recommendations as evidence of the degree to which the army was (or was not) addressing mental health issues. In practice, though, there were a variety of instances in which recommendations were simply unfeasible or impractical when considered within the context of multiple stakeholders and limited resources. In these instances, the decision not to implement a recommendation did not represent a failure; rather, it reflected the need to balance recommendations with other demands. A simple example is the MHAT V (2008) recommendation to hold quarterly behavioral health conferences in theater (Iraq) to facilitate dissemination of behavioral health information among providers. The fact that the recommendation specified "quarterly" implied that holding conferences twice a year was inadequate; nonetheless, the goal was dissemination of behavioral health information, not the specific number of conferences. Thus, over time the MHAT reports reflected a greater appreciation for the attention given to the recommendations.

The frequent nature of the MHAT deployments and other surveillance efforts played a key role in keeping combat-related mental health issues a priority for the U.S. military. This in turn produced an environment receptive to implementing preventive mental health programs. Broadly speaking, however, there are relatively limited options when it comes to broad-scale preventive programs; most programs can be classified into to one of two types. The first type includes selection and screening programs. These programs are designed to either select only certain types of individuals or to identify individuals with behavioral health problems and facilitate their care. We consider these programs in a separate chapter (see Chapter 7, this volume).

The second type of broad prevention program includes training interventions designed to teach skills and build resilience among service members. As occurred in World War II, the military has shown considerable willingness to implement these types of programs in support of service members engaged in the wars in Iraq and Afghanistan. We believe the military's implementation of behavioral health training programs to address the impact of conflicts in Iraq and Afghanistan represents one of the largest attempts to improve the behavior status of a large adult population. In the army, for instance, resilience-based training is targeted both across a soldier's career (i.e., basic training, progressive leadership courses) and across the deployment cycle (i.e., pre- and postdeployment). In any given year, these programs touch the lives of hundreds of thousands of individuals. The goals of these training programs are certainly worthwhile; they provide soldiers with cognitive skills that make them better able to adjust to combat and other stressors associated with military life. However, the military and the behavioral health community still need to determine the effectiveness of such programs, and so it is to this topic that we now turn. We do so, however, through a detailed examination of some of the surveillance data collected from MHAT VI (2009). We begin with these nonexperimental data because we believe the characteristics of these data provide valuable information for evaluating certain types of preventive programs; specifically, the information is valuable for those types of programs that are designed to work by leveraging small-group social processes.

NATURE OF BROAD-SCALE PREVENTIVE PROGRAMS

In many ways, the military provides an ideal setting to develop, implement, and test large-scale preventive behavioral health programs. Clearly there is a need for such programs: Military life places a number of stressors on service members and their families, as documented by a range of surveillance-type research. In addition, the military is institutionally capable of implementing large preventive programs given the hierarchical structure of the organization. That is, directives to implement such programs will be carried out, although the quality of program implementation may vary among subordinate units.

Scientifically, however, the main benefit the military has in terms of implementing broad-scale preventive mental health programs is its ability to leverage the social structure to affect the behavioral health of group members. The notion that group characteristics affect individual well-being is a well-established tenet of military psychology. Concepts such as unit cohesion, morale, and esprit de corps have been described as protective factors in a number of settings (e.g., Manning, 1991; Shils & Janowitz, 1948), and a variety of empirical studies have demonstrated the importance of the social context in soldier well-being (e.g., Bliese, 2006; Bliese & Britt, 2001; Bliese & Castro, 2000; Jex & Bliese, 1999).

Most of the empirical research demonstrating the importance of social context has been conducted in peacekeeping or training environments; however, the effects of social context are also evident in combat-based studies. Figure 4.1, for example, shows the relationship between combat experiences and the scores on the PTSD Checklist (PCL; Weathers, Litz, Herman, Huska, & Keane, 1993) for soldiers in 28 platoons (each cell in the figure represents a different platoon). These data were collected in Iraq in 2009 as part of MHAT VI and represent a subset of the different maneuver unit platoons.

As would be expected from the literature (e.g., Dohrenwend et al., 2006; Hoge et al., 2004), the relationship between combat experiences and the PCL scores presented in Figure 4.1 is generally positive, such that increases in combat experiences are associated with higher PCL scores. Nonetheless, Figure 4.1 shows that the relationship between combat experiences and PCL scores varies among platoons. In some platoons (e.g., Platoon 3), the relationship between PCL scores is strong and linear. In other platoons, the relationship

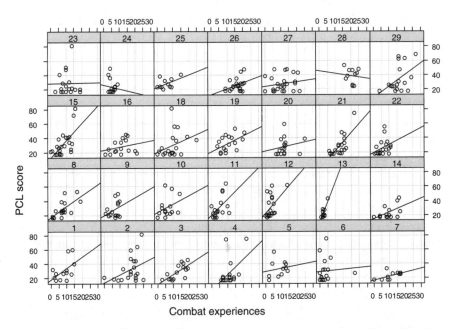

Figure 4.1. Relationship between number of combat experiences and Posttraumatic Stress Disorder Checklist (PCL) symptoms for 28 platoons.

is weaker. For instance, Platoon 16 has a relatively flat slope such that soldiers with high levels of combat experiences do not have elevated PCL scores.

It is important to note that statistical models indicate that the variability observed among platoons in the MHAT VI (2009) maneuver unit sample is greater than would be expected by chance; in other words, what Figure 4.1 shows is more than just random variability. This implies that there is a substantive reason why individuals in some platoons are particularly reactive to combat experiences, whereas individuals in other platoons are relatively nonreactive. In practical terms, we can consider platoons with flatter slopes to be ones that provide a more protective environment against the stressor of combat experiences. We can think of those protective platoons as being resilient against the negative effects of combat or, alternatively, as providing a protective setting for their members.

Unit-by-unit variability such as that observed in Figure 4.1 is not particularly rare in military mental health data. We routinely see group differences in the relationships between a range of combat-related stressors and a variety of outcomes such as anger and depression. When we see this type of variability, however, one of the central questions we ask is why units differ. Typically, the unit-level variability can be explained by some unit-level characteristic such as differences in the shared perceptions of cohesion, level of training, and perceptions of unit leaders. Of these shared unit variables, differences in how units perceive their leadership frequently emerge as a key predictor.

For instance, to explain the platoon-level variability in Figure 4.1, we examined four platoon-level characteristics: (a) shared perceptions of unit cohesion, (b) shared sense of being well trained, (c) shared perceptions of noncommissioned officer leadership, and (d) shared perceptions of commissioned officer leadership. Note that *shared* in these analyses refers to the average platoon rating of these constructs rather than the individual ratings. By using average ratings among platoon members, we are able to capture shared unit-level perceptions (Bliese, 2000). Of these four constructs, only shared perceptions of commissioned officer leadership showed evidence of being able to explain the unit-level variability. Figure 4.2 shows the form of this cross-level interaction.

Figure 4.2 is a classic stress-buffering interaction (e.g., Cohen & Wills, 1985) and shows that soldiers with low combat exposure report low PCL scores regardless of whether the platoon collectively rates their officers positively or negatively. As would be predicted, PCL scores increase as number of combat experiences increase; however, the strength of this relationship is weaker when the platoon perceives their officers positively. That is, soldiers are buffered from some of the negative effects of combat exposure when the officers are collectively perceived as engaging in positive behaviors. These positive leadership behaviors include exhibiting clear thinking and avoiding negative behaviors such as showing favoritism. We interpret Figure 4.2 as providing

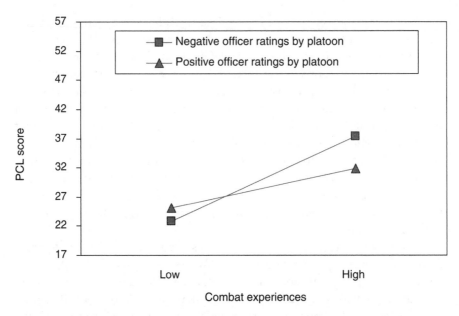

Figure 4.2. The relationship between combat experiences and Posttraumatic Stress Disorder Checklist (PCL) scores for a sample of 25 U.S. Army companies after returning from deployment to Iraq.

empirical evidence that competent and concerned leadership is a key factor in promoting resilience.

In a more global sense, we consider the identification of interactions such as those in Figure 4.2 to be central to how we operationalize *resilience factors*. In other words, resilience factors are variables that appear to make individuals less negatively reactive to stressors. Resilience factors might be shared group-level properties (e.g., shared perceptions of leadership) or individual factors (e.g., effective coping skills, the ability to maintain a sense of humor under stressful situations), but resilience factors are identified because they interact with a variety of stressors such that those individuals with the resilience factor deal with the stressor better than those without the factor. The identification of resilience factors plays a central role in providing an empirical basis for developing resilience-training programs. Specifically, factors that consistently emerge as resilience factors are excellent candidates for preventive training programs. With this in mind, it is not coincidental that many of the resilience training programs implemented in the army are targeted to leaders and incorporated in leadership schools.

There are other lessons that are important to learn from the data in Figure 4.1. Notice in Figure 4.1 how individual ratings of combat exposure cluster by platoon; soldiers in Platoon 28, for instance, consistently reported high levels of combat (notice how most responses from soldiers in Platoon 28 are on the right portion of the x-axis). In contrast, soldiers in Platoon 13 consistently reported low levels of combat experiences. Platoon 6 is also interesting because it shows that the entire platoon with the exception of one member reported few combat experiences. We do not really know why this one individual differed from his peers; it could reflect the somewhat random nature of combat, a reassignment of a soldier from another platoon, or inaccurate reporting by the respondent.

Even with clear cases where some individuals differ from their peers, we still find high levels of clustering when we estimate the intraclass correlation 1 or ICC(1). The ICC(1) provides a measure of the degree to which an individual's rating is related to or influenced by group membership (see Bliese, 2000). In the MHAT VI (2009) maneuver unit sample, the ICC(1) value for ratings of combat experiences is .43, indicating that 43% of the variance in any one individual's rating of personal combat experiences can be explained by the group to which the individual belongs. An ICC(1) value of .43 for items reported on a survey instrument represents a large amount of variance (Bliese, 2006) and suggests soldiers are reliably reporting similar levels of experiences within a platoon.

The high degree of clustering in the combat experiences ratings is all the more interesting when we contrast it with the low degree of clustering in PCL scores (i.e., the outcome). Logically, it would seem that if the main driver of an outcome (e.g., combat experiences driving PCL scores) clusters by platoon, then the outcome itself (e.g., PCL scores) should also cluster by platoon. An analogous circumstance could be found in an infectious disease model in which both the vector (e.g., anopheles mosquitoes) and the disease (e.g., malaria) cluster by geographic regions. Figure 4.1, though, provides no clear evidence that PCL scores cluster by platoon, and this is borne out by the low ICC(1) value of .026 (i.e., 2.6% of the variance in PCL ratings is related to platoon membership). That is, there is little consistency within platoons in PCL scores although there is high consistency in combat exposure within platoons.

Visually we see evidence of the low ICC(1) value for the outcome when we inspect the data. On each y-axis for the individual platoons we generally see most of the PCL scores between 20 and 40. Furthermore, each platoon appears to have a few individuals with high PCL scores regardless of whether the platoon had high or low combat exposure. Figure 4.1 does not tell us why there are three or four individuals in Platoon 6 with elevated PCL scores even though the platoon (with the exception of one member) reported low combat exposure; the figure just shows that PCL scores are highly variable within platoons.

IMPLICATIONS FOR PREVENTIVE PROGRAMS:
SOCIAL STRUCTURE

The detailed examination of mental health surveillance data provides several insights into large-scale preventive mental health programs, and although this example focused on MHAT VI (2009) data, these relationships are typical of surveillance data collected from other military samples. First, the examination shows that the social structure of the military affects individual mental health in two ways: (a) the nature of the link between stressors and a variety of mental health outcomes often varies depending on characteristics of the primary groups to which soldiers belong and (b) group membership and the cumulative experiences that occur within the group directly relate to mental health outcomes. In our example, we focused on the degree to which differences occurred among platoons; however, group effects occur at a variety of levels (e.g., squad, company, battalion). Typically, the measurable influence of social structure wanes as groups get larger, reflecting the fact that those individuals with whom one has the most contact (e.g., lower level units) exert the most influence.

These group-level findings suggest that one way the efficacy of universally applied preventive training programs in the military can be maximized is by directly tapping into components of the shared social structure. For example, training can emphasize skills designed to provide support to fellow unit members. Another example is to focus training on leaders and their behaviors and policies that promote resilience within entire groups. Both peer support and leadership strategies use aspects of the social context to enhance resilience training programs, and both strategies could produce direct results. For instance, training leaders could produce an overall reduction in levels of stress among service members. These strategies could also produce an indirect or interactive effect by, for example, training unit members to provide support in times of high stress, making service members more resilient to stressors. Such training could reinforce the development and sustainment of resilient squads, platoons, and companies.

IMPLICATIONS FOR PREVENTIVE PROGRAMS:
WIDE-SCALE IMPLEMENTATION

The second insight that can be drawn from the example in Figure 4.1 is the degree to which the causal mechanism underlying mental health problems fundamentally differs from the causal mechanism underlying many medical problems. Some medical problems can be connected to one or two key risk factors. Consequently, effective preventive programs can often be designed by specifically mitigating these risk factors. For example, if the risk factor for malaria (i.e., anopheles mosquitoes) is known to be present in East Africa, tourists going on safari to East Africa are given a malaria prophylactic, whereas tourists going to low-risk locations (e.g., skiing in the Alps) are not.

In contrast, Figure 4.1 illustrates the degree to which rates of mental health symptoms (e.g., those measured by the PCL) are affected by a variety of factors. Although the simple correlation between combat experiences and PCL scores in the MHAT VI (2009) data is moderately strong at .36, and the analyses show that platoons significantly differ in levels of combat experiences, PCL symptoms are also influenced by individual-level predictors (e.g., coping styles, previous experience with trauma). Thus ICC(1) values for PCL scores are low. If mental health symptoms were better predicted by group membership, as in the case with malaria, the ICC(1) values for the outcome would be higher, reflecting a consistent group score on the PCL.

These findings provide a rationale behind the decision to implement a broad public health model that affects both high-risk and low-risk groups in preventive mental health programs (often referred to as a *universal* vs. a *targeted* approach). Any program targeting only high-risk groups on a single factor such as combat exposure (e.g., targeting only Platoons 2, 28, and 29 in Figure 4.1) would inevitably miss a number of high-risk individuals in low-risk groups, and the consequences of missing even small numbers of individuals are potentially significant. Untreated mental health problems have the potential to lead to substantial distress and tragic outcomes such as suicide, spouse and child abuse, and violence. In this context, where the stakes are widely seen as being high, it is understandable why there is a perceived ethical duty to develop preventive measures and early intervention initiatives that can be applied to all service members regardless of risk. Furthermore, targeting only high-risk individuals (rather than groups) fails to build on the social structure inherent in the military setting in which battle buddies, units, and leaders are given the task of looking out for and caring for one another. Targeted programs aimed at individuals within groups also have the potential to be significantly more stigmatizing than programs directed at intact groups, and increases in stigma may inadvertently reduce program efficacy.

Given the difficulties of effectively identifying at-risk individuals and the consequences of unaddressed mental health problems, we believe the military's focus on universal preventive training programs is well advised. However, implementing preventive programs universally implies that large numbers of individuals who do not need the intervention are going to receive it. This, in turn, will have a direct impact on estimates of program efficacy. Specifically, if a program is being implemented on large numbers of individuals who are expected to receive little benefit, the estimated efficacy of the program will be significantly reduced, a finding evident in meta-analyses of prevention program efficacy (see, Brunwasser, Gillham, & Kim, 2009; Stice, Shaw, Bohon, Marti, & Rohde, 2009). This reduction in efficacy is one of the main reasons why the efficacy of programs is often examined using targeted approaches focused on high-risk individuals (e.g., Seligman, Schulman, & Tryon, 2007). The question, then, is what levels of efficacy should we expect from universally applied preventive programs in the military. We are specifically interested in those programs that are designed to work by leveraging the influence of the small-group social context.

IMPLICATIONS FOR PREVENTIVE PROGRAMS: EFFICACY AND EFFECT SIZES

One common way to address questions of efficacy is to design experimental studies and estimate effect sizes associated with the intervention. The gold standard for determining the efficacy of any program is a randomized trial. As a research team, the program at the Walter Reed Army Institute of Research conducted four large randomized trials between 2004 and 2009. One study was a randomized controlled trial on expressive writing at postdeployment, and three trials were group randomized trials (GRT) focused on a form of resilience training originally called *Battlemind Training* (now integrated into the army's resilience training program).

Our first GRT of resilience training involved four treatment arms and random assignment of over 2,000 U.S. soldiers returning from Iraq (Adler, Bliese, McGurk, Hoge, & Castro, 2009). The intervention involved hour-long training sessions provided to intact platoons, and both the Battlemind Training and the Battlemind Psychological Debriefing conditions relied on various aspects of the existing social structure to support the intervention. For instance, the postdeployment Battlemind Psychological Debriefing condition had platoon members identify key deployment-related events that members of the platoon experienced. Adler et al. (2009) found that Battlemind Training and Battlemind Psychological Debriefing led to lower symptom levels months later compared with standard stress education for individuals who had experienced high levels of combat (i.e., a high-risk group).

The study also provided estimated effect sizes for those individuals with low and moderate levels of combat experiences (i.e., low risk groups) and found no evidence to suggest that the intervention had negative consequences. Both pieces of evidence (i.e., the positive impact for the high-risk group and lack of negative impact for the low-risk groups) are important for interventions that are universally applied to service members. Subsequent analyses of data from the other two postdeployment Battlemind studies have also found evidence that the training is effective (Adler, Castro, Bliese, McGurk, & Milliken, 2007; Thomas et al., 2007).

Although the GRTs found that the resilience training interventions were effective, they also showed that the associated effect sizes tended to be small (d effects around .20). In the Adler et al. (2009) study, for example, the weak to moderate effect sizes were observed only for the group with high combat exposure. If the effect sizes had been calculated across all levels of combat exposure, they would have been negligible. In interpreting these findings, it is important to highlight that all treatment arms in the Adler et al. (2009) study involved active interventions. That is, the Battlemind conditions were compared with an alternative training brief rather than with a no-intervention control. This distinction is important because meta-analyses of other resilience training programs suggest that effect sizes are strongest when compared with no-intervention controls (e.g., Brunwasser, et al., 2009).

The d effect is a standardized calculation used to estimate and compare effect sizes across randomized trials and in meta-analyses. A d effect size of .21 (a typical effect size found in the high combat group by Adler et al., 2009, and on par with meta-analyses of other interventions such as Brunwasser et al., 2009) is equivalent to a correlation of .10, which in turn is equivalent to an r^2 of .01. An r^2 of .01 suggests that 1% of the variance in the mental health outcome was accounted for by the intervention condition tested in the randomized trial. Two related issues are raised by d effects of this magnitude. The first, and more obvious, issue is whether an effect size of this magnitude has enough practical significance to warrant implementing the program throughout the military. The second, and perhaps less obvious, issue is understanding the potential upper limits for broad-scale preventive training programs. That is, what is realistic to expect in terms of effect sizes for universally applied prevention programs designed to leverage small-group social context. Understanding realistic effect sizes for such programs does three things: (a) it helps avoid "overselling" programs, (b) it provides a basis for determining whether we should apply the same effect size criteria to large preventive programs that we apply to targeted preventive programs, and (c) it provides a basis for determining power for researchers considering conducting large randomized trials.

REALISTIC EFFECT SIZES AND GROUP PROPERTIES OF DATA

One way to frame answers to the upper-limit effect size question comes from what we know about the group-level properties of mental health related data. Figure 4.1 shows the high degree of individual variability in mental health outcomes within platoons. In that example, the ICC(1) results showed that over 97% of the variance in a variety of mental health measures was individually based (i.e., only 2.6% was related to unit membership). As noted, other studies find ICC(1) values for a variety of different mental health related outcomes that rarely exceed ICC(1) values of .10 (10%) and more realistically range around .05 or less (Bliese, 2006). The ICC(1) results for mental health outcomes in the military are congruent with results observed in other small-group settings such as classrooms in schools (Murray & Short, 1995).

We believe that these ICC(1) values provide an upper limit for what we can expect from universally applied, short-duration prevention programs provided to intact groups such as platoons. In our example, 2.6% of the variance in the PCL is related to group membership; therefore, with this sample we would expect universal programs targeting these platoons to hit this upper limit of 2.6%. We base this claim on the assumption that one of most plausible reasons why an hour-long, universally applied preventive program would have detectable effects 4 months later is that the program leveraged existing small-group dynamics. Our assertion that the upper limit for effect sizes is related to the ICC(1) is based on the observation that even with all the naturally occurring variability among groups in terms of combat experiences, leadership effectiveness, cohesion, and shared unit training, we still typically observe relatively low group-level properties associated with individual mental health outcomes. It is difficult to imagine that even the most effective large-scale training intervention will exert more influence than the combined influence of group factors such as a year of shared combat experience, shared experiences with the unit leaders, and shared benefits from being part of a cohesive unit.

From this perspective, we put the realistic upper limit for the impact of group-based interventions at around 5%. Although our example ICC(1) was 2.6% cumulatively across studies, we frequently observe ICC(1) values closer to .05 or 5% (see Bliese, 2006). As an upper limit, an effective group-based intervention that exerted as much combined influence as shared combat experiences, cohesion, leadership, and other group-level properties would still only explain 5% of the total variance in behavioral health scores. An upper limit of 5% corresponds to an effect size of .22 (as a correlation) and a d effect of .45. In practice, of course, group-level interventions are unlikely to reach this upper limit because of the host of other naturally occurring factors that influence groups and individuals. Thus, a more realistic d-effect size would be below the upper limit of .45. Based on our experiences with both surveillance data and randomized trials, we would expect a d-effect value of .20 to be a normative value for many programs. In the following section, we briefly review other factors that may influence d-effect values, along with results from meta-analyses of other programs.

It would be logical to expect that effect sizes will increase as the number of sessions increase and the concepts become reinforced over time. For instance, in an evaluation of the Penn Resiliency Program (PRP), Gillham et al. (2007) reported an average effect size of .34 for the reduction in depressive symptoms compared with controls (these values were from two schools, whereas a third school showed no evidence of efficacy for the PRP). The PRP described by Gillham et al. was designed as a 12-session program that provided more opportunities for individualized interaction for students who participated in the study (though participants completed only about half of the sessions and so could not have benefited from all 12 sessions).

Although the PRP effect size of .34 reported in Gillham et al. (2007) is stronger than the average Battlemind Training effect size, recall that a meta-analysis of the PRP reports d effects primarily in the .20 range (Brunwasser et al., 2009). Specifically, d effects comparing the PRP program with no-intervention controls are .21 (6- to 8-month follow-up) and .20 (12-month follow-up). When PRP is compared with active controls, the 6- to 8-month follow-up was 0.00 (no studies were available for the 12-month follow-up). It is not clear from these findings whether multiple sessions by themselves are sufficient to produce large effect sizes.

Presumably, effect sizes could also be increased by targeted interventions aimed only at high-risk individuals or groups. It is not a given fact, however, that targeted interventions with multiple sessions will always have more power. For instance, Brunwasser et al. (2009) reported that targeted studies of PRP had d effects of .23 at the 6- to 8-month follow-up and d effects of .22 at the 12-month follow-up. These values are not much different than the values of .21 and .20 based on the results from combining targeted and universal interventions at 6 to 8 months and at 12 months.

On the basis of our work with the group-level properties of surveillance data and our experiences with randomized trials, we believe that the strongest d effects would be associated with multiple session interventions aimed at high-risk intact groups. Such programs should be effective because they leverage social structure and reinforce key concepts to group members. Targeted, multiple-session interventions directed toward high-risk individuals within intact military units would not necessarily leverage existing social structure and thus would not necessarily optimize their effect sizes.

It is worth considering whether programs such as the PRP might show increased effect sizes if routinely implemented as group-based interventions with intact military units. Even though PRP is not routinely implemented with intact small groups (e.g., Gillham et al., 2007), Brunwasser and colleagues (2009) suggested that the PRP nonetheless may have a positive effect through its impact on group cohesion (p. 1052). If cohesion is an important causal variable, multiple-session programs such as the PRP might be particularly effective if implemented within the existing military social structure. When the PRP is implemented with individuals rather than intact groups, it would be necessary to have multiple sessions to form a sense of social identity among participants before factors such as cohesiveness could exert influence.

Our point is to highlight the need to establish realistic expectations when implementing and evaluating large-scale mental health training programs. On the basis of research examining the group-level characteristics of mental health data in the military, we do not believe it would be realistic to expect an hour-long, universal, group-based training intervention to produce d-effect sizes much above .20. Likewise, the evidence from meta-analyses from multiple-session, targeted programs leads one to conclude that effect sizes around .20 represent realistic values. In the military, we would expect stronger effects if multiple sessions were used with high-risk, intact groups such as platoons reporting high levels of combat exposure. Nonetheless, it is unlikely that training targeted at high-risk groups will replace universal programs, because leaders understand that there are numerous risk factors for psychological problems and so high-risk individuals are present even in low-risk groups.

EFFECT SIZES AND PRACTICAL SIGNIFICANCE

This discussion leads to an interesting juncture: Given what we know about the group-level properties of data and about large-scale preventive programs in general, we have to realistically assume that any effect sizes observed in universal large-scale preventive mental health programs will be small. Furthermore, in the military many preventive programs will (by logistic necessity) need to be group-based, with limited individualization and limited numbers of sessions. Do we therefore conclude that such efforts are a waste of time, or do we take a step back and ask whether small effect sizes are synonymous with being insignificant?

There is, of course, no simple answer to this question; however, we maintain that we do a disservice to the field by automatically applying conventional standards of practical significance without more thoughtful consideration of the specific goals of the training. One of the characteristics shared across a variety of large-scale preventive mental health programs is that each of the programs focuses on teaching sets of skills that are reinforced over time and in a variety of circumstances and thus generalize across time and across settings. For instance, the PRP often examines the effects of training for a period of up to 3 years postintervention (Gillham et al., 2007; Gillham & Reivich, 1999), under the assumption that the skills have longevity and relevance across stages of life (Gillham & Reivich, 1999). Even training with a shorter time horizon (e.g., postdeployment Battlemind) assumes that the skills will be relevant for a variety of social, family, and work situations that soldiers encounter in the months following deployment. Presumably, individuals who are successful in acquiring and applying resilient skills will be psychologically more resilient across a range of different situations. Implicit is the idea that training effects are likely to be cumulative; at any one time, training may or may not produce resilient behavior, but over time the effects of the training should be meaningful.

Abelson (1985) discussed this idea of small effect sizes, cumulative effects, and meaningful long-term differences in a seminal article titled "A Variance Explained Paradox: When a Little Is a Lot." Abelson's specific example uses archival baseball data to discuss the relationship between a miniscule effect size associated with any single at-bat baseball performance and long-term differences in batting averages. The central component of Abelson's argument was that batting skill explains about one third of 1% of the variance in any single batting performance (an r^2 of 0.00317, to be exact); however, because the batting average is a cumulative event, this miniscule difference produces meaningful differences in long-term performance, differences that are considered practically significant (at least to baseball players and team owners).

A similar idea, and perhaps more directly relevant to the idea of resilience training, can be drawn from the field of dynamical evolutionary psychology (Kenrick, Li, & Butner, 2003). Work in this field focuses on how new patterns in a group (what the authors call "structures") emerge from cumulative interactions among group members. For example, a group mixed with hostile and peaceful individuals might emerge with a composition of completely hostile individuals or with a composition of completely peaceful individuals. Kenrick et al. (2003) showed how seemingly inconsequential changes in interaction patterns among members can produce radically different outcomes for the group as a whole when simple rules and minor changes are cumulatively carried out over numerous iterations. One characteristic of this work is that, in the early stages of the data simulations, it is virtually impossible to predict how minor changes in initial starting values will affect the final outcome, yet it is clear that small, initial changes are important to these models.

Large-scale preventive mental health programs face a similar challenge. The intent of resilience training is to provide skills to individuals, unit members, and leaders to help them be successful across time and across a variety of settings. In terms of research design, however, we are often forced to try and measure the impact of the training in a fairly limited number of follow-ups. This is analogous to trying to reliably differentiate a player with a .214 batting average from a player with a .301 batting using data from only a few at-bats or trying to predict the final end state of a group based on the first few sets of interactions (e.g., early iterations of a dynamic simulation).

At any given follow-up occasion we have a small chance of detecting differences, but over time a soldier who has been taught a range of resilience skills should be a bit more likely than his or her peers to make the right decision (e.g., to walk away from a potential fight, to avoid being overly critical following a failure, to consider a spouse's point of view early in an argument, to step in to support a peer who is struggling). Over time and over different situations, we expect these cumulative events to produce more resilient individuals and also to affect the final states of the groups to whom the individual belongs, even if our ability to detect effects at any one specific time is poor.

If resilience training has a cumulative effect, then the research designs should examine multiple outcomes at different times. Consistent with this approach, in 2009 our group took the lead in a collaborative study with the Army Center for Enhanced Performance to determine whether undergoing multiple training sessions of sport psychology principles such as goal setting, self-confidence, attention control, energy management, and imagery would be associated with improved performance. The design was a GRT with random assignment of over 40 platoons in basic combat training (GRTs require numerous groups to ensure adequate statistical power). The skill training consisted of eight sessions, which permitted individual practice with various skills and repeated reinforcement of concepts. The strength of this kind of research is not so much tied to the effect sizes of any one particular outcome, as it is to whether over the course of basic combat training there is evidence of efficacy across a range of outcomes. Presumably, the skills will also generalize over the course of the soldier's career. Seen from this perspective, small effect sizes associated with any particular assessment period should not determine whether the training is in fact helpful; instead, the training be must be considered in terms of skill development as a whole.

What, then, do we see as necessary to provide evidence of efficacy for large-scale preventive training programs? We propose two criteria. Abelson (1985) provided the first criterion when he wrote that "one should not necessarily be scornful of miniscule values for percentage variance explanation, *provided there is statistical assurance that these values are significantly above zero*, and that the degree of potential cumulation is substantial" (p. 133, italics added). Abelson's quote makes it clear that although we should adjust our criteria about what constitutes significant effect sizes when facing cumulative phenomena, we cannot adjust the requirement for solid, empirical evidence of efficacy, the type of efficacy that is provided by randomized trials. Our second requirement for establishing efficacy of programs is that we believe statistical assurance of significance needs to be balanced with an examination of whether any proposed program might adversely affect those who would not be likely to need the program. For instance, recall that Adler et al. (2009) provided *d* effects showing efficacy for the group with high combat exposure; just as importantly, they also provided *d* effects for the groups with moderate and few combat exposures to show that there was little evidence of an adverse impact for this low-risk group. This latter addition is important because when programs are applied universally, they affect both those at risk and those not at risk. Given the practical realities of how preventive training is likely to be implemented, both pieces of evidence (i.e., efficacy for high risk, no harm for low risk) are necessary.

CONCLUSION

The military has embraced the idea that broad-scale preventive training programs are a valuable part of a much larger effort to support the mental health status of service members engaged in protracted combat in Iraq and Afghanistan. Nonexperimental surveillance-based data demonstrate that small-group, contextual effects play an important role in mental health outcomes and suggest that even short-term interventions can be effective if such programs leverage the power of peers and leaders. When knowledge of the group-level nature of data is coupled with military training designed to instill teamwork and a sense of responsibility for taking care of unit members, it is possible to see how a relatively brief, large-group training session has the potential to exert positive effects months later. At the same time, however, surveillance data, empirical evidence from randomized trials, and meta-analysis results suggest that the upper-limit effect sizes for many preventive programs will be quite small. Rather than dwelling on small effect sizes, we encourage researchers and practitioners to continue to focus on demonstrating statistically significant effects. Designing and executing solid research that demonstrates efficacy is time consuming and costly, but ultimately it is the only way to ensure that service members are provided with the best training possible.

REFERENCES

Abelson, R. P. (1985). A variance explained paradox: When a little is a lot. *Psychological Bulletin, 97*, 129–133. doi:10.1037/0033-2909.97.1.129

Adler, A. B., Bliese, P. D., McGurk, D., Hoge, C. W., & Castro, C. A. (2009). Battlemind Debriefing and Battlemind Training as early interventions with soldiers returning from Iraq: Randomization by platoon. *Journal of Consulting and Clinical Psychology, 77*, 928–940. doi:10.1037/a0016877

Adler, A. B., Castro, C. A., Bliese, P. D., McGurk, D., & Milliken, C. (2007, August). The efficacy of Battlemind Training at 3–6 months postdeployment. In C. A. Castro (Chair), *The Battlemind Training System: Supporting soldiers throughout the deployment cycle*. Symposium conducted at the meeting of the American Psychological Association, San Francisco, CA.

Berlien, I. C., & Waggoner, R. W. (1966). Selection and induction. In A. J. Glass & R. J. Bernucci, *Neuropsychiatry in World War II: Vol. I. Zone of the interior* (pp. 153–191). Washington, DC: Office of the Surgeon General.

Bliese, P. D. (2000). Within-group agreement, nonindependence, and reliability: Implications for data aggregation and analysis. In K. J. Klein & S. W. Kozlowski (Eds.), *Multilevel theory, research, and methods in organizations* (pp. 349–381). San Francisco, CA: Jossey-Bass.

Bliese, P. D. (2006). Social climates: Drivers of soldier well-being and resilience. In A. B. Adler, C. A. Castro, & T. W. Britt (Eds.), *Military life: The psychology of serving in peace and combat: Vol. 2. Operational stress* (pp. 213–234). Westport, CT: Praeger.

Bliese, P. D., & Britt, T. W. (2001). Social support, group consensus, and stressor–strain relationships: Social context matters. *Journal of Organizational Behavior, 22*, 425–436. doi:10.1002/job.95

Bliese, P. D., & Castro, C. A. (2000). Role clarity, work overload, and organizational support: Multilevel evidence of the importance of support. *Work and Stress, 14*, 65–73. doi:10.1080/026783700417230

Brunwasser, S. M., Gillham, J. E., & Kim, E. S. (2009). A meta-analytic review of the Penn Resiliency Program's effect on depressive symptoms. *Journal of Consulting and Clinical Psychology, 77*, 1042–1054. doi:10.1037/a0017671

Cabrera, O. A., Hoge, C. W., Bliese, P. D., Castro, C. A., & Messer, S. C. (2007). Childhood adversity and combat as predictors of depression and posttraumatic stress. *American Journal of Preventive Medicine, 33*, 77–82. doi:10.1016/j.amepre.2007.03.019

Cohen, S., & Wills, T. A. (1985). Stress, social support, and the buffering hypothesis. *Psychological Bulletin, 98*, 310–357. doi:10.1037/0033-2909.98.2.310

Dohrenwend, B. P., Turner, J. B., Turse, N. A., Adams, B. G., Koenen, K. C., & Marshall, R. (2006, August 18). The psychological risks of Vietnam for U.S. veterans: A revisit with new data and methods. *Science, 313*, 979–982. doi:10.1126/science.1128944

Eaton, K. M., Hoge, C. W., Messer, S. C., Whitt, A. A., Cabrera, O. A., McGurk, D., . . . Castro, C. A. (2008). Prevalence of mental health problems, treatment need, and barriers to care among primary care-seeking spouses of military service members involved in Iraq and Afghanistan deployments. *Military Medicine, 173*, 1051–1056.

Egan, J. R., Jackson, L., & Eanes, R. H. (1951). A study of neuropsychiatric rejectees. *JAMA, 145*, 466–469.

Gillham, J. E., & Reivich, K. J. (1999). Prevention of depressive symptoms in school children: A research update. *Psychological Science, 10*, 461–462. doi:10.1111/1467-9280.00188

Gillham, J. E., Reivich, K. J., Freres, D. R., Chaplin, T. M., Shatté, A. J., Samuels, B., . . . Seligman, M. E. P. (2007). School-based prevention of depressive symptoms:

A randomized controlled study of the effectiveness and specificity of the Penn Resiliency Program. *Journal of Consulting and Clinical Psychology, 75,* 9–19. doi:10.1037/0022-006X.75.1.9

Glass, A. J. (1966). Lessons learned. In A. J. Glass & R. J. Bernucci, *Neuropsychiatry in World War II: Vol. I. Zone of the interior* (pp. 735–759). Washington, DC: Office of the Surgeon General.

Hoge, C. W., Castro, C. A., Messer, S. C., McGurk, D., Cotting, D. I., & Koffman, R. L. (2004). Combat duty in Iraq and Afghanistan, mental health problems, and barriers to care. *The New England Journal of Medicine, 351,* 13–22. doi:10.1056/NEJMoa040603

Hoge, C. W., McGurk, D., Thomas, J., Cox, A., Engel, C. C., & Castro, C. A. (2008). Mild traumatic brain injury in U.S. soldiers returning from Iraq. *The New England Journal of Medicine, 358,* 453–463. doi:10.1056/NEJMoa072972

Jex, S. M., & Bliese, P. D. (1999). Efficacy beliefs as a moderator of the impact of work-related stressors: A multi-level study. *Journal of Applied Psychology, 84,* 349–361. doi:10.1037/0021-9010.84.3.349

Kenrick, D. T., Li, N. P., & Butner, J. (2003). Dynamical evolutionary psychology: Individual decision rules and emergent social norms. *Psychological Review, 110,* 3–28. doi:10.1037/0033-295X.110.1.3

Killgore, W. D. S., Cotting, D. I., Thomas, J. L., Cox, A. L., McGurk, D., Vo, A. H., . . . Hoge, C. W. (2008). Postcombat invincibility: Violent combat experiences are associated with increased risk-taking propensity following deployment. *Journal of Psychiatric Research, 42,* 1112–1121. doi:10.1016/j.jpsychires.2008.01.001

Manning, F. J. (1991). Morale, cohesion, and esprit de corps. In R. Gal & A. D. Mangelsdorff (Eds.), *Handbook of military psychiatry* (pp. 453–470). New York, NY: Wiley.

Mental Health Advisory Team. (2003). *Operation Iraqi Freedom (OIF) Mental Health Advisory Team (MHAT) Report.* Retrieved from http://www.armymedicine.army.mil/reports/mhat/mhat/mhat_report.pdf

Mental Health Advisory Team V. (2008). *Mental Health Advisory Team (MHAT) V Operation Iraqi Freedom 06-08: Iraq, Operation Enduring Freedom 8: Afghanistan.* Retrieved from http://www.armymedicine.army.mil/reports/mhat/mhat_v/MHAT_V_OIFandOEF-Redacted.pdf

Mental Health Advisory Team VI. (2009). *Mental Health Advisory Team (MHAT) VI Operation Iraqi Freedom 07-09.* Retrieved from http://MHAT_VI-OIF_EXSUM.pdf

Murray, D. M., & Short, B. (1995). Intraclass correlation among measures related to alcohol use by young adults: Estimates, correlates, and applications in intervention studies. *Journal of Studies on Alcohol, 56,* 681–694.

Seligman, M. E. P., Schulman, P., & Tryon, A. (2007). Group prevention of depression and anxiety symptoms. *Behaviour Research and Therapy, 45,* 1111–1126. doi:10.1016/j.brat.2006.09.010

Shils, E. A., & Janowitz, M. (1948). Cohesion and disintegration in the Wehrmacht in World War II. *Public Opinion Quarterly, 12,* 280–315.

Stice, E., Shaw, H., Bohon, C., Marti, C. N., & Rohde, P. (2009). A meta-analytic review of depressive prevention programs for children and adolescents: Factors that predict magnitude of intervention effects. *Journal of Consulting and Clinical Psychology, 77*, 486–503. doi:10.1037/a0015168

Thomas, J. L., Castro, C. A., Adler, A. B., Bliese, P. D., McGurk, D., Cox, A., & Hoge, C. W. (2007, August). The efficacy of Battlemind at immediate post-deployment reintegration. In C.A. Castro (Chair), *The Battlemind Training System: Supporting soldiers throughout the deployment cycle.* Symposium conducted at the meeting of the American Psychological Association, San Francisco, CA.

Thomas, J. L., Wilk, J. E., Riviere, L. R., McGurk, D., Castro, C. A., & Hoge, C. W. (2010). The prevalence and functional impact of mental health problems among active component and National Guard soldiers 3 and 12 months following combat in Iraq. *Archives of General Psychiatry, 67*, 614–623.

Weathers, F., Litz, B., Herman, D., Huska, J., & Keane, T. (October 1993). *The PTSD checklist (PCL): Reliability, validity, and diagnostic utility.* Paper presented at the meeting of the International Society for Traumatic Stress Studies, San Antonio, TX.

5

THE IMPACT OF COMBAT DEPLOYMENT ON MILITARY FAMILIES

LYNDON A. RIVIERE AND JULIE C. MERRILL

My transition to regular life has been weird. My wife tells me I changed and I have a shorter fuse. I make rash decisions and cannot stand stupid people.

—Anonymous U.S. soldier after returning from a 15-month deployment to Iraq

When I first returned from combat I felt like a stranger at home. My son had grown up so much and had really become independent. My wife was running my house and doing well at it. I felt that I had missed a lot with birthdays, anniversaries, holidays, and school activities. I had a pretty easy transition because I was able to take my time and slip back into my role in the family. We haven't encountered any major issues. We all became more mature people with the separation.

—Anonymous U.S. soldier after returning from a 15-month deployment to Iraq

Military families face several unique stressors. Yet despite these military-specific stressors, there is little evidence to suggest military families differ from civilian families in terms of functioning and well-being outcomes. This chapter reviews empirical literature on military family functioning and discusses challenges confronting military families. We review these stressors in terms of distinct classes (i.e., acute, chronic, and daily), with a focus on gaps in the literature and areas for future research.

The views expressed in this chapter are those of the authors and do not reflect the official position of the Walter Reed Army Institute of Research, the U.S. Army, or Department of Defense. This chapter was authored or coauthored by an employee of the United States government as part of official duty and is considered to be in the public domain. Any views expressed herein do not necessarily represent the views of the United States government, and the author's participation in the work is not meant to serve as an official endorsement.

The view that military families are not appreciably different from civilian families in terms of functioning and well-being outcomes is somewhat counterintuitive. We propose several explanations supporting this view. First, the perception that military families have poorer well-being outcomes may be a function of media coverage and a few empirical studies. Second, military families have a variety of institutionalized support programs not available to civilian families. These programs may reduce real or perceived levels of stress. Third, there may be some degree of self-selection among military families who continue with military service. These families may be better able to integrate into informal support networks, which can buffer some of the negative stressors military families encounter. These networks may be particularly valuable in helping families cope with the cumulative effects of chronic and daily stressors for which it is more difficult to provide formal support programs.

THE MILITARY FAMILY IN CONTEXT

When a family member decides to join the armed forces, an all-volunteer force, the newly defined military family makes an often tacit choice to accept the demands of military life. This change could result in a great deal of personal adjustment. Introduction to the military culture may be new and strange, particularly for the family member with a limited understanding of the military. Despite these sometimes radical life changes and myriad new stressors, most members of the new military family are at some level cognizant of the challenges commensurate with military service.

The media often simplistically portray military families as dysfunctional and faltering under the demands of military life. Stories garnering the most public attention often focus on the pain and loss associated with death or injury and problems such as child abuse or intimate partner violence (IPV). Despite the risk of creating or reinforcing a stereotype of military families as mentally unhealthy, focus on such problems can be an impetus for policy change. As described in Chapter 1 (this volume), news reports about a series of murder–suicides at Fort Bragg at the start of the war in Afghanistan focused public attention, and consequently military resources, on the issues of postcombat mental health problems.

Some academic literature bolsters the view of military families as more dysfunctional. LaGrone (1978), in an article titled "The Military Family Syndrome," asserted that children and adolescents of military families have more behavioral problems. According to LaGrone, the increase in behavioral disturbance was evidence of problems with the military's demands on service members and families and problems within military families. Other studies have also concluded that aspects of military family life, such as separations, result in higher rates of child behavioral problems (e.g., Hillenbrand, 1976). However, following these early studies, subsequent evidence has demonstrated that military families (of nondeployed service members) are comparable with civilian families in terms of mental and physical health despite often having to deal with unique demands such as foreign residence (e.g., Fernandez-Pol, 1988). In the following sections, we examine this contradiction with existing research and identify gaps in knowledge.

BENCHMARKING MILITARY FAMILY WELL-BEING

One of the challenges in military family research is that relatively few studies have documented the mental health status of military family members. Using an anonymous survey of 940 military spouses at one installation as part of the Walter Reed Army Institute of Research's (WRAIR) Land Combat Study (LCS), Eaton and colleagues (2008) found that 20% of the spouses reported symptoms exceeding criteria for major depressive disorder (MDD) or generalized anxiety disorder. We assessed a subset ($n = 341$) of the sample analyzed by Eaton et al. and found 10.3% to have symptoms exceeding criteria for posttraumatic stress disorder (PTSD). These surveys were conducted with spouses who were at various phases of the deployment cycle. Although the surveys were conducted with a convenience sample and may not generalize to the military spouse population, it is a starting point for understanding the epidemiology of military spouse mental health problems.

In terms of military children, Jensen, Xenakis, Wolf, and Bain (1991), found no evidence of greater psychopathology compared with national norms for civilian children. One epidemiological study specifically documenting mental health prevalence rates in military children (Jensen et al., 1995) revealed rates of depression, anxiety, attention-deficit/hyperactivity disorder, and conduct disorder similar to those found in the general population. Although noteworthy, this study was based on data collected at one military installation and may not generalize to all military children.

In terms of other indicators of family well-being, some evidence suggests that rates of child neglect and maltreatment increased in enlisted U.S. Army families during a combat deployment (Rentz et al., 2007). Subsequently, Rentz and colleagues (2008) found rates of child maltreatment in the military to be lower than in civilian cohorts (although they did not report deployment status). As Chamberlain, Stander, and Merrill (2003) cautioned, it is difficult to know how accurately incidents are reported, especially for military families. Some military family child maltreatment cases may go unreported because of potential adverse consequences to the service member's military career. Although the limited data may not show child maltreatment is more common in military families, the extant data might underestimate its occurrence.

The relationship between military stressors and IPV has also been studied in military families. Attention to this issue may stem from findings demonstrating higher rates of IPV among military veterans and active-duty service members compared with civilian samples (for a review, see Marshall, Panuzio, & Taft, 2005). Some research has focused on the specific impact of deployments on IPV rates, but the findings are inconsistent. McCarroll et al. (2000) found that deployed soldiers (the type of deployment was not specified) reported higher rates of severe IPV, and those rates, though small, significantly increased with deployment length (3 vs. 6 months and 6 vs. 12 months). Conversely, both McCarroll et al. (2003) and Newby et al. (2005) found that those who had deployed were at no greater risk of committing IPV. Of note, McCarroll et al. (2003) and Newby et al. used samples of active-duty soldiers deployed for 6 months to Bosnia on a peacekeeping mission, which may limit generalizability.

Combat deployments do align with increased rates of IPV (for a review, see Marshall et al., 2005). Researchers have noted that these rates may be indirectly related to the abusers' posttraumatic stress symptomatology (Byrne & Riggs, 1996). For example, Prigerson, Maciejewski, and Rosenheck (2002) found that despite the 21% of IPV episodes that were attributed to combat exposure in Vietnam veterans, the relationship between combat exposure and IPV only appeared in those veterans reporting PTSD symptomatology in the past year. In fact, PTSD, an outcome of military-related stress, appears to be a strong predictor of a variety of postdeployment marital problems in military families (Galovski & Lyons, 2004).

Another way to benchmark the mental health problems of military families is to examine marital dissolution rates. Karney and Crown (2007) conducted the most comprehensive analysis of military marital dissolution rates (mostly divorces, but including separations, interlocutory, and annulments) associated with the wars in Iraq and Afghanistan. This report contrasted marital dissolution rates from 1996 to 2000 with those from 2001 to 2005, the latter time period being one of intense combat deployments. Although trend data indicate a pattern of increasing marital dissolution rates since 2001, the rates in 2005 were identical to those of 1996, a year of relatively limited military engagements (Karney & Crown, 2007). They concluded that there was little empirical evidence that the intense combat deployment cycle between 2001 and 2005 aligned with increased marital dissolution rates. Given the systematic and detailed research design, it is difficult to dismiss this null finding despite anecdotal evidence to the contrary. However, marital dissolution can be considered a distal index of family problems because it may take several years before persistent family problems result in marital dissolution. Therefore, more proximal measures of family problems might be more sensitive to increased deployment tempo. Recent work by the WRAIR has begun to document more proximal indicators of military family well-being using LCS data. Work–family balance can be considered one such measure. For example, Castro and Clark (2005) found high levels of work–family conflict in soldiers and spouses associated with significantly lower levels of marital quality.

In addition, mental health concerns can affect overall satisfaction with the military lifestyle. The 341 military spouses in the sample referenced earlier were asked about perceived benefits associated with deployment as well as about mental health symptoms. Spouses who did not exceed criteria for MDD or PTSD (86.5% of the sample) reported benefits associated with deployment (see Figure 5.1). Although these data are cross-sectional, they demonstrate two key points. First, the majority of military spouses reported some benefits associated with deployment. These benefits are associated with opportunities for personal growth such as being more independent and self-confident in handling problems. Second, spouses who did not meet criteria for MDD or PTSD also were more likely to report these benefits, suggesting that resilience is associated with perceiving (or experiencing) these benefits.

Mental health concerns in soldiers have also been linked to military family outcomes. Cox, Eaton, and Allison-Aipa (2005) found that after a deployment, married soldiers' reports of symptoms of major depression were associated with lower marital quality, increased likelihood of soldier or spouse infidelity, decreased trust, and increased plans to separate or divorce. The relationship between marital quality and mental health status holds true for multiple populations according to LCS data. Mean marital quality ratings for

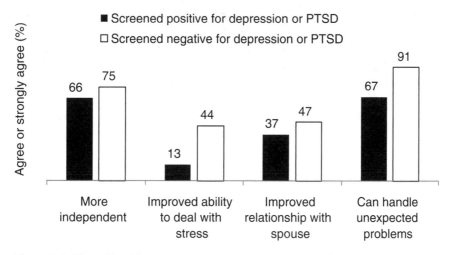

Figure 5.1. Mental health status and resilience indicators in spouses with deployment experience.

active-duty soldiers, National Guard soldiers, and army spouses exceeding criteria for MDD and PTSD were significantly lower than for those without mental health concerns.

IDENTIFYING MILITARY-RELATED STRESSORS

The characterization of military families as different from civilian families often centers on military families dealing with the threat of serious injury or death. This threat is even more pervasive during military deployments and serves as a backdrop for all other family stressors. In addition to the threat of serious death or injury, military families are faced with a variety of other significant stressors, which often occur simultaneously. These significant stressors can include relocation, separation and deployment, social isolation, and living in another country and necessitate considerable adaptation by the family.

Military-related stressors can be classified as acute, chronic, and daily. Despite being the focus of many studies of psychological stress, these stressors have not been specifically articulated in the context of research with military families. In terms of duration, acute stressors and daily hassles can be viewed as discrete stressors, whereas chronic stressors have a continuous duration (Serido, Almeida, & Wethington, 2004). The demarcations among the three types of stressors are not rigid. Although one stressor may begin as acute, prolonged duration will make it a chronic stressor (see Avison & Turner, 1988). These distinctions have important implications for designing resiliency-building programs and for providing meaningful support to military families.

Clearly, there is an individual element in the perception of stressors. For example, research has shown variability in what people consider a daily hassle and the degree to which these hassles affect psychological symptoms (Gruen, Folkman, & Lazarus, 1988). Because not all military families regard each demand as subjectively stressful, these demands might be positively appraised by military families. For example, spouses may experience a deployment positively through increased independence or negatively because of added roles and responsibilities. Understanding family members' expectations of military life and their positive perceptions can be useful in designing resiliency training. Such demands can serve as factors in determining the adjustment of military family members and deserve attention.

Acute Stressors

Acute stressors refer to "major life events" and have a more definite onset than chronic stressors (Eckenrode, 1984). These stressors, typically rare in most civilian settings, require significant adjustment (Serido et al., 2004) and can lead to disruptions of daily routines (Wagner, Compas, & Howell, 1988). Consequently, they have marked effects on well-being (Kessler, 1997). Military-relevant examples include relocation, separation, and injury or death of a loved one (see Serido et al., 2004; Wagner et al., 1988; Wheaton, 1999).

Relocation

In the military, service members, and therefore their families, relocate frequently. Indeed, military families typically relocate at least once every 3 years (Defense Manpower Data Center, 2007). Relocations force service personnel and family members to adapt to new situations, typically leaving behind more familiar environments. Further, relocations can disrupt access to regular sources of formal and informal support (Weiss, 1989). However, military families may not experience relocating as an acute stressor because of the self-selection for military service. Indeed, researchers have examined geographic mobility as a predictor of well-being in military children. After controlling for different measures of functioning, rate of mobility in military families was unrelated to various measures of child psychological adjustment (Kelley, Finkel, & Ashby, 2003). Relocation is an event that can be disruptive and can provide an opportunity for adventure, personal growth, professional advancement, and change.

Separation

Separations, particularly deployment-related ones, can be classified as acute stressors and are increasingly common in today's military. Long separations disrupt family routines and require significant adjustment from all family members. Some of the negative effects of long separations may even have a physiological basis. Functional magnetic resonance imaging has shown that social pains such as separation from a loved one activate the same part of the brain as physical pain (e.g., Panksepp, 2005). These results reflect what many military family members already know regarding the emotional pain and adjustment of separation.

Nevertheless, military families may also experience benefits associated with separations, including the development of greater independence and improvements in the quality of marital relationships (Wood, Scarville, & Gravino, 1995). Comparisons between military spouses with and without deployment experience (87% and 13%, respectively) using the LCS spouse data mentioned earlier demonstrate the relationship between deployment experience and self-reported competency (see Figure 5.2). Spouses with deployment experience were more confident in their ability to manage responsibilities and function effectively. Again, although these data are cross-sectional, it

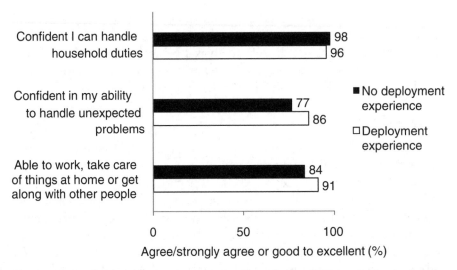

Confident I can handle
household duties **98** / 96

No deployment
experience

Confident in my ability
to handle unexpected
problems **77** / 86

Deployment
experience

Able to work, take care
of things at home or get
along with other people **84** / 91

0   50   100

Agree/strongly agree or good to excellent (%)

Figure 5.2. Resilience indicators in spouses with and without deployment experience.

suggests that deployment is associated with increased self-efficacy. For spouses who did not meet screening criteria for mental health problems, the deployment can also provide an opportunity for personal growth.

Injury or Death

Two of the most devastating acute stressors are the serious injury or death of a service member. Generally, in military conflicts from the Revolutionary War to present day, the number of U.S. service members wounded has been significantly greater than the number killed (Fischer, Klarman, & Oboroceanu, 2008). As of June 2010, for every one service member who has died since March 2003 in the Iraq and Afghanistan wars, about seven have been injured (Defense Manpower Data Center, 2010). Consequently, family members are much more likely to deal with injuries than deaths. Some injuries may lead to physical disabilities, which also may have chronic and daily stressor dimensions in adapting to new limitations (see Rena, Moshe, & Abraham, 1996). Few events are, however, as life changing for military families as the death of the serving family member. Over 58,000 U.S. service members died in the Vietnam War, close to 400 in the Persian Gulf War, and several thousand thus far in the wars in Iraq and Afghanistan (Fischer et al., 2008).

Chronic Stressors

Chronic stressors are persistent, open-ended problems (Avison & Turner, 1988; Serido et al., 2004). Compared with acute stressors, chronic stressors are not as dramatic in onset, but their intensity is greater than that of daily hassles. These stressors may arise as an individual tries to fill multiple potentially conflicting roles, such as being a spouse and an employee. Chronic stressors can also be environmental (Avison & Turner, 1988). Outlined as follows are six examples of chronic stressors that can affect military families: foreign residence, geographic isolation, spouse unemployment, risk of injury or death, deployment length and frequency, and marital and parental adjustments.

Foreign Residence

Although residential moves within one's home country may be demanding, taking up foreign residence adds additional demands. Living in a foreign country may be accompanied by homesickness and difficulty adjusting to the new environment and new routines (Van Tilburg, Vingerhoets, & Van Heck, 1996). Military families are 3 times more likely than nonmilitary families to migrate out of the country in a given year (Hosek, Asch, Fair, Martin, & Mattock, 2002). Although the service member may be busy with work-related demands, military spouses typically bear most of the burden of adjusting to the host country and a different cultural context (Shaffer & Harrison, 2001). Despite these demands, some family members can value the experience of living in another country and being exposed to new cultures. Still, research demonstrates foreign residence is a risk factor in the adjustment of family members. For example, Burrell, Adams, Durand, and Castro (2006) found foreign residence predicted poorer physical and mental health among military spouses.

Social Isolation

Military families experiencing frequent relocations and foreign residence may also be at risk of social isolation. This isolation entails a break from social networks, which provide emotional, instrumental, informational, and appraisal support. These types of support make up the larger construct of social support. When military families move to a new location, they often move away from extended family members, friends, and other social ties, which made up their previous social networks. The resulting social isolation is a risk factor for adjustment problems. For example, in one study, military spouses who had a close friend, a neighbor or a family member they could rely on were more likely to be well adjusted (Orthner & Rose, 2005b).

Spouse Unemployment and Underemployment

Frequent relocations can limit the employment opportunities of military spouses who are looking for work. Census data indicate that unemployment rates are higher in military spouses (both male and female) than in their civilian counterparts (Lim, Golinelli, & Cho, 2007). The 2008 Survey of Active Duty Spouses reported that 5% of male and 9% of female military spouses were unemployed (Defense Manpower Data Center, 2009). Further, moving has been linked to a 10% decline in employment among civilian female spouses of military personnel and a 6% drop in the employment of civilian male spouses (Cooke & Speirs, 2005).

Family members perceive a host of potential barriers to their employment. In one study, one in every three stay-at-home military spouses thought there were barriers to their employment, including a lack of day care facilities, limited job availability, and employer bias against military spouses (Harrell, Lim, Castaneda, & Golinelli, 2004). In fact, two thirds of the spouses surveyed in this same study stated that work opportunities were negatively affected by being a military spouse. Military life also negatively affected the educational goals of more than a third of these spouses (Harrell et al., 2004). Unemployment can be a chronic stressor (Cohen et al., 2007), with detrimental effects on both physical and psychological health (McKee-Ryan, Song, Wanberg, & Kinicki, 2005).

Studies with civilians have also found that underemployment negatively affects psychological well-being (Feldman, 1996). Studies controlling for education levels and location have found that military spouses not only have lower employment rates but also earn less than civilian spouses (Lim et al., 2007).

Risk of Injury or Death

Besides the possibility of actual injury or death of a service member, to varying degrees military families live with chronic fear about the risk of harm to a service member (Wright, Burrell, Schroeder, & Thomas, 2006). The chronic risk of injury or death is inherent in military life, although some military occupational specialties involve greater risk. The fear is probably greater during combat deployments compared with other kinds of separations. In fact, for military children a common concern is injury to a parent during a combat deployment (Orthner & Rose, 2005b). Family members, and spouses in particular, may face caregiving burdens as they attend to mentally and physically impaired combat veterans (Beckham, Lytle, & Feldman, 1996).

Deployment

Although we have classified deployment-related separation as an acute stressor, many of the characteristics of deployment are in fact chronic.

Separations require prolonged adjustments. Studies have found, for example, that service member mental health problems increased when deployments were longer or more frequent (Adler, Huffman, Bliese, & Castro, 2005; Mental Health Advisory Team IV, 2007). The subsequent impact of these deployment factors on the military family is also likely to increase. Furthermore, after a deployment, military families face the challenge of reestablishing emotional bonds and renegotiating roles and responsibilities. Military spouses have identified communicating with the deployed spouse, sharing parental responsibilities, and handling the service member's mood as difficult redeployment challenges (Orthner & Rose, 2005a).

Daily Stressors

Daily stressors or hassles are everyday annoyances, irritations, or frustrations (Kanner, Coyne, Schaefer, & Lazarus, 1981; Lepore, Palsane, & Evans, 1991; Serido et al., 2004). These stressors include relatively minor disruptive events such as lack of sleep, missing the bus, work deadlines, misplacing things, having to repair things around the house, or disputes with a friend (Lepore et al., 1991; Serido et al., 2004; Wheaton, 1999).

Although acute stressors clearly have the potential to place serious demands on individuals, studies consistently show that daily stressors have some of the strongest links to psychological (Kanner et al., 1981; Pillow, Zautra, & Sandler, 1996) and somatic symptoms (Jandorf, Deblinger, Neale, & Stone, 1986). The influence of daily stressors is found even after controlling for prior symptom levels (Lu, 1991). Daily stressors appear to better predict psychological symptoms than either acute or chronic stressors (Eckenrode, 1984). Indeed, military families may experience different or greater daily stressors than civilian families, especially during deployments; however, we are unaware of studies that have tested this hypothesis.

Of critical importance is the possibility of underestimating the effect of relatively minor hassles by both service personnel and military families. In a series of studies, Gilbert and colleagues (e.g., Gilbert, Pinel, Wilson, Blumberg, & Wheatley, 1998) found that people tend to overestimate the impact of major undesirable events on their (and others') happiness while underestimating the impact of minor events. People who face acute stressors such as the end of a romantic relationship or the failure to achieve academic tenure expected enduring effects. It is interesting, though, that individuals tend to ignore future experiences that may have equal or greater influence. Gilbert and colleagues contended that people are unaware of what they term the *psychological immune system*. When faced with a significant stressor, individuals typically use successful rationalizations and other mechanisms to lessen its effect (Gilbert et al., 1998). In the same way that the body's immune system fights disease, the psychological immune system fights stressors. Gilbert's research suggests that people automatically engage the psychological immune system to lessen the impact of major stressors but not for minor ones (Wilson & Gilbert, 2005). Other studies have also found that individuals are less likely to activate coping mechanisms when dealing with chronic stressors (Eckenrode, 1984; Wagner et al., 1988).

The insights from Gilbert and colleagues suggest that even among the most tested of military families, many will be able to cope with acute military stressors better than they expected. This resilience comes from an ability to engage the psychological immune system. In contrast, Gilbert's work suggests that chronic stressors and daily stressors may take an unexpectedly large toll on military families because families will underestimate their initial impact and thus the psychological immune system will not activate.

THE IMPACT OF STRESSORS ON MILITARY FAMILIES

More typically, however, the main characteristic of military family stressors is the potential accumulation of acute stressors, chronic stressors, and daily hassles. It is important that studies have found that acute, chronic, and daily stressors often interact with each other to affect well-being (e.g., Pillow et al., 1996). For example, chronic stressors can moderate the relationship between daily stressors and psychological symptoms (Serido et al., 2004) such that daily stressors have a stronger negative relationship to psychological symptoms in the presence of chronic stressors. In addition, stressors may lead to the development of psychological symptoms, and once symptomatic, an individual may perceive the presence of more stressors (Kanner et al., 1981; Kessler, 1997; Wagner et al., 1988).

MILITARY SUPPORT SYSTEMS

The conceptualization of stressors as acute, chronic, or daily is useful when considering institutionalized support systems. There is a host of formal military structures set up to counter the impact of both acute and chronic stressors. Indeed, the military likely has more institutionalized support programs to help address acute stressors than any other organization. For instance, in the most difficult circumstance of the death or serious injury of a military member, the military organization responds with a variety of formal mechanisms designed to provide both instrumental and emotional support (Wright et al., 2006). On a purely practical level, the military pays for medical care and/or the cost of burial. Survivor benefits, which include monthly payments and access to military facilities, are also provided to the family members of a deceased service member (see U.S. General Accounting Office, 2002). On an emotional level, the military responds by incorporating families into ceremonies and symbols to recognize the loss of the service member (Wright et al., 2006). These forms of assistance are part of the psychological contract between the military, service members, and families. Military families willingly endure hardships and military leaders provide support in the event of tragedy.

Institutionalized support programs are also in place to mitigate the impact of other acute and chronic stressors. In the United States, for example, the military provides health and child care services, relocation support, legal support, informational support, extra financial support during deployments, and practical support to help families manage demands (Karney & Crown, 2007). Although little research has specifically assessed the efficacy of these support programs, the provision of institutionalized support is clearly intended to lessen the negative effects of these acute and chronic stressors.

The military organization also has opportunities to significantly mitigate the impact of daily stressors. Support initiatives provided by Army Family Readiness Groups (which provide informational and emotional support over the course of a deployment) and Army Community Services (which provide instrumental support by managing relocation hassles, job searches, and finding good child care) are an important first step. Other examples of military emotional and instrumental support services include Military OneSource, which provides information and referral services for service personnel and dependents 365 days a year, 24 hours a day; the Family Readiness Campaign, whose goal is for junior enlisted service members and their spouses to practice financial stewardship; Child Development Centers, which serve over 200,000 children daily; and spouse educational and employment resources such as in-state tuition programs and the Spouse Telework Employment Program. Further, Family Centers and Family Assistance Centers are provided for both active-duty and reserve component families. These centers provide communication resources (e.g., videophone access) and deployment and postdeployment education, among other resources (U.S. Department of Defense, 2004).

In late 2007, the U.S. Army leadership instituted the Army Family Covenant, which will reportedly shore up existing family programs, improve the quality and accessibility of health care, and improve family housing (Army News Service, 2007). In 2008, this program was allotted $1.4 billion to accomplish its goals (Army News Service, 2007). In Europe, the program has saved U.S. military families over $1.8 million by providing free and low-cost child care and respite care, according to a July 2008 report (Millham, 2008). These efforts reinforce the idea that the military is cognizant of the demands that family members face. Whether these supports are optimal or even effective remains unclear, but they are in keeping with the military's efforts to meet its part of the psychological contract.

Informal social networks established by military families may also help mitigate the effect of daily stressors and some chronic stressors. For instance, for some families the burden of constant child care when a spouse is deployed may be alleviated more by an informal network of military families sharing child care rather than by formal child care. Although the military may encourage the development of such systems, the factors ultimately determining a family's willingness to be involved in the informal system are varied and often beyond the military's control. Families that do not participate in these informal military structures may self-select out of the military leaving behind those families that are more willing to access informal support systems.

EARLY INTERVENTIONS

Interventions provided by the military are currently prioritizing, and should continue to prioritize, services in support of families experiencing acute stress. This support is critical for humanitarian reasons and as part of the psychological contract of military service. However, because the evidence indicates that daily stressors are more predictive of lower levels of well-being, it is also important that support be provided to help families cope with chronic and daily stressors, particularly during periods of deployment-related separation.

Although not an intervention per se, unit leadership plays a notable role in communicating with families about resources and addressing any gaps in the system. This is critical for sustaining the military's side of the psychological contract. These efforts by unit leaders can have a significant and positive impact on the well-being of families. The intent of these efforts should be to acknowledge that both chronic and daily stressors have a demonstrable impact on family well-being and functioning.

A few notable early interventions in support of military family resilience include Spouse Battlemind Training and the Postdeployment Army Couples Expressive Writing Study. Spouse Battlemind Training is one of the components of the larger Battlemind Training System (for additional description, see Chapter 4, this volume). The army mandated that Spouse Battlemind Training be offered before and after a combat deployment. This training reviews the positive and negative aspects of life for military families, identifies and normalizes typical areas of deployment-related couples conflict, and emphasizes actions that both military spouses and soldiers can take to address the negative impact of deployment. Although the efficacy of soldier post-deployment modules has been assessed, Spouse Battlemind Training has thus far only been assessed in terms of satisfaction with training. Findings from such surveys of spouses who attended both versions of Spouse Battlemind Training indicated high ratings of user acceptability (see Figure 5.3; Riviere, Clark, Cox, Kendall-Robbins, & Castro, 2007).

One of the goals of the Battlemind Training System is learning how to communicate effectively about the deployment and how to tell one's story. As part of this effort, Bliese and Adler, two researchers at the WRAIR, initiated an expressive writing study for couples at postdeployment. The resulting randomized controlled study assessing postdeployment expressive writing in military couples was led by University of Texas researchers Pennebaker and Baddeley. In this study, couples were randomly assigned to an expressive writing task about the deployment, a neutral writing task, or a combination (i.e., only one partner is assigned to expressive writing and the other to a neutral topic). The objective of this 2008 study was to determine the efficacy of soldier and spouse expressive writing in mitigating the negative consequences of combat. An earlier civilian study on dating partners found that those who wrote expressively were more likely to be dating 3 months later compared with those assigned to the control condition (Slatcher & Pennebaker, 2006). Numerous other studies have demonstrated that expressive writing can enhance adjustment (e.g., Smyth & Pennebaker, 2008). Results from this military couples study can be used to guide army recommendations for helping military personnel and their families adjust to life after deployment. This study represents the standard for evidence-based interventions provided to military families.

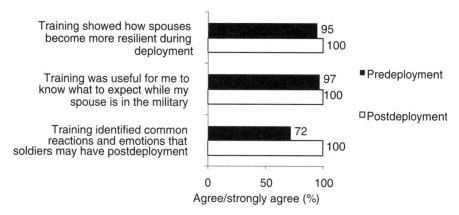

Figure 5.3. User acceptability for pre- and postdeployment Spouse Battlemind Training.

Despite efforts to promote resilience, there are some circumstances in which families are confronted with service members returning from combat with significant symptoms of traumatic stress. These critically important circumstances place families at risk of disruptions that require more than standardized mental health training to ameliorate. Policies and programs aimed at improving family resiliency should take this into account.

SPILLOVER

Clearly, all military families are not the same. The subpopulation of military families coping with physically and mentally ill service members is qualitatively different from and comparatively smaller than the majority who do not face such problems. Tanielian and Jaycox (2008) performed a thorough analysis and a critical review of the existing literature (including Hoge et al., 2004; Milliken, Auchterlonie, & Hoge, 2007). They found that the prevalence of U.S. service members returning from combat in Iraq with significant mental health problems ranged from 5% to 15%. Among the 229,000 U.S. veterans from Operation Iraqi Freedom and Operation Enduring Freedom seen at Veterans Affairs medical care facilities (a third of all eligible veterans), 37% have been seen for mental health problems (U.S. Congressional Budget Office Testimony, 2007). This subpopulation is at greater risk of negative outcomes and deserves separate attention.

Recent research supports the concept of spillover of service member negative outcomes on family member negative outcomes. In an investigation that studied couples following a recent Iraq or Afghanistan deployment, Goff, Crow, Reisbig, and Hamilton (2007) found that soldiers' trauma symptoms indirectly predicted low levels of relationship satisfaction in their spouses. These findings have been corroborated by Taft, Panuzio, Schumm, and Proctor (2008). International research on Israeli war veterans demonstrated that negative posttraumatic responses in military personnel adversely affect functioning in family members (e.g., Dekel & Solomon, 2006). There is also some evidence of higher depression levels in children of fathers who had deployed to the first Gulf War and had PTSD (Al-Turkait & Ohaeri, 2008).

PTSD specifically, and not combat, has been consistently identified as a predictor of family distress (Galovski & Lyons, 2004). In particular, PTSD symptoms such as emotional numbing and avoidance can negatively affect a service member's emotional involvement and family integration (Solomon, 1988). PTSD hyperarousal symptoms also increase the likelihood of engaging in aggressive behavior (Taft, Kaloupek, et al., 2007). Aggression may explain the relationship between PTSD and physical and psychological IPV noted earlier in this chapter (Taft, Street, Marshall, Dowdall, & Riggs, 2007). In addition, victims of IPV may be at greater risk of developing PTSD (Taft, Murphy, King, Dedeyn, & Musser, 2005).

Reserve families may also be more affected by service member mental health problems than active-duty families (Tanielian & Jaycox, 2008). Rates of PTSD in U.S. reservists were found to be 50% higher than rates in active-duty soldiers within 3 to 6 months after returning from Iraq and Afghanistan (Milliken et al., 2007; Milliken, Auchterlonie, & Hoge, 2007). Consequently, families of reservists may experience greater disruption from PTSD and other mental health problems. These reservist families may also have less institutional support than active-duty families.

FUTURE RESEARCH AND CONCLUSIONS

We have illustrated that military families are likely to face a number of stressors as a product of their occupation, and we have categorized these stressors as being acute, chronic, or daily. We have also argued that one of the defining characteristics of military stressors is the high probability of simultaneously experiencing a number of chronic and daily stressors and that these are not static within and between families. Clearly, these challenges can have negative consequences for the mental and physical health of military personnel and their spouses and children. As noted, however, the data suggest that many military families are able to cope successfully with the challenges that they face. We suggest that the resilience of military families may be in part due to their adaptive coping style and a variety of benefits of military life that cushion the impact of the stressors.

This chapter concludes by examining gaps in military family research and suggesting future directions. First, we need studies to document systematically the types of stressors military family members face and the impact of the three types of stressors on well-being. It is even more vital to study families coping with ill service members.

Second, the effectiveness of intervention programs needs to be understood. Are programs mitigating the effect of stressors on well-being? Do families of reserve service members face access issues that active-duty families do not face, and are the programs sufficiently tailored for the unique circumstances of these families? One conduit for interventions is the Internet, which may be particularly useful for geographically remote military families. For example, one web-based intervention among an active-duty U.S. military sample was successful at reducing alcohol consumption (Williams, Herman-Stahl, Calvin, Pemberton, & Bradshaw, 2009).

Evaluating the effectiveness of interventions is also complicated by the potential mismatch between self-report ratings of effectiveness and other ratings of effectiveness such as attrition from service. Interventions based on individual input would almost certainly be directed to major stressors, whereas ironically, interventions directed at more minor stressors may have a larger impact. However, interventions directed at daily stressors may fail to find evidence of effectiveness because individuals underestimate their influence stressors. These challenges and complications need to be addressed to effectively understand and improve intervention programs.

Third, epidemiological studies are needed that systematically document the prevalence rates of mental health problems in both active duty and reserve component military family members. Often, studies do not measure the prevalence of mental health disorders in spouses. Rather, general questions are asked about nonclinical depression, sadness, fear, aggression, or academic problems (see, e.g., SteelFisher, Zaslavsky, & Blendon, 2008). Although the WRAIR has begun to conduct some of this work with military spouses, much work remains to be done. There is a dearth of studies assessing the impact of deployment on children. Studying children is a difficult endeavor as they are a vulnerable population and cannot give informed consent. One option for studying children is the use of parental reporting; however, research indicates there are measurement problems when a parent's report is used as a proxy (Weissman et al., 1987).

Fourth, we need studies to better understand families coping with a service member's mental health problems. Family members may experience secondary traumatization or PTSD-related IPV. In addition, current PTSD treatments are provided to service members and veterans in a setting isolated from the family context. Perhaps, consistent with military culture and its emphasis on family readiness and responsibility, explicitly including the individual's family in the treatment process will prove to be an important adjunct to therapy.

Finally, what can be learned from those military families that cope well with the demands of military life? Research that can identify these coping mechanisms can be used as the basis for resiliency training. Such training then needs to be assessed in terms of its efficacy. Resiliency training should be developmental, providing basic concepts initially and building skills over time. Such training should also be targeted to the appropriate phase of the deployment cycle and be contextually appropriate to the military culture.

For their part, military families are repeatedly asked to organize their lives around the demands of the military. In turn, the military, through policy, programs, and leadership at all levels, has the obligation to provide military families with the best support possible. Sometimes instrumental support may not be available or may not be enough to offset the demands placed on the family. In these circumstances, it is particularly important that the military organization and military leaders acknowledge the sacrifices and losses endured by military families to maintain their part of the psychological contract. When there is a gap between what the organization provides and the expectations of families, there is potential for profound dissatisfaction. This dissatisfaction can negatively affect the family's well-being, the service member's mission performance, and the family's commitment to remaining a part of the military community. Using research to provide guidance for military family policy and programs can ensure that military families receive meaningful and effective support.

REFERENCES

Adler, A. B., Huffman, A. H., Bliese, P., & Castro, C. A. (2005). The impact of deployment length and experiences on the well-being of male and female soldiers. *Journal of Occupational Health Psychology, 10*, 121–137. doi:10.1037/1076-8998. 10.2.121

Al-Turkait, F. A., & Ohaeri, J. U. (2008). Psychopathological status, behavior problems, and family adjustment of Kuwaiti children whose fathers were involved in the first gulf war [Electronic version]. *Child and Adolescent Psychiatry and Mental Health, 2*, 2–12. doi:10.1186/1753-2000-2-12

Army News Service. (2007, October). *Army leaders sign covenant with families*. Retrieved from http://www.military.com

Avison, W. R., & Turner, R. J. (1988). Stressful life events and depressive symptoms: Disaggregating the effects of acute stressors and chronic strains. *Journal of Health and Social Behavior, 29*, 253–264. doi:10.2307/2137036

Beckham, J. C., Lytle, B. L., & Feldman, M. E. (1996). Caregiver burden in partners of Vietnam War veterans with posttraumatic stress disorder. *Journal of Consulting and Clinical Psychology, 64*, 1068–1072. doi:10.1037/0022-006X.64.5.1068

Burrell, L. M., Adams, G. A., Durand, D. B., & Castro, C. A. (2006). The impact of military lifestyle demands on well-being, army, and family outcomes. *Armed Forces and Society, 33*, 43–58. doi:10.1177/0002764206288804

Byrne, C. A., & Riggs, D. (1996). The cycle of trauma: Relationship aggression in male Vietnam veterans with symptoms of posttraumatic stress disorder. *Violence and Victims, 11*, 213–225.

Castro, C. A., & Clark, J. C. (2005, May). *Work–family balance in soldiers and their families*. Invited presentation for the Defense Department Advisory Committee on Women in the Services Business Meeting, Arlington, VA.

Chamberlain, H., Stander, V., & Merrill, L. L. (2003). Research on child abuse in the U.S. Armed Forces. *Military Medicine, 168*, 257–260.

Cohen, F., Kemeny, M. E., Zegans, L. S., Johnson, P., Kearney, K. A., & Stites, D. P. (2007). Immune function declines with unemployment and recovers after stressor termination. *Psychosomatic Medicine, 69*, 225–234. doi:10.1097/PSY. 0b013e31803139a6

Cooke, T. J., & Speirs, K. (2005). Migration and employment among the civilian spouses of military personnel. *Social Science Quarterly, 86*, 343–355. doi:10.1111/ j.0038-4941.2005.00306.x

Cox, A., Eaton, K. M., & Allison-Aipa, T. (2005, August). *Soldier and family dysfunction associated with combat-related PTSD.* Symposium conducted at the annual meeting of the American Psychological Association, Washington, DC.

Defense Manpower Data Center. (2007). *2006 Survey of Active Duty Spouses: Tabulations of responses.* Arlington, VA: Author.

Defense Manpower Data Center. (2009). *2008 Survey of Active Duty Spouses: Tabulations of responses.* Arlington, VA: Author.

Defense Manpower Data Center. (2010). *Military casualty information.* Retrieved from http://siadapp.dmdc.osd.mil/personnel/CASUALTY/castop.htm

Dekel, R., & Solomon, Z. (2006). Marital relations among former prisoners of war: Contribution of posttraumatic stress disorder, aggression, and sexual satisfaction. *Journal of Family Psychology, 20*, 709–712. doi:10.1037/0893-3200.20.4.709

Eaton, K. M., Hoge, C. W., Messer, S. C., Whitt, A. A., Cabrera, O. A., McGurk, D., . . . Castro, C. A. (2008). Prevalence of mental health problems, treatment need, and barriers to care among primary care-seeking spouses of military service members involved in Iraq and Afghanistan deployments. *Military Medicine, 173*, 1051–1056.

Eckenrode, J. (1984). Impact of chronic and acute stressors on daily reports of mood. *Journal of Personality and Social Psychology, 46*, 907–918. doi:10.1037/0022-3514. 46.4.907

Feldman, D. C. (1996). The nature, antecedents, and consequences of underemployment. *Journal of Management, 22*, 385–407. doi:10.1177/014920639602200302

Fernandez-Pol, B. (1988). Does the military family syndrome exist? *Military Medicine, 153*, 418–420.

Fischer, H., Klarman, K., & Oboroceanu, M. (2008). *American war and military operations casualties: Lists and statistics* (Order Code RL32492). Washington, DC: Congressional Research Service.

Galovski, T., & Lyons, J. A. (2004). Psychological sequelae of combat violence: A review of the impact of PTSD on the veteran's family and possible interventions. *Aggression and Violent Behavior, 9*, 477–501. doi:10.1016/S1359-1789(03)00045-4

Gilbert, D. T., Pinel, E. C., Wilson, T. D., Blumberg, S. J., & Wheatley, T. P. (1998). Immune neglect: A source of durability bias in affective forecasting. *Journal of Personality and Social Psychology, 75*, 617–638. doi:10.1037/0022-3514.75.3.617

Goff, B. S., Crow, J. R., Reisbig, A. M., & Hamilton, S. (2007). The impact of individual trauma symptoms of deployed soldiers on relationship satisfaction. *Journal of Family Psychology, 21*, 344–353. doi:10.1037/0893-3200.21.3.344

Gruen, R. J., Folkman, S., & Lazarus, R. S. (1988). Centrality and individual differences in the meaning of daily hassles. *Journal of Personality, 56*, 743–762. doi:10.1111/j.1467-6494.1988.tb00475.x

Harrell, M. C., Lim, N., Castaneda, L. W., & Golinelli, D. (2004). *Working around the military: Challenges of military spouse employment and education.* Santa Monica, CA: RAND Corporation.

Hillenbrand, E. D. (1976). Father absence in military families. *The Family Coordinator, 25*, 451–458. doi:10.2307/582860

Hoge, C. W., Castro, C. A., Messer, S. C., McGurk, D., Cotting, D. I., & Koffman, R. L. (2004). Combat duty in Iraq and Afghanistan, mental health problems, and barriers to care. *The New England Journal of Medicine, 351*, 13–22. doi:10.1056/NEJMoa040603

Hosek, J., Asch, B. J., Fair, C. C., Martin, C., & Mattock, M. (2002). *Married to the military: The employment and earnings of military wives compared with those of civilian wives.* Santa Monica, CA: RAND Corporation.

Jandorf, L., Deblinger, E., Neale, J. M., & Stone, A. A. (1986). Daily versus major life events as predictors of symptom frequency: A replication study. *The Journal of General Psychology, 113*, 205–218.

Jensen, P. S., Watanabe, H. K., Richters, J. E., Cortes, R., Roper, M., & Liu, S. (1995). Prevalence of mental disorder in military children and adolescents: Findings from a two-stage community survey. *Journal of the American Academy of Child and Adolescent Psychiatry, 34*, 1514–1524. doi:10.1097/00004583-199511000-00019

Jensen, P. S., Xenakis, S. M., Wolf, P., & Bain, M. W. (1991). The "military family syndrome" revisited: "By the numbers." *Journal of Nervous and Mental Disease, 179*, 102–107. doi:10.1097/00005053-199102000-00007

Kanner, A. D., Coyne, J. C., Schaefer, C., & Lazarus, R. S. (1981). Comparison of two modes of stress measurement: Daily hassles and uplifts versus major life events. *Journal of Behavioral Medicine, 4*, 1–39. doi:10.1007/BF00844845

Karney, B. R., & Crown, J. S. (2007). *Families under stress: An assessment of data, theory, and research on marriage and divorce in the military.* Santa Monica, CA: RAND Corporation.

Kelley, M. L., Finkel, L. B., & Ashby, J. (2003). Geographic mobility, family, and maternal variables as related to the psychosocial adjustment of military children. *Military Medicine, 168*, 1019–1024.

Kessler, R. C. (1997). The effects of stressful life events on depression. *Annual Review of Psychology, 48*, 191–214. doi:10.1146/annurev.psych.48.1.191

LaGrone, D. M. (1978). The military family syndrome. *The American Journal of Psychiatry, 135*, 1040–1043.

Lepore, S. J., Palsane, M. N., & Evans, G. W. (1991). Daily hassles and chronic strains: A hierarchy of stressors. *Social Science & Medicine, 33,* 1029–1036. doi:10.1016/0277-9536(91)90008-Z

Lim, N., Golinelli, D., & Cho, M. (2007). *"Working around the military" revisited: Spouse employment in the 2000 census data.* Santa Monica, CA: RAND Corporation.

Lu, L. (1991). Daily hassles and mental health: A longitudinal study. *The British Journal of Psychology, 82,* 441–447.

Marshall, A. D., Panuzio, J., & Taft, C. T. (2005). Intimate partner violence among military veterans and active duty servicemen. *Clinical Psychology Review, 25,* 862–876. doi:10.1016/j.cpr.2005.05.009

McCarroll, J. E., Ursano, R. J., Liu, X., Thayer, L. E., Newby, J. H., Norwood, A. E., & Fullerton, C. S. (2000). Deployment and the probability of spousal aggression by U.S. Army soldiers. *Military Medicine, 165,* 41–44.

McCarroll, J. E., Ursano, R. J., Newby, J. H., Liu, X., Fullerton, C. S., Norwood, A. E., . . . Osuch, E. A. (2003). Domestic violence and deployment in U.S. Army soldiers. *Journal of Nervous and Mental Disease, 191,* 3–9. doi:10.1097/00005053-200301000-00002

McKee-Ryan, F. M., Song, Z., Wanberg, C. R., & Kinicki, A. J. (2005). Psychological and physical well-being during unemployment: A meta-analytic study. *Journal of Applied Psychology, 90,* 53–76. doi:10.1037/0021-9010.90.1.53

Mental Health Advisory Team IV. (2007). *Mental Health Advisory Team (MHAT) IV Operation Iraqi Freedom 05-07.* Retrieved from http://www.armymedicine.army.mil/reports/mhat/mhat_iv/mhat-iv.cfm

Millham, M. (2008, July). Army Family Covenant's impact apparent to parents. *Stars and Stripes* (European ed.). Retrieved from http://www.stripes.com

Milliken, C. S., Auchterlonie, J. L., & Hoge, C. W. (2007). Longitudinal assessment of mental health problems among active and reserve component soldiers returning from the Iraq war. *JAMA, 298,* 2141–2148. doi:10.1001/jama.298.18.2141

Newby, J. H., Ursano, R., McCarroll, J., Liu, X., Fullerton, C., & Norwood, A. (2005). Postdeployment domestic violence by U.S. Army soldiers. *Military Medicine, 170,* 643–647.

Orthner, D. K., & Rose, R. (2005a). *SAF V survey report: Reunion adjustment among Army civilian spouses with returned soldiers.* Chapel Hill, NC: University of North Carolina.

Orthner, D. K., & Rose, R. (2005b). *SAF V survey report: Social support and adjustment among Army civilian spouses.* Chapel Hill, NC: University of North Carolina.

Panksepp, J. (2005). Why does separation distress hurt? Comment on MacDonald and Leary (2005). *Psychological Bulletin, 131,* 224–230. doi:10.1037/0033-2909.131.2.224

Pillow, D. R., Zautra, A. J., & Sandler, I. (1996). Major life events and minor stressors: Identifying meditational links in the stress process. *Journal of Personality and Social Psychology, 70,* 381–394. doi:10.1037/0022-3514.70.2.381

Prigerson, H. G., Maciejewski, D., K., & Rosenheck, R. A. (2002). Population attributable fractions of psychiatric disorders and behavioral outcomes associated with combat exposure among U.S. men. *American Journal of Public Health, 92,* 59–63. doi:10.2105/AJPH.92.1.59

Rena, F., Moshe, S., & Abraham, O. (1996). Couples' adjustment to one partner's disability: The relationship between sense of coherence and adjustment. *Social Science & Medicine, 43,* 163–171. doi:10.1016/0277-9536(95)00358-4

Rentz, E. D., Marshall, S. W., Loomis, D., Casteel, C., Martin, S. L., & Gibbs, D. A. (2007). Effect of deployment on the occurrence of child maltreatment in military and nonmilitary families. *American Journal of Epidemiology, 165,* 1199–1206. doi:10.1093/aje/kwm008

Rentz, E. D., Marshall, S. W., Martin, S. L., Gibbs, D. A., Casteel, C., & Loomis, D. (2008). The occurrence of maltreatment in active duty military and nonmilitary families in the state of Texas. *Military Medicine, 173,* 515–522.

Riviere, L. A., Clark, J. C., Cox, A. L., Kendall-Robbins, A., & Castro, C. A. (2007, August). Spouse Battlemind Training: Elements and strengths. In C. A. Castro (Chair), *The Battlemind Training System: Supporting soldiers throughout the deployment cycle.* Symposium conducted at the meeting of the American Psychological Association. San Francisco, CA.

Serido, J., Almeida, D. M., & Wethington, E. (2004). Chronic stressors and daily hassles: Unique and interactive relationships with psychological distress. *Journal of Health and Social Behavior, 45,* 17–33. doi:10.1177/002214650404500102

Shaffer, M. A., & Harrison, D. A. (2001). Forgotten partners of international assignments: Development and test of a model of spouse adjustment. *Journal of Applied Psychology, 86,* 238–254. doi:10.1037/0021-9010.86.2.238

Slatcher, R. B., & Pennebaker, J. W. (2006). How do I love thee? Let me count the words: The social effects of expressive writing. *Psychological Science, 17,* 660–664. doi:10.1111/j.1467-9280.2006.01762.x

Smyth, J. M., & Pennebaker, J. W. (2008). Exploring the boundary conditions of expressive writing: In search of the right recipe. *British Journal of Health Psychology, 13,* 1–7. doi:10.1348/135910707X260117

Solomon, Z. (1988). The effect of combat-related posttraumatic stress disorder on the family. *Psychiatry, 51,* 323–329.

SteelFisher, G. K., Zaslavsky, A. M., & Blendon, R. J. (2008). Health-related impact of deployment extensions on spouses of active duty army personnel. *Military Medicine, 173,* 221–229.

Taft, C. T., Kaloupek, D. G., Schumm, J. A., Marshall, A. D., Panuzio, J., King, D. W., & Keane, T. M. (2007). Posttraumatic stress disorder symptoms, physiological reactivity, alcohol problems, and aggression among military veterans. *Journal of Abnormal Psychology, 116,* 498–507. doi:10.1037/0021-843X.116.3.498

Taft, C. T., Murphy, C. M., King, L. A., Dedeyn, J. M., & Musser, P. H. (2005). Posttraumatic stress disorder symptomatology among partners of men in treatment for relationship abuse. *Journal of Abnormal Psychology, 114,* 259–268. doi:10.1037/0021-843X.114.2.259

Taft, C. T., Panuzio, J., Schumm, J. A., & Proctor, S. P. (2008). An examination of family adjustment among operation desert storm veterans. *Journal of Consulting and Clinical Psychology, 76,* 648–656. doi:10.1037/a0012576

Taft, C. T., Street, A. E., Marshall, A. D., Dowdall, D. J., & Riggs, D. S. (2007). Posttraumatic stress disorder, anger, and partner abuse among Vietnam combat veterans. *Journal of Family Psychology, 21,* 270–277. doi:10.1037/0893-3200.21.2.270

Tanielian, T., & Jaycox, L. H. (Eds.). (2008). *Invisible wounds of war: Psychological and cognitive injuries, their consequences, and services to assist recovery.* Santa Monica, CA: RAND Corporation.

U.S. Congressional Budget Office Testimony. (2007, October). *Statement of Mathew S. Goldberg, Deputy Assistant Director for National Security: Projecting the costs to care for veterans of U.S. military operations in Iraq and Afghanistan.* Washington DC: Congressional Budget Office.

U.S. Department of Defense. (2004). *Report of the first quadrennial quality of life review.* Retrieved from http://www.militaryhomefront.dod.mil/portal/page/mhf/MHF/MHF_DETAIL_1?content_id=168185

U.S. General Accounting Office. (2002). *Military personnel: Active duty benefits reflect changing demographics, but opportunities exist to improve* (GAO-02-935). Washington, DC: Author.

Van Tilburg, M. A. L., Vingerhoets, A. J. J. M., & Van Heck, G. L. (1996). Homesickness: A review of literature. *Psychological Medicine, 26,* 899–912. doi:10.1017/S0033291700035248

Wagner, B. M., Compas, B. E., & Howell, D. C. (1988). Daily and major life events: A test of an integrative model of psychological stress. *American Journal of Community Psychology, 16,* 189–205. doi:10.1007/BF00912522

Weiss, M. D. (1989). Relocating families: An overlooked market segment for nursing. *American Association of Occupational Health Nurses Journal, 37,* 454–458.

Weissman, M. M., Wickramaratne, P., Warner, V., John, K., Prusoff, B. A., Merikangas, K. R., & Gammon, G. D. (1987). Assessing psychiatric disorders in children. *Archives of General Psychiatry, 44,* 747–753.

Wheaton, B. (1999). The nature of stressors. In A. V. Horwitz & T. L. Scheid (Eds.), *A handbook for the study of mental health: Social contexts, theories, and systems* (pp. 176–197). Cambridge, England: Cambridge University Press.

Williams, J., Herman-Stahl, M., Calvin, S. L., Pemberton, M., & Bradshaw, M. (2009). Mediating mechanisms of a military Web-based alcohol intervention. *Drug and Alcohol Dependence, 100,* 248–257. doi:10.1016/j.drugalcdep.2008.10.007

Wilson, T. D., & Gilbert, D. T. (2005). Affective forecasting. *Current Directions in Psychological Science, 14,* 131–134. doi:10.1111/j.0963-7214.2005.00355.x

Wood, S., Scarville, J., & Gravino, K. (1995). Waiting wives: Separation and reunion among army wives. *Armed Forces and Society, 21,* 217–236. doi:10.1177/0095327 X9502100204

Wright, K. M., Burrell, L. M., Schroeder, E. D., & Thomas, J. L. (2006). Military spouses: Coping with the fear and the reality of service. In C. A. Castro, A. B. Adler, T. W. Britt (Eds.), *Military life: The psychology of serving in peace and combat: Vol. 3. The military family* (pp. 64–90). Westport, CT: Praeger.

II

TRANSITIONING HOME FROM DEPLOYMENT

6

THE PSYCHOLOGY OF TRANSITION: ADAPTING TO HOME AFTER DEPLOYMENT

AMY B. ADLER, MARK ZAMORSKI, AND THOMAS W. BRITT

> Coming from combat to home is not an easy task. It's hard to explain how I feel to anyone. . . . I have changed a lot—some for the better, some for the worse. Before Iraq I didn't have any plans or goals. Now I do. I might not be as happy as I used to be but I am getting there. Some days it's hard.
> —Anonymous U.S. soldier after returning from a 15-month deployment to Iraq

Returning home after a combat deployment can be both a relief and a challenge. Although military personnel are typically glad to be back, the transition home also involves a period of psychological adjustment. In this chapter, we explicitly broaden the traditional psychological focus on psychopathology in the aftermath of a combat deployment and focus instead on the overall transition process. Whether this period of adjustment is primarily positive, negative, or a combination of the two, all veterans must negotiate the psychological transition from combat to home. By broadening the conceptualization to include positive aspects of the transition process and adjustment issues that are not part of a psychiatric disorder, our goal is to reflect more accurately the psychological experience of service members following a deployment.

Typically, epidemiological studies find that significant mental health problems are reported by about 20% to 30% of individuals returning from combat (Dohrenwend et al., 2006; Hoge et al., 2004). Although these findings demonstrate that a significant number of returning service members report a mental health problem, many service members do not. To understand the transition process, domains beyond traditional clinical problems such as post-traumatic stress disorder, depression, and alcohol abuse must be considered.

The psychology of transition is worth attention for a number of reasons. First, how service members experience the transition home can have an impact on their quality of life and on their readiness to face future deployments. Second, many returning service members (and their families) find parts of the process difficult; therefore, making this process easier for people is the ethically correct thing to do. For example, it might help to normalize or predict certain transition experiences for returning service members and to train service members in specific skills to help them navigate potential transition pitfalls. Third, understanding the process of how service members benefit from their deployment experiences at postdeployment can help us develop ways to facilitate beneficial effects in military and other occupational settings. Finally, it may be that a difficult transition leads to subsequent mental health problems. Although scientific evidence has not completely documented this link, some analysts argue that by better managing the transition process (e.g., by offering a decompression program), future cases of deployment-related mental health problems or other outcomes such as divorce can be prevented. Although the complex interrelationship between transition problems and mental health problems is explored in detail later in this chapter, we introduce it now because it is a fundamental issue associated with examining the psychology of transition.

THE DEPLOYMENT CYCLE

In the military, the transition from combat to home is regarded as a phase of a larger deployment cycle. Militaries structure the deployment cycle to correspond to where an individual or unit is relative to the theater of operations (e.g., Norwood & Ursano, 1996). As a result, specific training, tasks, and supports can then be targeted to coincide with the needs of an individual or unit. For example, on an operational level, the U.S. Army divides the deployment experience into seven phases: train-up/preparation, mobilization, deployment, employment, redeployment, postdeployment, and reconstitution (Deputy Chief of Staff, 2009).

The U.S. Army further divides the transition home into three technical phases. First, the redeployment phase occurs when soldiers transfer from the theater of operations and return to their home station or a demobilization site. Second, the postdeployment phase occurs when soldiers arrive at their home station or demobilization site and undergo specific so-called recovery activities such as equipment accountability and return, block leave in which the unit is given time off, and certain training designed to orient the unit to living back in the home environment. Third, the reconstitution phase occurs when soldiers continue the process of reintegrating into their families, communities, and jobs. Each stage in the transition home involves specific administrative actions, briefings, training, counseling, and/or medical evaluations. Thus, on a technical level, the transition home can be characterized by specific military tasks. The psychological transition home, however, does not follow such a structured set of milestones.

Unlike physically relocating from one site to another, transitioning home is a psychological process, not an event, and as such it begins before the actual postdeployment phase of the deployment cycle. Service members begin thinking about, planning for, and fantasizing about their return home well before their actual return. Although the nature of this process and these phases have been described in research with military families (e.g., Wiens & Boss, 2006) and in conceptualizing the stress of homecoming (Yerkes & Holloway, 1996), little research has been conducted from the soldier perspective on the process of psychologically shifting from living in an operational combat zone to living at home.

THE PSYCHOLOGY OF TRANSITION

The process of making a psychological transition from a relatively dangerous and demanding environment to a relatively safe and comfortable environment requires service members to shift mentally. Borrowing from the concepts of narrative psychology (e.g., Crossley, 2002), it can be argued that returning service members are faced with the task of creating a coherent narrative to their lives and understanding the role that the deployment may have in shaping their identity. For some returning service members, this task will be relatively easy. They may not have experienced much during the deployment. For other service members, this task may be more challenging.

In this chapter, after briefly discussing the timing of transition processes within the entire deployment cycle, we detail a more comprehensive approach toward examining the transitioning process. We first provide a historical review of research on the transition process, highlighting the various transition issues that have faced service members in many prior military conflicts. This review highlights many examples of the issues veterans face in making the transition from combat to home and helps set the stage for an overall model of the transition process where we highlight the different dimensions on which service members experience the transition. We then discuss recent attempts to more systematically assess elements of the transition and describe factors that either facilitate or inhibit a successful transition. Finally, we discuss areas of the transition process that we believe are in need of future research.

The Transition Home: Research From World War II and Vietnam

In the United States, studies regarding the psychological transition of service members from combat to home can be traced back to World War II. At that time, studies published as part of Stouffer's *The American Soldier* (e.g., Stouffer et al., 1949; Stouffer, Suchman, DeVinney, Star, & Williams, 1949) identified the importance of this transition phase. Cottrell reported concerns that returning service members would be hostile and recommended the transition be a gradual process in which deployment experiences were discussed, and veterans were prepared mentally for the challenge of resuming civilian life. In the 1945 study *Men Under Stress*, Grinker and Spiegel reported returning service members needed family support, appropriate expectations, and a reorientation to civilian life (cited in Borus, 1973c).

Interview studies with Vietnam veterans underscore these and other key dimensions. For example, studies described how veterans had to disengage from their military experiences and intense friendships (Borus, 1973a; Faulkner & McGaw, 1977) and adjust to their garrison work environment which they perceived as meaningless, degrading, and inconsistent with their military training (Borus, 1973a). In interviews with Vietnam veterans, Borus (1973a) also found that veterans had developed close interracial friendships and had to adjust to racial tensions back home and the accompanying social divisions. Studies also found that veterans had to relearn how to control aggressive impulses that were acceptable in a war zone and manage their annoyance, survivor's guilt, and grief (e.g., Faulkner & McGaw, 1977; Shay, 2003; Solomon, 1993). Furthermore, veterans described feeling numb or emotionally shut down (Borus, 1973a). Finally, veterans consistently described the challenge of reconnecting with family members back home.

Taken together, the studies demonstrate the importance of considering homecoming as a process, not a discrete event. This process involves managing psychological changes in attitude, shifting one's self-concept, and placing deployment-related memories into the context of the home environment. The studies also demonstrate the importance of understanding the readjustment of combat veterans from both positive and negative perspectives. For example, Fontana and Rosenheck (1998) identified positive and negative reactions from Vietnam veterans related to patriotic beliefs (vs. disillusionment), self-improvement (vs. self-impoverishment), and solidarity with others (vs. alienation from others).

A Model of Transition

As seen in the review of research from veterans of World War II and Vietnam, the transition from combat to home has the potential to affect returning service members across a range of dimensions. Globally, these dimensions include a physical dimension, an emotional/cognitive dimension, and a social dimension. Although these dimensions may overlap or affect one another, for the sake of clarity, we present them as distinct domains in a model of transition. Figure 6.1 provides a schematic illustration of the postdeployment transition.

Note that the transition begins during the deployment and is influenced by deployment experiences. If the deployment has been long and arduous, the difficulty of the transition is likely to be affected. More physical and emotional adjustment may be needed. The anticipation of what the transition home will be like is also an important factor in the process. Research in other contexts has shown that people are notoriously bad about anticipating what will be difficult for them. They tend to overestimate the impact that large events have on their happiness and underestimate the impact that small annoyances have on them (Wilson & Gilbert, 2005). If the individual has unrealistic expectations about coming home, the transition will likely be more difficult. Meaningfulness of the work may also influence the transition process in various ways. Typically, deriving meaning from work is expected

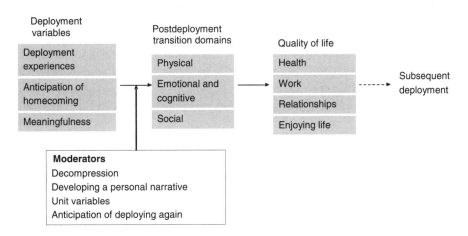

Figure 6.1. A model of deployment-to-home transition.

to enhance motivation and well-being (Britt, Dickinson, Moore, Castro, & Adler, 2007); however, if the work during deployment was meaningful but the work in garrison is not and that shift is not acknowledged by the organization, service members may feel frustrated and discontented. In contrast, if service members did not find meaning in their deployment, then sacrifices that were made may feel pointless, leading to anger and resentment.

Taken together, these deployment factors influence how the transition will be experienced across a variety of interrelated domains: the physical, emotional/cognitive, and social. There are, however, moderators of the transition process. Several moderators that have been emphasized in prior research are highlighted in the model and although introduced here, they are discussed in more detail later in the chapter. First, decompression is considered an important influence on the ability of service members to adapt following deployment, yet little is known about how this process actually influences the transition experience. A second moderator is the individual's implicit incorporation of deployment experiences into the development of a coherent narrative or sense of self. The importance of building such a narrative is included in the later section on facilitators of the transition process. Third, there are important unit variables, such as cohesion and leadership that are likely to influence how the transition is experienced. Fourth, in this model we have also included the potential presence of the next deployment as an influence on the transition process. As discussed later in this chapter, service members who anticipate another deployment may not be motivated to fully transition home physically, emotionally, mentally, or socially. Each of these domains is then regarded as having an impact on the service member's quality of life. In this model, the concept of quality of life encompasses health, relationships, work, and the ability to enjoy life. Note that for some service members, the transition home is temporary, and they will transition back to the deployment environment.

The primary purpose of the model is to integrate the myriad challenges and opportunities facing veterans into broad domains affecting them during the transition process. We believe the model is useful as a framework for research on transition processes. Many components of the model have been explored in research studies, but the model as a whole has not been systematically assessed. Note also that an individual may have both positive and negative experiences with the transition process and not all domains may transition at the same rate. Accordingly, the model is depicting a dynamic process. That is, there may be changes in the transition over time, with ups and downs, highs and lows, in the transition experience. After discussing the different domains of the model, we address emerging research on the transition process and assessing the transition. We then discuss factors that can either facilitate or inhibit a successful transition.

The Physical Component of the Transition

The physical dimension of transition refers to adjusting from the physical demands of deployed life. This adjustment can refer to relishing the comforts of home and appreciating the relatively mundane aspects life such as porcelain toilets, relief from extreme temperatures, privacy, and being able to prepare a meal. Clearly, these adjustments are examples of a positive aspect of transition, which underscores our point that when we address the issue of transition, we are not limiting that topic to negative concerns. Service members also adapt physically to the demands of the deployed environment and this adaptation may need to be reversed on homecoming. For example, service members are likely to become hypervigilant while deployed and will have learned to be aware of possible threats at all times. This adaptive heightened responsiveness to the environment is not required at home and needs to be reduced to avoid pitfalls such as exhaustion and irritability (see also Chapter 9, this volume). Service members may also learn to adapt their sleep to the deployed environment, which can mean not fully resting and always remaining somewhat alert. It may take service members time to reestablish nondeployed sleep cycles and learn how to relax.

The Emotional/Cognitive Component of the Transition

There is also an emotional or cognitive dimension to the psychological transition home. This dimension reflects the transition task of coming to terms with the emotional demands of the deployment and perhaps shifting the way in which veterans think about their environment. The transition may be characterized by positive emotions such as greater appreciation for relationships and by negative emotional states such as grief over the death of a unit member. The same transition domains may also be associated with positive emotion at one point and negative emotion at another. For example, the joy over being reunited with a spouse may yield to anger and frustration when old marital conflicts surface again. Some returning service members also report feeling intensely aware of the importance of their families and how much they value those around them. At the same time, despite this greater appreciation for life, service members typically note their tolerance for small complaints has diminished, and they report feeling easily irritated with those around them.

There may be other mixed emotions: For example, transition from the exciting and meaningful work activities on deployment to the more routine activities in garrison may be associated with equal measures of relief and boredom. Indeed, the prominence of such ambivalence (and the distress and confusion that it may cause) is a theme that has emerged in mental health training. In the U.S. postdeployment resilience training, for example, the *combat veteran's paradox*, is introduced as the state in which service members are both happy to be home and at the same time a bit edgy and angry.

The postdeployment transition may also mean coming to terms with deployment-related events that may have meant the loss of close friends and feelings of guilt. Guilt may be the result of actions service members now regret, or it may be associated with second-guessing decision making that led to injury or death. Service members may also become fatalistic about why they survived although others did not, using phrases such as "tempting fate" and "when your number's up, it's up." These comments sometimes address why they survived whereas others did not, and the question can shadow their return home. The degree to which killing has an impact on the postdeployment transition is likely related to the context under which the violence occurred and whether it was regarded as an atrocity or as a legitimate action consistent with the service member's professional identity. To assume that killing causes transition difficulties is not necessarily an accurate reflection of what service members experience. Although some authors describe that having killed leads to difficult emotional adjustment in the postdeployment phase (e.g., Grossman, 1996), others do not (see Gifford, 2006, for a discussion). Research is needed to identify the nature of the relationship between killing and subsequent adjustment.

Once home, individuals may need to integrate these experiences into their sense of self. Some service members may experience changes in their spiritual beliefs as well, and such changes will also need to be integrated into their postdeployment sense of self.

For many returning service members, the overall social adaptation is influenced by their ability to express their emotions appropriately and to moderate their underlying anger or rage. When deployed, many service members report repressing their emotional responses because of the danger that such responses could create. Once home, however, the returning service members may have to learn how to recognize and express emotions. Without this skill, the adjustment to home may be more difficult in terms of reestablishing and developing relationships, controlling emotions beyond feeling numbness or anger, and developing a personal narrative or story that supports an individual's identity.

Much of the emotional dimension overlaps with the way in which returning service members think about such issues as their actions in combat, their sense of responsibility regarding the death of unit members, and whether to share their story with family and friends at home. As described in the U.S. Army's postdeployment resilience training (formerly called *Battlemind Training*) conducted at reintegration and at 3 to 6 months postdeployment, certain cognitive patterns need to be adjusted during the transition. These thought patterns include service members remembering their right to enjoy life, their tolerance of mistakes, and the importance of sharing and reconnecting with loved ones.

The Social Component of the Transition

Besides the physical, emotional, and cognitive dimensions of transition, there is a social dimension as well. The social dimension incorporates several different aspects of the transition home. Service members returning from combat face the task of reestablishing relationships with friends and family when they return. These relationships may have shifted because the deployed individual as well as his or her friends and family are not the same as before. The returning service member and the people at home have had new experiences and have continued their lives to some extent without the other. Thus, these relationships need to be renewed, roles clarified, and the connection reestablished. Some service members experience these relationships as supportive; others report a chasm between their experience on deployment and what their friends and family are able to understand.

The service members also face a shift in terms of the cohesion that they felt with their units and buddies while deployed. This cohesion can be profound, and many service members describe how their battle buddies helped them cope or even survive the rigors of a combat deployment. The return home means a shift in the intense bonds that were created and in some cases a dispersion of the individuals to different units or geographical regions and what may almost feel like an intrusion of other primary relationships, such as those with family.

Another social shift in the transition is how individuals feel about returning to their work in garrison. For some, this return can be experienced as a respite from the life-or-death nature of the work required during a combat deployment. For others, this return means a decrease in decision-making autonomy that their small units had in remote areas. This return may also mean engaging in what can be perceived as less meaningful work. Some returning service members report feeling less patient with garrison duties and less patient with individuals who have not deployed and who cannot understand what the veteran service members have experienced.

Summary of the Transition Model

Thus, the transition is a time-driven process of multiple adaptations and iterative attempts to adjust to the new home environment. There is significant variation in the experiences of the transition process; each individual transitions home differently. Despite the fact that a return date occurs on a specific day, returning home is not a discrete event. As one soldier reflected on an open-ended questionnaire on returning from his second deployment to Iraq, "I . . . can see clearly that it is a process and not an event."

One common theme emerging from prior research and the transition model discussed here is the need to address both the positive and negative aspects of the transition process. Indeed, the field of psychology has increasingly recognized the importance of considering benefits associated with exposure to potentially traumatic events, exemplified by Tedeschi and Calhoun's (1996) introduction of a posttraumatic growth measure. Since then, numerous studies have examined benefit finding associated with stressful events (Helgeson, Reynolds, & Tomich, 2006), and studies have begun to examine postdeployment adjustment.

ASSESSING THE TRANSITION

Although previous studies on the transition from combat to home have largely been qualitative, these studies have provided important insights and have identified relevant themes and issues. The next step in assessing the transition process is to develop a scale measuring these facets of transition. In their development of a postdeployment scale, Canadian researchers Blais, Thompson, and McCreary (2009) called for an expansion of the conceptualization of the postdeployment transition and proposed a new scale based on interviews with returning veterans of Afghanistan.

In their Army Postdeployment Reintegration Scale, positive and negative aspects of three key areas are addressed: personal, family, and work reintegration. Analyses from a cross-sectional survey of Canadian soldiers 6 months after returning from Afghanistan provided support for the multidimensional approach. In addition, scores indicating negative reintegration attitudes correlated with measures of self-reported psychological distress, work-related stress, and less organizational commitment. Positive attitudes were essentially unrelated to symptom reporting but were correlated with affective commitment and positive job-related affect. These findings demonstrate the feasibility of assessing the transition using a type of transition scale. In addition, many of the items within the Blais et al. (2009) measure are consistent with the transition model presented earlier in the chapter. The authors included items addressing all four of the identified dimensions: physical (e.g., appreciation of conveniences), emotional (e.g., tension in relationships), cognitive (e.g., confused about experiences), and social (e.g., closer to family).

In parallel, U.S. researchers have also developed a Combat-to-Home Transition Scale measuring the positive and negative aspects of returning home from combat. Although some scale items reflect concepts addressed in the Canadian scale (e.g., a greater appreciation of things, feeling closer to family), there are also items that reflect some of the relatively bitter emotional experiences reported in focus groups by U.S. soldiers. On the basis of in-depth discussion groups with hundreds of soldiers returning from a year in Iraq, Walter Reed Army Institute of Research researchers compiled a list of items that described the phenomenological experience of transitioning home from combat (Adler, Bliese, McGurk, & Castro, 2008). Structural analysis on two independent samples of 1,651 and 636 active duty soldiers from Brigade Combat Teams surveyed 4 months after returning from Iraq yielded a consistent factor solution that included two benefit-finding factors (i.e., positive impact, appreciation) and two negative factors (i.e., anger/alienation, guilt). The items for the different factors are provided in Table 6.1.

The scale factors are consistent with the themes of transition identified in previous interview studies (e.g., Borus, 1973a; Faulker & McGaw, 1977; Fontana & Rosenheck, 1998). Specifically, anger and alienation were a consistent theme. The exact nature of this anger in veterans, the utility of the

TABLE 6.1
Frequency for the Combat-to-Home Transition Scale 4 Months
After Returning From Iraq

Factor	Scale item	Agree or strongly agree (%)
1	The recent deployment has had a positive effect on my life.	27.8
1	I feel pride from my accomplishments during the recent deployment.	60.0
1	My deployment was pointless.	22.2
1	What I did during the deployment helped improve life for Iraqis/Afghans.	32.5
1	I am able to find meaning in what happened during my deployment.	31.5
2	I cannot relate to people who have not deployed to combat.	25.0
2	Most of the concerns that others have seem trivial to me.	33.8
2	I have little patience for the stupid stuff people do.	71.2
2	I feel angry toward all Iraqi/Afghan people.	27.5
2	I would like to pay back the Iraqi/Afghan people for the death of my buddies.	27.3
3	I appreciate the little things in life more.	74.6
3	I appreciate my family and friends more than before I deployed.	66.9
3	I have matured as a result of my deployment.	64.9
4	I feel guilty about things that I did during deployment.	8.9
4	I have been second guessing the decisions I made during the deployment.	8.2
4	The deaths of my friends in combat have made it hard for me to get on with my life.	8.9

Note. Factor 1 was "positive impact," Factor 2 was "anger/alienation," Factor 3 was "appreciation," Factor 4 was "guilt." N = 1,651.

anger, the causal mechanisms that lead to such pervasive anger, and the resolution of this heightened anger need to be better understood. Underlying pervasive anger is important because it has the potential to serve as an impediment to reintegrating back with family and society at large. Such anger also has the potential to serve as a barrier in attempts to connect emotionally with others and to erupt in destructive and dangerous ways. Finally, guilt addresses challenges veterans face along the emotional, cognitive, and social dimensions of adjustment. In contrast, items reflecting benefit-finding demonstrated soldiers experienced positive outcomes associated with the deployment.

Developing a transition scale is essential for being able to benchmark key postdeployment experiences with consistency and for modeling these experiences over time. Although the transition scales do not address all components of the model, they can be useful for identifying moderators and mediators of a positive transition and for explicitly testing the relationship between transition and mental health problems. The various aspects of the postdeployment transition can be conceptualized as outcomes in their own right or as predictors of subsequent mental health problems.

From the service member's perspective, transition problems and postdeployment mental health problems may feel similar in that both may cause distress. But from the mental health provider's perspective, it is essential to distinguish between a clinical condition that will benefit from specific therapy and a nonclinical one that service members can solve on their own or for which limited help is needed.

It is as yet unclear whether transition problems follow the same increasing trajectory that has been found in postdeployment mental health problems (Bliese, Wright, Adler, Thomas, & Hoge, 2007; Milliken, Auchterlonie, & Hoge, 2007). In our survey of U.S. soldiers returning from combat, scores on the guilt and anger/alienation items increased significantly from 4 months postdeployment to 8 months postdeployment. At the same time, soldier perception that the deployment had a positive impact also increased over time.

Qualitative data from peacekeepers suggest that most peacekeepers feel that they have fully adjusted to home life after 4 months (Thompson & Gignac, 2001). Data from combat, however, suggest there may still be significant difficulties. Thus, the question of time course has yet to be adequately addressed. The question is important because the answers have implications for the timing of early interventions and the content of psychoeducational approaches.

In terms of research, future studies should assess and analyze transition problems as well as more traditional mental health concerns such as PTSD. In terms of clinical issues, interventions will need to target transition problems and mental health problems separately. Still, it may be helpful to describe postdeployment mental health problems as a reflection of the overall transition process to decrease stigma associated with seeking mental health and to explicitly acknowledge the role that occupational stressors can have in the development of mental health problems.

DECOMPRESSION AND MANAGING THE TRANSITION

The term *decompression* refers to bringing someone gradually back to a normal atmosphere. When the term is used with respect to deep-sea diving, it refers to the individual's relief from atmospheric pressure and acclimation to normal surface pressure. Used in the postdeployment context, the concept of decompression is similar in that it refers to a reduction in pressure and a return to normal. In the military, decompression encompasses the process of that initial adjustment, the period of time during which relief occurs, and the programs designed to facilitate this phase of transition. Such programs typically bring service members to a neutral, safe environment that is separate from the deployment and from home to facilitate decompression prior to reexperiencing the normal pressures of society.

Although decompression is considered to occur as service members exit the deployed environment and reenter the new (i.e., home) environment, how long this phase actually lasts has not been documented. We also do not know how the duration varies depending on the circumstances of deployment, but it is presumed that decompression would last longer in those who had had more difficult deployments (i.e., more pressure). Decompression programs typically assume that this process only lasts a few days.

In reviewing military decompression programs, Hacker Hughes and colleagues (2008) concluded that the formal idea of decompression in the military dates back to the Vietnam War. The Vietnam experience of decompression was different in a number of ways: First, many service members returned home by air, meaning they could be on the battlefield one day and back at home a day or two later; decompression thus occurred more rapidly and often in the presence of friends and family members who likely had little appreciation of what the veteran was experiencing. Second, service members often returned as individuals rather than as a unit, which prevented them from unwinding with people who were both important to them and had shared their experiences. Finally, the trip home occurred after a specified tour of duty rather than at the end of hostilities; as a result, many may have had mixed feelings about being home while their fellow unit members still remained in combat.

The idea of decompression may sound attractive in that it suggests that the return to normal can be directly facilitated by a few days of rest and relaxation. Currently, returning service members appear to value this relatively short decompression schedule because even if they acknowledge a need for a formal decompression program, they are eager to return home. For example, British soldiers returning from Iraq favorably evaluated a third-location decompression (TLD) program lasting only 36 hr. Of Canadian soldiers returning from a combat mission in Afghanistan who evaluated their 5-day TLD program, 64% felt that the duration was about right; only 8% felt that it should be longer.

In general, and across several studies, service members have been supportive of the concept of TLD programs. For example, after completion of a Canadian TLD program in Cyprus on the way home from a combat and peace support mission in Afghanistan, 92% of participants agreed with the statement "Some form of TLD is a good idea," and 87% agreed with the statement "I think letting off steam before going home was a good idea." Dutch military personnel returning from Iraq who had a 2-day "adjustment period" in Cyprus were also largely supportive of the concept of "letting off steam" and "having a breather" before going home; this group also demonstrated more favorable attitudes toward the TLD concept after having actually experienced it (Duel, 2008; Geerligs, 2005).

Despite these positive perceptions, formal decompression may not actually reduce the sense of pressure that service members experienced on the deployment. The limitation regarding the efficacy of decompression was supported by a recent observational study on a decompression program in garrison that showed that postdeployment mental health and well-being were identical in those who did not go through the postdeployment garrison program (Hacker Hughes et al., 2008). Although this study showed that spending a week or so on base did not confer an advantage relative to going on leave straight after returning home, the study did not use randomization and the decompression occurred on base, not in a third location.

Decompression Programs

The lack of conceptual clarity and sound research on the decompression phase of transition (and its consequences) has not dampened the enthusiasm for decompression programs. Such programs are typified by Canada's TLD program for service members returning from Afghanistan through Cyprus. Like the Canadian TLD program, these decompression programs tend to be brief (i.e., 1 to 5 days in duration), mandatory, likely to be established after "difficult" deployments, situated in a third location (i.e., not theater and not home), conducted with unit members, delivered with some educational component, and scheduled to include rest and recreation and some access to alcohol.

Given the seemingly spontaneous and inevitable nature of the relief associated with the end of a deployment, it is reasonable to ask why soldiers would need help with decompression. After all, the majority of service members returning from a deployment do not report mental health problems, suggesting that decompression may occur quickly with or without a decompression program. This issue demonstrates the importance of distinguishing between mental health problems and the quality of life associated with the transition home, reflected by the broader conceptualization of transition in the model offered earlier in the chapter. Many service members report that, independent of mental health problems, the transition home can be challenging. Thus, although there is no hard evidence that has demonstrated the mental health benefits associated with TLD, the transition may still be difficult, and service members who are eager to be home still view the concept of decompression quite positively. Such a perspective suggests that TLD addresses a need unique to the postdeployment transition process.

Evaluation of Decompression Programs

One question in evaluating decompression programs is whether decompression is more effective when conducted as part of a formal program and with fellow service members or when done informally at home in the company of friends and family. This question cannot be answered definitively without a group randomized trial, and no such trials have been performed. Evaluation of decompression programs has been limited to participant surveys and interviews done immediately after the program or at some point after return home.

In evaluating the impact of TLD programs it is also important to distinguish between the impact of the decompression program itself (i.e., the rest and recreation component) and the impact of the educational programming that is often delivered as part of the program. Qualitative research on two different Canadian TLD programs confirmed the positive attitudes toward the programs. It also documented the more favorable attitudes to the program over time: A number of respondents indicated that they were not looking forward to the experience and would have preferred to go straight home if given the choice. But nearly all reported favorable evaluations of the program both immediately after completion and many months after return, when the interviews were performed. For example, 80% of Canadian TLD participants agreed that it was a valuable experience immediately afterward, whereas 6 months later approximately 86% agreed that it was valuable and 83% felt that the program made the reintegration process easier for them. The specific aspects of the program that were felt (in retrospect) to be most valuable were the informal time spent with colleagues in a nonwork setting and the educational programming. Evaluation of the Dutch TLD program showed similar results and confirmed the tendency for satisfaction to increase over time after return home (Geerligs, 2005).

There is indirect evidence that family members may also find benefit from the soldier's participation in TLD. In one survey, 67% of Canadian TLD participants agreed that the TLD made reintegration easier for their families, and this TLD benefit also emerged as a theme in the qualitative study. The only direct assessment of spouses' attitudes about the TLD program comes from the Dutch experience: Spousal and TLD participant evaluations of the value of the experience showed nearly identically favorable results.

Thus, what can be said about the perceived impact of TLD programs is that participants are largely supportive of the concept (at least after difficult deployments), but they may not look forward to the experience. In addition, participants largely value the experience, and satisfaction with it seems to increase over the months after return. Furthermore, TLD programs are perceived by service members (and perhaps their families as well) to help in precisely the way they are intended; that is, they are seen as a way to ease the reintegration process for service members and for their families.

Finally, a cautionary note is in order: TLD programs have certain risks, particularly for the consequences of problematic behavior while intoxicated. Some nations allow service members limited access to alcohol during decompression as part of the transition back home after a deployment during which no alcohol was permitted. The Canadian experience with more than 7,000 TLD participants has included a number of episodes of alcohol poisoning, injuries, assaults, criminal acts (i.e., assault, larceny, vandalism), and disciplinary infractions. Implementation of various control measures appears to have been effective at decreasing (but not eliminating) these risks. The apparent benefits of TLD need to be interpreted within this context.

Research is needed in a number of key areas surrounding the decompression phase of transition. First, the psychology of the immediate postdeployment phase itself needs to be better characterized: What exactly are soldiers experiencing during this period? What is their time course? Second, how does the psychology of decompression relate to the psychology of transition as a whole (and to the emergence of deployment-related mental health problems)? Third, how do decompression programs influence the psychology of transition? More broadly, we need to understand the effects of transition programs on the physical, cognitive, emotional, and behavior dimensions identified earlier. Fourth, what aspects of decompression programs constitute the "active ingredient" underlying the observed effectiveness of the programs? Fifth, is having the decompression program in a third location necessary for program efficacy? If so, why? Finally, what aspects of the deployment make decompression programming particularly valuable? This information is essential because there is limited experience with decompression programs after less difficult operations to guide policy.

Transition in the Context of Deploying Again (Partial or Full Transition?)

Despite the emphasis on transitioning home, the reality is that many service members are called on to deploy multiple times. For example, in a sample of soldiers from one brigade returning from a deployment to Iraq, 35% had been previously deployed to Iraq or Afghanistan, and this rate is not atypical. Other research shows that multiple deployments are associated with worse mental health outcomes during (Mental Health Advisory Team V, 2008) or after (Rona et al., 2007) a combat deployment. However, there are also indications that some previous deployment experience may help individuals in their adjustment following peacekeeping operations (Adler, Huffman, Bliese, & Castro, 2005).

Still, the issue of multiple deployments raises an important challenge in tracking the transition process. What exactly defines a successful transition home if service members expect to deploy again within a year or two? What impact does the next deployment have on their transition home if the next deployment is never far from their thoughts? To what degree should they adjust to the garrison environment? Is there some degree to which service members should not fully transition physically, emotionally, cognitively, and socially to make the transition back into combat easier? These questions have not yet been examined but are important in understanding that for some the transition home is temporary.

Unit Variables as Predictors of a Successful Transition

Studies of readjusting veterans have found that being with other returning veterans facilitates adjustment. Star (as cited in Borus, 1973c) observed from the World War II experience that on returning home, veterans who were placed in units primarily composed of other veterans reported more job satisfaction, connection to their unit, and satisfaction with their leadership than veterans in units with a mix of veterans and nonveterans. Similarly, Borus (1973b) reported that Vietnam veterans found it easier to relate to other veterans, resulting in his recommending group sessions to talk about their experiences to facilitate their adjustment home. More recent studies have confirmed the correlation between unit cohesion and mental health outcomes in the 1st year following a combat deployment (e.g., Adler, Vaitkus, & Martin, 1996). Good leadership is also an important variable in predicting mental health adjustment (e.g., Adler et al., 1996; Mental Health Advisory Team IV, 2006). Leaders who help individuals derive meaning from the deployment may also have a more successful transition (e.g., Britt, Adler, & Bartone, 2001). Soldiers who find meaning in their deployment experiences may be able to manage the transition process, reorienting themselves to a civilian culture and perhaps being able to place feelings of guilt, grief, and second-guessing in perspective.

Homecoming and the Transition Process

Numerous studies have found that a positive homecoming reception is associated with better adjustment (e.g., Bolton, Litz, Glenn, Orsillo, & Roemer, 2002; Fontana, Rosenheck, & Horvath, 1997; King, King, Fairbank, Keane, & Adams, 1998; Koenen, Stellman, Stellman, & Sommer, 2003; Orsillo, Roemer, Litz, Ehlich, & Friedman, 1998). The homecoming reception sets the context for interpreting the combat-related events. It answers fundamental questions that service members face: Was the sacrifice worthwhile? Is the sacrifice acknowledged or appreciated? Is there a place for me back home? By establishing a positive homecoming, the returning service member can feel support at a larger, societal level. In turn, the veteran's family can also feel supported and that may enable family members to be more patient and accepting of the returning service member. The dynamic of homecoming receptions has not been systematically examined other than through surveys that find service members who report positive homecoming reception are more likely to report positive mental health adjustment. The question remains: What is the specific nature of the mechanism of the homecoming reception that sets the context for positive adjustment?

FUTURE DIRECTIONS

All service members returning home from combat face the challenge of transition. This challenge has remained consistent over time, suggesting that the act of moving psychologically from the deployment and toward home contains core elements of appreciation and maturity, the need to reestablish connections and a personal identity, and the need to tolerate frustrations, potentially meaningless work, and the minor hassles of life at home. Perhaps the deployment can be an opportunity for service members to redefine their lives, the meaning they find in work, connecting with others, and keeping perspective on what really matters.

By expanding the focus from postdeployment mental health to the transition as a whole, individual, work, and social variables that influence the transition process can be identified. This identification can then be useful in developing training programs for individuals and family members dealing with the postdeployment phase and in developing leaders and homecoming programs that can increase the positive aspects of the postdeployment transition while reducing the negative. Research should focus on identifying these variables, assessing the efficacy of decompression programs, and understanding the nature of the transition when the transition is only temporary.

Mental health training programs designed to facilitate the transition should emphasize service member strengths that helped them manage the demands of a deployment while reinforcing resilience skills. Such programs should also (a) emphasize and normalize the positive and negative aspects of transition, (b) address the perceived need for decompression, (c) emphasize the role of unit members and leaders, (d) encourage returning service members to tell their deployment story in some fashion, and (e) target particularly difficult emotional components of the transition related to guilt and grief. Each of these program components need to be assessed for efficacy not just in terms of how they influence the development of postdeployment mental health problems but in terms of the larger transition process. This transition process can, in turn, influence the service member's quality of life, their ability to enjoy life, return to work, find meaning in their sacrifice, and reconnect with people important to them.

REFERENCES

Adler, A. B., Bliese, P. D., McGurk, D., & Castro, C. A. (2008, March). Transitioning home: The role of combat experiences and leadership. In T. W. Britt & J. L. Thomas (Chairs), *Deriving benefits from stressful work: The case of combat veterans*. Symposium conducted at the 7th International Conference on Occupational Stress & Health, Washington, DC.

Adler, A. B., Huffman, A. H., Bliese, P. D., & Castro, C. A. (2005). The impact of deployment length and experience on the well being of male and female solders. *Journal of Occupational Health Psychology, 10*, 121–137. doi:10.1037/1076-8998.10.2.121

Adler, A. B., Vaitkus, M. A., & Martin, J. A. (1996). The impact of combat exposure on posttraumatic stress symptomatology among U.S. soldiers deployed to the Gulf War. *Military Psychology, 8*(1), 1–14. doi:10.1207/s15327876mp0801_1

Blais, A. R., Thompson, M. M., & McCreary, D. M. (2009). The development and validation of the army postdeployment reintegration scale. *Military Psychology, 21*, 365–386. doi:10.1080/08995600902914727

Bliese, P. D., Wright, K. M., Adler, A. B., Thomas, J. L., & Hoge, C. W. (2007). Timing of postcombat mental health assessments. *Psychological Services, 4*, 141–148. doi:10.1037/1541-1559.4.3.141

Bolton, E., Litz, B. T., Glenn, D. M., Orsillo, S., & Roemer, L. (2002). The impact of homecoming reception on the adaptation of peacekeepers following deployment. *Military Psychology, 14*, 241–251. doi:10.1207/S15327876MP1403_4

Borus, J. F. (1973a). Reentry I: Adjustment issues facing the Vietnam returnee. *Archives of General Psychiatry, 28*, 501–506.

Borus, J. F. (1973b). Reentry II: "Making it" back in the States. *The American Journal of Psychiatry, 130*, 850–854.

Borus, J. F. (1973c). Reentry III: Facilitating healthy readjustment in Vietnam veterans. *Psychiatry, 36*, 428–439.

Britt, T. W., Adler, A. B., & Bartone, P. T. (2001). Deriving benefits from stressful events: The role of engagement in meaningful work and hardiness. *Journal of Occupational Health Psychology, 6*, 53–63. doi:10.1037/1076-8998.6.1.53

Britt, T. W., Dickinson, J. M., Moore, D. M., Castro, C. A., & Adler, A. B. (2007). Correlates and consequences of morale versus depression under stressful conditions. *Journal of Occupational Health Psychology, 12*, 34–47. doi:10.1037/1076-8998.12.1.34

Crossley, M. L. (2002). Introducing narrative psychology. In C. Horrocks, N. Kelly, B. Roberts and D. Robinson (Eds.) *Narrative, memory, and life transitions* (pp. 1–13). Retrieved from http://www2.hud.ac.uk/hhs/nme/books/2002/Chapter_1_Michelle_Crossley.pdf

Deputy Chief of Staff. (2009). *Deployment cycle support process*. Retrieved from http://www.armyg1.army.mil/dcs/default.asp

Dohrenwend, B. P., Turner, J. B., Turse, N. A., Adams, B. G., Koenen, K. C., & Marshall, R. (2006, August 18). The psychological risks of Vietnam for U.S. veterans: A revisit with new data and methods. *Science, 313*, 979–982. doi:10.1126/science.1128944

Duel, J. (2008, September). *Participating in an adaptation program following deployment. Who benefits?* Paper presented at the meeting of the International Military Testing Association, Amsterdam, The Netherlands.

Faulkner, R. R., & McGaw, D. B. (1977). Uneasy homecoming: Stages in the reentry transition of Vietnam veterans. *Urban Life, 6*, 303–328.

Fontana, A., & Rosenheck, R. (1998). Psychological benefits and liabilities of traumatic exposure in the war zone. *Journal of Traumatic Stress, 11*, 485–503. doi:10.1023/A:1024452612412

Fontana, A., Rosenheck, R., & Horvath, T. (1997). Social support and psychopathology in the war zone. *Journal of Nervous and Mental Disease, 185*, 675–681. doi:10.1097/00005053-199711000-00004

Geerligs, E. (2005). Adaptatie te Cyprus [Adaptation at Cyprus] (Technical Report GW-05-062). The Hague, The Netherlands: Gedragswetenschappen [Behavioral Sciences Services Centre].

Gifford, R. (2006). Psychological aspects of combat. In T. W. Britt, C. A. Castro, & A. B. Adler (Eds.), *Military life: The psychology of serving in peace and combat: Vol. 1. Military Performance* (pp. 15–30). Westport, CT: Praeger.

Grossman, D. (1996). *On killing: The psychological cost of learning to kill in war and society*. New York, NY: Little, Brown.

Hacker Hughes, J. G., Earnshaw, N. M., Greenberg, N., Eldridge, R., Fear, N. T., French, C., . . . Wessely, S. (2008). The use of psychological decompression in military operational environments. *Military Medicine, 173,* 534–538.

Helgeson, V. S., Reynolds, K. A., & Tomich, P. L. (2006). A meta-analytic review of benefit finding and growth. *Journal of Consulting and Clinical Psychology, 74,* 797–816. doi:10.1037/0022-006X.74.5.797

Hoge, C. W., Castro, C. A., Messer, S. C., McGurk, D., Cotting, D., & Koffman, R. L. (2004). Combat duty in Iraq and Afghanistan, mental health problems, and barriers to care. *The New England Journal of Medicine, 351,* 13–22. doi:10.1056/NEJMoa040603

King, L. A., King, D. W., Fairbank, J. A., Keane, T. M., & Adams, G. A. (1998). Resilience-recovery factors in posttraumatic stress disorder among female and male Vietnam veterans: Hardiness, postwar social support, and additional stressful life events. *Journal of Personality and Social Psychology, 74,* 420–434. doi:10.1037/0022-3514.74.2.420

Koenen, K. C., Stellman, J. M., Stellman, S. D., & Sommer, J. F. (2003). Risk factors for course of posttraumatic stress disorder among Vietnam veterans: A 14-year follow-up of American Legionnaires. *Journal of Consulting and Clinical Psychology, 71,* 980–986. doi:10.1037/0022-006X.71.6.980

Mental Health Advisory Team IV. (2006). *Mental Health Advisory Team (MHAT) IV Operation Iraqi Freedom 05-07.* Retrieved from http://www.armymedicine.army.mil/reports/mhat/mhat_iv/MHAT_IV_Report_17NOV06.pdf

Mental Health Advisory Team V. (2008). *Mental Health Advisory Team (MHAT) V Operation Iraqi Freedom 06-08: Iraq, Operation Enduring Freedom 8: Afghanistan.* Retrieved from http://www.armymedicine.army.mil/reports/mhat/mhat_v/MHAT_V_OIFandOEF-Redacted.pdf

Milliken, C. S., Auchterlonie, J. L., & Hoge, C. W. (2007). Longitudinal assessment of mental health problems among active and reserve component soldiers returning from the Iraq war. *JAMA, 298,* 2141–2148. doi:10.1001/jama.298.18.2141

Norwood, A. E., & Ursano, R. J. (1996). The Gulf War. In R. J. Ursano & A. E. Norwood (Eds.), *Emotional aftermath of the Persian Gulf War: Veterans, families, communities, and nations* (pp. 3–21). Washington, DC: American Psychiatric Press.

Orsillo, S. M., Roemer, L., Litz, B. T., Ehlich, P., & Friedman, M. J. (1998). Psychiatric symptomatology associated with contemporary peacekeeping: An examination of postmission functioning among peacekeepers in Somalia. *Journal of Traumatic Stress, 11,* 611–625. doi:10.1023/A:1024481030025

Rona, R. J., Fear, N. T., Hull, L., Greenberg, N., Earnshaw, M., Hotopf, M., & Wessely, S. (2007). Mental health consequences of overstretch in the U.K. armed forces: First phase of a cohort study. *British Medical Journal, 335,* 603–607. doi:10.1136/bmj.39274.585752.BE

Shay, J. (2003). *Odysseus in America: Combat trauma and the trials of homecoming.* New York, NY: Scribner.

Solomon, Z. (1993). *Combat stress reaction: The enduring toll of war.* New York, NY: Plenum Press.

Stouffer, S. A., Lumsdaine, A. A., Williams, R. B., Smith, M. B., Janis, I. L., Star, S. A., & Cottrell, L. S. (1949). *The American soldier: Vol. 2. Combat and its aftermath.* Princeton, NJ: Princeton University Press

Stouffer, S. A., Suchman, E. A., DeVinney, L. C., Star, S. A., & Williams, R. A. (1949). *The American soldier: Vol. 1. Adjustment during army life.* Princeton, NJ: Princeton University Press.

Tedeschi, R. G., & Calhoun, L. G. (1996). The Posttraumatic Growth Inventory: Measuring the positive legacy of trauma. *Journal of Traumatic Stress, 9,* 455–471. doi:10.1002/jts.2490090305

Thompson, M. M., & Gignac, M. A. M. (2001). Adaptation to peace support operations: The experience of Canadian Forces augmentees. In P. Essens, A. Vogelaar, E. Tanercan, & D. Winslow (Eds.), *The human in command: Peace support operations* (pp. 235–263). Amsterdam, The Netherlands: Mets & Schilt/KMA.

Wiens, T. W., & Boss, P. (2006). Maintaining family resiliency before, during, and after military separation. In C. A. Castro, A. B. Adler, & T. H. Britt (Eds.), *Military life: The psychology of serving in peace and combat: Vol. 3. The military family* (pp.13–38) Westport, CT: Praeger.

Wilson, T. D., & Gilbert, D. T. (2005). Affective forecasting: Knowing what to want. *Current Directions in Psychological Science, 14,* 131–134. doi:10.1111/j.0963-7214.2005.00355.x

Yerkes, S. A., & Holloway, H. C. (1996). War and homecomings: The stressors of war and of returning from war. In R. J. Ursano & A. E. Norwood (Eds.), *Emotional aftermath of the Persian Gulf War: Veterans, families, communities, and nations* (pp. 25–42). Washington, DC: American Psychiatric Press.

7

PREVENTIVE MENTAL HEALTH SCREENING IN THE MILITARY

PAUL D. BLIESE, KATHLEEN M. WRIGHT, AND CHARLES W. HOGE

Routine screening for physical and mental health problems is widely practiced within the U.S. military. Service members are screened before joining the military, and service members receive a brief medical and mental health screen prior to deploying, followed by two screens on return (one conducted immediately on return and the second conducted 3 to 6 months later). Despite the fact that pre- and postdeployment screening is widely practiced within the U.S. military, the use of routine deployment screening has been controversial. Indeed, militaries from other countries have concluded that screening is of little value and have opted not to implement deployment-centered screening programs (Rona, Jones, French, Hooper, & Wessely, 2004).

Rona, Hyams, and Wessely (2005) provided a definition of *screening* based on Morrison (1992) as "the examination of a generally healthy population to classify individuals as likely or unlikely to have the condition that is the

The views expressed in this chapter are those of the authors and do not reflect the official position of the Walter Reed Army Institute of Research, the U.S. Army, or Department of Defense. This chapter was authored or coauthored by an employee of the United States government as part of official duty and is considered to be in the public domain. Any views expressed herein do not necessarily represent the views of the United States government, and the author's participation in the work is not meant to serve as an official endorsement.

object of screening" (p. 1257). This definition is broad, and when applied to mental health, screening typically uses survey-based procedures to identify at-risk individuals who are further evaluated for mental health problems. Fundamentally, however, all mental health screening programs contain some degree of error resulting in false positives and false negatives, and these errors in classification are a key source of controversy about the utility of these programs. Classification errors interact with the intended goals of the screening programs, and in some situations these errors are highly problematic, whereas in other situations they are relatively inconsequential.

In this chapter, we detail the use of mental health screening with U.S. service members and focus on the controversies surrounding these programs. Our emphasis is on the use of mental health screening programs as part of medical support surrounding military deployments (i.e., care-based screening); however, we also set the context by discussing the use of selection-based screening. In the interest of disclosure, we acknowledge that our research has played a central role in the U.S. military's decision to implement at least one care-based screening program; therefore, we cannot be considered unbiased, and we generally support deployment-centered screening programs. Nonetheless, in an attempt to provide a balanced treatment of the topic, we also recognize that concerns with screening programs cannot be lightly dismissed.

GOALS OF SCREENING PROGRAMS

Although all screening programs involve examining and classifying individuals, the purposes behind the programs vary. In World War II, psychiatric screening was used to select potential recruits for service. The goal was to implement an effective screen that would prevent psychologically vulnerable individuals from being able to join the service and help reduce postwar medical costs associated with treating psychiatric casualties (Berlien & Waggoner, 1966).

The attempt in World War II to use psychiatric screening for selection has generally been viewed as a failure (Berlien & Waggoner, 1966; Egan, Jackson, & Eanes, 1951; Glass, 1966; Rona et al., 2005); nonetheless, vestiges of this program continue. For instance, current selection procedures in the U.S. military rely on a detailed medical history that includes previous mental health treatment, hospitalizations, and medications. They also include tests of mental aptitude, a practice that originated during World War I and was continued in World War II (Cardona & Ritchie, 2006).

Somewhat parenthetically, one of the most influential criticisms of World War II screening was the 1951 JAMA article by Egan and colleagues. This study tracked a large cohort of individuals who had been initially rejected in the early years of the war and who were subsequently inducted because of a decline in available manpower in the latter part of the war. The central finding of this study was that the vast majority of the cohort who had been initially rejected performed well when they were subsequently inducted. The success of those who were initially rejected for service is interpreted as a failure of screening, although it is unclear what factors may have contributed to this finding. One potential confound may have been public attitude toward serving in World War II. For instance, one of the authors of this chapter recounts a story about a male family member concealing a physical ailment and lying about his age in order to join the military during World War II. If there was, in fact, a high motivation to serve, as exemplified by this family member, it is reasonable to imagine that a cohort of individuals who had originally been rejected would have been highly motivated to succeed when given the subsequent opportunity.

Currently, in terms of selection in the U.S. military, there is little support for screening for any psychological problem beyond severe mental illness (as identified in the comprehensive medical evaluation) and low general mental aptitude. Although it may at times be tempting to pursue the goals of World War II selection programs in an effort to increase the resiliency of recruits by screening out "the eccentric . . . the emotionally unstable . . . those with inadequate personalities that do not adapt readily, and those who are resentful of discipline" (Berlien & Waggoner, 1966, p. 162), there is a general consensus that broad-scale screening for psychological vulnerability during selection would be as ineffective today as it was in World War II (Cardona & Ritchie, 2006).

There are several reasons why the military has concluded that selection-based screening for a broad range of psychological vulnerabilities is ineffective. First, it is unclear how one would operationally define *psychological vulnerability*; recall the broad definition used in World War II included everything from "eccentric" to "resentful of discipline." Second, even if one could define psychological vulnerability, classification errors would continue to be highly problematic. From a statistical perspective, studies have repeatedly shown that the positive predictive values (PPV) of mental health screening instruments for even well-defined conditions such as depression, anxiety disorder, and posttraumatic stress disorder (PTSD) are low.

In a detailed analysis of the psychometric efficiency of the PTSD Checklist (PCL; Weathers, Litz, Herman, Huska, & Keane, 1993), Bliese et al. (2008) reported a range of PPVs that reached an asymptote at .62 and were generally in the .40 to .50 range for acceptable levels of sensitivity (i.e., the proportion of people positive for a mental health problem who scored above threshold on the screen) and specificity (i.e., the proportion of people negative for a mental health problem who scored below threshold on the screen).

Likewise, in an analysis of a screening instrument for the British military, Rona, Hooper, Jones, French, and Wessely (2004) reported PPVs of .47 and .48. Perhaps the most comprehensive analysis of screening instruments for PTSD was a study of the properties of the PCL by Terhakopian, Sinaii, Engel, Schnurr, and Hoge (2008). Results of this study indicate that PPVs are often in the .20 range when a validated instrument is applied on a population level (i.e., in a nonclinical setting).

In practical terms, PPVs of this magnitude mean that one fifth to one half of those identified via the screen instrument as being positive actually have the condition. For a selection screen, this would mean that 50% to 80% of those assessed as unfit would be expected to do fine. Psychometrically, the low PPVs do not simply reflect a need to develop better screening tools; they are fundamentally a reflection of the fact that the conditions being screened have relatively low prevalence. For instance, Bliese et al. (2008) showed that the PCL with a cutoff 30 had a sensitivity of .78 (i.e., the proportion of the sample referred for PTSD problems who scored above threshold on the PCL) and a specificity of .88 (i.e., the proportion of the sample not referred for PTSD problems who scored below threshold on the PCL). Despite these two reasonable sensitivity and specificity values, the PPV was only .38. In this case, the low PPV was a function of the low rate (5.8%) of individuals meeting the criterion established by the gold standard of a structured clinical interview for PTSD.

It is hard to precisely estimate the percentage of individuals who pass the current selection criteria for induction into service but who subsequently leave service because of existing psychological vulnerabilities. Cardona and Ritchie (2006) noted that, historically, the first-term attrition rate had been approximately 30%; however, recent modifications in training strategies have reduced the rate of attrition. Attrition occurs for a variety of reasons, most commonly orthopedic problems and administrative discharges such as a failure to meet retention standards. Discharges for mental health diagnoses are much less common than for administrative reasons but may interact with administrative problems such as misconduct and substance abuse. It has been estimated that, overall, 11% of soldiers leave military service as a result of mental health problems (see the 2008 Accession Medical Standards Analysis and Research Activity [AMSARA] report; Niebuhr et al., 2008).

If mental health problems contribute to approximately 11% of first-term attritions from the military, it is difficult to imagine how a screening instrument could be developed that would have PPVs high enough to make selection-based screens practical. For instance, if there was a test capable of identifying this 11% with a specificity of .90 and sensitivity of .75, then one could mathematically show that the resulting PPV would be .48. However, this value is a best-case scenario given the fact that mental health screening tools almost always have lower sensitivity and specificity values. In the end, one simply runs into a mathematical reality that any attempt to develop selection-based screens for psychological vulnerability would produce too many rejections of individuals who would have otherwise performed well. In this way, the screens would replicate the experiences of World War II. The bottom line is that screening for the purpose of rejecting psychologically vulnerable individuals has a history of being ineffective, and these failures would be repeated in attempts to apply screening for selection purposes.

CARE-BASED SCREENING TO FACILITATE DELIVERY OF CARE

We provide the background on selection-based screening to emphasize that the goals of population-wide screening of those already serving are different from the goals of selection-based screening. On the surface, population-based screening of those already serving may seem equivalent to World War II selection-based screening: It involves assessing a wide variety of mental health symptoms, such as depression, PTSD, and anxiety, for the purposes of identifying those at risk. At a functional level, however, the goal of population-wide screening is to facilitate access to health services, not to identify those who should not join the military. This distinction between screening to facilitate health care (care-based) and screening for selection purposes is critical even though both types of screening may fit under Morrison's (1992) definition of "the examination of a generally healthy population to classify individuals as likely or unlikely to have the condition that is the object of screening" (as cited in Rona et al., 2005, p. 1257).

In the U.S. military, population-wide, care-based screening in response to the wars in Afghanistan and Iraq began in 2003 with the implementation of the Department of Defense Form 2796, the Post-Deployment Health Assessment (PDHA) program, administered immediately on return from deployment. This was later expanded to include the Post-Deployment Health Reassessment (PDHRA) administered 3 to 6 months later. Both programs were designed to facilitate health care delivery.

Screening for the purposes of facilitating mental health care delivery is less controversial than screening for selection purposes, despite a relatively limited amount of data supporting its effectiveness. Using short screens to detect mental health symptoms such as depression or PTSD for the purposes of helping individuals receive care is based on the widely accepted premise that early detection and care for mental health problems is beneficial (Litz, & Gray, 2004). Based on this central tenet, there have been a number of calls to use short screens in primary care settings with the intent of detecting and treating depression and other mental health conditions (Agency for Healthcare

Research and Quality, 2002; Lang & Stein, 2005; McFarlane & Bryant, 2007). For instance, McFarlane and Bryant (2007) stated that "screening [for PTSD] should be considered for high-risk individuals, particularly following a major traumatic event or cumulative exposure" (p. 404). Despite the generally positive attitudes toward care-based screening, it is still worth stepping back and reviewing whether such programs meet generally agreed-on criteria for implementation.

SCREENING PROGRAM CRITERIA

Rona et al. (2005) provided six criteria for determining whether screening programs should be implemented: (a) Identified conditions should be important health problems; (b) screening tests should be clinically, socially, and ethically acceptable; (c) screening tests should be simple, precise, and validated; (d) high-quality research evidence should demonstrate the effectiveness of screening to reduce psychiatric morbidity; (e) adequate staffing and facilities for all aspects of psychological screening programs are critical; and (f) benefits from the screening program should outweigh potential harms. Each criterion is reviewed as follows in terms of postdeployment psychological screening.

Important Health Problems

Postdeployment care-based screening instruments have generally focused on detecting combinations of depression, suicidal and homicidal ideation, relationship problems, alcohol problems, PTSD, sleep problems, and anger problems (Bliese, Wright, Adler, Thomas, & Hoge, 2007). It is well documented that symptoms surrounding these problems are elevated following combat exposure (e.g. Dohrenwend et al., 2006; Hoge et al., 2004); however, Rona et al. (2005) made the valid point that elevated symptom reporting does not necessarily indicate the need for treatment.

It is not exactly clear what constitutes need for treatment in a screening context. More specifically, the question centers on identifying the level at which elevated symptoms constitute a problem necessitating treatment. One option would be to define need for treatment as those individuals who, at the time of screening, needed immediate care. Under the immediate care criterion, the prevalence of clinical disorders is so low (often less than 1%) that Rona et al. (2005) contended that the problems cannot be considered important health problems that can be realistically detected in screening. Clearly, screening for extremely low base-rate problems is impractical, even if there is a strong and well-intentioned desire to identify those needing immediate care because they are either suicidal or homicidal at the time of the screen. It is worth considering, however, whether the goals of detecting suicidal and homicidal service members (albeit imperfectly) might be addressed within a broader definition of what constitutes need for treatment.

An alternative criterion for the need for treatment is the percentage of screened individuals who were determined through the process to have severe enough symptoms to warrant a formal evaluation by a mental health provider. In postcombat studies of the U.S. military, referral rates have generally been high enough to justify screening. For example, Appenzeller, Warner, and Grieger (2007) summarized screening referrals for 12,817 soldiers screened at the PDHRA time point (i.e., 3 to 6 months postdeployment) and reported a mental health referral rate of 11.4%. Appenzeller et al. also reported that referrals for emergency services such as suicidal thoughts were 0.001% (nine of 12,817).

To date, the most comprehensive analysis of referral rates from screening has been conducted by Milliken, Auchterlonie, and Hoge (2007). This study is unique because it assessed both referrals and subsequent mental health visits for 56,350 soldiers over two time points: the PDHA time point (conducted on immediate return) and the PDHRA time point (3 to 6 months later). Milliken et al. reported that 4.4% of the 56,350 soldiers were referred at the PDHA time point and 9.3% were referred at the PDHRA time point. (We comment on this reporting difference across time in a later section.)

Milliken et al. (2007) further reported that 15.8% of the population were seen by mental health services within 90 days of the PDHA screening. Likewise, following the PDHRA screening, 21.8% were seen by mental health services within 90 days. The fact that rates seen by mental health services (15.8% and 21.8%) greatly exceed the rates referred (4.4% and 9.3% for PDHA and PDHRA, respectively) suggests that many soldiers who scored negatively on the screens subsequently self-referred, and usually the self-referral occurred within 30 days of the screen. Although these rates may seem high, particularly those at the PDHRA time point, they have been corroborated by others. In a study conducted at the PDHRA time point, Warner, Appenzeller, Jullen, Warner, and Grieger (2008) reported that 20.7% of previously deployed soldiers had sought care on their return, and Hoge, Auchterlonie, and Milliken (2006) reported that in the year after returning from Iraq, 35% of Iraq war veterans accessed mental health services.

Findings from the Milliken et al. (2007) study may raise questions about the sensitivity of the screens. However, the fact that this study and two others have found that between 11% and 35% of soldiers are seen by a mental health provider suggests that there is a significant need for mental health treatment and there is an important health problem that should be addressed. A substantial percentage of service members returning from a combat deployment have been screened and referred for a mental health interview and many more self-refer.

An interesting aside is that early in the Iraq and Afghanistan conflicts, the mental health burden of combat deployments was largely unknown. Empirical data were sparse; one piece of concrete data was a research report on screening for traumatic stress in one returning unit (Bliese, Wright, Adler, Thomas, & Hoge, 2004). This report noted the low percentage of soldiers meeting the full Mini-International Neuropsychiatric Interview criteria for PTSD (Sheehan et al., 1998). The low rate of PTSD in this small early sample screened within days of returning home from Iraq was incongruent with other research findings beginning to emerge (most notably Hoge et al., 2004) and prompted us to consider the utility of screening U.S. military personnel immediately after they returned from combat. Consequently, we conducted a reassessment of the same soldiers 4 months later and noted a marked increase in symptom reporting in the matched sample of 509 soldiers (Bliese et al., 2007). This follow-up study was a key piece of evidence that lead the Department of Defense to implement the original PDHRA program that screened all service members at 3 to 6 months postdeployment. As noted, Milliken et al. (2007) observed the same pattern, an increase in reported mental health symptoms from PDHA to PDHRA, in their larger sample of 52,350. The early work in PTSD screening also led us to question the value of the A2 criteria (i.e., intense fear, helplessness, or horror in response to a potentially traumatic event) for soldiers who frequently reported that their training "kicked in" when exposed to potentially traumatic events. Details surrounding the value of the A2 criteria for the occupational group of military service members are beyond this chapter but are provided in Adler, Wright, Bliese, Eckford, and Hoge (2008).

In summary, on the basis of an integrated analysis of the research data, we find compelling evidence that the problems facing U.S. service members at postdeployment are important and of sufficient prevalence to warrant screening as long as the criterion centers on overall referrals and not on immediate referrals for suicidal or homicidal thoughts. It is notable that the U.S. rates of postdeployment mental health problems are not necessarily consistent with rates reported elsewhere. Specifically, rates of mental health problems reported by service members in the United Kingdom have been significantly lower than rates reported by U.S. service members (e.g., Hacker Hughes et al., 2005). For instance, Hotopf et al. (2006) reported PTSD rates of 4% among U.K. veterans of Iraq, and Hacker Hughes et al. (2005) reported that 2% of their sample exceeded criteria on a trauma-screening questionnaire. It is not entirely clear why rates in the United Kingdom differed so markedly from U.S. rates; however, a likely explanation is that U.K. service members who deployed to Iraq did so for shorter periods of time (e.g., 4 months; Hacker

Hughes et al., 2005) and to a historically less violent region and so experienced significantly lower levels of combat than U.S. service members (Hoge & Castro, 2006). Indeed, Rona and colleagues (2007) reported that number of months in a combat deployment was a risk factor in the development of PTSD among U.K. service members. Furthermore, an analysis of U.K. data by Iversen et al. (2008) demonstrates the importance of combat experiences, particularly the appraisal of threat to life, in rates of PTSD. Thus, despite the different rates of postdeployment mental health between U.S. and U.K. service members, the same deployment-related factors appear to be important in driving rate elevations, suggesting that differences in rates between U.S. and U.K. service members are not driven by cultural factors.

Screening Tests Should Be Clinically, Socially, and Ethically Acceptable

A series of anonymous postscreening assessments has been conducted to determine whether screening tests are socially acceptable to soldiers. For instance, in 2005 we conducted a screening program evaluation using an anonymous survey of soldiers who had just completed screening. The screened population had returned from a year in Iraq 3 months earlier, and 739 completed the evaluation survey. In the program evaluation survey, 84% of the 739 respondents agreed or strongly agreed that screening could help soldiers get the care they need, 76% agreed or strongly agreed that mental health screening was a good way to take care of soldiers, and only 5% agreed or strongly agreed that mental health screening was a waste of time. We interpret these results as providing strong evidence that soldiers found screening acceptable.

Warner and colleagues (2008), who received anonymous program evaluation results from 2,678 of 3,294 soldiers being screened, conducted a study assessing perceptions of screening. This study focused on preferences for alternative screening approaches related to method, timing, screening personnel, and location and did not explicitly provide program evaluation items like those conducted in our 2005 program evaluation. Examining the results as a whole, the Warner et al. study provided evidence that screening procedures were clinically, socially, and ethically acceptable to soldiers. Indeed, one of Warner et al.'s main conclusions was that screening appeared to help reduce stigma and encourage care.

In considering the ethical nature of screening, perhaps the most important aspect of the screening instruments is that they are intentionally transparent. The instruments contain no checks for truthfulness, faking, or social desirability. Service members can easily identify the response pattern that will allow them to avoid a detailed secondary interview and subsequent referral for mental health problems. From our perspective, this transparency is a central, necessary component in a screening process designed to facilitate care and to provide opportunities for self-referral.

We consider it revealing that even with this transparency, a substantial proportion of service members provide response patterns that obviously lead to in-depth, face-to-face interviews with a clinical provider. Service members' willingness to endorse items indicating mental health concerns demonstrates that the screen is serving its purpose. Specifically, the screen gives service members a tool to raise with a provider a range of mental health and behavior issues, from sleep problems to relationship problems. This transparency also provides those service members who are not interested in receiving help with a simple way to respond, but even in this case, the screening process provides the opportunity for psychoeducation that may lead to help seeking voluntarily at a later date.

Screening Tests Should Be Simple, Precise, and Validated

Conducting validation tests of care-based screening instruments is difficult but possible. Between 2004 and 2005, the research staff at the U.S. Army Medical Research Unit–Europe conducted three validation tests. Two of these involved studies of soldiers who had recently returned home from deployment to Iraq, and one study was conducted predeployment to Iraq. In these three studies, soldiers completed an extensive primary screen that was scored on site. All soldiers with positive scores were subsequently interviewed by a trained provider. In addition, approximately 20% of those with negative scores were randomly selected to participate in a structured interview with a provider. Providers were unaware of the soldiers' responses on the primary screen.

Results of these studies show that it is possible to develop simple, precise, and validated care-based screening instruments. Specifically, Bliese et al. (2008) demonstrated that the PTSD measures used on the PDHA and PDHRA forms had reasonable diagnostic efficiency, and Wright et al. (2007) showed the utility of developing a screening instrument that contains items for distinct domains (i.e., PTSD, depression, and alcohol problems) rather than relying on single screening items or global distress scales.

Despite confirmation that current deployment screening measures are simple, precise, and validated, there are challenges in applying validated instruments developed in controlled settings to a population level. Consequently, it is hard to estimate the diagnostic efficiency of the U.S. screening programs as implemented. Not surprisingly, given the nature of screening in general, our best estimate is that the programs (as implemented) have relatively low specificity and low PPV. In an analysis of PDHA and PDHRA data, Milliken et al. (2007) showed that only approximately 20% of service members who screened positive for PTSD were referred for behavioral health evaluation. There are a variety of potential reasons why most service members who screen positive are not referred, including low severity of symptoms, lack of serious functional impairment, lack of willingness of the service member to receive mental health services, and inconsistencies in how screeners interpret the screening measures and conduct interviews. Nonetheless, it is clear that low predictive values will be an issue when conducting wide-scale, care-based screening.

In short, current screening instruments are valid compared with structured diagnostic interviews, but use of these screening instruments often leads to false positives and low PPVs. The consequences of low PPVs are not as significant in a care-based setting as in a selection setting; nonetheless, plans to implement care-based programs must acknowledge the demand to secondarily assess large numbers of individuals who will ultimately not need care. One way to facilitate the overall process would be to make both the interview and referral process as systematic as possible. In this regard, the *Structured Interview Guide* developed by the WRAIR team to accompany the PDHRA was designed to improve the screening process (see Wright, Adler, Bliese, & Eckford, 2008) by increasing the efficiency and consistency of the secondary interview process.

High-Quality Research Should Demonstrate Effectiveness in Reducing Psychiatric Morbidity

Of all the criteria, this requirement for high-quality research is perhaps the most important and simultaneously the most elusive. At the surface level, it would seem straightforward to design a study in which individuals were randomly selected to either receive screening or not receive screening and then follow these individuals for some period of time to see whether the screening group derives some benefit. The complexity does not revolve around designing the screening intervention itself; rather, it revolves around collecting and interpreting findings. In many randomized trials, it can be relatively simple to interpret results. For instance, in a study of an experimental vaccine, it would be logical to focus primarily on the number of individuals who contracted the disease after having received the vaccine relative to the placebo. The crux of the problem with mental health screening-based interventions is that in the short run the programs should be associated with an increase in care seeking rather than a decline in care seeking, thus making it difficult to rely on decreases in care-seeking rates as an indicator of screening success.

In the long term, successful care-based screening programs should be associated with fewer mental health-related problems and higher levels of functioning. That is, if care-based screening programs are effective, they should lead to early identification and effective treatment, resulting in reduced psychiatric morbidity. In this conceptualization, treatment serves as a direct mediator between screening and longer-term psychiatric morbidity outcomes. If treatments for mental health problems such as PTSD, depression, anger, and alcohol problems are ineffective, this would suggest that screening is also ineffective. In one sense, this conclusion would be accurate because individuals who were correctly identified could not be helped by that intervention; however, this actually relates to treatment effectiveness rather than the screening process specifically. The fact that screening is distally related to psychiatric morbidity through treatment efficacy virtually ensures (in a statistical sense) that any direct link between screening and the outcome will be small, further complicating attempts to detect programmatic effects associated with screening.

Perhaps an equally important way to consider the issue of effectiveness for care-based screening, however, is to focus on its role in reducing outcomes not necessarily mediated through treatment efficacy. For instance, a reduction in stigma associated with seeking mental health care is an important outcome related to developing effective preventive mental health initiatives. The act of providing care-based screening for all individuals may help lower stigma. In an anonymous postscreening survey, Warner et al. (2008) found that 17.8% of soldiers indicated an unwillingness to seek care for mental health problems because of concerns that they would be seen as weak. In contrast, the same stigma item collected in a nonscreening setting had a 35.4% endorsement rate (Hoge et al., 2004). Although the Warner et al. study was not a randomized trial, it nonetheless seems plausible that a process that involves routine mental health evaluations combined with normalization of reactions for all returning service members may help reduce stigma.

In summary, we acknowledge the need to have high-quality research demonstrate the effectiveness of care-based screening; however, we suggest that outcomes such as stigma reduction may be as important as reductions in psychiatric morbidity. A narrow focus on psychiatric morbidity runs the risk of missing the potential benefits of screening programs designed to promote opportunities for self-referral, to facilitate linking individuals with the mental health care system, and to change attitudes about how receiving mental health care is viewed.

Adequate Staffing and Facilities for All Aspects of Psychological Screening Programs Are Critical

In care-based screening interventions, there are three potential bottlenecks related to adequate staffing and facilities. First, the staffing and facilities must be sufficient to perform the actual screening. Second, there must be sufficient staffing and facilities to process the referrals and make a definitive determination about whether care is warranted. Third, there must be sufficient staffing to treat individuals effectively. These criteria, identified by Rona et al. (2005), are important to ensure that the goals of psychological screening programs are met.

Our experience has been that the initial screening process can be executed primarily with existing medical resources organic to army divisions and brigades. The original beta test for the PDHRA program at 3 to 6 months postdeployment was executed with a division of approximately 16,000 soldiers in Europe, using medical staff within the unit augmented with several case managers. Appenzeller et al. (2007) affirmed this approach in a large study of screening implementation in a division in the United States. Thus, it is certainly possible that existing mental health staffing levels are adequate for executing a large-scale screening process with success.

However, although the initial screening process in the United States appears to have been adequately staffed, there has been broad recognition that at some locations there are inadequate numbers of professionals for processing referrals and providing treatment. The Department of Defense Task Force on Mental Health (2007) reported the following:

> Available staffing data and findings from site visits to 38 military installations around the world clearly established that current mental health staff are unable to provide services to active members and their families in a timely manner, do not have sufficient resources to provide newer evidence-based interventions in the manner prescribed, and do not have the resources to provide prevention and training for service members or leaders that could build resilience and ameliorate the long-term adverse effects of extreme stress. (p. 43)

There are many reasons for this shortage, but it is likely that the need to process referrals from care-based screening programs has contributed to the strain on the system. The first stage of the screening process is not designed to provide a definitive diagnosis but to refer individuals for a more thorough evaluation. This processing is analogous to a primary care physician screening patients for depression, conducting a short interview, and then referring them to mental health care for a complete evaluation. The cumulative evidence from a variety of studies reviewed in this chapter indicates that PPVs are typically less than .50, so one would expect that half of those referred do not need definitive care. When service members show up at mental health clinics, however, the full evaluations are more detailed and time consuming than the brief interviews conducted as part of the initial screen.

Clearly, the challenge of providing adequate staffing for the full screening process is ongoing, and given the nature of screening instruments, this challenge is unlikely to be solved simply by improving the psychometrics of the screening instruments. The commitment to screen large groups of service members will always be associated with an increase in referrals, and the only way to mitigate shortages will be to increase the numbers of providers. If mental health professionals are used during the initial screening process, this can reduce their availability to provide effective treatment services.

Benefits From the Screening Program Should Outweigh Potential Harms

In our opinion, care-focused screening has considerably less potential to result in harm than does selection-based screening, particularly when care-focused screening uses transparent items that allow a respondent to self-refer. It is easy to forget that medical systems are complex and that young adult men (the primary population of the military) may not fully appreciate how to navigate these systems and initiate care. At a fundamental level, programs that facilitate bringing care to this population strike us as being beneficial. Care-based screening programs also have the ability to convey to service members that the military acknowledges potential service-related risks and is willing to devote resources to helping ameliorate these risks. This last point may not fit within a traditional medical model of benefit and risk; however, it is certainly important for maintaining morale in an all-volunteer organization.

Care-based screening programs, however, also carry risk. Care-focused screening has the potential to drain resources from where they are needed, thereby reducing the amount of effective care available for service members in need. Screening programs also run the risk of creating an expectation of pathology among service members that could result in iatrogenic effects. Specifically, screening might "medicalize" normal stress reactions that would have otherwise resolved on their own. Low specificity and a high rate of false positives can contribute to inappropriate diagnostic labeling and treatment. It is worth emphasizing that the contextual implications of this misclassification are important. It is, for instance, almost certainly more harmful for an individual to incorrectly believe that he or she was mentally unqualified for a job because of poor specificity on a screen (i.e., selection-based screening) than to be told that he or she might benefit from talking to a mental health professional following an intense combat deployment (i.e., care-based screen). Nonetheless, we cannot definitively conclude that the benefits of care-focused screening outweigh its harms because we have no definitive trails demonstrating program efficacy.

CONCLUSION

When we examine the six criteria as they relate to U.S. military care-based screens, we generally conclude that there is potentially considerable merit to such programs, counterbalanced by concerns that these programs can lead to iatrogenic risks and potentially overwhelm the health care delivery system. Rona et al.'s (2005) conclusion that screening programs have little, if any, value is too simplistic an interpretation of the data and not politically viable, knowing the importance of combat-related mental health problems.

The main reason why Rona et al. (2005) found little value in screening programs is that they approached the topic primarily from a selection-based perspective. Using a selection-based perspective on the six criteria led Rona et al. to question the value of screening. Given the well-documented difficulties with attempting to develop and implement selection-based screens, we concur with their reluctance to support such screens. At a basic level, however, it is important to realize that the overall context of the screening program (i.e., care-based vs. selection-based) has a large impact on how one approaches the six criteria. In general, we believe the consequences of screening attributes such as low PPVs are more of a concern in selection-based screening than in care-based screening.

In the U.S. military, care-based screening will almost certainly continue to be part of the preventive behavioral health program provided to service members. Given that these programs are unlikely to go away, we believe efforts need to continue to ensure that such programs are best able to meet service member needs and fit into the resource realities that face the behavioral health provider community. Research on the diagnostic efficiency of care-based screening alternatives, such as that conducted by Wright et al. (2007), has the potential to increase both the sensitivity and specificity of screens and thereby help facilitate care for those in need.

With this in mind, it is possible that there may be other alternatives to care-based screening in the military that would be as or more effective than current screening. For example, current screening efforts do not emphasize insomnia and sleep disturbance. Sleep disturbance, however, is frequently reported among service members returning from combat. In addition, service members appear to be willing to report sleep disturbance because it carries little behavioral health stigma. And, finally, there is evidence from some of our group's longitudinal studies that sleep disturbance causally precedes problems such as depression and PTSD. Given this background, early care-based screening and treatment for sleep problems may be an excellent way to facilitate behavioral health care.

Another area in which to continue research would be in testing for and reducing the potential for iatrogenic effects associated with screening. For example, screening programs might be integrated into resilience training programs to include overt statements of positive expectations regarding post-deployment mental health, a description of normal mental health effects of combat that do not require intervention, and information about healthy coping techniques. This positive screening approach could be contrasted with current methods to determine whether there were differences in referral rates and in long-term rates of mental health problems.

In conclusion, the debate regarding the role of psychological screening in addressing important public health problems is valuable (e.g., Wright et al., 2005). Such debate encourages critical thinking that can be used to drive programmatic improvements within a particular organizational culture and climate. And yet the debate itself exists in parallel with the needs of a military charged with delivering world-class health care to service members. Given this context, a balance must be maintained between (a) not harming individuals inadvertently and not overwhelming behavioral health resources and (b) implementing a program that actively demonstrates the organization's commitment to caring for service members returning from combat. Properly executed and maintained, we see care-based screening programs as playing a key role in helping deliver behavioral health care.

REFERENCES

Adler, A. B., Wright, K. M., Bliese, P. D., Eckford, R., & Hoge, C. W. (2008). A2 diagnostic criterion for combat-related posttraumatic stress disorder. *Journal of Traumatic Stress, 21*, 301–308. doi:10.1002/jts.20336

Agency for Healthcare Research and Quality. (2002). *Screening for depression: Recommendations and rationale*. Retrieved from http://www.ahrq.gov/clinic/3rduspstf/depression/depressrr.htm

Appenzeller, G. N., Warner, C. H., & Grieger, T. A. (2007). Postdeployment health reassessment: A sustainable method for brigade combat teams. *Military Medicine, 172*, 1017–1023.

Berlien, I. C., & Waggoner, R. W. (1966). Selection and induction. In A. J. Glass & R. J. Bernucci (Eds.), *Neuropsychiatry in World War II: Zone of the interior* (pp. 153–191). Washington, DC: Office of the Surgeon General.

Bliese, P. D., Wright, K. W., Adler, A. B., Cabrera, O. A., Castro, C. A., & Hoge, C. W. (2008). Validating the Primary Care Posttraumatic Stress Disorder screen and the Posttraumatic Stress Disorder Checklist with soldiers returning from combat. *Journal of Consulting and Clinical Psychology, 76*, 272–281. doi:10.1037/0022-006X.76.2.272

Bliese, P. D., Wright, K. M., Adler, A. B., Thomas, J. L., & Hoge, C. M. (2004). *Research report 2004-001: Screening for traumatic stress among redeploying soldiers*. Heidelberg, Germany: U.S. Army Medical Research Unit—Europe.

Bliese, P. D., Wright, K. M., Adler, A. B., Thomas, J. L., & Hoge, C. M. (2007). Timing of postcombat mental health assessments. *Psychological Services, 4*, 141–148. doi:10.1037/1541-1559.4.3.141

Cardona, R., & Ritchie, E. C. (2006). Psychological screening of recruits prior to accession in the U.S. military. In B. L. DeKoning (Ed.), *Textbooks of military medicine: Recruit medicine* (pp. 297–309). Washington, DC: Office of the Surgeon General.

Dohrenwend, B. P., Turner, J. B., Turse, N. A., Adams, B. G., Koenen, K. C., & Marshall, R. (2006, August 18). The psychological risks of Vietnam for U.S. veterans: A revisit with new data and methods. *Science, 313*, 979–982. doi:10.1126/science.1128944

Egan, J. R., Jackson, L., & Eanes, R. H. (1951). A study of neuropsychiatric rejectees. *JAMA, 145*, 466–469.

Glass, A. J. (1966). Lessons learned. In A. J. Glass & R. J. Bernucci (Eds.), *Neuropsychiatry in World War II: Zone of the interior* (pp. 735–759). Washington, DC: Office of the Surgeon General.

Hacker Hughes, J., Cameron, F., Eldridge, R., Devon, M., Wessely, S., & Greenberg, N. (2005). Going to war does not have to hurt: Preliminary findings from the British deployment to Iraq. *The British Journal of Psychiatry, 186*, 536–537. doi:10.1192/bjp.186.6.536

Hoge, C. W., Auchterlonie, J. L., & Milliken, C. S. (2006). Mental health problems, use of mental health services, and attrition from military service after returning from deployment to Iraq or Afghanistan. *JAMA, 295*, 1023–1032. doi:10.1001/jama.295.9.1023

Hoge, C. W., & Castro, C. A. (2006). Posttraumatic stress disorder in U.K. and U.S. forces deployed to Iraq [Letter to the editor]. *The Lancet, 368*, 837. doi:10.1016/S0140-6736(06)69315-X

Hoge, C. W., Castro, C. A., Messer, S. C., McGurk, D., Cotting, D., & Koffman, R. L. (2004). Combat duty in Iraq and Afghanistan, mental health problems, and barriers to care. *The New England Journal of Medicine, 351*, 13–22. doi:10.1056/NEJMoa040603

Hotopf, M., Hull, L., Fear, N. T., Browne, T., Horn, O., Iversen, A., . . . Wessely, S. (2006). The health of U.K. military personnel who deployed to the 2003 Iraq war: A cohort study. *The Lancet, 367*, 1731–1741. doi:10.1016/S0140-6736(06)68662-5

Iversen, A. C., Fear, N. T., Ehlers, A., Hacker Hughes, J., Hull, L., Earnshaw, M., . . . Hotopf, M. (2008). Risk factors for posttraumatic stress disorder among U.K. Armed Forces personnel. *Psychological Medicine, 38*, 511–522. doi:10.1017/S0033291708002778

Lang, A. J., & Stein, M. B. (2005). An abbreviated PTSD checklist for use as a screening instrument in primary care. *Behaviour Research and Therapy, 43*, 585–594. doi:10.1016/j.brat.2004.04.005

Litz, B. T., & Gray, M. J. (2004). Early intervention for trauma in adults. In B. T. Litz (Ed.), *Early intervention for trauma and traumatic loss* (pp. 87–111). New York, NY: Guilford Press.

McFarlane, A. C., & Bryant, R. A. (2007). Posttraumatic stress disorder in occupational settings: Anticipating and managing the risk. *Occupational Medicine*, 57, 404–410. doi:10.1093/occmed/kqm070

Milliken, C. S., Auchterlonie, J. L., & Hoge, C. W. (2007). Longitudinal assessment of mental health problems among active and reserve component soldiers returning from the Iraq War. *JAMA*, 298, 2141–2148. doi:10.1001/jama.298.18.2141

Morrison, A. S. (1992). *Screening in chronic disease* (2nd ed.). New York, NY: Oxford University Press.

Niebuhr, D. W., Cavicchia, M. A., Bedno, S. A., Cowan, D. N., Datu, B. D., Han, W., . . . Weber, N. S. (2008). *AMSARA: Accession medical standards analysis & research activity 2008 annual report* (Defense Technical Information Center Report ADA494071). Retrieved from http://handle.dtic.mil/100.2/ADA494071

Rona, R. J., Fear, N. T., Hull, L., Greenberg, N., Earnshaw, M., Hotopf, M., & Wessely, S. (2007). Mental health consequences of overstretch in the U.K. Armed Forces: First phase of a cohort study. *British Medical Journal.* Retrieved from http://www.bmj.com/cgi/content/full/bmj.39274.585752.BEv1

Rona, R. J., Jones, M., French, C., Hooper, R., & Wessely, S. (2004). Screening for physical and psychological illness in the British Armed Forces: I: The acceptability of the programme. *Journal of Medical Screening*, 11, 148–152. doi:10.1258/0969141041732193

Rona, R. J., Hooper, R., Jones, M., French, C., & Wessely, S. (2004). Screening for physical and psychological illness in the British Armed Forces: III: The value of a questionnaire to assist a medical officer to decide who needs help. *Journal of Medical Screening*, 11, 158–161. doi:10.1258/0969141041732210

Rona, R. J., Hyams, K. C., & Wessely, S. (2005). Screening for psychological illness in military personnel. *JAMA*, 293, 1257–1260. doi:10.1001/jama.293.10.1257

Sheehan, D. V., Lecrubier, Y., Sheehan, K. H., Amorim, P., Janavs, J., Weiller, E., . . . Dunbar, G. C. (1998). The MINI–International Neuropsychiatric Interview (M.I.N.I): The development and validation of a structured interview for *DSM–IV* and *ICD–10. The Journal of Clinical Psychiatry*, 59(Suppl. 20), 22–33.

Terhakopian, A., Sinaii, N., Engel, C. C., Schnurr, P. P., & Hoge, C. W. (2008). Estimating population prevalence of posttraumatic stress disorder: An example using the PTSD Checklist. *Journal of Traumatic Stress*, 21, 290–300. doi:10.1002/jts.20341

U.S. Department of Defense Task Force on Mental Health. (2007). *An achievable vision: Report of the Department of Defense Task Force on Mental Health.* Falls Church, VA: Defense Health Board.

Warner, C. H., Appenzeller, G. N., Jullen, K., Warner, C. M., & Grieger, T. A. (2008). Soldier attitudes toward mental health screening and seeking care upon return from combat. *Military Medicine*, 173, 563–569.

Weathers, F. W., Litz, B. T., Herman, D. S., Huska, J. A., & Keane, T. M. (1993, October). *The PTSD Checklist (PCL): Reliability, validity, and diagnostic utility.*

Paper presented at the annual meeting of the International Society for Traumatic Stress Studies, San Antonio, TX.

Wright, K. M., Adler, A. B., Bliese, P. D., & Eckford, R. D. (2008). Structured clinical interview guide for postdeployment psychological screening programs. *Military Medicine, 173,* 411–421.

Wright, K. M., Bliese, P. D., Adler, A. B., Hoge, C. W., Castro, C. A., & Thomas, J. L. (2005, July). Screening for psychological illness in the military [Letter]. *JAMA, 294,* 42–43. doi:10.1001/jama.294.1.42-b

Wright, K. M., Bliese, P. D., Thomas, J. L., Adler, A. B., Eckford, R. D., & Hoge, C. W. (2007). Contrasting approaches to psychological screening with U.S. combat soldiers. *Journal of Traumatic Stress, 20,* 965–975. doi:10.1002/jts.20279

8

THE PSYCHOLOGICAL RECOVERY OF PHYSICALLY WOUNDED SERVICE MEMBERS

MICHAEL J. ROY AND JENNIFER L. FRANCIS

Staff Sergeant Smith, a 28-year-old army soldier, reported a total of six significant blast exposures during his two deployments to Iraq. Blasts destroyed his vehicle on two different occasions. He transiently lost consciousness after one blast. He has residual shrapnel in his right arm. SSG Smith was medically evacuated from Iraq 10 months ago when an improvised explosive device (IED) explosion resulted in traumatic fractures of his right tibia and fibula as well as multiple fractures of the tarsal bones in his right foot. He has had nine surgeries to date to repair the bones and debride the traumatic wounds, in an attempt to preserve his right leg, but at this point the orthopedists have advised his medical team that the best option for him is to amputate his leg below the knee. SSG Smith has had persistent pain in the leg for months and is distraught at the thought that it has all been for naught. His sleep is impaired by pain as well as by nightmares relating to some of his combat experiences. SSG Smith has been diagnosed with posttraumatic stress disorder (PTSD), and his current medications include sertraline, quetiapine, prazosin, zolpidem, morphine, gabapentin, and naproxen.

—Case history of a wounded U.S. service member
at a major military hospital

The word *trauma* originates from the Greek for *bodily wound*. PTSD and other psychological sequelae often persist long after physical wounds have healed, preventing significant numbers of military service members from enjoying life as they otherwise would have. Although some researchers have

---

The views expressed in this chapter are those of the authors only and are not to be construed as those of the Department of the Army or Department of Defense. This chapter was authored or coauthored by an employee of the United States government as part of official duty and is considered to be in the public domain. Any views expressed herein do not necessarily represent the views of the United States government, and the author's participation in the work is not meant to serve as an official endorsement.

195

considered psychological and physical injuries as distinct entities, there is in fact a considerable body of evidence, both from military and civilian populations, that recovery from physical injuries is dramatically and adversely influenced by the presence of depression, PTSD, or other psychiatric conditions.

In this chapter, we review the available literature addressing the psychological recovery of physically wounded service members, with particular attention to the impact of amputation and traumatic brain injury (TBI) on the risk of PTSD, because these have been the most significant issues in the current conflicts in Iraq and Afghanistan. We then discuss factors influencing psychological recovery after amputation and TBI, and, finally, we address the impact of the physically wounded service member on the functioning of his or her family.

PSYCHOLOGICAL SEQUELAE WITH PHYSICAL INJURY IN A COMBAT SETTING

It is clear that the overall incidence of depression, PTSD, and other anxiety disorders has increased dramatically with deployment to Iraq or Afghanistan (Hoge, Auchterlonie, & Milliken, 2006; Hoge et al., 2004; Smith et al., 2008). However, there remains some controversy about the impact of physical injury on the risk of PTSD in the combat setting. On the one hand, some have argued that physical injury decreases the risk of PTSD because the physical injuries provide a focus for anxious energy, garner greater sympathy from others, and often lead to evacuation from theater, removing the injured from further threat or traumatization (Koren, Hemel, & Klein, 2006). Studies that have found relatively low rates of PTSD in wounded service members have supported this perspective (Merbaum & Hefez, 1976).

On the other hand, significant physical injury might bring home the reality of the life-threatening circumstances confronting the service member. Numerous studies have identified high rates of PTSD in injured civilian trauma survivors (Koren, Arnon, & Klein, 1999; Michaels et al., 1999; Shalev, Peri, Canetti, & Schreiber, 1996; Ursano et al., 1999), and injured Vietnam War veterans were reported to have two to three times the rate of PTSD as their noninjured fellow combatants (Pitman, Altman, & Macklin, 1989). More recently, Israeli researchers conducted a matched, case control study to directly compare 60 injured and 40 noninjured combat veterans. PTSD was diagnosed in 16.7% of the injured veterans compared with 2.5% of the noninjured; all PTSD subscale scores were significantly higher in the injured population (Koren, Norman, Cohen, Berman, & Klein, 2005). The authors noted that the 8-fold elevation in risk of PTSD attributable to physical injury may well be an underestimate because 35% of the injured soldiers (and none of the noninjured) declined participation for reasons that suggested avoidance.

In addition, mood-related disorders were identified in 36.4% of the injured compared with only 3.4% of the controls.

Koren et al. (2006) hypothesized three potential pathophysiological mechanisms to explain why physical injury might increase the likelihood of PTSD. First, there may be a direct effect of physical injury on PTSD whereby physical injury heightens the activation of the hypothalamic–pituitary–adrenal (HPA) axis and/or other endogenous pathways. The HPA axis is altered in many patients with PTSD, with studies documenting evidence such as lower baseline cortisol levels (Marshall & Garakani, 2002; Simeon et al., 2007), though further work is needed in this area. Second, the physical injury may activate mediators responsible for the link between physical injury and PTSD. That is, physical injury might be responsible for activating additional pathways other than those initially stimulated by the trauma. For example, substance P, endogenous opioids, and proinflammatory cytokines are potential mediators of the impact of physical trauma on psychological well-being, but again additional research is necessary to document the specific relationship between physical and psychological trauma and such factors. Third, injury might block the body's efforts to recover from the initial perturbations of such pathways that were induced by the trauma. For example, physical injuries and PTSD-related nightmares can interfere with sleep, adversely affecting both physical and psychological recovery.

Besides these three pathophysiological explanations, coping style is also an important variable in understanding the physical injury–PTSD link. An interesting study of civilian motor vehicle accident victims used diagnostic interviews at baseline and again 1, 6, and 12 months later to assess independent predictors of the development of PTSD symptoms (Dougall, Ursano, Posluszny, Fullerton, & Baum, 2001). Those with PTSD symptoms at 1 month actually had fewer severe injuries than those without PTSD symptoms, whereas there was no relationship between injury severity and PTSD at 6 and 12 months. Among demographic variables, the only association was that women were more likely to have PTSD symptoms at 1 and 6 months, and after regression analyses even this difference only remained significant at 1 month. Perception of a high degree of threat associated with the accident was an independent predictor of PTSD symptoms, but by far the strongest independent predictor was a coping style utilizing wishful thinking. According to the researchers, those who engage in wishful thinking often report wishing that a miracle would happen, that they could change what happened or how they felt, and that the situation would go away. They went on to postulate that such individuals might get wrapped up in this thinking or fantasizing in lieu of developing more positive coping mechanisms. Coping mechanisms need to be evaluated in other settings and with combat veterans to determine whether these findings can be replicated.

IMPACT OF PSYCHOLOGICAL DISORDERS ON OUTCOMES

There is a robust literature to document the adverse impact that PTSD and other psychological conditions have on functional status after injury. Most notably, the Trauma Recovery Project, a large, prospective epidemiologic study, was established to assess psychological and functional outcomes after significant physical trauma. Postinjury depression and PTSD, along with serious extremity injury and length of stay in the hospital, were found to be significantly associated with poor functional status at 6 months after injury. The identified associations persisted at 12 and 18 months after injury in this study of 1,048 patients with trauma (Holbrook, Anderson, Sieber, Browner, & Hoyt, 1999).

Another group of researchers found that the onset of PTSD was independently and inversely related to general health outcome 6 months later, assessed by the well-validated Short Form 36 (Michaels et al., 1999). After following patients with trauma for a full year, they also found that the development of PTSD, depression, or substance abuse was associated with poorer work status, poorer general health, and poorer overall satisfaction with recovery (Michaels et al., 2000). Thus, although Grieger et al. (2006) showed that physical injury adversely impacted psychological health, the converse is also true: Psychological injury adversely impacts physical health and overall functional status. It is important for physicians to be cognizant of this relationship and to be sure to address both body and mind throughout the care of returning service members.

In light of recent military operations, two categories of physical injuries deserve particular attention with regard to their impact on the psychological well-being of the military service member: TBI and amputations. Although these conditions occasionally coexist, we could identify no reports in the medical literature to date that address the comorbidity of TBI and amputation, so each are reviewed separately in this chapter.

Traumatic Brain Injury

TBI is a broad category, ranging from massive head injuries and prolonged coma to transient or no loss of consciousness with a feeling of being dazed or confused in the aftermath of a blast. Differentiation of TBI severity remains a matter of considerable debate, but one method of classification identifies mild TBI as that with no more than 30 min loss of consciousness (LOC), moderate TBI as that with more than 30 min LOC but no more than 24 hr, and severe TBI as that with more than 24 hr LOC. Unfortunately, some studies and corresponding publications do not clearly delineate the severity of TBI included in the sample and tend to lump all categories together, but when it is clear we identify the severity in this chapter.

In fact, the definition of mild TBI is especially problematic when considered in light of its relationship to PTSD and other psychological disorders. First, there is not yet a clear consensus on either the definition of mild TBI or the best instrument to use for diagnosis. In a mail survey of 2,235 U.S. military personnel returning from Iraq and Afghanistan, 12% of respondents indicated a history consistent with mild TBI, whereas 11% were positive for PTSD (Schneiderman, Braver, & Kang, 2008). In this population, even if overlapping symptoms were removed from the PTSD score, PTSD was more closely associated with residual TBI symptoms than any other factor. A similar pattern was found in survivors of motor vehicle accidents, indicating that postconcussive symptoms of mild TBI may be mediated by the interaction of neurological and psychological factors (Bryant & Harvey, 1999). Our own experience in an ongoing study is that the mild end of the TBI spectrum is particularly difficult to define because some of the persistent symptoms that have been attributed to mild TBI, including headaches, dizziness, memory problems, irritability, and sleep problems, are commonly reported by those with PTSD and other psychological conditions, and the identification of mild TBI in the absence of PTSD or related psychological disorders is exceedingly rare.

One instrument, the Defense and Veterans Brain Injury Center (DVBIC) TBI Screening Tool, incorporates the presence of such persistent symptoms as headaches, dizziness, memory problems, balance problems, tinnitus, irritability, and sleep problems in attempting to define mild TBI. Although the utility of the DVBIC instrument has been described in a small initial study of active duty service members who served in Iraq or Afghanistan (Schwab et al., 2006), how to establish the significance of being dazed or confused, or not remembering the injury, remains highly problematic. It is hard with such simple questions to identify a clear threshold that distinguishes inevitable surprise at being hit by a rocket propelled grenade or IED from significant confusion that represents likely concussive injury. Moreover, if persistent symptoms such as sleep or memory problems are temporally related to a blast exposure, are they manifestations of TBI or of PTSD? At present, there is really no way to discern this with any degree of confidence. Moreover, it is often difficult for service members to distinguish whether they were thrown to the ground by the force of a blast or went to the ground voluntarily as a reflex protective measure, and sometimes it is even hard to know whether they lost consciousness (e.g., some were asleep at the time of an explosion) and, if so, for how long. In the heat of battle or in the face of an explosion the most compelling needs are to carry out the mission and to protect oneself and one's buddies. Thus, asking about what symptoms were experienced, and for what duration, months or even years after the incident is not surprisingly a fool's errand. This results in widely varying estimates of TBI prevalence after deployment to Iraq and Afghanistan, from a fraction of a percentage up to a third of all service members.

TBI is really a point-of-injury diagnosis, based on what happened at the scene, whereas psychological conditions are largely based on persistence of symptoms over time. In this regard, two conditions, postconcussional disorder (PCD) and postconcussional syndrome (PCS), are worth commenting on because they represent persistent symptoms analogous to psychological disorders. PCD is identified in the *Diagnostic and Statistical Manual of Mental Disorders* (4th ed.; *DSM–IV*; American Psychiatric Association, 1994) as an area in which further research is necessary, with current evidence insufficient to support it as a diagnostic entity. The proposed *DSM–IV* criteria for PCD requires the history of a head trauma, followed by the onset of at least three of the following symptoms, which were not present prior to the trauma and have persisted at least 3 months: fatigue, headache, sleep disturbance, dizziness, irritability, anxiety or depression, personality changes, or apathy.

By comparison, the World Health Organization's (WHO) *International Classification of Diseases* (10th ed.; *ICD–10*; WHO, 1993) includes criteria for PCS that are less restrictive, only requiring a history of TBI and three or more of the following eight symptoms: headache, dizziness, fatigue, irritability, insomnia, difficulty with concentration, memory problems, and intolerance of stress, emotion, or alcohol. Because *DSM–IV* requires for a diagnosis of TBI that the head trauma cause significant cerebral concussion along with quantifiable impairment in memory or attention, it is not surprising that a study directly comparing the two sets of criteria for mild TBI found that the *ICD–10* criteria were met 3 times more frequently. However, neither set of criteria is ready for clinical use without further research. In fact, the WHO (1992) acknowledged the following in the description of PCS:

> These symptoms may be accompanied by feelings of depression or anxiety, resulting from some loss of self-esteem and fear of permanent brain damage. Such feelings enhance the original symptoms and a vicious circle results. Some patients become hypochondriacal, embark on a search for diagnosis and cure, and may adopt a permanent sick role. The etiology of these symptoms is not always clear, and both organic and psychological factors have been proposed to account for them. The nosological status of this condition is thus somewhat uncertain. There is little doubt, however, that this syndrome is common and distressing to the patient. (p. 67)

Perhaps as a result, most researchers continue to simply refer to the overall, albeit ill-defined, category of TBI rather than using either PCS or PCD.

Moderate to severe TBI appears to have an effect that is similar to that of other serious medical conditions, such as stroke or myocardial infarction: There is a significantly elevated risk of depression or other psychiatric disorder. Several studies document that at least one quarter to one half of those with TBI has major depression (Jorge et al., 2004; Kennedy et al., 2005; Seel et al., 2003).

However, moderate to severe TBI may, at least initially, provide some protection against the development of PTSD by obscuring the memory of the traumatic event. Further evaluation is necessary to better delineate the relationship between the severity of TBI and the risk of PTSD. In addition, it is important to emphasize the need for close attention to, and repeated formal assessment for, the potential evolution of PTSD symptoms as rehabilitation progresses and memory improves in individuals with moderate to severe TBI. A combination of serial neuropsychological testing along with the use of validated instruments such as the Clinician Administered PTSD Scale for PTSD (Blake et al., 1995) and Beck Depression Inventory (Beck, Steer, & Brown, 1996) or Patient Health Questionnaire for depression (Kroenke, Spitzer, & Williams, 2001) is advisable to best sort out improvement in TBI and potential onset of psychological disorders.

We are currently engaged in an effort to use functional magnetic resonance imaging to distinguish between service members returning from Iraq and Afghanistan with mild TBI alone, PTSD alone, both combined, or neither. However, it is too early at this point to say whether this approach will prove fruitful. What we have seen thus far is that mild TBI is rare in the absence of PTSD, suggesting that those who experience significant persistent symptoms after a blast exposure that does not result in more than transient loss of consciousness should have a thorough evaluation for PTSD and other psychological sequelae. This may be particularly beneficial to the individual patient because there is evidence-based treatment for PTSD, depression, and related conditions, which is not necessarily the case for mild TBI. A recent study supported this interpretation, identifying a significant association between mild TBI and psychiatric symptoms, including PTSD, in more than 40% of those who had loss of consciousness (Hoge et al., 2008). In fact, the investigators noted that the high rates of physical symptoms reported by soldiers could be attributed to PTSD and depression and that when these conditions were included in the analyses, there was no direct relationship between mild TBI and physical health problems (with the exception of a connection between those who had headaches and loss of consciousness). In addition, for two thirds of those in the study who met criteria for mild TBI, the diagnosis was based on an affirmative response to a question about whether they felt dazed or confused at the time of the injury.

The findings in our current study are similar; the question of feeling dazed or confused at the time of injury seems to capture large numbers of individuals who experience PTSD and depression related to blast exposure, but at least at this point in time, there is no evidence that this question distinguishes a unique category of patients with mild TBI who can be differentiated from others with PTSD or depression, regardless of whether there is any physical injury. Still more interesting and compelling is a recent study of hospitalized civilian trauma victims which compared 90 patients initially diagnosed with mild TBI to 85 non-brain-injured patients with trauma and found identical rates of PCS in both groups (Meares et al., 2008). These results suggest no relationship between actual brain injury and subsequent symptomatology; moreover, the strongest predictor of PCS was in fact a prior mood or anxiety disorder, with an odds ratio of 5.76.

Studies attempting to assess recovery from mild TBI indicate that overall it is a gradual process, with the majority of the cognitive recovery occurring in the first 6 months, and approximately 70% to 80% of individuals having few postinjury problems (Veterans Health Initiative, 2004). However, the remaining 20% to 30% have residual symptoms and impaired function associated with psychiatric symptoms (Veterans Health Initiative, 2004). Although depression, anxiety, and behavioral problems are commonly identified following TBI (Hoofien, Gilboa, Vakil, & Donovick, 2001; Kim et al., 2007), it is exceedingly difficult to discern whether persistent emotional and behavioral symptoms are directly related to the neurological damage, a secondary reaction to the cognitive deficits of the injury, or a comorbid psychological complication of the trauma itself (Prigatano, 2005).

A meta-analysis of the available medical literature on the impact of mild TBI across various cognitive domains raises some doubts regarding the likelihood that persistent difficulties can be attributed directly to the impact of mild TBI (Belanger, Curtiss, Demery, Lebowitz, & Vanderploeg, 2005). The investigators identified greater cognitive sequelae of mild TBI in clinic-based populations (i.e., convenience samples, or those seeking medical care for their symptoms) as well as in those individuals involved in litigation, as opposed to unselected or prospective samples. Litigation in particular was associated with stable or worsening cognitive function over time, which is perhaps not surprising—whether subconscious or not, functional improvement would presumably lessen reimbursement from pending litigation, serving as a disincentive to recovery.

In contrast, the investigators also found that studies with unselected populations or prospective designs found no evidence of residual neuropsychological impairment 3 months after injury. In an exception, one longitudinal study of veterans compared long-term neuropsychological outcomes in those with self-reported mild TBI after a motor vehicle accident with those who had a motor vehicle accident without TBI and those who had not had an accident. These comparisons were made an average of 8 years after the accidents had occurred (Vanderploeg, Curtiss, & Belanger, 2005). Comprehensive neuropsychological testing identified no significant differences between the three groups, though the authors argued that minor, borderline differences on the Paced Auditory Serial Learning Addition Test (Gronwall, 1977) and California Verbal Learning Test (Delis, Kramer, Kaplan, & Ober, 1987) suggested potential subtle attentional problems in the mild TBI population. Although this finding might indicate potential long-term adverse neuropsychological effects of mild TBI, it is quite conceivable that such differences are entirely due to psychiatric comorbidity, which should be carefully assessed in any studies that evaluate the impact of mild TBI. Regardless of the pathogenesis, it is clear that the residual emotional and behavioral changes have a significant impact on adjustment, including employment and social relationships (Draper, Ponsford, & Schonberger, 2007). Several factors influence this adjustment, such as injury severity (Tate & Broe, 1999), social support (Pelletier & Alfano, 2000), premorbid functioning (Godfrey & Smith, 1995), and coping styles (Kendall & Terry, 1996). For example, coping strategies such as avoidance, wishful thinking, worry, and self-blame are associated with higher levels of depression and anxiety in patients with TBI (Anson & Ponsford, 2006; Curran, Ponsford, & Crowe, 2000; Finset & Andersson, 2000). Coping strategies are an area that can be targeted for treatment intervention (Anson & Ponsford, 2006).

A recent systematic review of treatment for mild TBI found methodological limitations to the available literature, though there was some evidence to suggest potential benefit with educational interventions shortly after injury, particularly with those interventions that focus on providing accurate information about expected symptomatology (Freguson, Mittenberg, Barone, & Schneider, 1999). Thus, although there is considerable room for additional research in both the diagnosis and treatment of TBI, the effectiveness of treatment interventions in the military setting needs to be examined in returning soldiers (Lew et al., 2008). At first glance the military would appear to have the much-needed structure to assist soldiers who are struggling with poor concentration, attention, and memory. However, even with routine, things can go awry as one struggles with postdeployment issues. Military structure can be relatively unforgiving of mistakes, forgetfulness, or poor attention to detail, and soldiers may receive a counseling statement (i.e., an administrative document in the personnel file that can be considered a warning) or an Article 15 (i.e., nonjudicial military discipline) for infractions related to their symptoms. This punitive response can lead to increased psychosocial stress, which exacerbates existing symptoms and may contribute to further maintenance of TBI symptoms. Rank structure can be an additional complication because military hierarchy demands more from those of higher rank. Anecdotally, some higher ranking soldiers have reported trying to "pass" as if they are not having difficulties to preserve pride and to meet expectations they believe are being placed on them. Intervention research may also need to include specific education for military leaders in how to handle TBI symptoms in the workplace as more soldiers resume their military duties.

Limb Amputation

Traumatic loss of one or more limbs is a frequent, some would even say signature, wound in the Global War on Terror. This is in part due to the nature of IEDs, but it is also a testament to the success of protective measures that have left the torso relatively unscathed as well as a testament to the quality of medical care. Just as prior wars have resulted in significant medical advances that have benefited society at large, amputee care and the quality of prostheses has improved dramatically as a result of the efforts to provide amputees with maximum function and mobility. Amputees are remaining on active duty and making valuable contributions to the war effort in ways that were simply not conceived of in prior wars. However, loss of a limb neverthe-less profoundly influences one's self-image and can be associated with psychological sequelae.

Depression is not uncommon following amputation, and a review of the literature found evidence for a bimodal peak (Horgan & MacLachlan, 2004). Individuals within 2 years after amputation had depression rates ranging from 30% to 58%, a prevalence comparable with that in individuals who experienced a severe medical complication such as a heart attack or stroke. Elevated rates (22% to 28%) were also seen among individuals 10 to 20 years after amputa-tion, though individuals 2 to 10 years postamputation had rates of depression no greater than the general population. Anxiety has not been as thoroughly assessed after amputation, but the available evidence indicates high initial rates that diminish within 2 years after amputation. Recent studies have reaffirmed high prevalence rates for depression and anxiety following ampu-tation (Atherton & Robertson, 2006), especially in those with phantom or residual limb pain (Desmond & MacLachlan, 2006). In summary, although psychological symptoms appear to be a common reaction following amputation, methodological weaknesses such as cross-sectional designs and self-report outcome measures limit confidence, and there is a need for well-designed longitudinal studies.

Horgan and MacLachlan (2004) identified mixed results regarding an association between phantom limb pain and psychological conditions, with some evidence that depression is more common in those with more persistent pain, an association similar to the one that has been shown between depression and chronic pain of diverse etiologies. However, there is no convincing evidence of an association between the cause of the amputation (usually trauma vs. vascular disease) and particular psychological sequelae. Nor is there evidence that demographic factors such as age and gender significantly influence psycho-logical adjustment to amputation.

A number of cognitive factors that do impact adjustment to amputation have been identified. Body image is one of the more salient factors. Rybarczyk,

Nyenhuis, Nicholas, Cash, and Kaiser (1995) developed the Amputation Related Body Image Scale (ARBIS) to specifically assess body image in amputees. The ARBIS contains questions such as "I avoided looking at my prosthesis" and "I thought that my prosthesis was ugly." Using this instrument, the investigators found an association between adjustment to amputation and depressive symptoms. Additionally, overall body image of amputees predicted quality of life, depression, and self-rated health. Dimensions that are closely tied to body image such as self-consciousness and perceived stigma also play a role in adjustment. Individuals with an amputation who have more public self-consciousness are more likely to be distressed (Atherton & Robertson, 2006) and have increased risk of functional disability (Williamson, 1995). Perceived stigma—the belief that others hold negative attitudes toward one because of the disability—is also associated with depressive symptoms (Rybarczyk et al., 1995). In laboratory studies, individuals without disability demonstrate behavioral avoidance when interacting with individuals with disabilities (Snyder, Kleck, & Strenta, 1979).

Further research is needed to determine whether physically wounded service members have the same perceptions as civilian amputees. The acuity and severity of the trauma; the need for immediate medical attention, often compounded by the need for removal from imminent continuing danger and long-distance evacuation; and the frequent need for multiple surgical procedures all may diminish the focus on body image during the initial periods of adjustment. In addition, proximity to other amputees in the context of the military medical setting may normalize body image concerns and reduce the likelihood of perceived stigma during the initial period of adjustment.

We know little about other variables that may be important to understanding adjustment to amputation in military personnel. For example, concerns about independence and physical prowess may prove more important than body image. Technological advances in prosthetics and rehabilitation, including the use of virtual reality, make it possible to more closely approximate prior levels of function, in turn enabling consideration of a much wider range of activities, including remaining on active duty. Striving for these goals with the benefit of the camaraderie and spirit inherent in the military environment may trump concerns about appearance. However, military service members may also be more reluctant to acknowledge concerns about body image because of feelings of guilt or stigmatization. Research must first establish a better understanding of the significance of such complex factors involved in the adjustment to amputation and then develop and evaluate corresponding therapeutic interventions.

Just as for TBI, coping styles are a mediator of emotional distress and are significantly associated with improved well-being and psychosocial adjustment after amputation (Desmond, 2007; Desmond & MacLachlan, 2006). Livneh,

Antonak, and Gerhardt (2000) espoused a three-dimensional model: active/confronting approaches as opposed to passive/avoidant coping styles on the first axis, optimistic/positivistic coping versus pessimistic/fatalistic on the second, and social/emotional versus cognitive on the third axis. Each axis is best viewed as a spectrum, and some have more distinct differences than others.

Given that the first axis is the most sharply delineated, we focus on the importance of active versus passive coping style in understanding recovery from amputation. Active coping, planning, positive reframing, and acceptance are on the adaptive end, and alcohol and drug use, disengagement, self-criticism, and social withdrawal are at the maladaptive end. Actively addressing problems is associated with improved psychosocial outcomes (Livneh et al., 2000), whereas avoidance is associated with increased psychological distress and poor adjustment (Desmond, 2007). The need to identify positive aspects of coping was also highlighted by Dunn (1996). Dunn examined three cognitive coping styles: finding positive meaning in amputation, perceiving control over amputation, and adopting a positive outlook. All three had an inverse relationship with the level of depressive symptoms. The incorporation of these ideas into rehabilitation strategies may be beneficial.

Adjustment to amputation can also be examined as a series of phases or stages (Livneh & Sherwood, 1991). Loss of a limb has been compared with grieving (Parkes, 1975), and Kubler-Ross's (1969) five stages of grief, initially a conceptualization of the process that a dying patient goes through when informed of his or her prognosis, has potential relevance in the case of amputees or other injured individuals as well. The first stage is *denial*, in which individuals refuse to acknowledge that they have such a condition. The second stage is *anger*, when individuals might lash out verbally or in other ways against those around them, out of frustration with their condition. The third stage is *bargaining*, in which individuals might promise to do something better in return for resolution or improvement in their condition. The fourth stage is *depression*, when individuals seem to give up hope to a certain extent, becoming more passive about their condition. Finally, there is *acceptance*, when individuals seem ready to acknowledge the condition they have and are ready to move on in as productive a manner as possible. Physicians and psychologists should not expect that all amputees will go through each of these stages or that amputees will experience these stages in a consistent sequence, but an understanding of these stages as potential reactions may help to better assist amputees in their efforts to cope with their loss of limb(s).

The Amputee Coalition of America (2005) describes six phases in the process of recovery after amputation: enduring, suffering, reckoning, reconciling, normalizing, and thriving. *Enduring* occurs as the individual is getting through the surgery and pain. *Suffering* is a phase of questioning and experiencing emotion related to the loss. *Reckoning* is coming to terms with the implications of the loss. The final three phases (i.e., *reconciling, normalizing,* and *thriving*) symbolize positive aspects of change, including putting the loss in perspective, reordering priorities, and living life to the fullest. Again, it is important to reiterate that not all patients will experience all these stages, and some patients may experience elements of more than one phase simultaneously. Further studies are needed to assess the validity of these models in the military population, but it can be a useful framework for clinicians to use in working with injured service members. Among the positive aspects of the Amputee Coalition model is that it focuses on adaptive functioning and providing specific behavioral descriptions of adjustment. It provides a mechanism for beginning to understand what amputees are going through emotionally and provides some hope for improvement in those who are having more difficulty. However, this is a broad brush, and the individuality of each amputee, both physically and emotionally, must be taken into account in the development of specific, realistic, and attainable goals.

IMPACT OF PHYSICALLY WOUNDED SERVICE MEMBERS ON THEIR FAMILIES

Although the tremendous impact that caring for wounded service members has on families is well recognized, there is little empirical research addressing the emotional impact the returning soldiers have on their families. Several factors have the potential to increase stress reactions and affect coping resources in military families: disruption of family dynamics already induced by the deployment, the young age of many service members and their spouses (if married), and the loss of military environment and culture (Collins & Kennedy, 2008). Although not explicitly limited to military families, one study of the impact of having a father with PTSD on other family members was recently conducted in Bosnia and Herzegovina, where most of the male population fought in the civil war (Zalihić, Zalihić, & Pivic, 2008). In comparison with control families, depression was more common in wives in the PTSD families. The impact of fathers with PTSD on their children was profound, resulting in the children missing more school, being more easily upset, having greater eating and breathing problems, and experiencing more abdominal pain.

Indeed, it is well documented that PTSD symptoms compound difficulties in family adjustment following war zone deployments (Evans, McHugh, Hopwood, & Watt, 2003; Galovski & Lyons, 2004). In addition, the physical, cognitive, emotional, and behavioral changes experienced by physically wounded service members directly affect the family. For example, there are often changes in family roles, an increase in financial burden, a loss of intimacy, and a loss of employment due to changes in functioning (Curtiss, Klemz, & Vanderploeg, 2000). Some unique aspects of military culture also influence the impact that PTSD might have on families. Large military communities such as Fort Bragg, North Carolina, and Fort Hood, Texas, can provide built-in support structures composed of other families who understand the impact of deployment-related stressors, but this is a trade-off because the posts are often far from their family of origin, diminishing that potential source of support. In fact, many families from remote posts such as Fort Riley, Kansas, have elected to return to their families of origin in instances when the military units deployed to Iraq for a year and knew that they would be deployed again after only 1 year at home. The resulting prolonged geographic separation, wherein service members might only see their family for a month of vacation over a 3-year period, can greatly exacerbate intrafamily conflict and may make it even more difficult for family members to appreciate the impact that physical or psychological injuries might be having on the life of a service member. Not surprisingly, divorce rates have been significantly higher in such instances. Significant physical injuries such as moderate to severe TBI and amputation may exacerbate matters if prolonged hospitalization and/or repeated surgical intervention is required, especially if performed at distant facilities, perpetuating the estrangement of service members and their families. Military medical centers do have some housing available for family members, including Fisher Houses, specifically established for this purpose, but prolonged separation from home, school, and/or employment may not be practical for many families.

Dealing with moderate to severe TBI is a particular challenge. Caregivers of persons with more severe TBI have been found to demonstrate significant emotional distress in response to the traumatic injury (Brooks, 1991; Florian, Katz, & Lahav, 1991; Kreutzer, Marwitz, & Kepler, 1992). Some family members already had a history of emotional distress and maladaptive family functioning prior to the impact of moderate to severe TBI (Sander, 2005). Nevertheless, a focus on family adjustment is important because it correlates with the length and degree of recovery from the injury (Serio, Kreutzer, & Gervasio, 1995). Basic education regarding symptoms of brain injury and an understanding of the emotional and behavioral consequences of moderate to severe TBI and how to manage them is extremely important, particularly in long-term management (Larøi, 2003; Rotondi, Sinkule, Balzer, Harris, & Moldovan, 2007). Specific educational elements geared toward children should be considered, and some, such as educational coloring books, have already been implemented by the military, although a study of their efficacy would be useful. Without proper education, family members may personalize and blame the individual with any grade of TBI for symptoms such as frequent fatigue, lack of motivation, memory loss, or angry outbursts.

With regard to marital relationships, high rates of divorce and separation after moderate to severe TBI have been reported (Wood & Yurdakul, 1997), and as alluded to earlier, marital problems are already a challenge for military families due to the high operations tempo in recent years. A variety of factors are associated with relationship satisfaction, including the severity of the injury, the duration of the relationship, and time since injury. In a study examining relationships in the face of severe TBI, patient mood swings were a strong predictor in dissolution of the relationship (Wood, Liossi, & Wood, 2005). Interventions oriented toward families have typically been educational, supportive, or therapy-based, but little evidence is available to document the effectiveness of such approaches (Sander, 2005). Some limited data support the utility of educating family members regarding moderate to severe TBI, and teaching behavioral management techniques for use with injured service members may also be effective (Sander, 2005), but future research examining family interventions is warranted. We are currently working on an Internet-based intervention featuring educational elements targeted toward improving knowledge and generating behavioral changes in family members, using before and after testing to assess efficacy.

FUTURE DIRECTIONS

Psychological conditions, including depression, PTSD, and other anxiety disorders, are common after physical injury in a combat setting. Physicians seeing combat veterans in military hospitals, Veterans Affairs facilities, and elsewhere need to be aware of, and screen for, these conditions because physical outcomes are significantly worse when the psychological conditions are present. Effective psychological treatments are available, and treatment should proceed alongside treatment of the physical complications of war, rather than being set aside until after the medical complications are addressed, to most rapidly and effectively improve the functional status of patients. Given the significance that coping strategies appear to have in TBI, amputations, and other physical injuries, cognitive behavior therapy (CBT), which in part seeks to identify and implement more effective coping strategies, is likely to be particularly valuable. CBT has been shown to be effective in a wide range of medical conditions that frequently have comorbid psychological disorders, but its efficacy should be specifically studied in this population. There is a growing body of literature addressing various aspects of the care of injured service members, including psychological comorbidity, but there is a glaring need for well-designed studies seeking to validate and improve on diagnostic and therapeutic modalities.

The focus of this chapter has been on the psychological recovery of physically wounded soldiers, but it can be difficult to fully grasp what the impact of war looks like in returning soldiers, until you have seen it firsthand. As clinicians at Walter Reed Army Medical Center, we often represent the first mental health encounter for soldiers, as well as definitive medical and psychiatric care. It is clear that the consequences of war do not end when one leaves the battlefield. It may require 10, 20, or more trips to the operating room, as surgical teams battle to preserve a shrapnel-riddled limb. However, the psychological impact of the war, and threatened or actual loss of limb, career, and livelihood, is invariably of even greater impact and duration, so it should come as no surprise that at least as many visits to a mental health professional may be necessary to support psychological recovery. It is important to have well-integrated, holistic, multidisciplinary care that considers the entire context of the service member and his or her injuries, and includes their family and unit structure, to achieve successful outcomes.

REVISITING THE CASE OF "SSG SMITH": BATTLING THE CONSEQUENCES OF INJURY

Although the name and some other details have been changed to protect the confidentiality of the individual, a patient similar to SSG Smith presented to us for evaluation, and a diagnosis of PTSD was confirmed. SSG Smith's constant pain and use of crutches were daily reminders of the life-threatening IED explosion he experienced in Iraq. From the moment he awoke until the moment he went to bed, these thoughts did not escape him. Civilians did not have any qualms about asking him what happened to his leg. Multiple times over the course of a typical day SSG Smith found himself providing some semblance of an answer, waffling between the truth and jest to avoid getting angry and saying something he might regret. Sometimes his thoughts would race, jumping from elements of his Iraq experiences to questions about whether to proceed with his amputation. Many days it was just easier to not get out of bed to avoid it all.

SSG Smith was treated with virtual reality exposure therapy, following a protocol that incorporates multiple cognitive behavioral techniques including activity scheduling, cognitive restructuring, imaginal and in vivo exposure, and immersion in a "virtual Iraq" environment. SSG Smith learned about his symptoms and the connection between trauma, PTSD, and depression. While undergoing exposure, SSG Smith was also learning to examine his thought patterns through use of cognitive techniques. Many of his thoughts involved worry about whether to have the amputation. He learned to break down these thoughts, evaluate them, and examine the pros and cons of having the amputation. He ultimately decided to undergo the amputation and described a sense of relief with the decision. After four 90-min sessions, he began to demonstrate significant improvement in his PTSD symptoms, which progressed to remission despite the intervening loss of his leg. SSG Smith's treatment focused on exposure and cognitive work that incorporated a direct focus on his physical wounds. The physical wounds of soldiers from Operation Iraqi Freedom and Operation Enduring Freedom are tightly interwoven with their trauma symptoms and cannot be ignored.

REFERENCES

American Psychiatric Association. (1994). *Diagnostic and statistical manual of mental disorders* (4th ed.). Washington, DC: Author.

Amputee Coalition of America. (2005). *First step: A guide for adapting to limb loss*. Retrieved from http://www.amputee-coalition.org/aca_first_step.html

Anson, K., & Ponsford, J. (2006). Coping and emotional adjustment following traumatic brain injury. *The Journal of Head Trauma Rehabilitation, 21*, 248–259. doi:10.1097/00001199-200605000-00005

Atherton, R., & Robertson, N. (2006). Psychological adjustment to lower limb amputation amongst prosthesis users. *Disability and Rehabilitation, 28*, 1201–1209. doi:10.1080/09638280600551674

Beck, A. T., Steer, R. A., & Brown, G. K. (1996). *Beck Depression Inventory* (2nd ed.). San Antonio, TX: Psychological Corporation.

Belanger, H. G., Curtiss, G., Demery, J. A., Lebowitz, B. K., & Vanderploeg, R. D. (2005). Factors moderating neuropsychological outcomes following mild traumatic brain injury: A meta-analysis. *Journal of the International Neuropsychological Society, 11*, 215–227. doi:10.1017/S1355617705050277

Blake, D. D., Weathers, F. W., Nagy, L. M., Kaloupek, D. G., Gusman, F. D., Charney, D. S., & Keane, T. M. (1995). The development of a clinician-administered PTSD scale. *Journal of Traumatic Stress, 8*, 75–90. doi:10.1002/jts.2490080106

Brooks, D. (1991). The head-injured family. *Journal of Clinical and Experimental Neuropsychology, 13*, 155–188. doi:10.1080/01688639108407214

Bryant, R. A., & Harvey, A. G. (1999). Postconcussive symptoms and posttraumatic stress disorder after mild traumatic brain injury. *Journal of Nervous and Mental Disease, 187*, 302–305. doi:10.1097/00005053-199905000-00006

Collins, R. C., & Kennedy, M. C. (2008). Serving families who have served: Providing family therapy and support in interdisciplinary polytrauma rehabilitation. *Journal of Clinical Psychology, 64*, 993–1003. doi:10.1002/jclp.20515

Curran, C. A., Ponsford, J. L., & Crowe, S. (2000). Coping strategies and emotional outcome following traumatic brain injury: A comparison with orthopedic patients. *The Journal of Head Trauma Rehabilitation, 15*, 1256–1274. doi:10.1097/00001199-200012000-00006

Curtiss, G., Klemz, S., & Vanderploeg, R. D. (2000). Acute impact of severe traumatic brain injury on family structure and coping responses. *The Journal of Head Trauma Rehabilitation*, *15*, 1113–1122. doi:10.1097/00001199-200010000-00005

Delis, D. C., Kramer, J. H., Kaplan, E., & Ober, B. A. (1987). California Verbal Learning Test (rev. ed.). New York, NY: Psychological Corporation.

Desmond, D. M. (2007). Coping, affective distress, and psychosocial adjustment among people with traumatic upper limb amputations. *Journal of Psychosomatic Research*, *62*, 15–21. doi:10.1016/j.jpsychores.2006.07.027

Desmond, D. M., & MacLachlan, M. (2006). Affective distress and amputation-related pain among older men with long-term, traumatic limb amputations. *Journal of Pain and Symptom Management*, *31*, 362–368. doi:10.1016/j.jpainsymman.2005.08.014

Dougall, A. L., Ursano, R. J., Posluszny, D. M., Fullerton, C. S., & Baum, A. (2001). Predictors of posttraumatic stress among victims of motor vehicle accidents. *Psychosomatic Medicine*, *63*, 402–411.

Draper, K., Ponsford, J., & Schonberger, M. (2007). Psychosocial and emotional outcomes 10 Years following traumatic brain injury. *The Journal of Head Trauma Rehabilitation*, *22*, 278–287. doi:10.1097/01.HTR.0000290972.63753.a7

Dunn, D. S. (1996). Well-being following amputation: Salutary effects of positive meaning, optimism, and control. *Rehabilitation Psychology*, *41*, 285–302. doi:10.1037/0090-5550.41.4.285

Evans, L., McHugh, T., Hopwood, M., & Watt, C. (2003). Chronic posttraumatic stress disorder and family functioning of Vietnam veterans and their partners. *The Australian and New Zealand Journal of Psychiatry*, *37*, 765–772.

Finset, A., & Andersson, S. (2000). Coping strategies in patients with acquired brain injury: Relationships between coping, apathy, depression, and lesion location. *Brain Injury*, *14*, 887–905. doi:10.1080/026990500445718

Florian, V., Katz, S., & Lahav, V. (1991). Impact of traumatic brain damage on family dynamics and functioning: A review. *International Disability Studies*, *13*, 150–157.

Freguson, R. J., Mittenberg, W., Barone, D. F., & Schneider, B. (1999). Postconcussion syndrome following sports-related head injury: Expectation as etiology. *Neuropsychology*, *13*, 582–589. doi:10.1037/0894-4105.13.4.582

Galovski, T., & Lyons, J. A. (2004). Psychological sequelae of combat violence: A review of the impact of PTSD on the veteran's family and possible interventions. *Aggression and Violent Behavior*, *9*, 477–501. doi:10.1016/S1359-1789(03)00045-4

Godfrey, H. P., & Smith, L. M. (1995). *Family support programs and rehabilitation*. New York, NY: Plenum Press.

Grieger, T. A., Cozza, S. J., Ursano, R. J., Hoge, C., Martinez, P. E., Engel, C. C., & Wain, H. J. (2006). Posttraumatic stress disorder and depression in battle-injured soldiers. *The American Journal of Psychiatry*, *163*, 1777–1783. doi:10.1176/appi.ajp.163.10.1777

Gronwall, D. (1977). Paced Auditory Serial Addition Test: A measure of recovery from concussion. *Perceptual and Motor Skills*, *44*, 367–373.

Hoge, C. W., Auchterlonie, J. L., & Milliken, C. S. (2006). Mental health problems, use of mental health services, and attrition from military service after returning from deployment to Iraq or Afghanistan. *JAMA, 295*, 1023–1032. doi:10.1001/jama.295.9.1023

Hoge, C. W., Castro, C. A., Messer, S. C., McGurk, D., Cotting, D. I., & Koffman, R. L. (2004). Combat duty in Iraq and Afghanistan, mental health problems, and barriers to care. *The New England Journal of Medicine, 351*, 13–22. doi:10.1056/NEJMoa040603

Hoge, C. W., McGurk, D., Thomas, J. L., Cox, A. L., Engel, C. C., & Castro, C. A. (2008). Mild traumatic brain injury in U.S. soldiers returning from Iraq. *The New England Journal of Medicine, 358*, 453–463. doi:10.1056/NEJMoa072972

Holbrook, T. L., Anderson, J. P., Sieber, W. J., Browner, D., & Hoyt, D. B. (1999). Outcome after major trauma: 12-month and 18-month follow-up results from the trauma recovery project. *The Journal of Trauma, 46*, 765–773. doi:10.1097/00005373-199905000-00003

Hoofien, D., Gilboa, A., Vakil, E., & Donovick, P. J. (2001). Traumatic brain injury (TBI) 10–20 years later: A comprehensive outcome study of psychiatric symptomatology, cognitive abilities, and psychosocial functioning. *Brain Injury, 15*, 189–209. doi:10.1080/026990501300005659

Horgan, O., & MacLachlan, M. (2004). Psychosocial adjustment to lower-limb amputation: A review. *Disability and Rehabilitation, 26*, 837–850. doi:10.1080/09638280410001708869

Jorge, R. E., Robinson, R. G., Moser, D., Tateno, A., Crespo-Facorro, B., & Arndt, S. (2004). Major depression following traumatic brain injury. *Archives of General Psychiatry, 61*, 42–50. doi:10.1001/archpsyc.61.1.42

Kendall, E., & Terry, D. J. (1996). Psychosocial adjustment following closed head injury: A model for understanding individual differences and predicting outcome. *Neuropsychological Rehabilitation, 6*, 101–132. doi:10.1080/713755502

Kennedy, R. E., Livingston, L., Riddick, A., Marwitz, J. H., Kreutzer, J. S., & Zasler, N. D. (2005). Evaluation of the neurobehavioral functioning inventory as a depression screening tool after traumatic brain injury. *The Journal of Head Trauma Rehabilitation, 20*, 512–526. doi:10.1097/00001199-200511000-00004

Kim, E., Lauterbach, E. C., Reeve, A., Arciniegas, D. B., Coburn, K. L., Mendez, M. F., . . . Coffey, E. C. (2007). Neuropsychiatric complications of traumatic brain injury: A critical review of the literature (a report by the ANPA Committee on Research). *The Journal of Neuropsychiatry and Clinical Neurosciences, 19*, 106–127. doi:10.1176/appi.neuropsych.19.2.106

Koren, D., Arnon, I., & Klein, E. (1999). Acute stress response and posttraumatic stress disorder in traffic accident victims: A one-year prospective, follow-up study. *The American Journal of Psychiatry, 156*, 367–373.

Koren, D., Hemel, D., & Klein, E. (2006). Injury increases the risk for PTSD: An examination of potential neurobiological and psychological mediators. *CNS Spectrums, 11*, 616–624.

Koren, D., Norman, D., Cohen, A., Berman, J., & Klein, E. M. (2005). Increased PTSD risk with combat-related injury: A matched comparison study of injured and uninjured soldiers experiencing the same combat events. *The American Journal of Psychiatry, 162,* 276–282. doi:10.1176/appi.ajp.162.2.276

Kreutzer, J. S., Marwitz, J. H., & Kepler, K. (1992). Traumatic brain injury: Family response and outcome. *Archives of Physical Medicine and Rehabilitation, 73,* 771–778.

Kroenke, K., Spitzer, R. L., & Williams, J. B. W. (2001). The PHQ-9. Validity of a brief depression severity measure. *Journal of General Internal Medicine, 16,* 606–613. doi:10.1046/j.1525-1497.2001.016009606.x

Kubler-Ross, E. (1969). On death and dying. New York, NY: Macmillan.

LarØi, F. (2003). The family systems approach to treating families of persons with brain injury: A potential collaboration between family therapist and brain injury professional. *Brain Injury, 17,* 175–187. doi:10.1080/0269905021000010140

Lew, H. L., Vanderploeg, R. D., Moore, D. F., Schwab, K., Friedman, L., Yesavage, J., . . . Sigford, B. J. (2008). Guest editorial: Overlap of mild TBI and mental health conditions in returning OIF/OEF service members and veterans. *Journal of Rehabilitation Research and Development, 45*(3), xi–xvi.

Livneh, H., Antonak, R. F., & Gerhardt, J. (2000). Multidimensional investigation of the structure of coping among people with amputations. *Psychosomatics, 41,* 235–244. doi:10.1176/appi.psy.41.3.235

Livneh, H., & Sherwood, A. (1991). Application of personality theories and counseling strategies to clients with physical disabilities. *Journal of Counseling and Development, 69,* 525–538.

Marshall, R. D., & Garakani, A. (2002). Psychobiology of the acute stress response and its relationship to the psychobiology of posttraumatic stress disorder. *The Psychiatric Clinics of North America, 25,* 385–395. doi:10.1016/S0193-953X (01)00005-3

Meares, S., Shores, E. A., Taylor, A. J., Batchelor, J., Bryant, R. A., Baguley, I. J., . . . Marosszeky, J. E. (2008). Mild traumatic brain injury does not predict acute postconcussion syndrome. *Journal of Neurology, Neurosurgery, and Psychiatry, 79,* 300–306. doi:10.1136/jnnp.2007.126565

Merbaum, M., & Hefez, A. (1976). Some personality characteristics of soldiers exposed to extreme war stress. *Journal of Consulting and Clinical Psychology, 44,* 1–6. doi:10.1037/0022-006X.44.1.1

Michaels, A. J., Michaels, C. E., Moon, C. H., Smith, J. S., Zimmerman, M. A., Taheri, P. A., . . . Peterson, C. (1999). Posttraumatic stress disorder after injury: Impact on general health outcome and early risk assessment. *The Journal of Trauma, 47,* 460–467. doi:10.1097/00005373-199909000-00005

Michaels, A. J., Michaels, C. E., Smith, J. S., Moon, C. H., Peterson, C., & Long, W. B. (2000). Outcome from injury: General health, work status, and satisfaction 12 months after trauma. *The Journal of Trauma, 48,* 841–850. doi:10.1097/ 00005373-200005000-00007

Parkes, C. M. (1975). Psychosocial transitions: Comparison between reactions to loss of a limb and loss of a spouse. *The British Journal of Psychiatry, 127,* 204–210. doi:10.1192/bjp.127.3.204

Pelletier, P. M., & Alfano, D. P. (2000). Depression, social support, and family coping following traumatic brain injury. *Brain and Cognition, 44,* 45–49.

Pitman, R. K., Altman, B., & Macklin, M. L. (1989). Prevalence of posttraumatic stress disorder in wounded Vietnam veterans. *The American Journal of Psychiatry, 146,* 667–669.

Prigatano, G. P. (2005). Therapy for emotional and motivational disorders. In W. M. High, A. M. Sander, M. A. Struchen, & K. A. Hart (Eds.), *Rehabilitation for traumatic brain injury* (pp. 118–130). New York, NY: Oxford University Press.

Rotondi, A. J., Sinkule, J., Balzer, K., Harris, J., & Moldovan, R. (2007). A qualitative needs assessment of persons who have experienced traumatic brain injury and their primary family caregivers. *The Journal of Head Trauma Rehabilitation, 22,* 14–25. doi:10.1097/00001199-200701000-00002

Rybarczyk, B., Nyenhuis, D. L., Nicholas, J. J., Cash, S. M., & Kaiser, J. (1995). Body image, perceived social stigma and the prediction of psychosocial adjustment to leg amputation. *Rehabilitation Psychology, 40,* 95–110. doi:10.1037/0090-5550.40.2.95

Sander, A. M. (2005). Interventions for caregivers. In A. S. W. M. High, M. A. Struchen, & K. A. Hart (Eds.), *Rehabilitation for traumatic brain injury* (pp. 156–175). Oxford, England: Oxford University Press.

Schneiderman, A. I., Braver, E. R., & Kang, H. K. (2008). Understanding sequelae of injury mechanisms and mild traumatic brain injury incurred during the conflicts in Iraq and Afghanistan: Persistent postconcussive symptoms and post-traumatic stress disorder. *American Journal of Epidemiology, 167,* 1446–1452. doi:10.1093/aje/kwn068

Schwab, K., Baker, G., Ivins, B., Sluss-Tiller, M., Lux, W., & Warden, D. (2006). The brief traumatic brain injury screen (BTBIS): Investigating the validity of a self-report instrument for detecting traumatic brain injury (TBI) in troops returning from deployment in Afghanistan and Iraq. *Neurology, 66,* A235.

Seel, R. T., Kreutzer, J. S., Rosenthal, M., Hammond, F. M., Corrigan, J. D., & Black, K. (2003). Depression after traumatic brain injury: A national institute on disability and rehabilitation research model systems multicenter investigation. *Archives of Physical Medicine and Rehabilitation, 84,* 177–184. doi:10.1053/apmr.2003.50106

Serio, C., Kreutzer, J., & Gervasio, A. (1995). Predicting family needs after traumatic brain injury: Implications for intervention. *The Journal of Head Trauma Rehabilitation, 10,* 32–45. doi:10.1097/00001199-199504000-00005

Shalev, A. Y., Peri, T., Canetti, L., & Schreiber, S. (1996). Predictors of PTSD in injured trauma survivors: A prospective study. *The American Journal of Psychiatry, 153,* 219–225.

Simeon, D., Knutelska, M., Yehuda, R., Putnam, F., Schmeidler, J., & Smith, L. M. (2007). Hypothalamic–pituitary–adrenal axis function in dissociative disorders, posttraumatic stress disorder, and healthy volunteers. *Biological Psychiatry, 61*, 966–973. doi:10.1016/j.biopsych.2006.07.030

Smith, T. C., Ryan, M. A., Wingard, D. L., Slymen, D. J., Sallis, J. F., & Kritz-Silverstein, D. (2008). New onset and persistent symptoms of posttraumatic stress disorder self-reported after deployment and combat exposures: Prospective population based U.S. military cohort study. *British Medical Journal, 336*, 366–371. doi:10.1136/bmj.39430.638241.AE

Snyder, M. L., Kleck, R. E., & Strenta, A. (1979). Avoidance of the handicapped: An attributional ambiguity analysis. *Journal of Personality and Social Psychology, 37*, 2297–2306. doi:10.1037/0022-3514.37.12.2297

Tate, R. L., & Broe, G. A. (1999). Psychosocial adjustment after traumatic brain injury: What are the important variables? *Psychological Medicine, 29*, 713–725. doi:10.1017/S0033291799008466

Ursano, R. J., Fullerton, C. S., Epstein, R. S., Crowley, B., Kao, T. C., Vance, K., . . . Baum, A. (1999). Acute and chronic posttraumatic stress disorder in motor vehicle accident victims. *The American Journal of Psychiatry, 156*, 589–595.

Vanderploeg, R. D., Curtiss, G., & Belanger, H. G. (2005). Long-term neuropsychological outcomes following mild traumatic brain injury. *Journal of the International Neuropsychological Society, 11*, 228–236. doi:10.1017/S1355617705050289

Veterans Health Initiative. (2004). *Traumatic Brain Injury*. Retrieved from U.S. Department of Veterans Affairs website: www1.va.gov/vhi/docs/TBI.pdf

Williamson, G. M. (1995). Restriction of normal activities among older adult amputees: The role of public self-consciousness. *Journal of Clinical Geropsychology, 1*, 229–242.

Wood, R. L., Liossi, L., & Wood, L. (2005). The impact of head injury neurobehavioral sequelae on personal relationships: Preliminary findings. *Brain Injury, 19*, 845–851. doi:10.1080/02699050500058778

Wood, R. L., & Yurdakul, L. (1997). Change in relationship status following traumatic brain injury. *Brain Injury, 11*, 491–502.

World Health Organization. (1993). *The ICD-10 classification of mental and behavioral disorders: Diagnostic criteria for research*. Geneva, Switzerland: Author.

Zalihić, A., Zalihić, D., & Pivic, G. (2008). Influence of posttraumatic stress disorder of the fathers on other family members. *Bosnian Journal of Basic Medical Sciences, 8*, 20–26.

9

RECONCEPTUALIZING COMBAT-RELATED POSTTRAUMATIC STRESS DISORDER AS AN OCCUPATIONAL HAZARD

CARL ANDREW CASTRO AND AMY B. ADLER

> Coming home from deployment, I find myself on the edge a lot. Whether it's being jumpy when I hear a loud noise or when someone pisses me off I'm real quick to react now in a defensive way.
> —Anonymous soldier after returning
> from a 15-month deployment to Iraq

Posttraumatic stress disorder (PTSD) following combat is relatively common. The popular understanding in the literature, however, is that PTSD affects less than a quarter of combat veterans. These rates are based on calculations that typically include all service members regardless of their specific mission and combat experiences. An underlying assumption in these estimates is that every deployed service member is at equal risk of developing PTSD. In fact, surveys of U.S. troops deployed to Iraq and Afghanistan have shown that it is those soldiers and marines who spend significant time outside of the base camps conducting combat operations who are at the most risk (Mental Health Advisory Team [MHAT] IV, 2007; MHAT V, 2008). The rates based on these samples are more than double the typical estimates. Approximately 40% of soldiers and marines who spend more than 40 hours a week, 7 days a week, outside of the base camp report significant symptoms of

The views expressed here are those of the authors only and are not to be construed as those of the Department of the Army or Department of Defense. This chapter was authored or coauthored by an employee of the United States government as part of official duty and is considered to be in the public domain. Any views expressed herein do not necessarily represent the views of the United States government, and the author's participation in the work is not meant to serve as an official endorsement.

PTSD. Service members from the same units who do not spend time outside of the base camp report rates at the same low level as service members back in garrison who have never deployed (7% to 8%). This point highlights the fact that not all soldiers and marines are at equal risk of developing PTSD because not all of them are equally exposed to combat. Deployment itself is not a risk factor for developing PTSD; it is the combat experiences on the deployment that drive the development of the disorder. Nevertheless, for the one third of the soldiers and marines who are exposed to high levels of combat, PTSD symptoms are a typical reaction.

Combat is clearly an occupational hazard with direct implications for mental health. In the case of the military, the mission dictates how often a service member leaves the base camp and is exposed to the combat conditions that can result in PTSD. Those in other occupations, such as firefighters and police officers, face risky environments as well. This issue of occupational risk associated with PTSD has gone largely unrecognized as it relates to the diagnostic conceptualization of the disorder. Unfortunately, the current diagnostic criteria for PTSD do not adopt an occupational health model. Instead, the criteria are based on a victim-based medical model. This decision to combine occupational risk with victimhood has obscured the critical differences between the two and has limited the examination of their unique diagnostic and prognostic pathways. The purpose of this chapter is to propose a reconceptualization of combat-related PTSD. This reconceptualization reviews the role of the definition of trauma, the context of symptoms, and the understanding of functional impairment.

VIEWING POSTTRAUMATIC STRESS DISORDER WITHIN AN OCCUPATIONAL MODEL

The current approach to PTSD fails to distinguish between individuals who develop PTSD as a result of some traumatic event from individuals who develop the disorder as part of an occupation for which they are trained. Thus, victims of natural disasters, personal violence (e.g., rape, physical assault), and accidents (e.g., car crashes) are placed in the same diagnostic category as service members exposed to combat. Victim-based PTSD makes several fundamental assumptions that are not consistent with an occupational health approach to PTSD. Figure 9.1 depicts the key differences between the current victim-based approach and an occupational-based approach of PTSD.

First, the victim model views the individual as a passive victim of a potentially traumatic event, whereas an occupational model views potentially traumatic events as part of the job. An occupational model views the individual as an active participant in the events. These professionals are trained

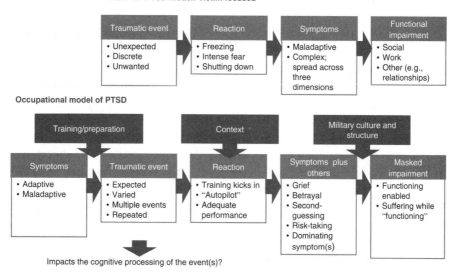

DSM–IV PTSD model: Victim focused

Traumatic event	Reaction	Symptoms	Functional impairment
• Unexpected • Discrete • Unwanted	• Freezing • Intense fear • Shutting down	• Maladaptive • Complex; spread across three dimensions	• Social • Work • Other (e.g., relationships)

Occupational model of PTSD

Training/preparation		Context		Military culture and structure	
Symptoms	Traumatic event	Reaction	Symptoms plus others	Masked impairment
• Adaptive • Maladaptive	• Expected • Varied • Multiple events • Repeated	• Training kicks in • "Autopilot" • Adequate performance	• Grief • Betrayal • Second-guessing • Risk-taking • Dominating symptom(s)	• Functioning enabled • Suffering while "functioning"

Impacts the cognitive processing of the event(s)?

Figure 9.1. Occupational health model. *DSM–IV = Diagnostic and Statistical Manual of Mental Disorders* (4th ed.).

for the potentially traumatic events that they may experience, and they expect these kinds of events to occur. There are many features of the occupation that make hazards associated with serving in the military explicit. For example, in the military, the primary job of a combat soldier or marine is to kill the enemy. Soldiers and marines also understand that the enemy is trying to kill them. Everything they do in training is to confront these two eventualities. There is also an institutional awareness in the military that service members may be required to give their life in service of their country. This awareness is not minimized; it permeates the military community from the practical to the conceptual. The awareness of occupational danger is integrated in the military's life insurance system, in the mandatory banking of individual DNA to facilitate identification of personal remains, in the memorials to fallen service members, and in the warrior ethos. Service members expect danger, they are prepared for danger, and they are trained to respond to danger by taking action. All of this is missing in a victim model. Thus, service members face potentially traumatic events with a different mindset and a different level of preparedness that fundamentally changes their perception of potentially traumatic events and the nature of the symptoms that can occur.

Second, the victim-based approach described in the *Diagnostic and Statistical Manual of Mental Disorders* (4th ed.; *DSM–IV*; American Psychiatric Association, 1994) presumes exposure to a single discrete event at one point in time. In contrast, an occupational model accounts for the fact that deployments can involve exposure to numerous and varied potentially traumatic events over time. At-risk service members are continuously exposed to the threat of death or serious injury every time they leave the base camp. For example, in combat, soldiers report experiencing a wide range of potentially traumatic events such as being in a firefight, being attacked by improvised explosive devices (IEDs), handling human remains, and witnessing the death of fellow service members (e.g., Hoge et al., 2004; Killgore et al., 2008; MHAT V, 2008). This unremitting onslaught has implications for the service member's ability to remain resilient in the face of multiple combat experiences. The fact that there are multiple combat events also means that any treatment plan needs to be adapted to include several events rather than focusing on one specific event, as is typically the case of most exposure therapies (e.g., Bryant, Moulds, Guthrie, Dang, & Nixon, 2003; Ehlers, Clark, Hackmann, McManus, & Fennell, 2005).

Third, *DSM–IV* ignores the social context of the traumatic event. In an occupational model, this social context is critical. In the case of the military, traumatic events do not just occur to individuals but to teams of service members who have formed strong personal relationships with one another. The teams have typically trained together and lived together in close quarters for months prior to any traumatic events occurring. As a result, traumatic events are processed not only at the individual level but at the group level as well. This group processing has implications for how the traumatic experiences are regarded by the individual. The team implicitly and explicitly reacts to the traumatic events, assigning meaning to the experiences, determining who is to blame, evaluating individual and team performance, and providing a context for talking about the experiences. Recognizing that other team members are expressing similar symptoms and reactions serves to normalize one's response to traumatic events. This social context, therefore, has implications for how posttraumatic reactions can be addressed therapeutically.

Without an occupational model, interventions would tend to focus on individuals or on groups of unrelated individuals who share symptoms. In an occupational model, early interventions can be built around the team to take advantage of natural supports and common understandings of the traumatic experiences and to use the team members to reinforce adaptive behaviors in the team as a whole (see Chapter 3, this volume). Furthermore, team and unit leaders also have a significant role in the mental health of team members and how they respond to traumatic combat events. Numerous studies have identified the importance of noncommissioned officers and officers in influencing individual well-being. Thus, early interventions should take advantage of the organizational structure in facilitating the health of service members faced with a combat deployment.

Fourth, the *DSM–IV* model assumes that all of the symptoms follow exposure to a traumatic event. This makes sense in the case of a victim-based approach in which the individual is surprised by a traumatic event for which they are not prepared. Within the military deployment context, however, many of the symptoms for PTSD exist prior to the occurrence of a specific traumatic event. For example, hypervigilance is normal in the deployed context because service members are explicitly trained to continuously look for signs of danger and are warned not to become complacent. Difficulty sleeping is another normal response to the deployed context because the field conditions, noise, lack of privacy, and 24/7 routines are likely to disrupt sleep. Restricted range of affect is also a normal response to the military context because of the cultural emphasis on suppressing emotions to maintain military professionalism on combat operations. Thus, the *DSM–IV* ignores the occupational setting that can lead to symptoms and reactions commonly associated with a diagnosis of PTSD. This gap has significant implications for treatment because many symptoms and reactions that service members display are independent or unrelated to the experiences of traumatic events and instead reflect elements of the military occupational setting. Treatment approaches need to take this occupational context into account so that symptoms are addressed as part of a larger response to deployment rather than as a specific response to a traumatic event.

Given the relevance of an occupational model for understanding combat-related PTSD, the diagnostic conceptualization of PTSD needs to be reexamined. This is not the first time that the diagnostic criteria for PTSD have been critically considered. Before the inclusion of PTSD in the *DSM*, clinicians had described disorders much like the current understanding of PTSD. Depending on the historical context, these disorders were given different terms, such as *trench fever*, *shell shock*, and *combat fatigue* (for a historical overview, see Jones & Wessely, 2001; McFarlane & Girolamo, 1996; van der Kolk, Weisaeth, & van der Hart, 1996).

The understanding of what constitutes PTSD was then refined over several decades until it became a universally accepted diagnosis when it appeared in the third edition of the *Diagnostic and Statistical Manual of Mental Disorders* (*DSM–III*; American Psychiatric Association, 1980). At that time, the PTSD diagnostic criteria required that there be a traumatic event considered outside the range of usual human experience that would be distressing to almost everyone. Criticism of this criterion centered on three issues (Breslau & Davis, 1987; McFarlane & Girolamo, 1996): (a) such experiences were actually relatively frequent and not necessarily outside the range of usual experience, (b) events involving threat to life had more of an impact on well-being than other kinds of potentially traumatic events, and (c) the relative importance of how an individual responded to the potentially traumatic event in predicting the development of symptoms. Thus, in the subsequent iteration of the *DSM*, the criteria shifted to include a focus on threat-related events and a subjective response of fear, helplessness, or horror.

Each version of the *DSM* has attempted to refine and explain the experience of individuals dealing with the aftermath of trauma. This chapter is designed to highlight one way in which the current understanding of PTSD limits its utility with a key population for which it was designed. It should be noted that we may not be the first to question the appropriateness of including combat veterans under this global diagnosis. The goal of the next section, however, is to reconceptualize PTSD criteria within the occupational health framework, particularly as it pertains to combat.

RECONSTRUCTING THE CONCEPT OF EXPOSURE TO TRAUMA

The current diagnostic criteria are separated into six sections. The first section refers to the traumatic event itself and has two components. The first criterion (A1) defines the traumatic event, and the second criterion (A2) defines the individual's response to that event (or to those events). Both of these criteria have to be present for an individual to receive the diagnosis of PTSD.

A1 Criterion

The event itself is defined in *DSM–IV* as involving "actual or threatened death or serious injury, or a threat to the physical integrity of self or others" (p. 427). *DSM–IV* implies that there is one discrete event responsible for subsequent symptoms, but in combat there may be many traumatic events separated by weeks or months. This repeated exposure to different events makes any link between traumatic experiences and subsequent symptoms difficult to determine. In the combat context, there is not necessarily a one-to-one correspondence between exposure to a specific traumatic event and the development of a specific set of PTSD symptoms. For example, a service member may have had trouble sleeping before the first event, nightmares after the second event, and flashbacks after the fifth event. This kind of accumulation of symptoms reflects the complexity of understanding combat-related PTSD and reflects the research that has found that the overall number of combat experiences is related to reports of PTSD symptoms (Bliese, Adler, Castro, Thomas, & Hoge, 2008).

This finding also underscores the occupational health argument that the more service members spend time outside of the base camp conducting combat operations, the more at risk they are of developing PTSD. Given enough combat exposure, service members are eventually likely to develop symptoms consistent with PTSD whether or not they receive the diagnosis (Milliken, Hoge, & Auchterlonie, 2007). This does not mean that every soldier will receive a diagnosis of PTSD but that a vast majority will display symptoms consistent with PTSD and perhaps even remain highly functioning. Therefore, the traumatic event criteria for combat PTSD needs to be viewed in terms of multiple stressors and the overall context of combat in which those stressors are experienced.

It is conceivable that the *DSM–IV*'s A1 criterion of being "threatened" is broad enough to include the fact of deployment itself. Deploying involves a degree of threat because of the exposure to potential danger of any kind, such as being on a base camp that can be mortared or on a patrol. As it stands now, however, if the A1 criterion related to being threatened is interpreted in this way, then an argument could be made that driving on a highway would also meet the A1 criterion because the risk of an accident is present. Such a broad operational definition of A1 is unhelpful and does not tell us what to consider risky. Still, the issue of defining A1 is important because it creates an expectation that the A1 event is responsible for the emergence of symptoms, an assumption that is inconsistent with combat-related PTSD.

A2 Criterion

The second PTSD event-related criterion relates to the subjective response to the traumatic event. In the *DSM–IV*, this response entails fear, helplessness, or horror. On the basis of findings from previous research on the A2 criterion, however, it appears that limiting the subjective response to these three reactions does not adequately describe the experience of military personnel in combat who develop PTSD symptoms.

Although reports of A2 may be diagnostically useful for victims of potentially traumatic events (e.g., Breslau & Kessler, 2001; Brewin, Andrews, & Rose, 2000; Creamer, McFarlane, & Burgess, 2005), the A2 criterion appears to be of narrow utility when applied to individuals trained to respond to potentially traumatic occupational stressors. In fact, as Creamer et al. (2005) noted, it may be that experiencing an A1 event as part of one's occupational role affects one's initial response. This initial occupationally related response does not necessarily preclude the development of emotional responses or the development of PTSD symptoms. Nevertheless, the response of professionals may differ significantly from the response of victims because professionals expect to encounter occupationally related potentially traumatic events. They want the opportunity to use their skills, to test themselves, and to provide meaningful help to others.

Research has confirmed this supposition. In a study of 202 soldiers who had returned from a year of combat in Iraq, the majority who reported an A1 combat event did not report an A2 response (Adler, Wright, Bliese, Eckford, & Hoge, 2008). Although reporting an A2 response was associated with higher PTSD symptom scores on a continuous measure, there were no significant differences in the percentage of subjects who met cutoff criteria for PTSD. In interviews, soldiers who did not endorse an A2 response were asked how they did respond. Of the 159 who were asked, 98 (62%) said that they responded in a way that reflected their military training. This occupationally based response was epitomized by statements such as "My training kicked in" and "I did what I was trained to do." The second most common response reported by soldiers was anger (Adler et al., 2008).

The fact that service members responded first with an occupationally based reaction may reflect their level of training or perhaps their profession's cultural bias against emotional responses other than anger. However, their immediate occupationally related response did not preclude their development of PTSD symptoms. It is notable that exploratory analyses found that responding with anger was associated with increased rates of endorsing reexperiencing and hyperarousal symptoms of PTSD. Similarly, studies of police officers have also found that professionals encountering traumatic events as part of their occupation report training-related responses and anger reactions (Brunet et al., 2001; Sims & Sims, 1998).

Taken together, these studies demonstrate that PTSD criteria requiring an A2 response for occupational groups such as military personnel systematically underestimate the PTSD in these populations. The current A2 criterion makes sense for a victim-focused model of PTSD in which the individual is naturally horrified or shocked by an unexpected event. The A2 criterion does not, however, fit the subjective experience of service members and misjudges the subjective experience of service members encountering traumatic events in combat. Soldiers do not see themselves as victims. They see themselves as agents of action, and they are trained to respond, to return fire, to focus on what must be done in a given situation. Although at times they might consider themselves a victim of bad leadership or policy, they do not necessarily see themselves as victims when faced with a traumatic event in combat. That is why it is important to use an occupational approach that allows for the individual's initial response to be focused on trained action without eliminating the possibility that at some later date the individual might develop emotional difficulties akin to PTSD.

Besides meeting criteria for the traumatic event, the DSM–IV diagnosis of PTSD reviews three major symptom clusters that must be present for the diagnosis to be made: the A cluster, or reexperiencing of symptoms associated with recollections of the event; the B cluster, or avoidance of stimuli associated with the traumatic event and emotional numbing; and the C cluster, or symptoms of hyperarousal.

RECONSTRUCTING THE SYMPTOMS AFTER COMBAT

Each of the PTSD symptom clusters needs to be considered within an occupational health framework. Deconstructing these clusters makes it clear that many responses that are regarded as symptoms of PTSD are in fact normal and adaptive responses to combat. Thus, the symptoms themselves become examples of normal behavior rather than a pathological set of behaviors requiring immediate intervention. The struggle that mental health professionals may face in understanding these symptoms is that in the combat environment the symptoms are normal and adaptive, but in the civilian environment they can appear destructive and pathological. Therefore, understanding these symptoms can serve as a starting point for developing meaningful interventions during a combat deployment, after returning from a combat deployment, and before returning to a combat environment. This analysis can also serve to identify what symptoms may be more important than others in understanding the psychological response to combat.

Reexperiencing

In the *reexperiencing* cluster, five symptoms are identified in the *DSM–IV*, and an individual must have at least one of these to meet the criteria for a diagnosis of PTSD. These five symptoms include intrusive and distressing memories of the traumatic event, distressing dreams of the traumatic event, the sense that the traumatic event is reoccurring, and intense psychological distress and physiological reactivity to cues that remind the individual of the traumatic event.

These last two symptoms of reactivity to cues that are similar to the event are not necessarily pathological. Service members are trained to look for environmental cues that can potentially lead to danger (i.e., a traumatic event), once more underscoring the importance of understanding these reactions within an occupational framework. This occupational reactivity is normal, encouraged, and essential to surviving a combat deployment. For example, service members look for places where IEDs might be hidden, and when on patrol they look for anything out of the ordinary that could signal danger. It is important to note that service members are likely to be psychologically and physiologically reactive to these cues before being exposed to their first combat-related traumatic event. Experiencing the actual danger associated with a particular set of cues will likely strengthen the link between the cues and psychological and physiological reactivity. Even intense memories of the event may help individuals become more aware of combat-related dangers and develop strategies to avoid such deadly situations in the future. This focus on learning from critical incidents is institutionally supported by such military procedures as after-action reviews in which units examine what went wrong and devise corrective actions to take the next time a similar event occurs.

Although psychological and physiological reactivity and strong memories can be adaptive in combat, several PTSD symptoms in the reexperiencing cluster can be maladaptive. Specifically, intense and distressing memories of the events, dreams, and flashbacks (as they are commonly known) are likely to be maladaptive. Distressing memories are likely to be disruptive and may even endanger a service member who is distracted by memories and flashbacks when on combat operations. In considering the way in which reexperiencing symptoms are triggered, it is important to remember that there are typically multiple combat-related traumatic events. These multiple events may create multiple cues, or a single cue may trigger multiple memories, thus resulting in a more complex understanding of the way in which reexperiencing symptoms occur.

Reexperiencing symptoms may also be triggered when service members are preparing to deploy to combat for a second or third time. This predeployment period may be experienced quite differently by those who have already been to combat. Killgore, Stetz, Castro, and Hoge (2006) showed that combat veterans preparing to deploy again report more PTSD-related symptoms compared with those soldiers who are deploying for the first time. In contrast, soldiers who are deploying for the first time report more physical symptoms than those who have already been to combat. Thus, the experience of predeployment anticipation is manifested differently in these two populations. It is not clear why this difference occurs. It may be that for veterans the anticipation of deploying back to combat triggers memories and accompanying PTSD symptoms or it may be that veterans have not had the chance to reset psychologically. Anecdotally, units report that they see a spike in the number of veterans seeking behavioral health services before deploying again. Although some may view this delayed help-seeking as a means to avoid deploying again, it is quite possible that PTSD symptoms are being triggered by the anticipation of combat. Heretofore, this phenomenon has been unexplored but is deserving of comprehensive examination.

Avoidance

The second major symptom cluster in the *DSM–IV* is *avoidance*. There are seven avoidance symptoms, and according to the *DSM–IV* at least three of them need to be present to meet the criterion for this cluster. These symptoms are (a) attempts to avoid thoughts, feelings, or conversations about the trauma; (b) attempts to avoid activities, places, or people that result in memories of the trauma; (c) gaps in recall regarding aspects of the traumatic event; (d) reduced interest in personal activities; (e) feelings of detachment from others; (f) limited range of emotions; and (g) a sense of a foreshortened future (American Psychiatric Association, 1994).

The *DSM–IV* requires that these symptoms are "not present before the trauma" to qualify for the diagnosis (American Psychiatric Association, 1994, p. 428). However, as in the case of reexperiencing symptoms, several of these avoidance symptoms are likely to be present before a service member is exposed to a combat-related traumatic event. Indeed, three of these symptoms are considered adaptive elements of the occupational setting. Specifically, deployed service members are expected to narrow their focus to the needs of the deployment to the exclusion of outside distractions. This narrowing of interests can be seen as an aspect of the avoidance symptom of diminished interest in significant activities but may in fact be more a reflection of the 24/7 work cycle. On deployment, there is limited ability to contact home, limited time to engage in recreation, limited outlets for recreation, and a cultural emphasis on staying focused on the mission.

Another symptom that can occur before exposure to a traumatic event is feeling detached from others. This estrangement is normal because of the geographical isolation, lack of physical contact with family and friends back home, and limited communication with family and friends back home. Feelings of estrangement are a normal aspect of any deployment because service members are functionally cut off from family and friends for a long period of time, and there is a cumulative lack of shared experiences. These feelings can occur even in the absence of a specific traumatic event. This detachment is also consistent with the increased focus on the importance of the small teams that will help individual service members survive combat. Thus, detachment from others is a means for service members to focus all their attention and energy on the combat mission. Although contact home is possible, it is met with some ambivalence; service members sometimes find that hearing about family events is burdensome or distressing when they cannot be home to take care of family problems, such as fixing a car, or to handle financial issues (MHAT IV, 2007).

The third symptom of avoidance that is likely to exist prior to exposure to any traumatic event is having a restricted emotional range. The military culture explicitly encourages service members on deployment to control their emotions. The typical service member interprets this control as not expressing emotions other than anger. Feeling numb or, at the most, angry is considered acceptable, whereas other feelings are considered distractions that might limit a service member's ability to exercise judgment in critical situations. Arguably, trying to avoid thoughts, feelings, or conversations about the traumatic event may be adaptive in an occupational setting in which the individual needs to remain focused on job performance because the stakes are so high. However, some degree of attention needs to be paid to the details of the event to reduce the risk of danger in the future. The military reinforces this awareness through after-action reviews, so blocking out memories entirely or not recalling specific aspects of the traumatic event may be maladaptive. Clearly, trying to avoid activities that remind service members of the traumatic event is maladaptive in terms of military performance. Service members are likely to be required to return to duty shortly after exposure to a traumatic event. This may include patrolling in the area where friends have been killed.

According to the *DSM–IV*, the final symptom of avoidance in this cluster is a sense of a foreshortened future. The assumption appears to be that this is a pathological, irrational response to a traumatic event. In the military context, however, this sense of a foreshortened future is quite rational. When service members see their friends killed or wounded, this experience forces the realization that they are in an occupation that is dangerous. They realize that they can be killed or wounded at any time so their belief that life can be cut short is not irrational or necessarily pathological. In a way, the sense of foreshortened future reflects a fatalistic belief. Service members often feel that survival is a matter of luck and that there is little that can be done. This belief is reflected in statements such as, "When your number's up, it's up" and "The third time's a charm."

The understanding that death in combat is essentially random may in fact be adaptive, particularly if the service member is likely to face additional danger or future deployments. This fatalism needs to be understood within a larger context. Certainly, if it leads to reckless behavior or lack of attention to cues signaling danger, then it is maladaptive. However, if the fatalism leads to acceptance of the real risk faced by service members spending time outside the base camp, then this may help reduce feelings of guilt and second-guessing. Wanting to exert control when the context is not under one's control is problematic, much like being highly engaged in one's military job leads to more health symptoms for service members encountering work overload (Britt, Castro, & Adler, 2005). That is, there may be a limit in terms of how much uncontrollable stress service members can absorb while still engaging in active coping strategies; fatalism may play a role in helping service members cope with the demands of combat.

Hyperarousal

The third cluster of PTSD symptoms in the *DSM–IV* is related to increased arousal or *hyperarousal*. These five symptoms include difficulty sleeping, irritability or anger, difficulty concentrating, hypervigilance, and an exaggerated startle response. To meet the criteria for this cluster, at least two of these symptoms must be present, and these symptoms must not have been present before the traumatic event.

Similar to the other symptom clusters, at least three of these symptoms are likely to be present before the trauma in an occupational setting such as deployment. As mentioned previously, difficulty sleeping is prevalent on a deployment because of the physical conditions. In addition, hypervigilance and an exaggerated startle response are also seen as adaptive because they increase tactical awareness of the combat environment. All three of these symptoms are thus likely to occur before any specific combat-related traumatic event. It is interesting to note that several of the symptoms in this dimension are difficult to assess as problematic in a combat environment because they represent a normal state for service members in combat. Similarly, many of these symptoms are normal for service members when they return home from combat because it takes a while for their bodies to adjust to the lower state of arousal. This is why these symptoms may not be particularly useful in distinguishing service members with postdeployment adjustment difficulties.

One avoidance symptom that is central to the service member's experience during and after deployment is anger. Pervasive anger is a predominant emotion, and although service members may have a restricted emotional range, this range surely includes anger. Service members frequently mention that they are angry (Adler et al., 2008; Wright et al., 2005); their anger is not focused on any one thing. It is nonspecific, and they report feeling angry (or irritated) at everything (see also Chapter 6, this volume). This pervasive anger can include being angry because of having missed a year of their lives as a result of the deployment, being upset with their leaders for not meeting their expectations, and being easily irritated by the little things in life. Certainly, being easily angered and highly irritable can lead to relationship problems, difficulty at work, and difficulty enjoying life. A case could be made that anger merits inclusion as a symptom required for the diagnosis of combat-related PTSD.

Besides the three symptom clusters, the diagnostic criteria for PTSD also includes a duration and functional impairment criterion. That is, symptoms need to be present for at least 1 month and need to cause significant distress or problems in daily functioning. Although the *DSM–IV* provides a strong description of PTSD from a victim model perspective, some of the symptoms are not only misapplied in an occupational context, but there are also several relevant categories missing from the current model.

UNDERSTANDING THE MENTAL HEALTH RESPONSE TO COMBAT

Using an occupational model to understand reactions to traumatic events leads to several new issues that need to be addressed. These issues include the development of symptoms over time; the way in which exposure to traumatic events changes a service member's outlook; the role of other emotions such as grief, guilt, and regret; and the way in which the service member's adjustment affects job performance and readiness for future deployments.

Time Course of Symptom Development

The current *DSM* assumes a relatively linear symptomatic response to a traumatic event. However, in the occupational context of a combat deployment, this response begins prior to exposure to events, is affected by the deployment cycle, and is shaped by the need to reset for future deployments. Thus the entire course of the development of combat-related PTSD is affected.

First, in an occupational model in which service members are trained for the likelihood that they will encounter traumatic events, symptoms are likely to develop prior to any specific traumatic event experience. As we mentioned previously, these symptoms may be adaptive given the context (e.g., hypervigilance) or may be understandable (e.g., sleeping difficulties). Thus, any time course established for the development of combat-related PTSD may begin at the start of a deployment.

Second, when service members first return from a deployment, their levels of distress may in fact be minimized. They may just feel numb or be so relieved at arriving home safely that they experience little discomfort. Service members may therefore unintentionally minimize the extent and severity of their symptoms. They may also discount their symptoms as remnants of the deployed environment that will quickly dissipate now that they are home. This initial euphoria is like a kind of postdeployment optimism that may make it difficult to ascertain the presence of maladaptive reactions. Therefore, any effective postdeployment assessment program needs to take into account the fact that few symptoms are likely to be reported when service members initially return home. However, these symptoms are likely to be more prevalent a few months later and formal assessments should also include this time frame (Bliese et al., 2008). One may view this typical postdeployment time frame as indicative of a delayed onset of combat-related PTSD. A less common form of combat-related PTSD occurs in a combat environment or within the 1st month of postdeployment. In fact, Milliken et al. (2007) found that service members reporting symptoms during the late deployment or early redeployment time frame reported more symptoms at follow-up, suggesting that early onset PTSD symptoms may be more difficult to treat. A reconceptualization of PTSD for service members needs to take into account this typical delay for purposes of assessment, predicting course over time, and treatment.

Rapid Maturation

There are two ways in which the outlook of service members may change following a combat deployment. The first change is that the individual may mature rapidly. Although this rapid maturation may not appear to be symptomatic in the sense that it is dysfunctional, it can lead to an individual feeling out of step with his or her peers. Combat veterans describe feeling disconnected from friends who have not deployed. This disconnection reflects differences in priorities; service members who have deployed may view the concerns of their friends back home as relatively trivial. This maturation has a positive component in that service members may appreciate or value life differently, but it leaves them out of step with their same-age peers.

This same maturation may be seen physically in how they walk, their body posture, and self-reported physical complaints. Their gait and the way in which they hold themselves can become similar to an elderly person's style of movement. Although we only have anecdotal data that describe this physical maturation, Boscarino's research (1997) on Vietnam veterans being more at risk of various physical health problems is consistent with this point. Similarly, Hoge, Terhakopian, Castro, Messer, and Engel (2007) found a link between somatic concerns and PTSD in combat veterans. In the combat-to-home transition scale described in Chapter 6 of this volume, 65% of returning service members reported feeling as though the deployment to Iraq made them mature. This subjective sense of aging should be examined directly in research and should be considered for inclusion in the diagnostic description of combat-related PTSD.

Risk Taking

The second way in which outlook changes following a combat deployment is that service members may have a different attitude toward risk taking. As Killgore and colleagues noted in their 2008 paper, service members who reported intense combat exposure were more likely to report a propensity for risk taking. In a separate study, Adler et al. (2008) also found that intense combat exposure is associated with increased likelihood of engaging in risky behaviors, such as carrying an unnecessary weapon and looking to start a fight. Thus, prolonged exposure to combat may result in physiological changes that alter the way in which service members process emotional experiences.

Although not directly addressed in the Killgore et al. (2008) study, it may be that service members are driven to increased risk taking through three mechanisms. First, they may be seeking what is commonly referred to as an "adrenaline high." Safe activities may not be enough to break through the overall numbness. Only through high-risk activities can the individual experience a satisfying emotional response. Second, service members who survive the dangers of combat may feel invincible. Thus, what others may regard as dangerous, they may dismiss as merely exciting. This outlook is typified by statements such as, "If combat didn't kill me, this won't either." Third, service members may have developed a fatalistic attitude. That is, they may feel that their fate is determined by factors outside their control and that taking part in high-risk activities provides them some control. The exact mechanism leading to increased risk taking needs to be better understood and considered for inclusion in the diagnostic criteria for combat-related PTSD.

Grief, Guilt, and Second-Guessing

The third way in which service members are affected by combat is that they often have to deal with the emotional load of grief, guilt, and second-guessing. These themes are conspicuously absent from the current conceptualization of PTSD, although numerous researchers have identified these areas as important (e.g., Brunet et al., 2001; Henning & Frueh, 1998; Kubany, 1994; Sims & Sims, 1998; Weathers & Keane, 2007).

Within the military context, the impact of the death or serious injury of a fellow unit member is compounded by the fact that the service members know each other well and may even be friends. Service members often describe the pain associated with the loss of a respected leader or friend. They recount how they worked with the person, trained with the person, lived with the person, and shared personal stories with him or her. These deaths are not abstract; they hit close to home.

Grieving for the death of a fellow service member can be manifested in several ways. In theater, the time allotted for mourning is measured in hours, not days or weeks. The memorial service is brief, and understandably the focus quickly returns to the combat mission. Service members often report going back on patrol immediately after a memorial service. Thus, time for reflection is likely to be limited and incomplete. Instead of being expressed through sadness, grief may become manifested in anger. This anger can be directed toward a unit leader and, in more extreme cases, toward enemy combatants and innocent civilians (e.g., Castro & McGurk, 2007; MHAT IV, 2007). After returning home, this anger is expressed more generally and can lead to a disruption in social and occupational functioning. It becomes an essential symptom in combat-related PTSD and a key challenge in the recovery process.

Guilt and second-guessing also take an emotional toll. In the military, individuals are trained to take responsibility, to be accountable for what happens, and to identify and correct deficiencies. This strong sense of duty is an integral part of the occupational identity of service members. When a unit member is injured or killed, which is one of the risks of combat, this same sense of duty can result in devastating guilt and second-guessing. Service members recognize that combat is chaotic and that death and injury in combat are random; survival depends on luck. The paradox, however, is that service members are also trained to control their behaviors and actions in this chaotic environment, as if these behaviors can prevent all deaths and injuries. This paradox fuels guilt and second-guessing. Second-guessing and guilt can result in service members being unwilling or unable to forgive themselves for some action or lack of action that they think contributed to the death or injury of someone. Again, other PTSD researchers have identified the importance of guilt (e.g., Henning & Frueh, 1998; Kubany, 1994), although it is absent from the current conceptualization of PTSD.

Functionality and Impairment

The current conceptualization of PTSD does not consider the occupational setting in assessing an individual's impairment in functioning. This conceptualization assumes that an individual's adjustment following trauma exposure is independent of the occupational context, although the diagnostic criteria include disruption of occupational functioning as well as disruption of social and interpersonal relations. The structure of the military culture is so pervasive that it can implicitly sustain service members who may have combat-related PTSD symptoms in their efforts to remain highly functioning. This structure includes specific proscriptions regarding grooming, physical fitness, and clothing. The rigid hierarchy dictates or influences social behavior and social interactions. The job provides a predictable daily routine. This structure provides a fundamental support by making it easier to meet expectations in terms of job performance and social interactions.

When service members leave the military, they lose this structure, and this loss may precipitate a decline in functioning. In extreme cases, this loss of structure may lead to homelessness. We hypothesize that the transition to the less structured civilian world may result in higher levels of treatment seeking in the Veterans Affairs health care system. Thus, the loss of structure may explain why some cases of PTSD have a delayed onset. Service members may have symptoms of PTSD while on active duty but show no marked impairment in functioning until leaving the military structure. A proactive response to these issues would suggest that veterans be routinely assessed for combat-related PTSD 3 to 6 months after leaving active duty instead of waiting until they seek Veterans Affairs care themselves.

The flip side of the support provided by the military culture is that symptoms of PTSD may be dismissed because certain behaviors (e.g., drinking, relationship problems) may be considered a normal part of military life. Ironically, this military structure, which enables symptomatic service members to function, ensures that they will be eligible to deploy again where they will be at risk of being further traumatized. Evidence for what is termed the *multiple-deployer effect* in MHAT IV (2007) and MHAT V (2008) shows that soldiers on their first combat deployment report fewer symptoms of PTSD compared with soldiers on their second combat deployment. Indeed, each additional combat deployment raises the odds that an individual will report more PTSD symptoms. These issues of functioning are complex, but they should be accounted for in an occupational model of combat-related PTSD. The issue of structure also has implications for understanding what it means to return to combat.

THE WAY AHEAD AND CONCLUSION

Using an occupational model to understand psychological reactions to potentially traumatic events can change the way in which PTSD is conceptualized. This reconceptualization creates a need to reexamine each of the symptoms associated with PTSD and provides a basis from which the criteria for diagnosis can be redefined. Fundamentally, we are arguing that psychologists need to move away from rigid sequencing in which PTSD symptoms are expected to be the consequence of exposure to a potentially traumatic event. Adopting an occupational model introduces the concept of anticipatory reactions and symptoms and the adaptive nature of those symptoms in combat. However, it is important to note that these symptoms may become exacerbated or more intransigent once one is exposed to combat-related traumatic events. This occupational model also has implications for prevention, early intervention, and treatment of combat-related PTSD. Professionals working with combat-related PTSD issues should not rely solely on victim-based interventions as a guide for conceptualizing or treating combat-related PTSD. Finally, this occupational model has implications for future research efforts designed to understand combat-related PTSD.

Implications for Prevention, Early Intervention, and Treatment

Attempts to identify ahead of time those individuals who will develop PTSD after being exposed to a potentially traumatic event have met with singular failure (Rona, Hyams, & Wessely, 2005). During World War II, for example, psychiatric interviews were used to try to select out individuals at risk of combat-related mental health problems. These attempts lacked both specificity and sensitivity and resulted in literally hundreds of thousands of individuals being unnecessarily excluded from military service. Despite these exclusions, combat exhaustion still represented a significant proportion of casualties during World War II (Ginzberg, 1959; Harris, Mayer, & Becker, 1955).

Early attempts to select out individuals who were at risk of developing PTSD focused on psychosocial markers; the focus has now shifted to identifying biomarkers. As mentioned at the beginning of this chapter, when combat is viewed as an occupational hazard, the incidence of severe PTSD symptoms approaches 40%, and another 20% to 35% report at least moderate PTSD symptoms. Thus, any attempt to select out individuals who will go on to develop moderate or severe PTSD symptoms would effectively eliminate three quarters of the population interested in serving in the military.

If 75% go on to develop moderate to severe PTSD symptoms when confronted with combat-related traumatic events, the problem becomes a population issue, not a selection issue. That is, 75% represents the majority of individuals and reinforces the point that the predominant risk factor for developing combat-related PTSD is in fact combat. This perspective has consequences for how prevention and early intervention efforts are developed. Focusing on developing individual-level risk factors such as psychosocial and biochemical markers as selection tools will not be helpful in preventing PTSD symptoms in service members exposed to combat unless we are ready to select only 25% of the available pool or unless we develop effective prevention strategies that can overcome psychosocial and biochemical predispositions.

In reality, we do send these individuals into combat, and we do not have sufficiently sophisticated intervention strategies that prevent at-risk individuals from developing significant PTSD symptoms. Thus, at this point in time, identifying individual-level risk factors should not be a focus of prevention efforts.

Besides the lack of intervention efforts that can be used to counter individual-level risk factors, there is another problem with focusing research efforts on identifying individual risk factors. This kind of research can inadvertently send an implicit message that the problem of PTSD symptoms lies with the individual rather than with the occupational hazards associated with combat. This message appears to blame service members for things outside their control, which may just compound their difficulties because it encourages self-blame, stigma, and a sense of hopelessness.

Conceptualizing the problem at the population level fundamentally changes the way in which we as a society focus on helping individuals deal with occupational hazards. We believe addressing these problems from a population perspective should include three levels of intervention. First, because so many individuals are at risk, mental health training needs to be provided before exposure to occupational hazards as well as after. All individuals at risk of exposure to occupationally related traumatic events should receive this kind of training. This mental health training should address topics such as appropriate occupationally related reactions, how to move between states of hypervigilance and calm, and how to manage anger as a normal response to combat-related events. These behaviors need to be taught within a tough, realistic training environment, reinforced by buddies and leaders, and framed for the military culture.

Prevention should also involve the training of leaders so that they can learn ahead of time to exhibit positive leadership behaviors, to avoid negative leadership behaviors, and to understand their impact on unit functioning. These leaders should also be trained to manage stress reactions in their units using techniques such as cognitive restructuring, to provide opportunities for recovery from hypervigilance, and to learn how to listen effectively. This training should be integrated into their traditional leadership courses as well as integrated into their realistic training exercises.

Second, besides predeployment mental health training, there should also be effective early intervention strategies that are population-based, unit-based, and individual-based, depending on the level of risk. A population-based approach recognizes that a vast majority of service members may have some degree of problems adjusting postdeployment and would benefit from training. For example, all service members returning from deployment could be provided training in how to manage the normal stress of transitioning from combat to home. Training the entire population in these kinds of skills might reduce the number of adjustment difficulties, including the number of PTSD symptoms overall. Through this kind of training, even individuals who do not have problems can benefit by becoming aware of problems their fellow unit members may be experiencing, better enabling them to support unit members during the transition. In the U.S. Army, this system of training falls under *Battlemind Training* (see Chapter 1, this volume). In Battlemind, service members are taught about what kinds of reactions they or others may experience and learn what might be a sign of transition difficulty, and they are encouraged to look out for themselves and others.

Besides population-based training, at-risk military units can also be provided with additional training. Targeting at-risk units recognizes the reality that not all units are exposed to the same level of combat. For example, units that are conducting patrols every day may be more at risk than those working at the base camp (Castro & McGurk, 2007). This unit-based training can take a variety of forms, from structured group interaction to more traditional classes. For example, Battlemind Psychological Debriefing can be used during and after deployment to discuss difficult deployment-related experiences within small units and how to manage reactions to these experiences (Adler, Castro, & McGurk, 2009). Other interventions can target high-risk units with additional mental health training modules. For example, at-risk units can be trained in managing intrusive thoughts through brief acceptance therapy exercises (e.g., Shipherd & Salters-Pedneault, 2008). Peers can also receive specialized training in mental health assessment and education to support fellow unit members. The United Kingdom's TRiM program (see Chapter 3, this volume) and the United States' Battlemind Warrior Resiliency Training, a type of psychological first aid for medics, are two examples of this kind of intervention model.

Third, individuals in need of additional help can be targeted for treatment. A proactive psychological assessment program is one mechanism to identify symptomatic service members and refer them for follow-up care. This kind of assessment can also be used to reduce stigma and potential barriers to care, although the timing of this kind of assessment is critical, and such assessments need to be conducted at several different points in the deployment cycle. For instance, it might prove to be beneficial to conduct routine mental health assessments throughout the deployment, with the goal of providing the service members with any needed mental health support to sustain them throughout the deployment rather than having to wait until after they return before any mental health support is provided.

The treatment itself needs to be adapted to take into account the occupational model proposed here because the development and maintenance of PTSD-related symptoms are directly and indirectly affected by the occupational context. For example, traditional treatment models assume the sequential nature of the development of PTSD. That is, individuals are exposed to a discrete event and that exposure causes subsequent symptoms. By recognizing that combat-related traumatic events are imposed on top of prolonged physiological stress, the treatment would need to emphasize this physiological component. Furthermore, treatment models need to be developed to take into account that the treatment may be provided in the midst of an ongoing combat deployment. Thus, treatment needs to be adapted; long-term therapy sessions, homework, and relaxation techniques may not necessarily be appropriate or even healthy in a combat setting. In turn, treatment provided following a combat deployment needs to take into account the fact that treatment is delayed and that several potentially traumatic combat-related events may have occurred across the deployment (see Chapter 2, this volume). Service members may also be expecting to return to combat, and thus their concerns about safety and their avoidance of emotions may serve an important function. Furthermore, traditionally accepted treatments for PTSD, such as cognitive behavior therapy and prolonged exposure therapy, typically focus on specific events, not on the global aspects of the combat environment. Not much is known about how treatment should be optimally designed to address these concerns or how to adapt existing treatment models to deal with occupational realties for veterans with PTSD.

The difficulty is knowing when to focus on the dysfunction of the veteran's response and when to focus on the environmental context of combat. By making this distinction, mental health professionals working with service members in the combat context can orient their interventions to team-based supports as well as understand which responses may in fact be adaptive to the combat environment and which ones may be disruptive. For instance, hypervigilance in a combat environment is adaptive and should not be treated. However, sleep difficulties, although normal and understandable, can impair performance and therefore should be treated, albeit in a manner that does not impair military performance.

Across all three types of support, prevention, early intervention, and treatment, organizational policies need to be created to institutionalize and facilitate the delivery of these supports. Although beyond the scope of this chapter, these policies include establishing adequate time between deployments, mandatory mental health training, and psychological screening (for a discussion of how policies can impact the provision of mental health services, see Chapter 2, this volume). In addition, policies that support the empirical validation of interventions can support the development of effective strategies for reducing combat-related PTSD. Such research can be used to establish an agenda for what needs to be addressed in this occupational context and to establish evidence-based best practices for this population.

Future Research

Research in the area of combat-related PTSD should address several key questions. First, to what extent does the experience of combat affect personality? If the assumption is that combat can lead to character development, then it follows that combat should also be powerful enough to lead to character impairment. Although personality disorders may have existed prior to a combat deployment, it may also be that exposure to combat in fact changes one's personality. Combat can serve as a powerful life-changing experience capable of altering one's character and personality both in a positive and negative way. To date, this area has received little scientific attention in service members following combat, although it has important implications for personality theory and personality disorder diagnosis. This area also has implications for resolving compensation claims. In the military, individuals who only receive a personality disorder diagnosis are not entitled to disability compensation because the presumption is that the personality disorder existed prior to entering active duty. Thus, this area has both practical implications and is important in terms of broadening our understanding of how combat deployment affects service members.

A second research area that should be addressed is defining when combat-related PTSD symptoms become part of a disorder and when they are adaptive for the occupation. Paradoxically, as stated earlier, the same PTSD symptoms in one context (e.g., combat) can be adaptive, whereas in another (e.g., garrison) they can be maladaptive. Whether these symptoms will lead to disruption in functioning depends on the context. Research is needed to understand the optimal way for service members to transition the adaptive PTSD symptoms to the garrison setting.

A third research area should address the issue of delayed onset combat-related PTSD. Military structure and social support provide service members with the context that can allow them to be high functioning even when they have PTSD symptoms. Once these service members leave the military, however, these same symptoms can lead to impairment. Thus, diagnosing veterans after they leave active duty does not necessarily represent a failure of the military medical system to diagnose the service members while they were on active duty as much as the fact that the impairment may not have manifested itself until after the service members separated from active duty. Thus, research is needed to understand the ways in which service members can be supported while on active duty and how these same supports can be used to bridge their adjustment to civilian life. This emphasis is particularly important given that a disproportionate number of veterans become homeless, engage in criminal activity, and are at risk for suicide.

We appreciate that incorporating an occupational model into the diagnosis and treatment of combat-related PTSD is complex. The goal of this chapter has been to provide a basis from which this reconceptualization can begin. A proper diagnosis, early intervention, and treatment strategy for combat veterans cannot take place unless there is recognition as a field that PTSD as it is currently understood does not address the needs of combat veterans. Many professionals working with combat veterans implicitly recognize the limits of the diagnosis and adapt their work accordingly. It is up to the medical community as whole, however, to continue to refine our understanding of combat-related PTSD.

REFERENCES

Adler, A. B., Castro, C. A., & McGurk, D. (2009). Time-driven Battlemind psychological debriefing: A group-level early intervention in combat. *Military Medicine*, *174*, 22–28.

Adler, A. B., Wright, K. M., Bliese, P. D., Eckford, R., & Hoge, C. W. (2008). A2 diagnostic criterion for combat-related posttraumatic stress disorder. *Journal of Traumatic Stress*, *21*, 301–308. doi:10.1002/jts.20336

American Psychiatric Association. (1980). *Diagnostic and statistical manual of mental disorders* (3rd ed.). Washington, DC: Author.

American Psychiatric Association. (1994). *Diagnostic and statistical manual of mental disorders* (4th ed.). Washington, DC: Author.

Bliese, P. D., Adler, A. B., Castro, C. A., Thomas, J. L., & Hoge, C. W. (2008, August). The impact of combat experiences on mental health over time. In A. B. Adler & C. A. Castro (Chairs), *Managing the psychological impact of combat: Soldiers, units, and leaders*. Symposium conducted at the meeting of the American Psychological Association, Boston, MA.

Boscarino, J. A. (1997). Diseases among men 20 years after exposure to severe stress: Implications for clinical research and medical care. *Psychosomatic Medicine, 59,* 605–614.

Breslau, N., & Davis, G. C. (1987). Posttraumatic stress disorder: The etiologic specificity of wartime stressors. *The American Journal of Psychiatry, 144,* 578–583.

Breslau, N., & Kessler, R C. (2001). The stressor criterion in *DSM–IV* posttraumatic stress disorder: An empirical investigation. *Biological Psychiatry, 50,* 699–704. doi:10.1016/S0006-3223(01)01167-2

Brewin, C. R., Andrews, B., & Rose, S. (2000). Fear, helplessness, and horror in posttraumatic stress disorder: Investigating *DSM–IV* criterion A2 in victims of violent crime. *Journal of Traumatic Stress, 13,* 499–509. doi:10.1023/A:1007741526169

Britt, T. W., Castro, C. A., & Adler, A. B. (2005). Self-engagement, stressors, and health: A longitudinal study. *Personality and Social Psychology Bulletin, 31,* 1475–1486. doi:10.1177/0146167205276525

Brunet, A., Weiss, D. S., Metzler, T. J., Best, S. R., Neylan, T. C., Rogers, C., . . . Marmar, C. R. (2001). The peritraumatic distress inventory: A proposed measure of PTSD criterion A2. *The American Journal of Psychiatry, 158,* 1480–1485. doi:10.1176/appi.ajp.158.9.1480

Bryant, R. A., Moulds, M. L., Guthrie, R. M., Dang, S. T., & Nixon, R. D. V. (2003). Imaginal exposure alone and imaginal exposure with cognitive restructuring in treatment of posttraumatic stress disorder. *Journal of Consulting and Clinical Psychology, 71,* 706–712. doi:10.1037/0022-006X.71.4.706

Castro, C. A., & McGurk, D. (2007). The intensity of combat and behavioral health status. *Traumatology, 13,* 6–23. Retrieved from http://tmt.sagepub.com/cgi/content/abstract/13/4/6

Creamer, M., McFarlane, A. C., & Burgess, P. (2005). Psychopathology following trauma: The role of subjective experience. *Journal of Affective Disorders, 86,* 175–182. doi:10.1016/j.jad.2005.01.015

Ehlers, A., Clark, D. M., Hackmann, A., McManus, F., & Fennell, M. (2005). Cognitive therapy for posttraumatic stress disorder: Development and evaluation. *Behaviour Research and Therapy, 43,* 413–431. doi:10.1016/j.brat.2004.03.006

Ginzberg, E. (1959). *The lost divisions.* New York, NY: Columbia University Press.

Harris, F. G., Mayer, J., & Becker, H. A. (1955). *Experiences in the study of combat in the Korean theater: I. Psychiatric and psychological data.* Washington, DC: Walter Reed Army Institute of Research.

Henning, K. R., & Frueh, B. C. (1998). Combat guilt and its relationship to PTSD symptoms. *Journal of Clinical Psychology, 53,* 801–808. doi:10.1002/(SICI)1097-4679(199712)53:8<801::AID-JCLP3>3.0.CO;2-I

Hoge, C. W., Castro, C. A., Messer, S. C., McGurk, D., Cotting, D. I., & Koffman, R. L. (2004). Combat duty in Iraq and Afghanistan, mental health problems, and barriers to care. *The New England Journal of Medicine, 351,* 13–22. doi:10.1056/NEJMoa040603

Hoge, C. W., Terhakopian, A., Castro, C. A., Messer, S. C., & Engel, C. C. (2007). Association of posttraumatic stress disorder with somatic symptoms, health care visits, and absenteeism among Iraq war veterans. *The American Journal of Psychiatry, 164,* 150–153. doi:10.1176/appi.ajp.164.1.150

Jones, E., & Wessely, S. (2001). Psychiatric battle casualties: An intra and interwar comparison. *The British Journal of Psychiatry, 178,* 242–247. doi:10.1192/bjp.178.3.242

Killgore, W. D. S., Cotting, D. I., Thomas, J. L., Cox, A. L., McGurk, D., Vo, A. H., . . . Hoge, C. W. (2008). Postcombat invincibility: Violent combat experiences are associated with increased risk-taking propensity following deployment. *Journal of Psychiatric Research, 42,* 1112–1121. doi:10.1016/j.jpsychires.2008.01.001

Killgore, W. D., Stetz, M. C., Castro, C. A., & Hoge, C. W. (2006). The effects of prior combat experience on the expression of somatic and affective symptoms in deploying soldiers. *Journal of Psychosomatic Research, 60,* 379–385. doi:10.1016/j.jpsychores.2006.02.012

Kubany, E. S. (1994). A cognitive model of guilt typology in combat-related PTSD. *Journal of Traumatic Stress, 7,* 3–19. doi:10.1002/jts.2490070103

McFarlane, A. C., & Girolamo, G. D. (1996). The nature of traumatic stressors and the epidemiology of posttraumatic stress reactions. In B. A. van der Kolk, A. C. McFarlane, & L. Weisaeth (Eds.), *Traumatic stress: The effects of overwhelming experience on mind, body and society* (pp. 129–154). New York, NY: Guilford Press.

Mental Health Advisory Team IV. (2007). *Mental Health Advisory Team (MHAT) IV Operation Iraqi Freedom 05-07.* Retrieved from http://www.armymedicine.army.mil/reports/mhat/mhat_iv/mhat-iv.cfm

Mental Health Advisory Team V. (2008). *Mental Health Advisory Team (MHAT) V Operation Iraqi Freedom 06-08: Iraq, Operation Enduring Freedom 8: Afghanistan.* Retrieved from http://www.armymedicine.army.mil/reports/mhat/mhat_v/mhat-v.cfm

Milliken, C. S., Hoge, C. W., & Auchterlonie, J. L. (2007). Longitudinal assessment of mental health problems among active and reserve component soldiers returning from the Iraq War. *JAMA, 298,* 2141–2148. doi:10.1001/jama.298.18.2141

Rona, R. J., Hyams, K. C., & Wessely, S. (2005). Screening for psychological illness in military personnel. *JAMA, 293*, 1257–1260. doi:10.1001/jama.293.10.1257

Shipherd, J., & Salters-Pedneault, K. (2008). Attention, memory, intrusive thoughts, and acceptance in PTSD: An update on the empirical literature for clinicians. *Cognitive and Behavioral Practice, 15*, 349–363.

Sims, A., & Sims, D. (1998). The phenomenology of posttraumatic stress disorder: A symptomatic study of 70 victims of psychological trauma. *Psychopathology, 31*, 96–112. doi:10.1159/000029029

van der Kolk, B. A., Weisaeth, L., & van der Hart, O. (1996). History of trauma in psychiatry. In B. A. van der Kolk, A. C. McFarlane, & L. Weisaeth (Eds.), *Traumatic stress: The effects of overwhelming experience on mind, body, and society* (pp. 47–74). New York, NY: Guilford Press.

Weathers, F. W., & Keane, T. M. (2007). The criterion A problem revisited: Controversies and challenges in defining and measuring psychological trauma. *Journal of Traumatic Stress, 20*, 107–121. doi:10.1002/jts.20210

Wright, K. M., Thomas, J. L., Adler, A. B., Ness, J. W., Hoge, C. W., & Castro, C. A. (2005). Psychological screening procedures for deploying U.S. forces. *Military Medicine, 170*, 555–562.

10

ADDRESSING POSTTRAUMATIC STRESS DISORDER IN VETERANS: THE CHALLENGE OF SUPPORTING MENTAL HEALTH FOLLOWING MILITARY DISCHARGE

TERENCE M. KEANE, BARBARA L. NILES, JOHN D. OTIS, AND STEPHEN J. QUINN

I moved home to Boston after being discharged from the army and immediately lacked the communal and structural support of both a military installation and fellow soldiers. Within a matter of weeks I realized that I had been significantly impacted psychologically by my experiences spanning 5 years and two tours in Iraq. I was angry, depressed, suffering from anxiety, and felt that no one at home—family, friends, coworkers—could relate. Making the first step towards treatment was the most difficult; that is, acknowledging that (1) I *had* been psychologically affected and (2) I could not control what I was feeling. Furthermore, I lacked the tools to address my troublesome thoughts and emotions. Through one-on-one sessions at the VA I have come to address many of the issues I now battle in everyday life. I now know that this road is a long one and professional establishments, such as the VA, that specialize in PTSD are instrumental to helping me and other veterans live happy, healthy lives despite our experiences.

—U.S. Army veteran

The current conflicts in Afghanistan and Iraq have been the largest U.S. combat operations since our involvement in the Vietnam War. Given the need for highly skilled and seasoned personnel on the battlefield, soldiers are being asked to complete multiple tours of duty or to extend the time of their

This chapter was authored or coauthored by an employee of the United States government as part of official duty and is considered to be in the public domain. Any views expressed herein do not necessarily represent the views of the United States government, and the author's participation in the work is not meant to serve as an official endorsement.

current tour of duty. Although this approach has created an experienced fighting force, there is growing concern that extending the amount of time a soldier is engaged in combat will place more stress on soldiers and their families and that this added stress will contribute to mental health problems and related psychosocial problems well into the future. Indeed, it is clear from the literature that veterans of Operation Enduring Freedom (OEF) and Operation Iraqi Freedom (OIF) are experiencing high rates of mental health disorders, including posttraumatic stress disorder (PTSD), depression, and alcohol use disorders (Hoge et al., 2004; Seal, Bertenthal, Miner, Sen, & Marmar, 2007). Given these statistics and the knowledge gained from treating veterans of past conflicts, Veterans Affairs (VA) has mobilized a major effort designed to disseminate evidence-based treatments for mental health disorders and to make these treatments highly accessible to OEF and OIF veterans nationwide.

The aim of this chapter is to provide a critical review and synthesis of the existing literature investigating the mental health issues, particularly PTSD, often faced by returning veterans. The chapter begins with a presentation of the diagnostic criteria, prevalence, and risk and resiliency factors associated with PTSD. Research is then presented describing evidence-based assessment and treatment practices, as well as efforts to identify and engage OEF and OIF veterans in need of mental health care. The specific needs of veterans who have been sexually assaulted are addressed, and the impact of physical injury, specifically traumatic brain injury (TBI) and chronic pain, on recovery is reviewed. Finally, the chapter closes with a section on future directions for treatment as well as a call for continued research to further refine existing treatments.

DIAGNOSTIC CRITERIA FOR POSTTRAUMATIC STRESS DISORDER

PTSD can occur following exposure to an event that is, or is perceived to be, threatening to one's own well-being or that of another person. The distinctive profile of symptoms in PTSD include (a) exposure to a traumatic event that involved the threat of death or serious injury (Criterion A); (b) reexperiencing the event in the form of intrusive thoughts, nightmares, flashbacks to the traumatic event, and psychophysiological reactivity to cues of the traumatic event (Criterion B); (c) avoidance of thoughts, people, and places that resemble the traumatic event, emotional numbing, and an absence of emotional attachments (Criterion C); and (d) symptoms of hyperarousal, including heightened startle sensitivity, sleep problems, attentional difficulties, hypervigilance, and the presence of irritability and anger (Criterion D; American Psychiatric Association, 1994).

EPIDEMIOLOGY OF POSTTRAUMATIC STRESS DISORDER IN WAR

Individuals who are engaged in military combat are at significant risk of exposure to traumatic events and the subsequent development of PTSD. The National Vietnam Veterans Readjustment Survey (NVVRS) estimated the prevalence and effects of PTSD in the Vietnam War veteran population. Conducted between November 1986 and February 1988, the NVVRS comprised interviews of 3,016 American veterans selected to provide a representative sample of those who served in the armed forces during the Vietnam era. In total, 1,632 Vietnam theater veterans, 716 Vietnam era veterans, and 668 civilian comparison subjects participated in the survey. The analyses indicated that 15.2% of all male Vietnam theater veterans met criteria for current PTSD. PTSD was significantly higher in participants who had been exposed to combat and other war zone stressors. Among Vietnam theater veteran women 8.5% of the 7,200 women who served met criteria for current PTSD. The NVVRS analyses also indicated that over one third (30.6%) of male Vietnam era veterans (over 960,000 men) and over one fourth (26.9%) of women serving in the Vietnam theater (over 1,900 women) met lifetime criteria for PTSD (Kulka et al., 1990a, 1990b).

More recently, a number of studies examined the prevalence of PTSD and other mental health disorders in OEF and OIF veterans. Hoge et al. (2004) conducted a survey of 3,671 OEF and OIF veterans after they returned from active duty in Afghanistan or Iraq. The results suggested a strong relationship between the number of combat experiences (e.g., being shot at) and the prevalence of PTSD. Seal et al. (2007) studied 103,788 OEF and OIF veterans to assess the proportion of veterans seen at VA facilities who received mental health and/or psychosocial diagnoses. Overall, 25% (25,658) received one or more distinct mental health diagnoses, with the median number being three. The single most common mental health diagnosis was PTSD, which was coded in 52% of those receiving mental health diagnoses and 13% of all OEF and OIF veterans in the study population. Depression was seen in 5%, and substance use disorder was seen in another 5% of the study population.

RISK AND RESILIENCY FACTORS

Although many people will experience a traumatic event over the course of their lifetime, most people do not develop PTSD as a consequence of the event. In an effort to explain the development of PTSD, Keane and Barlow (2002) described a model of PTSD that is based on the triple vulnerability model of anxiety (Barlow, 2000, 2002). According to the triple vulnerability model of anxiety, an integrated set of three vulnerabilities needs to be present for developing an anxiety disorder: a generalized biological vulnerability, a generalized psychological vulnerability based on early experiences of lack of control over salient events, and a more specific psychological vulnerability in which one learns to focus anxiety on specific situations. Although the triple vulnerability model applies to the development of anxiety in general, Keane and Barlow (2002) extended this model to the development of PTSD specifically. According to their model, persons who are more likely to develop PTSD or other anxiety disorders may inherit a biological or genetic vulnerability for developing an anxiety disorder (Ozer, Best, Lipsey, & Weiss, 2003). When persons are exposed to a traumatic event (e.g., a life and death situation) they often experience a basic and intense emotional response that can be classified as a "true alarm." However, the experience of "alarm" or other intense emotions is not sufficient for the development of PTSD. Given the nature of some traumatic events, "learned alarms" can develop in situations that resemble aspects of the traumatic event. To develop PTSD, one must develop anxiety or the sense that these situations, including one's own emotional reactions to them, are proceeding in an unpredictable and uncontrollable manner. Thus, when negative affect and a sense of uncontrollability develop, PTSD may emerge (see Figure 10.1). Although this model implies that a psychological

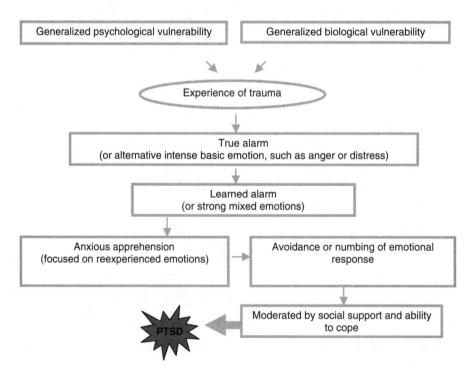

Figure 10.1. A model of the etiology of posttraumatic stress disorder (PTSD).

and biological vulnerability to develop the disorder exists, anxiety is always moderated to some extent by variables such as the availability of social support and the presence of adequate coping skills (Keane & Barlow, 2002).

Considerable research has also identified other factors associated with either increased risk of or resiliency against developing PTSD. There are three types of risk factors: pretraumatic, peritraumatic, and posttraumatic. One demographic factor that is related to the development of PTSD is age. In a study of OEF and OIF veterans, Seal et al. (2007) found that among veterans of active duty service, those who were younger (18 to 24 years) had significantly increased risk of mental health and PTSD diagnoses. One reason for this finding may be that younger soldiers are more likely to be of lower rank and have more combat exposure. These findings replicate the NVVRS results suggesting that younger soldiers are more likely to develop PTSD.

In another study on risk factors for PTSD, Breslau, Chilcoat, Kessler, Peterson, and Lucia (1999) found that the risk of developing PTSD in women was twice that in men, even when the type of trauma was taken into account. Although the nature of the mechanism involved is not known, such a finding regarding sex differences is consistent across many anxiety and mood disorders (Barlow, 2002). Peritraumatic factors are related to the nature of the traumatic event and one's reaction to it. For example, degree of combat exposure and the number of traumatic stressors experienced appears to predict PTSD (Hoge et al., 2004; Ozer et al., 2003). Of those factors that can be classified as posttraumatic, the availability of social support and personal hardiness appear to be most important, with the potential of providing resiliency to those who have experienced a traumatic event (Friedman, Keane, & Resick 2007; King, King, Fairbank, Keane, & Adams, 1998). Thus, the assessment of risk factors, particularly psychological strength and availability of social support, should be part of every PTSD diagnostic interview.

ASSESSMENT OF POSTTRAUMATIC STRESS DISORDER

Clinicians working in military and veterans health care systems are interested in the accurate assessment of patients with PTSD because they recognize that many of their patients have experienced traumatic events and can present with PTSD symptoms as either primary or secondary diagnoses. Obviously, PTSD is assessed for many different purposes, and the goals of a particular assessment determine the approach selected by the clinician. The objective of many mental health clinicians is to diagnose a patient by conducting an evaluation that includes a differential diagnosis, a functional assessment, and the collection of other related data that can be helpful in case conceptualization and in treatment planning. Other practitioners may be involved in forensic assessments or compensation evaluations where diagnostic accuracy is critical. Clearly, different assessment contexts require different assessment approaches, depending on the particular assessment goals of the professional (see Wilson & Keane, 2004, for reviews of available techniques for the assessment of PTSD within various contexts).

Since the inclusion of PTSD in the *Diagnostic and Statistical Manual of Mental Disorders* (American Psychiatric Association, 1994), there has been excellent progress in developing sound measures to assess trauma symptoms and PTSD in adults (Keane & Barlow, 2002; Keane, Weathers, & Foa, 2000; Weathers, Keane, & Davidson, 2001). We have recommended a multi-method approach to the assessment of PTSD since the inception of our clinical and research programs (Keane, Fairbank, Caddell, Zimering, & Bender, 1985). These different methods may include (a) structured diagnostic interview to assess PTSD and other comorbidities, (b) self-report psychological questionnaires, and (c) psychophysiological measures.

Structured diagnostic interviews are considered extremely valuable tools for assessing PTSD symptoms (Keane et al., 1998). Although it is standard practice in research settings to use structured diagnostic interviews, the use of structured interviews in the clinical setting is less common, except in a clinical forensic practice (Keane, 1995; Keane, Buckley, & Miller, 2003). This likely is due to time and cost burdens, as well as the need for specialized training to administer many of these interviews. Nonetheless, the use of structured diagnostic interviews for PTSD in clinical settings has been recommended to improve diagnostic accuracy and aid in treatment planning (Litz & Weathers, 1994). Here, we provide information on several structured interviews that were developed to measure PTSD symptoms either as modules of comprehensive diagnostic assessment tools or as independent PTSD measures.

Self-report measures provide information on the presence or absence of PTSD, trauma symptoms, and their severity. Several measures provide specific cutoffs that are indicative of a diagnosis of PTSD, whereas the majority incorporate continuous indicators of symptom severity. In general, self-report measures are more time and cost efficient than diagnostic interviews and are of particular utility in clinical settings in which a structured interview is not feasible or practical. Clinicians are encouraged to use those measures that have been normed in the population for which they will be used, to maximize accuracy and efficiency (Keane & Barlow, 2002). We also highlight some of those self-report measures that we recommend in practice.

Over the past 20 years, research on biologically based measures of PTSD has established a foundation for a psychobiological description of PTSD (Orr, Metzger, Miller, & Kaloupek, 2004). Researchers have found that PTSD alters a wide range of physiological functions (Yehuda, 1997) and may affect structural components of the brain (particularly the hippocampus; Bremner et al., 1995). Overall, the most consistent neurobiological finding in PTSD is that psychophysiological reactivity to trauma-specific cues is elevated in individuals with PTSD but not in trauma-exposed individuals without PTSD (for reviews, see Orr et al., 2004; Prins, Kaloupek, & Keane, 1995). Although psychophysiological assessment can provide unique information, widespread use of this approach in a clinical environment is not anticipated because it is expensive and requires equipment and specialized training on the part of the clinician. In the majority of cases, more time- and cost-efficient methods of assessment, such as diagnostic interviews or self-report measures, are more than adequate. As psychophysiological methods are not accessible to the majority of clinicians, we refer the interested reader to Orr et al. (2004) for an excellent review.

In addition, the clinician may want to review medical records and interview collateral sources regarding the patient's behavior and experiences, particularly when the accuracy of self-report is questioned or there is suspicion of malingering (e.g., during a compensation evaluation). In this chapter, we review measures of PTSD and their utility for diagnostic purposes, case conceptualization, treatment planning, and treatment monitoring and outcome.

OVERALL EVALUATION OF POSTTRAUMATIC STRESS DISORDER

Efforts to diagnose and assess patients for PTSD symptoms best include the use of a range of standardized assessment methods in addition to reviewing medical records, accessing collateral sources, and taking a thorough history. The gold standard in PTSD assessment is the Clinician Administered PTSD Scale structured interview (Blake et al., 1995), given that it is a sound, widely used measure that possesses excellent psychometric properties. As an adjunct, or in cases in which administering a structured interview is not feasible or practical, we recommend the use of self-report measures.

INITIAL IDENTIFICATION OF TREATMENT NEEDS

The number of Iraq and Afghanistan military returnees eligible for VA services for their health care needs is increasing continually as men and women who served in those combat theaters separate from active duty. A VA report identified that as of February 2008, just over half of the 1.7 million personnel who have served in the Global War on Terror (GWOT) have separated from the military and have access to veterans' benefits as OEF and OIF veterans (Veterans Health Affairs Office of Public Health and Environmental Hazards, 2008). As of January 1, 2008, only 39% of these new veterans had sought treatment through VA for medical or mental health problems; the need for VA to meet the health care needs of OEF and OIF veterans will likely continue to grow as those veterans already in the VA system remain there and the 61% who have not yet used VA services begin to use them.

Veterans with PTSD or other trauma-related psychological disorders present unique challenges for VA because these veterans commonly avoid seeking services for psychological problems. Although the presence of trauma and PTSD is associated with increased health care use in both veteran and civilian samples (Elhai, North, & Frueh, 2005; Hidalgo & Davidson, 2000; Kartha et al., 2008; Kessler, 2000; Solomon & Davidson, 1997), patients who are traumatized are less likely in the short term to seek mental health treatment. Despite reports of significant symptoms of psychological disorders and emotional distress in returning veterans, studies indicate that as many as half of the returning veterans who have PTSD do not seek mental health assistance (Hoge et al., 2004; Tanielian & Jaycox, 2008). Hoge and colleagues (2004) identified a number of perceived barriers to care that may contribute to the low rates of mental health assistance provided to active duty military, including difficulty with access to treatment and the stigma associated with seeking mental health treatment.

Specific concerns related to treatment-seeking among veterans with PTSD symptoms include the following:

- Fear that admitting to having psychological or interpersonal problems of any kind could lead to the diagnosis of a mental disorder with associated stigma. A commonly expressed sentiment in reaction to the possibility of being diagnosed with a psychiatric disorder or needing professional help is "I'm not crazy" or "I should be able to take care of my own problems."
- Fear that documented mental health related treatment could cause loss of employment or inability to obtain employment or would impede advancement.
- Fear of legal prosecution if any event is discussed that could have legal implications and is recorded in the medical record.

In the majority of cases, issues of stigma and confidentiality are easily handled with some education once a person takes the step to obtain help, but these issues may provide a barrier precluding help-seeking in the first place.

Despite the many barriers to care faced by newly returning veterans, a substantial proportion of the almost 325,000 OEF and OIF veterans currently in the VA system have PTSD. Over 20% of these veterans have received a diagnosis of PTSD by their VA care providers. If these symptoms remain untreated, the negative impact of PTSD on the psychosocial functioning of these veterans will grow. PTSD adversely affects relationships, employment, physical health, and overall quality of life. In addition, PTSD is often accompanied by increased rates of comorbid disorders, such as depression, anxiety, substance abuse, and chronic pain.

CURRENT VETERANS AFFAIRS PROGRAMS AND OUTREACH

VA, recognizing that many traumatized veterans will initially seek services for nonmental health problems, has instituted a number of interventions to identify veterans returning from OEF/OIF who may need referral for treatment of PTSD and common comorbidities such as depression or substance abuse. Each VA has a designated returning veterans coordinator. All newly returned veterans who may be having psychological problems are routed to this person as they enter the system. The coordinator is a clinician who can screen for psychiatric or readjustment problems, concerns, and symptoms; discuss benefits; and make referrals for treatment. Based on the Veterans Health Administration's (VHA) Uniform Mental Health Services Plan (Department of Veterans Affairs, 2008), each VA is also tasked with conducting outreach to military units, as guard and reserve veterans rotate back from deployment and prepare to return to civilian life, and to active duty soldiers, especially those with life altering injuries.

Veterans who enter the system through a primary care medical clinic will encounter medical professionals who are cued by VA's electronic medical record to screen for PTSD, depression, alcohol abuse, and TBI during initial visits. All VA medical centers also have designated clinics with staff expertise in the treatment of returning OEF and OIF veterans, either through an OEF/OIF specific team or though an established PTSD program. The role of clinicians through these initial contacts is to provide a first line of mental health care while supporting resilience and expected adjustment to the transition home to civilian life.

Since the findings of the NVVRS (Kulka et al., 1990b) confirmed the high prevalence of PTSD in returning Vietnam theater veterans, VA medical facilities have been equipped with specialty programs targeting the treatment of PTSD through psychotherapy and pharmacological interventions. There are outpatient and residential PTSD treatment programs across the VA health care system. Since 2007, VA's PTSD specialized treatment programs have consisted of 122 outpatient treatment teams and 41 intensive (day hospital or residential) treatment programs (Fontana, Rosenheck, Spencer, & Gray, 2008). In addition, VA's parallel system of readjustment counseling centers, called *Vet Centers* (Department of Veterans Affairs, 2008), consists of 232 treatment teams across the United States. The Vet Center system was created in 1979 in the aftermath of the Vietnam War to mitigate the reluctance of some veterans to seek mental health treatment. This was accomplished by moving the Vet Centers out of medical centers and into small storefront clinics. This increased sense of separation and privacy remains important to veterans today.

MILITARY SEXUAL TRAUMA

Beginning with the Navy's Tailhook incident in 1991, the issue of sexual harassment and sexual assault in the military became publically visible and openly debated. Several studies confirmed high rates of sexual assault and sexual harassment in military populations and even higher rates among VA patients (Bastian, Lancaster, & Reyst, 1996; Coyle, Wolan, & Van Horn, 1996; Skinner et al., 2000). According to VA's 2002 surveillance data results, military sexual trauma (MST) is much more common among women, but given the male and female base rates in the VA population, over 50% of identified MST cases in VA are male (Veterans Health Initiative, 2004).

Because of the often hidden nature of sexual trauma, veterans can apply for treatment at VA hospitals, clinics, or Vet Centers without charge and without need to demonstrate that the assault occurred. If providers conclude that medical or psychological symptoms are consistent with MST, those problems are treated without charge. All veterans are screened for MST through mental health or primary care contacts, and each facility has a designated MST coordinator to ensure that identified patients are referred for treatment and that they are not inadvertently billed for those services. Data for 2003, covering over 4.3 million VA patients, showed completed screening for 70% of patients, with increased odds across all categories of mental disorder comorbidities for those who screened positive for MST (Kimerling, Gima, Smith, Street, & Frayne, 2007).

SUICIDE PREVENTION

Outreach and treatment of PTSD require attention to the management of suicidal thoughts and behavior. Nearly 5% of the general population will at some point make a suicide attempt. An additional 17.5% will have suicidal thoughts, and 3.9% will progress to the point of having a plan and means of accomplishing it (Kessler, Borges, & Walters, 1999). Also concerning are the rates of suicide in the veteran population, which are approximately twice as high as those in the general population (Kaplan, Huguet, McFarland, & Newsom, 2007). A recent study of suicide mortality among veterans treated for depression in VA concluded that, unlike the general population, younger age was identified as a factor for increased risk, a finding of significant importance as a new and younger cohort of veterans returns from Iraq and Afghanistan (Zivin et al., 2007).

Veterans with PTSD are likely to manifest several risk factors that increase the probability of suicidal thinking and suicide attempts, including depression and feelings of hopelessness, substance abuse, estrangement from social supports, chronic anxiety and anger, and employment or financial difficulties (Chiles & Strosahl, 2005). Each VA has a suicide prevention coordinator who can track and follow cases of known suicide risk to ensure that needed care is accessed.

EVIDENCE-BASED TREATMENTS AND DISSEMINATION EFFORTS

Providing treatment with a strong evidence base for efficacy is a high priority in VA. A June 2008 VA directive for mental health services stated that VA medical centers and outpatient clinics nationwide "must provide adequate staff capacity to allow the delivery of evidence-based psychotherapy to their patients" (U.S. Department of Veterans Affairs, 2008, p. 29). A brief review of the salient issues and current state of the art in the treatment of PTSD in VA follows.

Posttraumatic Stress Disorder Treatment Literature

Over 20 controlled clinical trials of psychotherapy for PTSD have been published since the International Society for Traumatic Stress Studies (ISTSS) published practice guidelines in 2000 (Foa, Keane, & Friedman, 2000; for a recent review, see Resick, Monson, & Gutner, 2007). These studies demonstrated that short-term, goal-directed cognitive behavior therapy (CBT) is more efficacious than nonspecific therapy or no treatment. Studies comparing two or more short-term focused therapies indicated that there are few clear differences in efficacy among various available CBT treatments. More sophisticated and fine-grained recent treatment outcome studies have focused on identifying the active ingredients or specific mechanisms of change in PTSD treatments, and they have suggested that cognitive restructuring (Resick, Galovski, Uhlmansiek, Scher, Clum, & Young-Xu, 2008) and exposure (Bryant, Moulds, Guthrie, Dang, & Nixon, 2003; Foa et al., 2005) are important components of successful treatment.

Cognitive restructuring, an essential component of any CBT treatment, is the process of learning to alter one's maladaptive thinking patterns. In CBT, this is done in a systematic way: Clients are assigned homework "thought records" in which they identify their dysfunctional thoughts, write them down, and dispute their validity. For clients with PTSD, typical dysfunctional thoughts that are identified and challenged are, "I should have known it was going to happen and prevented it" or "It was all my fault."

Prolonged exposure is a technique for reducing fear and anxiety, in which the client confronts a feared situation, object, or memory that he or she has been avoiding. In PTSD treatment, the therapist guides the client to recall the traumatic event in a controlled fashion, either through actively imagining it in session (i.e., *imaginal exposure*) or writing about it in or out of session. Repeated exposure to the traumatic memories results in a reduction of fear and a reduction of avoidance of these memories (Keane, Fairbank, Caddell, & Zimering, 1989; Keane & Kaloupek, 1982).

For the past decade, exposure has been considered an important component of effective treatment for PTSD. In 1999, an expert consensus panel for PTSD recommended exposure-based psychotherapy for the treatment of multiple PTSD symptoms, including intrusive thoughts, flashbacks, trauma-related fears, panic attacks, avoidance, and generalized anxiety. Exposure therapies were considered to be the quickest acting and also one of the most effective psychotherapies for PTSD.

Challenges of Dissemination

Dissemination to practitioners of empirically validated treatments has been an important focus in the recent PTSD literature because it has become clear that the transition from clinical research to incorporation in clinical practice is much more difficult than had been formerly assumed (Cook, Schnurr, & Foa, 2004). This is a problem not only for exposure-based therapies, where therapists are often reluctant to require that clients directly face their feared memories and are concerned the exposure might frighten clients, but also for all psychotherapies generally. At the time the American Psychiatric Association's practice guidelines for empirically supported treatments were published (American Psychiatric Association Task Force on Promotion and Dissemination of Psychological Procedures, 1995), a number of objections appeared in the literature, the most prominent of these expressing concerns regarding the perceived reduction of clinical expertise in decision making. Specifically, opponents of using evidence-based manuals in psychotherapy argued that the challenge of treating patients as they appear in the consultation room is a more complex affair than allowed by scripted treatments (Seligman, 1995). Opponents also complained that their role in guiding treatment would be greatly reduced if they were required to follow a manual; they feared that specific techniques would replace theoretical grounding, and reliance on diagnostic classifications would fail to capture case complexity

(Addis & Krasnow, 2000). Thus, although there is clear empirical support for CBT treatments for PTSD, it is less clear how to encourage therapists to use them.

Health care scholars have examined the validity of several of the objections to manualized therapy in recent studies of PTSD treatment. Common objections to the routine use of exposure therapy include concerns that it will increase symptoms and cause clients—particularly those with comorbid disorders, who may be viewed as most fragile—to drop out of treatment. In a review of this literature, Hembree et al. (2003) found no difference in dropout rates when comparing exposure therapy with other CBT interventions across 25 controlled studies. Furthermore, treatment of patients with characteristics of borderline personality disorder, usually considered to present multiple treatment difficulties (Linehan, 1993), did not result in greater dropout or reduction in treatment benefit (Clarke, Rizvi, & Resick, 2008).

A temporary symptom exacerbation has also been described as a predictable and expected aspect of exposure-based treatments of PTSD (Nishith, Resick, & Griffin, 2002) because the usual avoidance strategies are deliberately thwarted. Several studies have investigated adverse outcomes and treatment dropouts to examine the possibility that exposure-based treatments could be poorly tolerated or even harmful to some clients, and none has identified significant problems in using exposure-based interventions (Chard, 2005; Foa et al., 2005; Monson et al., 2006). Several outcome studies have drawn samples from the community with fewer exclusion criteria than might be expected. Chard (2005), in studying child abuse survivors with PTSD, allowed a number of inclusion criteria, including ongoing pharmacological intervention, substance abuse, personality disorders, multiple traumas across the life span, suicidal ideation, and self-injurious behavior (as long as it was not considered life-threatening). Foa et al. (2005), treating a sample of female assault survivors with PTSD, noted that one third of their sample were unemployed or on disability, with almost half of participants reporting annual income of $15,000 or less and two thirds of the sample diagnosed with at least one comorbid Axis I disorder. Monson et al. (2006), in a study using cognitive processing therapy (CPT) treatment of veterans, reported that half of the CPT-treated cohort were receiving VA disability payments for PTSD at the time of the study and that disability status was not associated with outcome.

The challenge of successfully disseminating exposure therapies for PTSD so that VA clinicians will use them routinely in practice may be one of the greatest challenges the VA faces in providing top-notch treatment for veterans with PTSD. Although the VA was on the cutting edge in the development of exposure therapy (Keane & Kaloupek, 1982; Keane et al., 1989), VA clinicians as a whole have not embraced it in their clinics. One survey (Rosen et al., 2004) found that among VA clinicians who identify themselves as PTSD specialists, fewer than 20% conduct repeated exposure to traumatic memories, and fewer than 10% do so routinely. As clinicians continue to express reservations about using exposure therapy, interventions that specifically target therapist use of exposure are needed (Cook et al., 2004). VA has begun to tackle this challenge by (a) hiring hundreds of new mental health clinicians to address the needs of newly returning veterans with PTSD and (b) providing in-depth training and ongoing support for all VA mental health clinicians for two evidence-based exposure treatments via the VA "rollout," discussed next.

VA ROLLOUT OF EVIDENCE-BASED TREATMENT

The recently published VA guidelines on mental health services mandates evidence-based treatment for PTSD (Department of Veterans Affairs, 2008), with the recommendation that all veterans in the VA system have access to one or both of two empirically supported, manualized CBTs that include an exposure element: CPT, or prolonged exposure (PE) therapy. Rather than simply providing manuals to VA therapists, an elaborate rollout with extensive training has been designed and implemented for both CPT and PE. As reviewed by Davis et al. (1999), the struggle to bring science into practice is not unique to psychology but is common throughout medicine, where traditional continuing education activities such as the provision of educational materials have relatively little impact on practice. In reviewing several successful community implementation projects, Cook et al. (2004) noted that effective strategies include contact between clinicians and treatment experts, organizational support for the treatment, adaptability of the intervention, and provision of data on its success. VA's rollout of PE and CPT was designed with these elements to maximize the transmission of knowledge as well as clinician and client buy-in for these provocative treatments.

CPT was originally developed by Resick and colleagues to treat female rape victims with PTSD (Resick & Schnicke, 1993), and there is strong empirical support for its efficacy in that population (Resick, Jordan, Girelli, Hutter, & Marhoefer-Dvorak, 1998; Resick, Nishith, Weaver, Astin, & Feuer, 2002). More recently CPT has been adapted for use with veterans with combat-related PTSD, and a recent study indicates efficacy with this population as well (Monson et al., 2006). This 12-session treatment includes a written exposure component, where clients are required to write an account of their trauma, read it to the therapist, and reread it daily. Cognitive restructuring is also a critical part of the therapy, and therapists work with clients on challenging false beliefs around themes of safety, trust, power and control, esteem, and intimacy.

Exposure therapy was applied to PTSD by Keane and his colleagues working with combat veterans (Black & Keane, 1982; Fairbank & Keane, 1982; Keane & Kaloupek, 1982). They also conducted the first randomized clinical trial examining the effects of exposure therapy in treating PTSD (Keane et al., 1989, 1985). In that clinical trial, symptoms of PTSD and related conditions were greatly improved following the use of exposure therapy. Next, Foa and Rothbaum (1998) applied this treatment to PTSD secondary to sexual assault and rape. These researchers completed multiple clinical trials substantiating the effects of exposure therapy in successfully treating the symptoms of PTSD (e.g., Foa, Riggs, Massie, & Yarczower, 1995; Foa et al., 2005). In vivo exposure to trauma reminders was also emphasized in this nine- to 12-session treatment.

CPT and PE are being disseminated in an unprecedented national educational campaign across the VA system in 3- to 5-day workshops led by a cadre of trained clinicians who are traveling to different regions around the country to instruct VA clinicians on how to conduct these treatments. To address education, skills training, treatment adherence, and fidelity issues, both therapies are offered in intensive training formats with follow-up supervision and discussion forums. PE training consists of 5 days of didactics and role-play followed by consultation on two PE cases that include review of therapy tapes (National Center for Posttraumatic Stress Disorder, n.d.). Training in CPT is similarly structured, consisting of 2- to 3-day training sessions for individual and group CPT followed by consultation by telephone on four individual cases or two groups (National Center for Posttraumatic Stress Disorder, n.d.). Intensive training in workshop format is then followed by telephone case consultation available 25 hr per week; other support is provided to clinicians in an effort to promote maintenance of the skills (e.g., advanced lectures, discussion board, downloadable materials).

UNIQUE CHALLENGES OF TREATING COMBAT VETERANS

The good news is that there are no identifiable differences in what works in exposure therapies. Although it is sometimes assumed that there are important, if not critical, differences across various kinds of traumas, such as rape versus combat, car accident, or hurricane, there is no empirical evidence that supports this contention. In fact, exposure therapies were shown to be effective with combat veterans before large-scale treatment studies of PE and CPT were conducted (Keane et al., 1989; Keane & Kaloupek, 1982). Recent PTSD treatment studies with positive outcomes include those using a sample of war veterans with chronic PTSD over decades (Monson et al., 2006) as well as those using a sample of women who have been victimized in a variety of ways, with violent histories that span their lives and contain a number of potentially traumatic events (Chard, 2005; Foa et al., 2005; Resick et al., 2008). One advantage of the treatment rollout in VA is that the training and ongoing support for therapists can address common misconceptions regarding PE and CPT and can also address the skill sets necessary for the successful treatment of PTSD. Naive therapists will often assume that all potentially traumatic events must be treated individually for a treatment effect to be seen, when in fact all the evidence shows that a positive generalization effect is to be expected after treating one, or possibly two, events.

Another issue facing VA clinicians treating returning service members is that their clients may be serving in the National Guard or reserves and may be redeployed in the near future. Monthly reserve or guard duty, where clients interact and train with the units with which they served in the war zone, can serve as a strong trigger that worsens PTSD symptoms. Clients may feel acute loss for their buddies who died in combat or who are in recovery for devastating injuries from the war zone. These events can also serve as opportunities for in vivo exposure and psychological growth, however, because these military personnel are exposed to vivid reminders and can work in therapy to find adaptive ways to cope with the strong emotions that are triggered.

Clients who are facing potential or certain redeployment also pose unusual challenges for VA therapists. On some occasions, clinicians may be asked by military commanders to provide information on fitness for duty. This may have a negative effect on the therapeutic alliance because clients may be either reluctant to disclose the severity of their symptoms or may be inclined to amplify their difficulties to attain their desired outcome. The timing of redeployment may also affect whether exposure therapy is used because clinicians may be reluctant to commence with a protocol when there may not be time to complete it.

EMERGING TREATMENTS FOR POSTTRAUMATIC STRESS DISORDER

Seeking Safety is a treatment developed to address both PTSD and a common comorbid problem: substance abuse or dependence (Najavits, 2002). This CBT-based treatment touches on 25 different topics in the cognitive, behavioral, and interpersonal domains. For each topic a new coping skill is introduced that encourages alternatives to substance use and other destructive behavior. Outcome studies with small numbers of participants indicate that as a result of this focused treatment, patients improve both in terms of PTSD symptoms and substance use (e.g., Hien, Cohen, Miele, Litt, & Capstick, 2004; Najavits, Schmitz, Gotthard, & Weiss, 2005). Historically in VA, a diagnosis of current substance abuse disorder would frequently cause a patient to be excluded from CBT or exposure therapy for PTSD; these patients would routinely be referred for focused substance abuse treatment instead. In Seeking Safety, these two disorders are addressed concurrently, allowing greater continuity of care while stressing the development of coping skills to manage trauma symptoms early in the treatment process.

Other treatments under development that may hold promise for PTSD are those influenced by Eastern healing traditions of meditation and mindfulness combined with CBT. Dialectical behavior therapy, developed by Linehan (1993) for chronically suicidal clients with borderline personality disorder, contains components of more traditional CBT (e.g., cognitive restructuring, building skills to help regulate emotion) and has a strong emphasis on acceptance of negative emotion. Similarly, another approach to treatment, acceptance and commitment therapy (ACT; Hayes, Strosahl, & Wilson, 1999), promotes the acceptance of painful private experiences as part of the human condition that should not be avoided. ACT is also premised on principles of CBT. Although these treatments and other mindfulness approaches have not been adequately tested for PTSD, they may prove to be important adjuncts to evidence-based exposure therapy. Mindfulness approaches might usefully prepare clients to tolerate the unpleasant emotions that trauma exposure generates.

In addition, eye movement desensitization and reprocessing (EMDR; Shapiro, 1995) is a treatment that possesses some clear support from randomized clinical trials in the treatment of PTSD (Spates, Koch, Cusack, Pagoto, & Waller, 2009). This approach also works directly on the symptoms of PTSD (i.e., thoughts and images of the traumatic event) and thus bears a resemblance to other forms of CBT. The primary difference between EMDR and exposure therapy is the use of facilitated eye movements as one recalls the images of the traumatic event and the relative brevity of the exposure itself. EMDR also emphasizes the identification and use of alternative cognitive beliefs about the event itself. As a result, EMDR appears to use at least two treatment components that in themselves are effective treatments of PTSD. More research is needed on EMDR as it is applied to active duty military and war veterans who have developed PTSD secondary to their military service.

IMPACT OF INJURY ON RECOVERY

Given advances in protective equipment, a higher percentage of soldiers are surviving physical injuries that would have been fatal in the past (Okie, 2005; Warden, 2006). Yet chronic pain is a significant problem among injured OEF and OIF veterans, with commonly reported pain sites including the head, legs, and shoulders (Clark, Bair, Buckenmaier, Gironda, & Walker, 2007).

Although blast injuries caused by improvised explosive devices and suicide bombers can result in injuries that one can see (i.e., physical injuries), they can also cause injuries that may be less visually apparent but equally debilitating (i.e., mild traumatic brain injury, PTSD). Head and neck injuries such as TBI have been reported in a significant number of veterans who have been evacuated from Iraq and Afghanistan (Tanielian & Jaycox, 2008; Xydakis, Fravell, Nasser, & Casler, 2005). The overlap among some symptoms associated with chronic pain, PTSD, and TBI can make it difficult to correctly attribute symptoms to one condition versus another; however, the ability to make such distinctions has important implications for treatment planning and expected outcome for our returning veterans. Thus, the following section provides a brief review of our current understanding of the potential interactions among these three commonly co-occurring conditions.

POSTTRAUMATIC STRESS DISORDER AND PAIN

Although pain is typically a transient experience, for some people pain persists past the point where it is considered an adaptive reaction to an acute injury and results in emotional distress and increased use of health care system resources. Consistent with a biopsychosocial model of illness, individuals with chronic pain often report that pain interferes with their ability to engage in occupational, social, or recreational activities. Their inability to engage in these activities may contribute to increased isolation, negative mood (e.g., feelings of worthlessness and depression), and physical deconditioning, all of which in turn can exacerbate or contribute to the experience of pain.

Pain that persists for an extended period of time (i.e., months or years), that accompanies a disease process, or that is associated with a bodily injury, and that has not resolved over time may be referred to as *chronic pain* (International Association for the Study of Pain, 1994). Pain is one of the most common complaints made to primary care providers (Gureje, Van Korff, Simon, & Gater, 1998; Otis, Reid, & Kerns, 2005) and has significant implications for health care costs. In fact, the National Institute of Health identified chronic pain as the costliest medical problem in America, affecting nearly 100 million individuals (Byrne & Hochwarter, 2006).

The co-occurrence of chronic pain and PTSD may have serious negative implications for the adaptive functioning of OEF and OIF veterans who have experienced a traumatic combat event. Research suggests that patients with chronic pain and PTSD experience more intense pain and affective distress (Geisser, Roth, Bachman, & Eckert, 1996), higher levels of life interference (Turk & Okifuji, 1996), and greater disability (Sherman, Turk, & Okifuji, 2000) than patients with either pain or PTSD alone. Although rates vary, it has been reported that 45% to 85% of patients who report for the treatment of PTSD also have a significant chronic pain condition (Beckham et al., 1997; Shipherd et al., 2007). The association between pain and PTSD is likely to be stronger among OEF and OIF veterans when compared with Vietnam era veterans because the traumatic event and the pain condition are more likely to have a recent onset and to be associated with the same event. Theoretically driven research regarding the reasons for the high comorbidity between pain and PTSD is currently underway.

Otis, Keane, and Kerns (2003) proposed that the triple vulnerability model for anxiety (Barlow, 2000, 2002) might also be used to account for the high rates of chronic pain in this population. Otis et al. suggested that, similar to the development of anxiety and PTSD, there may also be underlying biological, psychological, and specialized psychological vulnerabilities related to the development of chronic pain. For example, pain may have a biological basis, and persons may have a genetic predisposition to develop certain pain conditions such as headache (Larsson, Bille, & Pedersen, 1995; Russell, 2008). Also, pain can be the result of a physical injury or the gradual deterioration of tissue over time. However, the presence and extent of physical pathology by themselves are often not sufficient to account for the report of pain. For example, there is a low correlation between abnormal magnetic resonance imaging and pain report and functional impairment (Wood, Garvey, Gundry, & Heithoff, 1995).

Thus, just as a biological vulnerability is one risk factor in the development of anxiety yet is not sufficient to cause an anxiety disorder, pain too may have a biological basis, but the presence of structural pathology alone may not be sufficient to cause a chronic pain condition. Similar to the triple vulnerability model developed for anxiety and PTSD, a generalized psychological vulnerability may also be present prior to the development of a chronic pain condition. Numerous studies indicate that many patients with chronic pain do experience perceptions of low social support, poorly developed coping skills, failed past attempts to cope with stressful life events (e.g., job stressors, marital stressors), and perceptions of lack of control over life events (DeGood & Tait, 2001). More specifically, it is possible that for some people to develop a chronic pain condition, they must also develop a belief that the pain is proceeding in an unpredictable and uncontrollable manner. When combined with a previous experience of coping poorly with a painful condition, this could contribute to decreased self-efficacy and low expectations of adaptively coping with future experiences of pain, which may constitute a specific psychological vulnerability to developing chronic pain.

Numerous studies indicate that many individuals with chronic pain do, in fact, typically perceive a lack of personal control over their pain (Turk &

Rudy, 1988). The relationship between perceived controllability and pain has been demonstrated in a variety of chronic pain syndromes, including migraine headache (Mizener, Thomas, & Billings, 1988), low back pain, and rheumatoid arthritis (Flor & Turk, 1988), to name a few. When persons perceive their pain to be uncontrollable, feelings of low self-efficacy may develop, along with negative affect. Thus, a fear may develop of entering situations or performing activities in which pain may occur, leading to avoidance of situations in daily life. This avoidance will further fuel negative affect, feelings of uncontrollability, and low self-efficacy, and result in increased disability. Similar to findings in the PTSD literature, it has been found that pain is always moderated to some extent by variables such as the presence of adequate coping skills and social support (Kerns, Otis, & Wise, 2002; Kerns, Rosenberg, & Otis, 2002). Thus, whether the alarm is a trauma reminder or pain reminder, the development of a sense of uncontrollability may precede the development of both disorders. On the basis of this model of the development of chronic pain and PTSD, efforts to teach active military personnel to develop strong coping skills and to use them effectively in the face of stressors, and efforts to encourage the establishment of a supportive operating environment appear warranted.

In an effort to develop more effective treatments for returning military personnel with comorbid chronic pain and PTSD, Otis and Keane are conducting a randomized clinical trial of an integrated treatment for veterans with chronic pain and PTSD (Otis, Keane, Kerns, Monson, & Scioli, 2009). Some of the treatment elements were chosen for use in this trial on the basis of evidence-based, cognitive–behaviorally oriented treatments for pain management (Otis, 2007) and PTSD (Resick et al., 2002). The resulting 11-session treatment manual and workbook emphasizes goal setting and increasing patient activity levels and teaching patients ways to cope with stress and to challenge maladaptive thoughts and beliefs related to pain and PTSD. Results of the study thus far have been positive; although participants in all three active treatment conditions manifested clinically significant decreases in their self-reported pain and PTSD symptoms, initial data suggest that those who received the integrated treatment showed the most substantial changes from pre- to posttreatment. Following this line of research, a follow-up study is exploring the efficacy of a brief and intensive (i.e., 3-week) version of treatment. Because many returning OEF and OIF veterans have significant pain and PTSD, an intensive and integrated treatment approach could be particularly beneficial to help these veterans return to healthy functioning as soon as possible. As similar studies are launched and treatment strategies are tested on patients with comorbid pain and PTSD, we may then begin to refine our existing treatment protocols.

POSTTRAUMATIC STRESS DISORDER
AND TRAUMATIC BRAIN INJURY

TBI diagnoses can range from mild to severe depending on the severity of injury. Mild TBI and concussion may be characterized by symptoms including irritability, memory problems, difficulty concentrating, or altered mental status and is often referred to as *postconcussive syndrome* (PCS; Lew et al., 2008). Given the large number of injured soldiers who have experienced external blows to the head, been in close proximity to an explosion, or experienced other combat hazards, mild TBI has been labeled a signature injury in the wars in Iraq and Afghanistan (Defense and Veterans Brain Injury Center, n.d.). Although mild TBI can resolve quickly (often within a month of the injury; Belanger, Curtiss, Demery, Lebowitz, & Vanderploeg, 2005), for some people the symptoms can last for months or years. Complicating the clinical picture further is the fact that psychiatric conditions such as PTSD can interfere with normal cognitive function and moderate PCS. Furthermore, mild TBI may increase the risk of developing psychiatric conditions such as PTSD (Lew et al., 2008).

A recent survey conducted by the RAND Corporation provided some insight into the scope of the problem the VA health care system is likely to face in the coming years in terms of the health-related needs of OEF and OIF veterans related to depression, PTSD, and TBI. The survey of 1,965 OEF and OIF veterans found that 14% screened positive for PTSD, 14% for major depression, and 19.5% reported symptoms consistent with a mild TBI during deployment; of those experiencing TBI, over a third (37.4%) also had overlapping PTSD or depression. Assuming that the prevalence found in this study is representative of the 1.7 million service members who had been deployed for OEF and OIF as of October 2007, these findings suggest that approximately 300,000 returning service members are currently experiencing PTSD or major depression and about 320,000 may have experienced a mild TBI during deployment (Tanielian & Jaycox, 2008).

Hoge et al. (2008) shed new light on the relationship between combat-related mild TBI during deployment and postdeployment health related outcomes, including PTSD. Hoge et al. surveyed 2,225 U.S. Army infantry soldiers 3 to 4 months postdeployment to Iraq. Of the 124 (4.9%) soldiers reporting injuries with loss of consciousness, 43.9% met criteria for PTSD. Analyses indicated that soldiers with mild TBI were more likely to report health related problems such as poor general health, missed workdays, medical visits, and a high number of somatic and postconcussive symptoms than were soldiers with other injuries. However, after adjusting for PTSD and depression, mild TBI was no longer associated with these physical health outcomes or symptoms, except for headache. This study was significant because it raised critical questions regarding the impairments that can be attributed to mild TBI versus those that are perhaps more accurately attributable to PTSD and depression.

FUTURE DIRECTIONS

The GWOT remains an active war across multiple war zones, and it is distinctly possible that American troops will continue to serve in these war zones for the indefinite future. The number of individuals serving multiple tours of duty is increasing, and with this increase comes greater exposure to traumatic stressors and the likelihood of acquiring PTSD and other trauma-related conditions. The true prevalence of PTSD secondary to these wars is unknown; research to date has used only screening measures for PTSD. We consider the statistics cited to date to be the best estimates. However, large numbers of patients are seeking treatment for psychological problems from the Department of Defense health care system and from the Department of Veterans Affairs health care system. This help seeking is likely to continue.

Central questions do remain and await research to inform public policy and clinical practice. For example, do patients with PTSD and TBI access psychological treatments, and are their outcomes comparable with those without TBI? Do patients with chronic pain and PTSD respond consistently to the evidence-based treatments available? How can psychopharmacological agents be useful in treating patients with PTSD, TBI, and chronic pain? These are important questions that need to be addressed.

Yet, accessing mental health treatment carries with it a stigma in contemporary society. Can interventions be used to reduce this stigma so that individuals can obtain treatment early in the course of their condition and mitigate the impact that these symptoms have on their lives' trajectory? More work is needed in this area. The key to prevention will be based on the capacity of individuals to access services early; interventions designed to mitigate stigma within systems, communities, and in individuals would be most welcome.

Similarly, the availability of the Internet offers an incredible opportunity for treatment delivery, but it also presents challenges. Surely the web can be one component of a multipronged effort to get treatments to individuals when and where they need it. Evaluation of an Internet-based therapy to address PTSD in Pentagon employees after the September 11 attack indicates that this mode of therapy offers great promise in reducing symptomatology (Litz, Engel, Bryant, & Papa, 2007). In addition, the web mitigates the stigma with which mental health treatment is often associated. The key questions will be the extent to which informational and educational models of intervention will promote positive adjustment and whether other types of interventions (e.g., chat rooms) can be useful in promoting the emotional processing often seen as fundamental to behavior change. In any case, the web offers war veterans a unique opportunity for the first time to reach out to others who have experienced similar war trauma, whether it is psychological or physical. Such support can be pivotal in maintaining the motivation to engage in rehabilitative activities so that veterans with a wide range of disabilities can optimize their recovery.

Finally, policies and procedures adopted by military and veterans' organizations can themselves be important interventions that improve the lives of affected veterans. Standardizing high-quality compensation and pension examinations nationwide would be one policy that would enhance the experience of veterans and military members facing these difficult and stressful processes. Similarly, policies that enhance the integration of the health care systems associated with DOD and VA would greatly improve the initial care received by wounded servicemen when they transition to VA care. These are all eminently achievable practices; they are surely important ones for all administrators involved to consider.

REFERENCES

Addis, M. E., & Krasnow, A. D. (2000). A national survey of practicing psychologists' attitudes toward psychotherapy treatment manuals. *Journal of Consulting and Clinical Psychology, 68*, 331–339. doi:10.1037/0022-006X.68.2.331

American Psychiatric Association. (1994). *Diagnostic and statistical manual of mental disorders* (4th ed.). Washington, DC: Author.

American Psychiatric Association Task Force on Promotion and Dissemination of Psychological Procedures. (1995). Training in and dissemination of empirically validated psychological treatments: Report and recommendations. *Clinical Psychologist, 48*, 3–23.

Barlow, D. H. (2000). Unraveling the mysteries of anxiety and its disorders from the perspective of emotion theory. *American Psychologist, 55*, 1247–1263. doi:10.1037/0003-066X.55.11.1247

Barlow, D. H. (Ed.). (2002). *Anxiety and its disorders.* New York, NY: Guilford Press.

Bastian, L., Lancaster, A., & Reyst, H. (1996). Department of Defense 1995 Sexual harassment survey (Report No. 96-014). Arlington, VA: Defense Manpower Data Center.

Beckham, J. C., Crawford, A. L., Feldman, M. E., Kirby, A. C., Hertzberg, M. A., Davidson, R. J. T., & Moore, S. (1997). Chronic posttraumatic stress disorder and chronic pain in Vietnam combat veterans. *Journal of Psychosomatic Research, 43*, 379–389. doi:10.1016/S0022-3999(97)00129-3

Belanger, H. G., Curtiss, G., Demery, J. A., Lebowitz, B. K., & Vanderploeg, R. D. (2005). Factors moderating neuropsychological outcomes following mild traumatic brain injury: A meta-analysis. *Journal of the International Neuropsychological Society, 11*, 215–227. doi:10.1017/S1355617705050277

Black, J. L., & Keane, T. M. (1982). Implosive therapy in the treatment of combat related fears in a World War II veteran. *Journal of Behavior Therapy and Experimental Psychiatry, 13*, 163–165. doi:10.1016/0005-7916(82)90061-1

Blake, D. D., Weathers, F. W., Nagy, L. M., Kaloupek, D. G., Gusman, F. D., Charney, D. S., & Keane, T. M. (1995). The development of a clinician-administered PTSD scale. *Journal of Traumatic Stress, 8*, 75–90. doi:10.1002/jts.2490080106

Bremner, J. D., Randall, P. K., Scott, T. M., Bronen, R. A., Seibyl, J. P., Southwick, S. M., . . . Innis, R. B. (1995). MRI-based measurement of hippocampal volume in patients with combat-related posttraumatic stress disorder. *The American Journal of Psychiatry, 152*, 973–981.

Breslau, N., Chilcoat, H. D., Kessler, R. C., Peterson, E. L., & Lucia, V. C. (1999). Vulnerability to assaultive violence: Further specification of the sex difference in posttraumatic stress disorder. *Psychological Medicine, 29*, 813–821. doi:10.1017/S0033291799008612

Bryant, R. A., Moulds, M. L., Guthrie, R. M., Dang, S. T., & Nixon, R. D. V. (2003). Imaginal exposure alone and imaginal exposure with cognitive restructuring in treatment of posttraumatic stress disorder. *Journal of Consulting and Clinical Psychology, 71*, 706–712. doi:10.1037/0022-006X.71.4.706

Byrne, Z. S., & Hochwarter, W. A. (2006). I get by with a little help from my friends: The interaction of chronic pain and organizational support and performance. *Journal of Occupational Health Psychology, 11*, 215–227. doi:10.1037/1076-8998.11.3.215

Chard, K. M. (2005). An evaluation of cognitive processing therapy for the treatment of posttraumatic stress disorder related to childhood sexual abuse. *Journal of Consulting and Clinical Psychology, 73*, 965–971. doi:10.1037/0022-006X.73.5.965

Chiles, J. A., & Strosahl, K. D. (2005). *Clinical manual for assessment and treatment of suicidal patients.* Washington, DC: American Psychiatric Publishing.

Clark, M. E., Bair, M. J., Buckenmaier, C. C., Gironda, R. J., & Walker, R. L. (2007). Pain and combat injuries in soldiers returning from Operations Enduring Freedom and Iraqi Freedom: Implications for research and practice. *Journal of Rehabilitation Research and Development, 44*, 179–194. doi:10.1682/JRRD.2006.05.0057

Clarke, S. B., Rizvi, S. L., & Resick, P. A. (2008). Borderline personality characteristics and treatment outcome in cognitive–behavioral treatments for PTSD in female rape victims. *Behavior Therapy, 39*, 72–78. doi:10.1016/j.beth.2007.05.002

Cook, J. M., Schnurr, P. P., & Foa, E B. (2004). Bridging the gap between posttraumatic stress disorder research and clinical practice: The example of exposure therapy. *Psychotherapy, 41*, 374–387. doi:10.1037/0033-3204.41.4.374

Coyle, B. S., Wolan, D. L., & Van Horn, A. S. (1996). The prevalence of physical and sexual abuse in women veterans seeking care at a Veterans Affairs Medical Center. *Military Medicine, 161*, 588–593.

Davis, D., Thomson-O'Brien, M. A., Freemantle, N., Wolf, F. M., Mazmanian, P., & Taylor-Vaisey, A. (1999). Impact of formal continuing medical education: Do conferences, workshops, rounds, and other traditional continuing education activities change physician behavior or health care outcomes? *JAMA, 282*, 867–874. doi:10.1001/jama.282.9.867

Defense and Veterans Brain Injury Center. (n.d.). *Understanding traumatic brain injury.* Retrieved from http://www.dvbic.org/Providers/DVBIC-Educational-Materials.aspx

DeGood, D. E., & Tait, R. C. (2001). Assessment of pain beliefs and pain coping. In D. C. Turk & R. Melzack (Eds.), *Handbook of pain assessment* (pp. 320–345). New York, NY: Guilford Press.

Elhai, J. D., North, T. C., & Frueh, B. C. (2005). Health service use predictors among trauma survivors: A critical review. *Psychological Services, 2*, 3–19. doi:10.1037/1541-1559.2.1.3

Fairbank, J. A., & Keane, T. M. (1982). Flooding for combat-related stress disorders: Assessment of anxiety reduction across traumatic memories. *Behavior Therapy, 13*, 499–510. doi:10.1016/S0005-7894(82)80012-9

Flor, H., & Turk, D. C. (1988). Chronic back pain and rheumatoid arthritis: Predicting pain and disability from cognitive variables. *Journal of Behavioral Medicine, 11*, 251–265. doi:10.1007/BF00844431

Foa, E. B., Hembree, E. A., Cahill, S. E., Rauch, S. A. M., Riggs, D. S., Feeny, N. C., & Yadin, E. (2005). Randomized trial of prolonged exposure for posttraumatic stress disorder with and without cognitive restructuring: Outcome at academic and community clinics. *Journal of Consulting and Clinical Psychology, 73*, 953–964. doi:10.1037/0022-006X.73.5.953

Foa, E. B., Keane, T. M., & Friedman, M. J. (2000). *Effective treatments for PTSD, practice guidelines from the International Society for Traumatic Stress Studies.* New York, NY: Guilford Press.

Foa, E. B., Riggs, D. S., Massie, E. D., & Yarczower, M. (1995). The impact of fear activation and anger on the efficacy of exposure treatment for posttraumatic stress disorder. *Behavior Therapy, 26*, 487–499. doi:10.1016/S0005-7894(05)80096-6

Foa, E. B., & Rothbaum, B. O. (1998). *Treating the trauma of rape: Cognitive–behavioral therapy for PTSD.* New York, NY: Guilford Press.

Fontana, A., Rosenheck, R., Spencer, H., & Gray, S. (2008). The long journey home XVI: Treatment of posttraumatic stress disorder in the Department of Veterans Affairs: Fiscal Year 2007 Service Delivery and Performance. In M. J. Friedman, T. M. Keane, & P. A. Resick (Eds.), *Handbook of PTSD: Science and practice* (pp. 540–561). New York, NY: Guilford Press.

Friedman, M. J., Keane, T. M., & Resick, P. A. (Eds.). (2007). *Handbook of PTSD: Science and practice*. New York, NY: Guilford Press.

Geisser, M. E., Roth, R. S., Bachman, J. E., & Eckert, T. A. (1996). The relationship between symptoms of posttraumatic stress disorder and pain, affective disturbance, and disability among patients with accident and nonaccident related pain. *Pain, 66*, 207–214. doi:10.1016/0304-3959(96)03038-2

Gureje, O., Van Korff, M., Simon, G. E., & Gater, R. (1998). Persistent pain and well-being: A World Health Organization study in primary care. *JAMA, 280*, 147–151. doi:10.1001/jama.280.2.147

Hayes, S. C., Strosahl, K., & Wilson, K. G. (1999). *Acceptance and commitment therapy: An experimental approach to behavior change*. New York, NY: Guilford Press.

Hembree, E. A., Foa, E. B., Dorfan, N. M., Street, G. P., Kowalski, J., & Tu, X. (2003). Do patients drop out prematurely from exposure therapy for PTSD? *Journal of Traumatic Stress, 16*, 555–562. doi:10.1023/B:JOTS.0000004078.93012.7d

Hidalgo, R. B., & Davidson, J. R. T. (2000). Posttraumatic stress disorder: Epidemiology and health-related considerations. *The Journal of Clinical Psychiatry, 61*, 5–13.

Hien, D. A., Cohen, L. R., Miele, G. M., Litt, L. C., & Capstick, C. (2004). Promising treatments for women with comorbid PTSD and substance use disorders. *The American Journal of Psychiatry, 161*, 1426–1432. doi:10.1176/appi.ajp.161.8.1426

Hoge, C. W., Castro, C. A., Messer, S. C., McGurk, D., Cotting, D. I., & Koffman, R. L. (2004). Combat duty in Iraq and Afghanistan, mental health problems, and barriers to care. *The New England Journal of Medicine, 351*, 13–22. doi:10.1056/NEJMoa040603

Hoge, C. W., McGurk, D., Thomas, J. L., Cox, A. L., Engel, C. C., & Castro, C. A. (2008). Mild traumatic brain injury in U.S. soldiers returning from Iraq. *The New England Journal of Medicine, 358*, 453–463. doi:10.1056/NEJMoa072972

International Association for the Study of Pain. (1994). Forensic Psychological Assessment in PTSD. In H. Merskey & N. Bogduk (Eds.), *IASP Task Force on Taxonomy* (pp. 209–214). Seattle, WA: IASP Press.

Kaplan, M. S., Huguet, N., McFarland, B. H., & Newsom, J. T. (2007). Suicide among male veterans: A prospective population-based study. *Journal of Epidemiology and Community Health, 61*, 619–624. doi:10.1136/jech.2006.054346

Kartha, A., Brower, V., Saitz, R., Samet, J. H., Keane, T. M., & Liebschutz, J. (2008). The impact of trauma exposure and posttraumatic stress disorder on healthcare utilization among primary care patients. *Medical Care, 46*, 388–393. doi:10.1097/MLR.0b013e31815dc5d2

Keane, T. M. (1995). Guidelines for the forensic psychological assessment of posttraumatic stress disorder claimants. In R. I. Simon (Ed.), *Posttraumatic stress disorder in litigation: Guidelines for forensic assessment* (pp. 99–115). Washington, DC: American Psychiatric Association.

Keane, T. M. (2008). Posttraumatic stress disorder: Future directions in science and practice. *Journal of Rehabilitation Research and Development, 45*, vii–ix.

Keane, T. M., & Barlow, D. H. (2002). Posttraumatic stress disorder. In D. H. Barlow (Ed.), *Anxiety and its disorders* (pp. 418–453). New York, NY: Guilford Press.

Keane, T. M., Buckley, T. C., & Miller, M. W. (2003). Part 1. Topics and codes. In R. I. Simon (Ed.), *Posttraumatic stress disorder in litigation: Guidelines for forensic assessment* (2nd ed., pp. 119–140). Washington, DC: American Psychiatric Publishing.

Keane, T. M., Fairbank, J. A., Caddell, J. M., & Zimering, R. T. (1989). Implosive (flooding) therapy reduces symptoms of PTSD in Vietnam combat veterans. *Behavior Therapy, 20*, 245–260. doi:10.1016/S0005-7894(89)80072-3

Keane, T. M., Fairbank, J. A., Caddell, J. M., Zimering, R. T., & Bender, M. E. (1985). A behavioral approach to assessing and treating posttraumatic stress disorder in Vietnam veterans. In C. R. Figley (Ed.), *Trauma and its wake: Vol. I. The study and treatment of posttraumatic stress disorder* (pp. 257–294). New York, NY: Brunner/Mazel.

Keane, T. M., & Kaloupek, D. G. (1982). Imaginal flooding in the treatment of posttraumatic stress disorder. *Journal of Consulting and Clinical Psychology, 50*, 138–140. doi:10.1037/0022-006X.50.1.138

Keane, T. M., Kolb, L. C., Kaloupek, D. G., Orr, S. P., Blanchard, E. B., Thomas, R. G., . . . Lavori, P. W. (1998). Utility of psychophysiology measurement in the diagnosis of posttraumatic stress disorder: Results from a department of Veterans Affairs cooperative study. *Journal of Consulting and Clinical Psychology, 66*, 914–923. doi:10.1037/0022-006X.66.6.914

Keane, T. M., Weathers, F. W., & Foa, E. B. (2000). Diagnosis and assessment. In E. B. Foa, T. M., Keane, & M. J. Friedman (Eds.), *Effective treatments for PTSD: Practice guidelines from the International Society for Traumatic Stress Studies* (pp. 18–36). New York, NY: Guilford Press.

Kerns, R. D., Otis, J. D., & Wise, E. (2002). Treating Families of Chronic Pain Patients: Application of a cognitive–behavioral transactional model. In R. J. Gatchel & D. C. Turk (Eds.), *Psychological approaches to pain management* (pp. 256–275). New York, NY: Guilford Press.

Kerns, R. D., Rosenberg, R., & Otis, J. D. (2002). Self-appraised problem-solving competence and pain relevant social support as predictors of the experience of chronic pain. *Annals of Behavioral Medicine, 24*, 100–105. doi:10.1207/S15324796 ABM2402_06

Kessler, R. C. (2000). Posttraumatic stress disorder: The burden to the individual and to society. *The Journal of Clinical Psychiatry, 61*, 4–12.

Kessler, R. C., Borges, G., & Walters, E. E. (1999). Prevalence of risk factors for lifetime suicide attempts in the National Comorbidity Survey. *Archives of General Psychiatry, 56*, 617–626. doi:10.1001/archpsyc.56.7.617

Kimerling, R., Gima, K., Smith, M. W., Street, A. E., & Frayne, S. M. (2007). The Veterans Health Administration and military sexual trauma. *American Journal of Public Health, 97*, 2160–2166. doi:10.2105/AJPH.2006.092999

King, L. A., King, D. W., Fairbank, J. A., Keane, T. M., & Adams, G. (1998). Resilience-recovery factors in posttraumatic stress disorder among female and male Vietnam veterans: Hardiness, postwar social support, and additional stressful life events. *Journal of Personality and Social Psychology, 74*, 420–434. doi:10.1037/0022-3514.74.2.420

Kulka, R. A., Schlenger, W. E., Fairbank, J. A., Hough, R. L., Jordan, B. K., Marmar, C. R., & Weiss, D. S. (1990a). *The national Vietnam veterans readjustment study: Tables of findings and technical appendices.* New York, NY: Brunner/Mazel.

Kulka, R. A., Schlenger, W. E., Fairbank, J. A., Hough, R. L., Jordan, B. K., Marmar, C. R., & Weiss, D. S. (1990b). *Trauma and the Vietnam War generation: Report of findings from the national Vietnam veterans readjustment study.* New York, NY: Brunner/Mazel.

Larsson, B., Bille, B., & Pedersen, N. L. (1995). Genetic influence in headaches: A Swedish twin study. *Headache, 35*, 513–519. doi:10.1111/j.1526-4610.1995.hed3509513.x

Lew, H. L., Vanderploeg, R. D., Moore, D. F., Schwab, K., Friedman, L., Yesavage, J., . . . Sigford, B. J. (2008). Guest editorial: Overlap of mild TBI and mental health conditions in returning OIF/OEF service members and veterans. *Journal of Rehabilitation Research and Development, 45*, xi–xvi.

Linehan, M. M. (1993). *Cognitive–behavioral treatment for borderline personality disorder.* New York, NY: Guilford Press.

Litz, B. T., Engel, C. C., Bryant, R. A., & Papa, A. (2007). A randomized, controlled proof-of-concept trial of an Internet-based, therapist-assisted self-management treatment for posttraumatic stress disorder. *The American Journal of Psychiatry, 164*, 1676–1684. doi:10.1176/appi.ajp.2007.06122057

Litz, B. T., & Weathers, F. W. (1994). The diagnosis and assessment of posttraumatic stress disorder in adults. In M. B. Williams & J. F. Sommer (Eds.), *Handbook of posttraumatic therapy* (pp. 19–37). Westport, CT: Greenwood Press.

Mizener, D., Thomas, M., & Billings, R. (1988). Cognitive changes of migraineurs receiving biofeedback training. *Headache, 28*, 339–343. doi:10.1111/j.1526-4610.1988.hed2805339.x

Monson, C. M., Schnurr, P. P., Resick, P. A., Friedman, M. J., Young-Xu, Y., & Stevens, S. P. (2006). Cognitive processing therapy for veterans with military-related posttraumatic stress disorder. *Journal of Consulting and Clinical Psychology, 74*, 898–907. doi:10.1037/0022-006X.74.5.898

Najavits, L. M. (2002). *Seeking safety: A treatment manual for PTSD and substance abuse.* New York, NY: Guilford Press.

Najavits, L. M., Schmitz, M., Gotthard, S., & Weiss, R. D. (2005). Seeking safety plus exposure therapy: An outcome study on dual diagnosis men. *Journal of Psychoactive Drugs, 37*, 425–435.

National Center for Posttraumatic Stress Disorder. (n.d.). *Research and education on posttraumatic stress disorder.* Retrieved from http://www.ptsd.va.gov/index.asp

Nishith, P., Resick, P. A., & Griffin, M. G. (2002). Pattern of change in prolonged exposure and cognitive-processing therapy for female rape victims with post-traumatic stress disorder. *Journal of Consulting and Clinical Psychology, 70,* 880–886. doi:10.1037/0022-006X.70.4.880

Okie, S. (2005). Traumatic brain injury in the war zone. *The New England Journal of Medicine, 352,* 2043–2047. doi:10.1056/NEJMp058102

Orr, S. P., Metzger, L. J., Miller, M. W., & Kaloupek, D. G. (2004). Psychophysiological assessment of PTSD. In J. P. Wilson & T. M. Keane (Eds.), *Assessing psychological trauma and PTSD* (pp. 289–343). New York, NY: Guildford Press.

Otis, J. D. (2007). *Managing chronic pain: A cognitive–behavioral therapy approach.* New York, NY: Oxford University Press.

Otis, J. D., Keane, T. M., & Kerns, R. D. (2003). An examination of the relationship between chronic pain and posttraumatic stress disorder. *Journal of Rehabilitation Research and Development, 40,* 397–406. doi:10.1682/JRRD.2003.09.0397

Otis, J. D., Keane, T., Kerns, R. D., Monson, C., & Scioli, E. (2009). The development of an integrated treatment for veterans with comorbid chronic pain and post-traumatic stress disorder. *Pain Medicine, 10,* 1300–1311.

Otis, J. D., Reid, M. C., & Kerns, R. D. (2005). The management of chronic pain in the primary care setting. In L. C. James & R. A. Folen (Eds.), *Primary care clinical health psychology: A model for the next frontier* (pp. 41–59). Washington, DC: American Psychological Association. doi:10.1037/10962-003

Ozer, E. J., Best, S. R., Lipsey, T. L., & Weiss, D. S. (2003). Predictors of posttraumatic stress disorder and symptoms in adults: A meta-analysis. *Psychological Bulletin, 129*(1), 52–73. doi:10.1037/0033-2909.129.1.52

Prins, A., Kaloupek, D. G., & Keane, T. M. (1995). Psychophysiological evidence for autonomic arousal and startle in traumatized adult populations. In M. J. Friedman, D. S. Charney, & A. Y. Deutch (Eds.), *Neurobiological and clinical consequences of stress: From normal adaption to posttraumatic stress disorder* (pp. 291–314). Philadelphia, PA: Lippincott-Raven.

Resick, P. A., Galovski, T. E., Uhlmansiek, M. O., Scher, C. D., Clum, G. A., & Young-Xu, Y. (2008). A randomized clinical trial to dismantle components of cognitive processing therapy for posttraumatic stress disorder in female victims of interpersonal violence. *Journal of Consulting and Clinical Psychology, 76,* 243–258. doi:10.1037/0022-006X.76.2.243

Resick, P. A., Jordan, C. G., Girelli, S. A., Hutter, C. K., & Marhoefer-Dvorak, S. (1988). A comparative outcome study of behavioral group therapy for sexual assault victims. *Behavior Therapy, 19,* 385–401. doi:10.1016/S0005-7894(88)80011-X

Resick, P. A., Monson, C. M., & Gutner, C. A. (2007). Psychosocial treatments for PTSD. In M. J. Friedman, T. M. Keane, & P. A. Resick (Eds.), *Handbook of PTSD: Science and Practice* (pp. 330–358). New York, NY: Guilford Press.

Resick, P. A., Nishith, P., Weaver, T. L., Astin, M. C., & Feuer, C. A. (2002). A comparison of cognitive-processing therapy with prolonged exposure and a waiting list condition for the treatment of chronic posttraumatic stress disorder in female rape victims. *Journal of Consulting and Clinical Psychology, 70,* 867–879. doi:10.1037/0022-006X.70.4.867

Resick, P. A., & Schnicke, M. K. (1993). *Cognitive processing therapy for rape victims: A treatment manual.* Newbury Park, CA: Sage.

Rosen, C. S., Chow, H. C., Finney, J. F., Greenbaum, M. A., Moos, R. H., Sheikh, J. I., & Yesavage, J. A. (2004). Practice guidelines and VA practice patterns for treating posttraumatic stress disorder. *Journal of Traumatic Stress, 17,* 213–222. doi:10.1023/B:JOTS.0000029264.23878.53

Russell, M. B. (2008). Is migraine a genetic illness? The various forms of migraine share a common genetic cause. *Neurological Sciences, 29,* 52–54. doi:10.1007/s10072-008-0887-4

Seal, K. H., Bertenthal, D., Miner, C. R., Sen, S., & Marmar, C. (2007). Bringing the war back home: Mental health disorders among 103,788 U.S. veterans returning from Iraq and Afghanistan seen at Department of Veterans Affairs facilities. *Archives of Internal Medicine, 167,* 476–482. doi:10.1001/archinte.167.5.476

Seligman, Z. (1995). Trauma and drama: A lesson from the concentration camps. *The Arts in Psychotherapy, 22,* 119–132. doi:10.1016/0197-4556(95)00017-Y

Shapiro, F. (1995). *Eye movement desensitization and reprocessing: Basic principles, protocols, and procedures.* New York, NY: Guilford Press.

Sherman, J. J., Turk, D. C., & Okifuji, A. (2000). Prevalence and impact of posttraumatic stress disorder-like symptoms on patients with fibromyalgia syndrome. *The Clinical Journal of Pain, 16,* 127–134. doi:10.1097/00002508-200006000-00006

Shipherd, J. C., Keyes, M., Jovanic, T., Ready, D. J., Baltzell, D., Worley, V., . . . Duncan, E. (2007). Veterans seeking treatment for posttraumatic stress disorder: What about comorbid chronic pain? *Journal of Rehabilitation Research and Development, 44,* 153–166. doi:10.1682/JRRD.2006.06.0065

Skinner, K. M., Kressin, N., Frayne, S. M., Tripp, T. J., Hankin, C. S., Miller, D. R., & Sullivan, L. M. (2000). The prevalence of military sexual assault among female Veterans' Administration outpatients. *Journal of Interpersonal Violence, 15,* 291–310. doi:10.1177/088626000015003005

Solomon, S. D., & Davidson, J. R. T. (1997). Trauma: Prevalence, impairment, service use, and cost. *The Journal of Clinical Psychiatry, 58,* 5–11.

Spates, C. R., Koch, E., Cusack, K., Pagoto, S., & Waller, S. (2009). Eye movement desensitization and reprocessing. In E. Foa, T. Keane, M. Friedman, & J. Cohen (Eds.), *Effective Treatments for PTSD* (2nd ed., pp. 279–305). New York, NY: Guilford Press.

Tanielian, T., & Jaycox, L. H. (Eds.). (2008). *Invisible wounds of war: Psychological and cognitive injuries, their consequences, and services to assist recovery* (RAND Monograph MG-720-CCF). Santa Monica, CA: RAND Corporation.

Turk, D. C., & Okifuji, A. (1996). Perception of traumatic onset, compensation status, and physical findings: Impact on pain severity, emotional distress, and disability in chronic pain patients. *Journal of Behavioral Medicine, 19,* 435–453. doi:10.1007/BF01857677

Turk, D. C., & Rudy, T. E. (1988). Toward an empirically derived taxonomy of chronic pain patients: Integration of psychological assessment data. *Journal of Consulting and Clinical Psychology, 56,* 233–238. doi:10.1037/0022-006X.56.2.233

U.S. Department of Veterans Affairs. (2008). *VHA Handbook 1160.01: Uniform mental health services in VA medical centers and clinics.* Washington, DC: Author.

U.S. Department of Veterans Affairs. (2008, May 27). *Vet center: Keeping the promise.* Retrieved from http://www.vetcenter.va.gov/

Veterans Health Affairs Office of Public Health and Environmental Hazards. (2008). *May 2008 analysis of VA health care utilization among U.S. Global War on Terrorism (GWOT) veterans: Operation Enduring Freedom/Operation Iraqi Freedom.* Washington, DC: Author.

Veterans Health Initiative. (2004). *Military sexual trauma.* Washington, DC: Department of Veterans Affairs.

Warden, D. (2006). Military TBI during the Iraq and Afghanistan wars. *The Journal of Head Trauma Rehabilitation, 21,* 398–402. doi:10.1097/00001199-200609000-00004

Weathers, F. W., Keane, T. M., & Davidson, J. R. T. (2001). Clinician-Administered PTSD Scale: A review of the first ten years of research. *Depression and Anxiety, 13,* 132–156. doi:10.1002/da.1029

Wilson, J. P., & Keane, T. M. (2004). *Assessing psychological trauma and PTSD* (2nd ed.). New York, NY: Guilford Press.

Wood, K. B., Garvey, T. A., Gundry, C., & Heithoff, K. B. (1995). Magnetic resonance imaging of the thoracic spine: Evaluation of asymptomatic individuals. *Journal of Bone and Joint Surgery, 77,* 1631–1638.

Xydakis, M. S., Fravell, M. D., Nasser, K. E., & Casler, J. D. (2005). Analysis of battlefield head and neck injuries in Iraq and Afghanistan. *Otolaryngology—Head and Neck Surgery, 133,* 497–04.

Yehuda, R. (1997). Sensitization of the hypothalamic–pituitary–adrenal axis in posttraumatic stress disorder. In R. Yehuda & A. C. McFarlane (Eds.), *Psychobiology of posttraumatic stress disorder* (pp. 57–75). New York, NY: New York Academy of Sciences.

Zivin, K., Kim, M., McCarthy, J. F., Austin, K. L., Hoggatt, K. J., Walters, H., & Valenstein, M. (2007). Suicide mortality among individuals receiving treatment for depression in the Veterans Affairs health system: Associations with patient and treatment setting characteristics. *American Journal of Public Health, 97,* 2193–2198.

INDEX

Assessment(s), *continued*
   of posttraumatic stress disorder,
      247–249
   psychophysiological, 249
   in public health epidemiology, 29–30
   of service member's ability to
      perform, 62
   of transition, 162–165
Attitudes
   of leaders, 76
   resilience-based, 94
   of soldiers in theater, 44
   toward others' mental health
      problems, 85–88
   toward risk taking, 231–232
Attrition, 178
Auchterlonie, J. L., 181
Authenticity, 28
Autonomy, 70
Availability, 39, 40, 76
Avoidance, 226–228
Axis II personality disorders, 27

Bain, M. W., 127
Barlow, D. H., 245–246
Barrier(s)
   to family member employment, 134
   for newly returning veterans,
      250–251
   to providing psychoeducation, 43
   to seeking help, 84–87
   stigma as, 20
   symptom-based, 28
Battlefield circulation, 45–47
Battlefield ethics, 22
Battlemind Psychological Debriefing,
   51–52
Battlemind Training, 22–23
   development of, 9–10
   as early intervention strategy, 236
   effectiveness of, 114–115
   and mental health support, 94–95
   as psychoeducation, 42–43
   for spouses, 138–139
   transitioning home in, 76
Beehr, T. A., 72
Behavioral responses, 37–38
Behaviors
   alcohol-related problematic, 168
   maladaptive, 57

   misconduct, 36–37
   violent, 54–55
Belonging, sense of, 76
Benchmarks
   for family well-being, 127–130
   for key postdeployment experiences,
      164
Bennett, M. M., 72
Bereavement groups, 57
Biofeedback, 58
Biologically-based measures, 248–249
Biomarkers, 235
Biopsychosocial model of illness, 260
Blais, A. R., 162
Blast exposure, 199, 201
Bliese, P. D., 139, 178, 182, 184
Body image, of amputees, 204–205
Borus, J. F., 156, 169
Boscarino, J. A., 231
Bosnia, 23
Boundaries, 63–65
Bowling, N. A., 72
Breslau, N., 247
Brewin, C. R., 88
Briefings, 43–44
Britt, T. W., 84, 87
Broad-scale preventive programs,
   107–111
Brunwasser, S. M., 117
Bryant, R. A., 180
Buddy system, 83
Burrell, L. M., 133

Calhoun, L. G., 162
Campise, R., 87
Canadian Armed Forces, 86
Cardona, R., 178
Care-based screening
   for delivery of mental health care,
      179–180
   efficiency of, 189
   selection-based screening vs., 188
   successful, 185–186
Career, military, 84, 87
CARE framework, 35–66
   and disposition from theater,
      59–60
   elements of, 39–41
   forward psychiatry in, 53–55
   medication management in, 58–59

Immune system, psychological, 136
Impairment
    after active duty, 239
    functional, 229, 233–234
    neuropsychological, 202–203
Individual-level predictors, 113
Individual screening, 47–49
Informal support systems, 138
Informational support, 133, 138
Inpatient psychiatry, 62
"In-session homework," 56
Institute of Medicine (IOM), 25–26
Institutionalized support systems,
    136–138
Instrumental support, 133, 137
Integrated treatment, 262
Internal stigma, 81
*International Classification of Diseases
    (ICD–10)*, 200
International Society for Traumatic
    Stress Studies (ISTSS), 253
Internet-based treatment, 264–265
Intervention(s)
    for daily stressors, 142
    for dangerous patients, 61
    early. *See* Early intervention
    for families, 138–142, 208–209
    group-based, 116, 117
    homework as, 56
    targeted, 117
    VA-based, 251
Interviews
    psychiatric, 234–235
    structured diagnostic, 248
Intimate partner violence (IPV), 128
Intoxication, 168
Intraclass correlation 1 (ICC[1]), 111,
    115–116
Invincibility, 232
IOM (Institute of Medicine), 25–26
IPV (intimate partner violence), 128
Iraq, war in. *See also* Operation Iraqi
    Freedom
    effects of evacuation from, 59–60
    Mental Health Advisory Teams in,
        21–23, 105–106
    mental health impact of, 29, 140,
        182, 245
    and military behavioral health
        programs, 107

multiple tours of duty in, 243–244
    population-wide, care-based screen-
        ing for, 179
    psychological effects of combat in,
        104–105
    PTSD risks for troops in, 196–197,
        217–218
    results of research data from, 29
    service members in. *See* Service
        members (Iraq)
    TBI as signature injury of, 263
    TBI rates after deployment to, 199
Isolation, 59–60, 133–134
ISTSS (International Society for
    Traumatic Stress Studies), 253

Jaycox, L. H., 140
Jensen, P. S., 127
Job performance, 88
Johnson, W. B., 86
Jullen, K., 181

Kaiser, J., 204–205
Karney, B. R., 128
Keane, T. M., 245–246, 257, 261, 262
Kenrick, D. T., 119
Kerns, R. D., 261
Kessler, R. C., 247
Killgore, W. D., 226, 231
Killing, 160, 219
Koren, D., 197
Koshes, R. J., 50
Kosovo, 23
Kubler-Ross, E., 206
Kulka, R. A., 245

Labuc, S., 80
LaGrone, D. M., 126
Land Combat Study, 19–21, 127
Leaders
    attitudes toward mental health care,
        86
    as mental health support, 89–90
    mental health support for, 76–77
    prevention training for, 236
    protective effect of, 22
    roles and responsibilities of, 70–71, 89
    as source of informational support,
        138
    and stress buffering, 109–110

"Learned alarms," 246
Lebanon War, 53
Life changes, 3–4
Limb amputation, 204–207
Linehan, M. M., 259
Livneh, H., 205–206
Loss of consciousness (LOC), 198
Lucia, V. C., 247

MacLachlan, M., 204
Main effect hypothesis, 74, 79–80
Major depressive disorder (MDD),
    52–53, 127
Maladaptive behaviors, labeling, 57
Maladaptive responses, 36–39
Maladaptive symptoms (PTSD), 226,
    228, 239
Maltreatment, of children, 127–128
Marital relationships. *See also* Spouses
    after traumatic brain injury, 209
    and depression, 128
    and geographic separation, 57,
        131–132, 208
    military-related stressors in, 128–129
    negative outcome spillover in, 140
Marshall, S. L. A., 50, 78
Masculinity, 82–83, 87
Maturation, rapid, 231
McCarroll, J. E., 128
McCreary, D. M., 162
McFarlane, A. C., 180
McGurk, D., 51
McNally, S. T., 73
MDD. *See* Major depressive disorder
Meaningfulness, 157–158, 161
Mechanisms
    causal, 112–113
    pathophysiological, 197
Medical centers, 251–252
Medical evaluations, 47
Medication management, 47–48, 58–59
Membership, group, 74
Memorial services, 42
Memories, 201, 225, 226
Menninger, W. C., 38
Mental health, 70–73
    advisory teams for, 21–23, 105–106
    advocacy for, 46
    comorbid physical health and,
        24–25, 27

comparison of statistics for, 106
deployment-related problems, 18,
    21–22
of family members, 127–130
of leaders, 76, 86
preventive, 41–42
research programs in military, 8–9
and resilience, 41–42
response to combat, 229–234
social support detrimental to, 72
standard for deployment, 47–48
and stigma, 81–82
Mental Health Advisory Teams
    (MHATs), 21–23, 105–106
Mental health care services
    attitudes about leaders using, 86
    continuity of, 48–49
    screening to facilitate delivery of,
        179–180
    stigma as barrier to, 20
    symptom-based barriers to, 28
Mental health disorders
    impact of, on outcomes, 198
    in OEF/OIF veterans, 245
    preexisting, 52–53
    trauma-related, 250
Mental health problems
    care-based screening for, 180–183
    discharges for, 178
    evidence-based prevention
        attempts, 5
    nonclinical vs. clinical conditions,
        164
    in others, 85–88
    pervasiveness of, 142
    physical injuries vs., 88
    in postdeployment service members,
        182–183
    and quality of life, 167
    rates of, 182–183
    veterans with, 250
    when returning from combat, 140,
        154
Mental health providers
    allocation of, 22
    authority of, 61
    in battlefield circulation, 45–46
    in CARE framework, 39–41
    and decision to treat, 59
    ethical concerns of, 60–65

Medications (Assistant Secretary of Defense),48
Population-based screening, 179, 236
Population-level conceptualization, 235–236
Porter, T. L., 86
Positive predictive values (PPV), 177–178, 184–185
Postconcussion disorder (PCD), 200
Postconcussion syndrome (PCS), 200, 263
Postdeployment
    assessment programs for, 230
    benchmarks for, 164
    and expressive writing, 139–140
    mental health problems in, 182–183
    optimism, 230
    phase of, 155
    and resilience training, 160–161
    screening programs, 18, 20–21, 23–24
Postdeployment Army Couples Expressive Writing Study, 138–140
Post-Deployment Health Assessment (PDHA), 18
    positive predictive values of, 184–185
    referral rates with, 181
    research on, 23–24
    as response to wars in Iraq and Afghanistan, 179
Post-Deployment Health Reassessment (PDHRA), 23–24
    to facilitate health care delivery, 179
    implementation of, 182
    positive predictive values of, 184–185
    referrals rates with, 181
    staffing for, 187
Postinjury depression, 198
Posttraumatic stress disorder (PTSD), 217–239, 243–265
    and anxiety disorders, 246
    assessment of, 247–249
    combat-related, 28–29
    comorbidity with, 25
    early intervention strategies for, 236–237
    epidemiology of, 245
    evidence-based treatment for, 27–28, 253–257
    and exposure to trauma, 222–224

    fathers with, 207
    future research directions, 238–239, 264–265
    health concerns associated with, 21–22
    and marital relationships, 127–129
    and mild TBI, 199
    in occupational model, 218–222
    in OEF/OIF veterans, 263
    and pain, 260–263
    and physical injuries, 196–197, 259–260
    postdeployment rates of, 182
    postscreening referrals for, 185
    prediction of, 25, 140–141
    preexisting symptoms of, 221
    prevention strategies for, 234–236
    and response to combat, 229–234
    risk and resilience factors in, 245–247
    selective serotonin reuptake inhibitors for, 26
    and suicide prevention, 252–253
    symptom clusters in, 225–229
    and traumatic brain injury, 263–264
    treatment of, 25–26, 237–238, 249–251, 257–259
    and unit cohesion, 79
    VA programs and outreach, 251–253
    in Vietnam War veterans, 245
Potential patients, 63
PPV. *See* Positive predictive values
Predeployment, 47–49, 226, 236
Predictors
    individual-level, 113
    of posttraumatic stress disorder, 25, 140–141
    of successful transition, 169–170
Preexisting mental health disorders, 52–53
Preexisting symptoms, 227
Preparation, for trauma exposure, 83
Preplanning, 92–93
Pressures, 165–166
Prevention. *See also* Resiliency and preventive training (CARE framework)
    for posttraumatic stress disorder, 234–236
    primary, 42–47
    secondary, 47–52

Secondary prevention, 47–52
Second-guessing, 232–233
Seeking help
   attitudes about, in leaders, 86
   barriers to, 84–87
   and masculinity, 82–83
   and military career, 84, 87
   with multiple deployments, 226
   and screening transparency, 184
   and stigma, 81–82, 264
   in veterans with PTSD, 250–251
Seeking Safety, 258–259
Selection-based screening, 179, 188,
         189. *See also* Screening programs
Selection programs, 103–104, 106–107
Selective serotonin reuptake inhibitors
         (SSRIs), 26
Self, sense of, 160
Self-report measures, 248
Self-stigma, 81
Senior officers, 63–64
Sense of duty, 232–233
Sense of self, 160
Sequelae, psychological, 196–197
Service members (general)
   ability to perform, 62
   death of fellow, 232–233
   as detainee guards, 65
   disposition from theater, 59
   maladjustment of, 103–104
   mental health of, 70–73
   normal states for, 229
   occupational danger awareness of,
         219
   perceptions of physical injury in,
         205
   postdeployment mental health
         problems in, 182–183
   postdeployment optimism in, 230
   rapid maturation of, 231
   risk taking in, 231–232
   social context of, 220
   in United Kingdom, 182–183
Service members (Afghanistan)
   access to VA benefits, 249
   adaptive functioning in, 260–261
   chronic pain in, 259–260
   depression in, 263
   effects of evacuation on, 59–60
   mental health of, 140, 245

   posttraumatic stress disorder in,
         196–197, 217–218, 263
   resilience training for, 107
   traumatic brain injury in, 199,
         263
Service members (Iraq)
   A2 criterion in, 223–224
   access to VA benefits, 249
   adaptive functioning in, 260–261
   chronic pain in, 259–260
   depression in, 263
   effects of evacuation on, 59–60
   levels of combat for, 160–161
   mental health of, 140, 245
   mental health services for, 20
   posttraumatic stress disorder in,
         196–197, 217–218, 263
   resilience training for, 107
   time in combat of, 243–244
   traumatic brain injury in, 199,
         263
Sessions, therapy, 64
Sexual trauma, 252
Shell shock, 54
Sightseeing, 60–61
Simplicity, 54–55
Sinaii, N., 178
Single-session model, 55–56
Sleep disturbance, 189, 221
Slogans, for recruitment, 80
Small group motivation, 80
Social adaptation, 160
Social component, of transition, 161
Social context, 108–111, 219
Social environment, 41
Social isolation, 133–134
Socialization, military, 71–72
Social networks, 138
Social relationships, 63
Social structure
   of military, 107–108
   and preventive programs, 112
Social support
   in immediate aftermath of traumatic
         events, 88–89
   as mental health support, 71–77
   and the military, 79–80
   for occupational hazards, 69–70
Social ties, 73, 75
Soldier adaptation model, 91–92

ABOUT THE EDITORS

Amy B. Adler, PhD, is a clinical research psychologist and chief of science at the U.S. Army Medical Research Unit–Europe, Walter Reed Army Institute for Research. She is the manager of the army's medical research on psychological resilience training, has led several of the army's randomized trials on psychological resilience training, and has worked on psychological health issues related to deployment for more than 15 years. Besides serving as a U.S. representative on NATO research groups, Dr. Adler has also been invited to speak and to consult with militaries in several other nations. She has published more than 40 articles and has coedited five books, including the series *Military Life: The Psychology of Serving in Peace and Combat.*

Paul D. Bliese, PhD, is the director of the Center for Military Psychiatry and Neuroscience at the Walter Reed Army Institute of Research (WRAIR), Silver Spring, Maryland. Dr. Bliese has served as the commander of the U.S. Army Medical Research Unit–Europe, located in Heidelberg, Germany, and as the chief of the Department of Military Psychiatry at WRAIR. In 2005, 2007, and 2009, he deployed to Iraq as part of the annual Mental Health Advisory Team (in the latter 2 years as team leader). Dr. Bliese has published numerous scientific articles, has developed and maintains the multilevel library for the open-source statistical language R, and serves as an associate editor for the *Journal of Applied Psychology*. He is a fellow of the American Psychological Society and a colonel in the U.S. Army.

Carl Andrew Castro, PhD, is director of the Military Operational Medicine Research Program at the U.S. Army Medical Research and Material Command at Fort Detrick, Maryland, where he oversees a wide range of research programs, including Psychological Health and Resilience, Injury Prevention, Environmental Medicine, and Physiological Health and Well-Being. Most recently, Dr. Castro has served as the commander of the U.S. Army Medical Research Unit–Europe, located in Heidelberg, Germany, and as the chief of the Department of Military Psychiatry. He was the original author and developer of the Battlemind Training System, the U.S. Army's resilience training program. His operational experience includes serving tours of duty in Bosnia, Kosovo, and Iraq. In 2003 and 2006, he deployed to Iraq as part of the annual Mental Health Advisory Team (first as senior science officer and then as team leader). Dr. Castro has published more than 60 scientific articles and has served as coeditor of the four-volume series *Military Life: The Psychology of Serving in Peace and Combat*. He also leads several NATO research groups and other international activities. He is a colonel in the U.S. Army.